D0560341

Freedom in the World

Political Rights and Civil Liberties
1986–1987

A FREEDOM HOUSE BOOK

Greenwood Press issues the Freedom House series "Studies in Freedom" in addition to the Freedom House yearbook *Freedom in the World*.

Strategies for the 1980s: Lessons of Cuba, Vietnam, and Afghanistan
Philip van Slyk. Studies in Freedom, Number 1

Escape to Freedom: The Story of the International Rescue Committee
Aaro Levenstein. Studies in Freedom, Number 2

Forty Years: A Third World Soldier at the UN
Carlos P. Romulo with Betty Day Romulo. Studies in Freedom, Number 3

Will of the People: Original Democracy in Non-Western Societies
Raul S. Manglapus. Studies in Freedom, Number 4

Freedom in the World

Political Rights and Civil Liberties
1986–1987

Raymond D. Gastil

With an Essay by

Leonard R. Sussman

GREENWOOD PRESS

New York • Westport, Connecticut • London

Library of Congress Catalog Card Number: 82-642048
ISBN: 0-313-25906-2
ISSN: 0732-6610

First published in 1987

Greenwood Press, Inc.
88 Post Road West, Westport, Connecticut 06881

Printed in the United States of America

∞

The paper used in this book complies with the
Permanent Paper Standard issued by the National
Information Standards Organization (Z39.48-1984).

10 9 8 7 6 5 4 3 2 1

Contents

Contents

PART IV. COUNTRY SUMMARIES

Map

Tables

Preface

Americans have many foreign policy interests. For most citizens our economic and security relations are foremost, and our foreign policy is directed primarily to securing these interests. However, in the long run the future of our country will only be secured in a free and democratic world. From this perspective achieving this world is both a vital interest of Americans and a vital interest of all peoples. To help us in understanding where we are in the struggle to achieve this world and to keep the relevance of this issue before the public, Freedom House has supported the Comparative Survey of Freedom since 1972.

This yearbook marks the fourteenth year of the Comparative Survey and is the ninth edition in the Freedom House series of annual publications. Previous yearbooks, in addition to focusing on the Comparative Survey, have emphasized different aspects of freedom and human rights. The first yearbook, the 1978 edition, examined basic theoretical issues of freedom and democracy and assessed the record of the Year of Human Rights. The second yearbook reported extensively on a conference devoted to the possibilities of expanding freedom in the Soviet Union. The 1980 yearbook considered international issues in press freedom, aspects of trade union freedom, the struggle for democracy in Iran, elections in Zimbabwe, and the relationship between human rights policy and morality. The 1981 yearbook contained essays and discussions from a Freedom House conference on the prospects for freedom in Muslim Central Asia. The 1982 yearbook emphasized a variety of approaches to economic freedom and its relation to political and civil freedom. The 1983-84 yearbook addressed the problems of corporatism, and the health of democracy in the third world. It also incorporated the papers and discussions of a conference held at Freedom House on supporting democracy in mainland China and Taiwan. The 1984-85 yearbook came back to the themes of the definition of freedom, and the conditions for the development of freedom that were first addressed in the 1978

ix

yearbook. It also looked at the particular problem of developing democracy in Central America. The 1985-86 yearbook considered America's role in the worldwide struggle for democracy, and reported the results of a conference on supporting liberalization in Eastern Europe.

In addition to the ratings and tables produced by the Survey, the discussion of criteria and definitions at the beginning of the 1986-87 yearbook again includes the checklist for political rights and civil liberties. Discussion of the communication policies of the United States and the Soviet Union forms a special theme in this year's summary of the international struggle for free and informative news media. To give a greater degree of concreteness to the often abstract summaries of democratic problems and conditions, the 1986-87 yearbook also examines some common problems of democracies, and explores these in the context of first as well as third world democracies.

We acknowledge, once again, the contribution made by the advisory panel for the Comparative Survey. The panel consists of: Robert J. Alexander, Richard W. Cottam, Herbert J. Ellison, Seymour Martin Lipset, Lucian W. Pye, Leslie Rubin, Giovanni Sartori, Robert Scalapino, and Paul Seabury. We also express our appreciation to those foundations whose grants have made the Survey and the publication of this yearbook possible. Major support for the Survey has again been provided by the J. Howard Pew Freedom Trust. We thank the Earhart Foundation for its additional support. All Freedom House activities are also assisted by the generous support of individual members of the organization as well as trade unions, corporations, and public foundations that contribute to our general budget. No financial support from any government—now or in the past—has been either solicited or accepted.

We gratefully acknowledge the research and editorial assistance of Jeannette C. Gastil in producing this yearbook.

PART I

The Survey in 1986

Freedom in the
Comparative Survey:
Definitions and Criteria

Freedom, like democracy, is a term with many meanings. Its meanings cover a variety of philosophical and social issues, many of which would carry us far beyond the discussion of political systems with which the Comparative Survey of Freedom has been principally concerned. Unfortunately, linguistic usage is such that the meanings of freedom infect one another, so that a "free society" may be taken to be a society with no rules at all, or a free man may be taken to be an individual with no obligations to society, or even another individual. It is this global sense of individual freedom that leads many Americans to scoff at the idea that theirs is a free society. Not primarily concerned with politics, most Americans apply the word "free" to their personal relationships, sensing correctly, but for our purposes irrelevantly, the necessity to work at a job, or to drive at a certain speed on the highway. To these individuals, "freedom" sounds like a wonderful goal, but hardly a goal that their society has achieved. Yet freedom, when addressed in a narrow political sense, is the basic value, goal, and, to a remarkable degree, attainment of successful democratic regimes.

Freedom as independence is important to the Survey, but this too is not a primary basis of judgment. When the primary issue for so many countries in the colonial era was to become free from a colonial or occupying power, "freedom" meant that a country had emerged from control by another state, much as the United States had achieved freedom in the 1780s. This sense of freedom was applied to the term "the free world" after World War II because the Soviet Union forced satellization on so many countries of Eastern Europe. By contrast those beyond this sphere were said to be free. In this sense Spain was part of the free world, but at the time only in its relative independence. Still, for a people to accept rule by leaders of their own nationality rather than by foreign leaders is an aspect of political freedom—self-determination is a democratic right. But the fact, for example, the dictators of

Haiti have been Haitians has done little for the freedom or democratic rights of their people.

Since democratic freedoms and human rights are often considered together it has often been assumed that the Survey of Freedom is equivalent to a survey of human rights. However, in spite of the considerable overlap of the two, concern for democracy and concern for human rights are distinct. A free people can deny human rights to some of their number, and they can certainly deny human rights to others. Thus, the Japanese tendency to exclude foreigners, and to discriminate against those who come to Japan, is unfortunate but does little to affect its democracy. If people are beaten cruelly in the jails of Arkansas, this too is a violation of human rights, but the ill-treatment may both be passively approved by the people of the state and be of little consequence for those requirements for free speech and nonviolent pluralism necessary for the expression of political democracy.

One concern that many have felt with the human rights movement has been its tendency to proliferate as "rights" an ever-lengthening list of desirabilia, a list that mixes general principles of natural rights with the particular concerns of modern intellectuals. This weakens the proposition that there are basic natural rights that all peoples in all places and times should feel incumbent upon themselves and their societies. It also leads to an increasing opposition between expanding democratic freedoms (that is, the ability of a people to decide its own fate) and expanding human rights.

In the Survey, freedom or democracy is taken to mean "liberal democracy." It is surprising how many well-informed persons believe that since the "German Democratic Republic" also uses the term democracy in its label, we must include regimes of this type within our definition. It would be like saying that since the German fascists called their party "National Socialist," discussions of socialism must use definitions that would include the Nazis. Words can be appropriated to many uses, and no one can stop the appropriation, but when an extension of meaning adds little but confusion, and begins to call black white, it should be rejected.

In rejecting the Marxist-Leninist or extreme leftist usage of the word democracy, as in "people's democracy," we do not mean to imply that there is not a range of acceptable meanings of

4

"democracy" that must be taken into account in any survey of democratic freedoms. We have explicitly addressed in previous volumes of the Survey the question of how "economic freedom" might be defined.[1] Our conclusion was that a system was free primarily to the extent that the people were actually given a choice in determining the nature of the economic system. Therefore, a system that produces economic equality, if imposed, is much less democratic than a more unequal system, if freely chosen. Of course, questions must always be asked about the extent to which a system is freely chosen by any people. Economic measures such as land reform in a poor peasant economy may play a significant fact in improving the ability of people to take part in the political process fairly, and thereby choose the economic strategies that they desire.

The Comparative Survey was begun in the early 1970s as an attempt to give a more standardized and relativized picture of the situation of freedom in the world than could be provided by essays of individuals from different backgrounds that had formed, and in part still form, Freedom House's annual review of the condition of freedom in the world. My own experience had been that the world media and, therefore, informed opinion often misevaluated the level of freedom in countries with which Westerners had become particularly involved. In many countries oppressions were condemned as more severe than they were in comparative terms. On the other hand, the achievements of the postwar period in expanding freedom were often overlooked. Many small countries had quietly achieved and enjoyed democracy with relatively little media attention. The most oppressive states were those about which there was the least news in the media. Although these imbalances are still present, it is possible that some improvement in the presentation of the state of freedom in the world has resulted from the development of these Surveys.

The Comparative Survey of Freedom was hardly the first survey. There had been a number of other surveys. Bryce had listed the number of democracies in the world in about 1920.[2] An extensive cross-comparison of societies on social and cultural variables was published in the early sixties by Banks and Textor.[3] Based on an analysis of qualitative and quantitative data for all nations in the period 1960-62, the authors ranked and categorized polities on a wide variety of indices. These included economic

5

development, literacy, and degree of urbanization, as well as political and civil rights. Since the authors' purpose was ultimately to discover correlations among the variables, their indices were more specific than those used in the Comparative Survey. They were interested primarily in presenting detailed information on items such as the nature of the party system, the presence or absence of military intervention, the freedom of opposition groups to enter politics, or the freedom of the press.

The next major effort, by Robert Dahl and colleagues at Yale, was much closer in intent to the Comparative Survey.[4] In updating Banks and Textor's work they placed all significant states along a variety of scales relating to democracy. The resulting scales were then aggregated into scales representing the two fundamental dimensions of "polyarchy" according to Dahl: opportunities for political opposition and degree of popular participation in national elections. Dahl's lists of polyarchies and near-polyarchies were very similar to our lists of free states. A similar rating of democratic systems was developed about the same time by Dankwart Rustow.[5] In both cases, and especially that of Rustow, there seemed to be an overemphasis on the formal charac-teristics of participation in elections and too little regard for the civil liberties that must complement elections if they are to be meaningful. Nevertheless, the resulting lists were very similar to those produced a few years later in the first Comparative Survey of Freedom.

The essential difference between the Comparative Survey and the other attempts of the last generation has been its annual presentation of the evidence and rankings, as opposed to what are essentially one-shot presentations. The latter often represent much more detailed study, but they suffer from the lack of experience with repeated judgments and changes over a period of years that has served to improve the Comparative Survey.

In many ways more comparable to the Survey are the annual reports on human rights to Congress of the State Department's Bureau of Human Rights and Humanitarian Affairs.[7] Presenting detailed information on the state of human rights in every country, the reports consider political and civil liberties as well as other issues. They are, of course, influenced by America's foreign policy concerns, but with this caveat they are remarkably informative. Improving in coverage and comparability are also the annual reports of Amnesty International.[8] Amnesty's concerns in the area are much narrower, but information on Amnesty's issues—execution, political imprisonment, and torture—often has a wider significance. Both of these efforts have now become basic sources of information for the Comparative Survey.

The purpose of the Comparative Survey, then, is to give a general picture of the state of political and civil freedoms in the world. By taking a consistent approach to the definition of freedom, distinctions and issues that are often overlooked are brought out. In particular, its comparative approach brings to the reader's attention the fact that the most publicized denials of political and civil liberties are seldom in the most oppressive states. These states, such as Albania and North Korea, simply do not allow relevant information to reach the world media. There may or may not be hundreds of thousands in jail for their beliefs in North Korea: few care because no one knows.

Besides giving a reference point for considering the performance of independent countries, by its existence the Survey stands for the importance of democracy and freedom in an often cynical world. Too often, Westerners believe that democracy is impossible outside of a few Western countries, and consign the rest of the world to perpetual despotism. The story of the struggle for democratic freedoms is a much more complicated one, and needs to be told. In a sketchy manner the Survey records the advances and retreats of democracy, and alerts the world to trends that should be resisted and those that should be supported.

The Categories of the Survey

The two dimensions of the Survey are political rights and civil liberties. **Political rights** are rights to participate meaningfully in the political process. In a democracy this means the right of all adults to vote and compete for public office, and for elected representatives to have a decisive vote on public policies. **Civil liberties** are rights to free expression, to organize or demonstrate, as well as rights to a degree of autonomy such as is provided by freedom of religion, education, travel, and other personal rights.

Political rights and civil liberties are rated on seven-point scales, with (7) the least free or least democratic and (1) the most free. With no exact definition for any point on these scales, they are constructed comparatively: countries are rated in relation to other countries rather than against absolute standards. The purpose of the rating system is to give an idea of how the freedoms of one state compare with those of others. Different persons with different information, or even with the same information, might compare countries differently. But unless the results of such comparisons are wildly different, there should be no concern. For example, if the Survey rates a country a (3) on political rights, and another person, accepting the criteria of the Survey, rates it a (4), this is an acceptable discrepancy. If judgments of two persons should turn out to be more than one point off, however, then either the Survey's methods are faulty, or the information of one of the judges is faulty.

The generalized checklist for the Comparative Survey is outlined in the accompanying Checklist for Freedom Ratings. The following discussion of some checklist items is keyed to the tabular presentation of the checklist.

Discussion of Political Rights.

(1-2)   Political systems exhibit a variety of degrees to which they offer voters a chance to participate meaningfully in the process. Let us briefly consider several levels of political participation and choice.

At the antidemocratic extreme are those systems with no process, such as inherited monarchies or purely appointive communist systems. Little different in practice are those societies that hold elections for the legislature or president, but give the voter no alternative other than affirmation. In such elections there is neither the choice nor possibility—in practice or even sometimes in theory—of rejecting the single candidate that the government proposes for chief executive or representative. In elections at this level the candidate is usually chosen by a secretive process involving only the top elite. More democratic are those systems, such as Zambia's, that allow the voter no choice, but suggest that it is possible to reject a suggested candidate. In this case the results may show ten or twenty percent of the voters actually voting against a suggested executive, or, rarely, rejecting an individual legislative candidate on a single list. In some societies

8

Checklist for Freedom Ratings

Political Rights

1. Chief authority recently elected by a meaningful process

2. Legislature recently elected by a meaningful process

   Alternatives for (1) and (2):

   a. no choice and possibility of rejection
   b. no choice but some possibility of rejection
   c. government or single-party selected candidates
   d. choice possible only among government-approved candidates
   e. relatively open choices possible only in local elections
   f. open choice possible within a restricted range
   g. relatively open choices possible in all elections

3. Fair election laws, campaigning opportunity, polling and tabulation

4. Fair reflection of voter preference in distribution of power
   —parliament, for example, has effective power

5. Multiple political parties
   —only dominant party allowed effective opportunity
   —open to rise and fall of competing parties

6. Recent shifts in power through elections

7. Significant opposition vote

8. Free of military or foreign control

9. Major group or groups denied reasonable self-determination

10. Decentralized political power

11. Informal consensus; de facto opposition power

Civil Liberties

12. Media/literature free of political censorship

    a. Press independent of government
    b. Broadcasting independent of government

13. Open public discussion

14. Freedom of assembly and demonstration

15. Freedom of political or quasi-political organization

16. Nondiscriminatory rule of law in politically relevant cases

    a. independent judiciary
    b. security forces respect individuals

17. Free from unjustified political terror or imprisonment

    a. free from imprisonment or exile for reasons of conscience
    b. free from torture
    c. free from terror by groups not opposed to the system
    d. free from government-organized terror

18. Free trade unions, peasant organizations, or equivalents

19. Free businesses or cooperatives

20. Free professional or other private organizations

21. Free religious institutions

22. Personal social rights: including those to property, internal
    and external travel, choice of residence, marriage and family

23. Socioeconomic rights: including freedom from dependency
    on landlords, bosses, union leaders, or bureaucrats

24. Freedom from gross socioeconomic inequality

25. Freedom from gross government indifference or corruption

there is a relatively more open party process for selecting candidates. However the list of preselected candidates is prepared, there is seldom any provision for serious campaigning against the single list.

The political system is more democratic if multiple candidates are offered for each position, even when all candidates are government or party selected. Popular voting for alternatives may exist only at the party level—which in some countries is a large proportion of the population—or the choice may be at the general election. Rarely do such systems extend voter options to include choice of the chief authority in the state. Usually that position, like the domination by a single party, is not open to question. But many legislators, even members of the cabinet, may be rejected by the voters in such a system, although they must not go beyond what the party approves. Campaigning occurs at this level of democracy, but the campaigning is restricted to questions of personality, honesty, or ability; for example, in Tanzania campaigning may not involve questions of policy. A further increment of democratic validity is effected if choice is possible among government-approved rather than government-selected candidates. In this case the government's objective is to keep the most undesirable elements (from its viewpoint) out of the election. With government-selected candidates there is reliance on party faithfuls, but self-selection allows persons of local reputation to achieve office. More generally, controlled electoral systems may allow open, self-selection of candidates for some local elections, but not for elections on the national scale. It is also possible for a system, such as that of Iran, to allow an open choice of candidates in elections, but to draw narrow ideological limits around what is an acceptable candidacy.

Beyond this, there is the world of free elections as we know them, in which candidates are both selected by parties and self-selected. It could be argued that parliamentary systems, such as are common outside of the United States, reduce local choice by imposing party choices on voters. However, independents can and do win in most systems, and new parties, such as the "Greens" in West Germany and elsewhere, test the extent to which the party system in particular countries is responsive to the desires of citizens.

(3) In most of the traditional western democracies there are fair election laws, at least on the surface. This is not true in many aspiring democracies. Senegal, for example, did not allow opposition parties to join together for the last general election, a regulation the government seems determined to maintain. Since effective oppositions often emerge from coalitions, this regulation is a useful device for preventing fragmented opposition groups from mounting a succesful challenge. Election laws in Egypt and South Korea have been devised so that the size of the majority of the governing party is artificially inflated after its victory.[9] This is a useful device where there is a danger of excessive fragmentation leading to majorities too weak to govern, but it seems in these cases to be intended to reduce the size of the opposition.

Political scientists dispute whether it is fairer to allow people to contribute to candidates as they like, or whether the government should disburse all campaign funds. Obviously, if the former system is allowed there will be advantages for the more wealthy. However, if the latter is allowed there will be advantages for those who already have power, since governmental disbursement systems must allow funds to be spent in accordance with past patterns (and impoverished campaigns favor incumbents who initially are better known). If outcomes of elections were determined simply by the amounts spent, then depending on government financing would support a quite unchanging vote distribution. One example of this tendency on a restricted scale is the use of the public media for electioneering, usually by giving the parties, or candidates, or at least the major parties and candidates, specified and equal time on television or radio.

Perhaps the most common accusation against the fairness of elections is the extent to which the government takes advantage of the resources of office to defeat its opponents. Incumbents and government officials can often issue statements and make appearances related to the campaign that are not strictly described as campaigning. "News," whatever its origin, is likely to favor incumbents simply because as long as they are incumbents their actions are more newsworthy. Other practices that continue in the less-advanced democracies, but were common in all democracies until recently, are various forms of "vote buying," whether this be by actually distributing money, the promise of large projects, or the promise of future positions to well-placed influentials in critical districts. The use of government equipment such as jeeps and helicopters has often been alleged in campaigns in the third world, such as those of Congress (I) in India or of Barletta in Panama in 1984.

Few democracies are now seriously plagued by direct manipulation of votes, except occasionally on the local level. However, new democracies and semidemocracies are plagued both by such manipulations and equally by accusations that they have occurred. Elections recently in Bangladesh, Guyana, Panama, and Mexico have been marred by such accusations, and with justification. One test of a democracy is the extent to which it has effective machinery in place to prevent flagrant cheating. Such methods generally include genuinely neutral election commissions and poll watchers from all major parties to observe the voting and tabulation of results.

Given the advantages of the incumbents, and thereby generally the government and its party, any campaigning rules that restrict the campaign are likely to affect opposition candidates or parties most severely. The very short campaigns prescribed by many democratic systems might seem unfair to Americans—yet many countries have a fully competitive system with such limited campaigns (probably because their strong parties are, in effect, continuously campaigning). More serious are restrictions placed on campaigning or party organization, such as Indonesia's restriction of opposition party organization to the cities.

(4) Even though a country has a fair electoral process, fair campaigning, and meaningful elections, it will not be a functioning democracy unless those elected have the major power in the state. The most common denial of such power has come through the continued domination of the political system by a monarch or a self-selected leader, as in Morocco or Pakistan. Another common denial of real parliamentary power is occasioned by the continued direct or indirect power of the military—or military and king as in Thailand. In Latin America it is common even in otherwise functioning democracies for the military services not to be effectively under the control of the civilian and elected government. By tradition, ministers of defense in most Latin American countries are appointed from the military services rather than being civilians as is the practice in more mature democracies. In countries such as Guatemala and El Salvador, the problem has gone beyond that of

the military not being under civilian control. In such cases, at least until recently, an economic elite has been unwilling to let elected governments rule. Such an elite may directly and indirectly struggle against its opponents through violent internal warfare outside the control of the system—although elements of the system may be used to implement the desires of these shadowy rulers.

(5) In theory it should be quite possible for democracy to be perfected without political parties. Certainly the founding fathers of the American Republic did not think parties were necessary. The leaders of many countries that have moved from liberal democratic models to single parties argue for the necessity to reduce the adversarial spirit of parties; they claim to be able to preserve democracy by bringing the political struggle within the confines of one party. However, in practice policy is set in single parties by a small clique at the top; those in disfavor with the government are not allowed to compete for office by legal means—indeed, they are often ejected from the single party all together, as in Kenya.

The conclusion of the Survey is that while parties may not be necessary for democracy in very small countries such as Tuvalu, for most modern states they are necessary to allow alternatives to a ruling group or policy to gain sufficient votes to make a change. Therefore, the existence of multiple parties is important evidence for the existence of democracy, but is not absolutely conclusive. We are waiting for demonstrations of the ability of one-party or nonparty systems to achieve democracy. (Nepal's experiment with a nonparty system is worth watching in this connection.)

"Dominant Party" structures such as those of Malaysia or Mexico allow oppositions to mobilize to the extent that they can publicize alternative positions and effectively criticize government performance, but not to the extent that they represent a realistic threat to the group in power. Controls over campaigning, expression of opinion, patronage, and vote manipulation, as well as "punishment" of areas that vote against the government are methods used in such systems to make sure that the governing party remains in power.

(6-7) An empirical test of democracy is the extent to which there has been a recent shift in power occasioned through the operation of the electoral process. While it is true that the people of a country may remain relatively satisfied with the performance of one party for a long period of time, it is also true that a party in power may be able over time to entrench itself in multiple ways to such a degree that it is next to impossible to dislodge it by legitimate means. For a time in the first years of the Survey there was the suspicion that the social democratic party of Sweden had accomplished this. However, in 1976 social democratic domination was ended after forty-four years. The extent of democratic rights can also be empirically suggested by the size of an opposition vote. While on rare occasions a governing party or individual may receive overwhelming support at the polls, any group or leader that regularly receives seventy percent or more of the vote indicates a weak opposition, and the probable existence of undemocratic barriers in the way of its further success. When a government or leader receives over ninety percent of the vote this indicates highly restrictive freedom for those opposing the system: over ninety-eight percent indicate that elections are little more than symbolic.

(8) A free, democratic society is one that governs itself through its own official processes. The two most blatant means of denying the control of a society by its elected leaders are military or foreign control. Since control of violent force is a basic requirement of all governments, when those who directly have this power begin to affect the political process, this aspect of government is turned on its head. The traditional democracies have long since been able to remove the military from power; at the opposite extreme are purely military regimes, as in much of Africa. A few countries remain under a degree of foreign control or influence. For example, in Europe, Finland, and to a lesser extent Austria, must remain neutral because of the pressure of the Soviet Union. Mongolia and Afghanistan are under direct Soviet occupation.

There are many vague accusations that one or another country is under military or foreign control. In this spirit the United States is said to be "ruled" by a military-industrial complex or Mexico is said to be under American control. But there is simply too much evidence that these "controllers" are frequently ignored or slighted for such accusations to be taken too seriously. To a degree every country in the world is influenced by many others—large and small. (While smaller countries generally have less power of self-determination than larger countries, for most issues the power of the individual voter in the smaller states to control his life through the ballot is likely to be greater than that of people in larger countries.) The Survey's position in regard to both of these kinds of "outside" control is to record only the most flagrant cases, and to not enter the area of more complex interpretations.

(9) A democratic polity is one in which the people as a whole feel that the process is open to them, and that on important issues all individuals can be part of a meaningful majority. If this is not true, then the democratic polity must either divide, or devise methods for those who feel they are not part of the system to have reserved areas, geographical or otherwise, in which they can expect that their interests will be uppermost. In other words there must be either external or internal self-determination. Most democracies are relatively homogeneous. But even here, without some forms of elected local or regional government, people in some areas will feel crushed under a national majority that is unable to understand their particular problems or accept their values. Federal democracies, such as India or the United States, have devised elaborate methods for separate divisions of the country to be in important degrees self-governing. The problems of over-centralization in Europe have recently been addressed by countries such as France, Spain, and the United Kingdom, but in the case of Northern Ireland, current subdivisions or political boundaries continue to make a section of the people feel like foreigners in their own land.

(10) The question of self-determination is closely related to the extent to which political power has been decentralized. Since it would be possible for a country to have an elaborate degree of decentralization and still hand down all the important decisions from above, we must test empirically the extent to which persons or parties not under control of the center actually succeed politically. The fact, for example, that Japanese-Americans are able to play a leading role in Hawaiian politics, or that the Scots nation-

alists are able to achieve a significant vote in Scotland suggest an authentic devolution of political power.

(11)   Finally, the Survey wants evidence for the extent to which the political decision process depends not only on the support of majorities at the polls, but also on a less adversarial process involving search for consensus among all groups on issues of major public interest. A democracy should be more than simply a society of winners and losers. The most common way for this to be demonstrated is for the opposition to be taken into account in major decisions and appointments, even when it does not have to be consulted in terms of the formal requirements of the system. The unwillingness of Malta's governing party to treat its opposition in this way, in spite of the fact that the governing party received less than a majority of the popular votes in the last election (but a slight majority of the seats), has made that country's political life into the struggle of two warring camps.[10]   Obviously, this test of informal power is particularly important in judging the degree of success of one-party "democracies" that base their claim to legitimacy on their willingness to achieve national consensuses.

Discussion of Civil Liberties.

(12) The potential checklist for civil liberties is longer and more diffuse than that for political rights. While many civil liberties are considered in judging the atmosphere of a country, primary attention is given to those liberties that are most directly related to the expression of political rights, with less attention given to those liberties that are likely to primarily affect individuals in their private capacity.

At the top of the list are questions of freedom for the communications media. We want to know whether the press and broadcasting facilities of the country are independent of government control, and serve the range of opinion that is present in the country. Clearly, if a population does not receive information about alternatives to present leaders and policies, then its ability to use any political process is impaired. In most traditional democracies there is no longer any question of censoring the press: no longer are people imprisoned for expressing their rational views on any matter—although secrecy and libel laws do have a slight affect in some democracies. As one moves from this open situation, from ratings of (1) to ratings of (7), a steady decline in freedom to publish is noticed: the tendency increases for people to be punished for criticizing the government, or papers to be closed, or censorship to be imposed, or for the newspapers and journals to be directly owned and supervised by the government.

The methods used by governments to control the print media are highly varied. While pre-publication censorship is often what Westerners think of because of their wartime experience, direct government ownership and control of the media and post-publication censorship through warnings, confiscations, or suspensions are more common. Government licensing of publications and journalists and controls over the distribution of newsprint are other common means of keeping control over what is printed. Even in countries with some considerable degree of democracy, such as Malaysia, press controls of these sorts may be quite extensive, often based on an ostensible legal requirement for "responsible journalism." Control of the press may be further extended by requiring papers to use a government news agency as their source of information, and by restricting the flow of foreign publications.[11]

Broadcasting—radio or television—are much more frequently owned by the government than the print media, and such ownership may or may not be reflected in government control over what is communicated. It is possible, as in the British case, for a government-owned broadcasting corporation to be so effectively protected from government control that its programs demonstrate genuine impartiality. However, in many well-known democracies, such as France or Greece, changes in the political composition of government affects the nature of what is broadcast to the advantage of incumbents. The government-owned broadcasting services of India make little effort to go beyond presenting the views of their government.

In most countries misuse of the news media to serve government interests is even more flagrant. At this level, we need to distinguish between those societies that require their media, particularly their broadcasting services, to avoid criticism of the political system or its leaders, and those that use them to "mobilize" their peoples in direct support for government policies.

In the first case the societies allow or expect their media, particularly their broadcasting services, to present a more or less favorable picture; in the second, the media are used to motivate their peoples to actively support government policies and to condemn or destroy those who oppose the governing system. In the first, the government's control is largely passive; in the second it is directly determinative of content.[12]

The comparison of active and passive control by government brings us to the most difficult issue in the question of media freedom—self-censorship. It is fairly easy to know if a government censors or suspends publications for content, or punishes journalists and reporters by discharge, imprisonment, or worse; judging the day-to-day influence of subtle pressures on the papers or broadcasting services of a country is much more difficult. Perhaps the most prevalent form of government control of the communications media is achieved through patterns of mutual assistance of government and media that ensure that, at worst, reports are presented in a bland, non-controversial manner—a common practice in Mexico and Pakistan.

Some critics believe that most communications media in the West, and especially in the United States, practice this kind of censorship, either because of government support, or because this is in the interest of the private owners of the media. In the United States, for example, it is noteworthy that National Public Radio, financed largely by the state, is generally much more critical of the government in its commentaries than are the commercial services. The critics would explain this difference by the greater ability of commercial stations to "police" their broadcasts and broadcasters. The primary explanation, however, lies in the gap between the subculture of broadcasters and audience for public radio and the subculture of broadcasters and especially audience for commercial stations.[13]

(13) Open public discussion is at least as important a civil liberty as free communications media. The ultimate test of a democracy is the degree to which an atmosphere for discussion in public and private exists free of fear of reprisal by either the government or opposition groups. Even in the relatively free communist society of Yugoslavia people are still being imprisoned for the expression of critical opinions in private.[14] Certainly Iranians have had to be

careful in the early and mid 1980s not to express too openly opinions that go against the prevailing climate of opinion in their country.

(14-15) Open discussion expressed through political organization, public demonstration, and assemblies is often threatening to political incumbents. There are occasions in which such assemblies may be dangerous to public order and should be closely controlled or forbidden. But in many societies this hypothetical danger is used as a pretense to deny opposition groups the ability to mobilize in support of alternative policies or leaders. In Malaysia, for example, the government's denial of public assembly to the opposition has been one of the main ways to restrict the ability of the opposition to effectively challenge the rule of the government.[15] Obviously, denial of the right to organize freely for political action is the most generalized form of the attempt to prevent the effective mobilization of opposition to government policies. Control over political organization is a distinguishing characteristic of one-party states, but many multiparty states place limits on the kinds or numbers of political parties that may be organized. Controls over extremist parties that deny the legitimacy of democratic institutions, such as many fascist or communist parties, are understandable—still, they represent limits on freedom. (Obviously, political and civil freedoms overlap closely on the right to political organization. The distinction is between denying the right to participate in elections and denying the right to organize to present alternative policies or arguments for and against change in other ways.)

(16) A democratic system is not secured unless there is a legal system that can be relied on for a fair degree of impartiality. The electoral process, for example, needs to be supervised by electoral commissions or other administrative systems that ultimately can be checked or overruled by the judicial system. People accused of actions against the state need to have some hope that their cases will be tried before the courts of the society and that the process will be fair. One of the tests that the author often applies to a country is whether it is possible to win against the government in a political case, and under what conditions. A reliable judicial system requires a guarantee of the permanence of judicial tenure,

20

particularly at the highest levels, as well as traditions of executive noninterference developed over a period of years. Of course, in no society are all trials fair or all judges impartial; but in this respect there are vast differences between democracies and nondemocracies.

A significant but less striking difference exists between the ways in which security services treat the public in democracies and nondemocracies. Since the people of a democracy are the sponsors of the system,[16] in theory the security services are their hired employees, and these employees should treat them with the utmost respect. However, because of the nature of the task of police and army, and their monopoly over force, in larger societies, at least, this relationship is often forgotten. Even in full-fledged democracies many security services have a reputation, for example in France or certain parts of the United States, of treating people with carelessness and even brutality. But it is clearly true that to the degree that security forces are the employees even in theory of a smaller group than the people as a whole, then their behavior will be even less "democratic."

(17) Certainly democracy requires that people be free from fear of the government, especially in regard to their politically related activities. To this degree, the emphasis of organizations such as Amnesty International on the extent of imprisonment, execution, or torture for reasons of conscience is closely related to any measurement of democracy. Oppressive countries imprison their opponents, or worse, both to silence the particular individuals, and to warn others of the dangers of opposing the system. Recently, exile and disappearances have been used as a further deterrent. "Disappearance" is generally a form of extra-judicial execution, often carried out in support of the ruling system. Such terrorism may or may not be directly under the orders of government leaders. These practices underscore the fact that a great deal of such internal state terrorism does not involve the normal legal process; frequently opponents are incarcerated through "detentions" that may last for years. In the Soviet Union and some other communist countries, the practice of using psychiatric institutions to incarcerate opponents has been developed on the theory that opposition to a people's state is itself a form of mental illness.

It is important in this regard to distinguish between the broader category of "political imprisonment" and the narrower "imprisonment for reasons of conscience." The former includes all cases that informed opinion would assume are related to political issues, or issues that can be defined politically in some states (such as religious belief in communist or some Islamic societies). It includes those who have written articles that the regime finds offensive as well as those who have thrown bombs or plotted executions, or even caused riots, to dramatize their cause. Since clearly the latter actions cannot be accepted by any government, all states, at whatever level of freedom, may have some "political prisoners." But if we take the category of political prisoners and separate out those who appear to have not committed or planned, or been involved in supporting, acts of violence, then we have the smaller category of "prisoners of conscience." Their existence must be counted against the democratic rating of any country. This is not to say that the existence of prisoners of conscience who have been involved in violence cannot also be taken in many countries as an indication that a system may not be sufficiently responsive to demands expressed nonviolently—too often there may be no effective means to express opposition without violence. The distinction between prisoners by reason of conscience and political prisoners is in practice often blurred by the outsider's difficulty in deciding whether particular incarcerated individuals have or have not committed or planned acts of violence. Nevertheless, by looking at the pattern of a regime's behavior over a period of years it is possible to estimate the degree to which a regime does or does not have prisoners of conscience.

Anti-dissident terror undertaken by groups that support the general system of a country but are not, or may not be, under government control is often difficult to evaluate in determining a country's rating. In the case where the terrorism is carried out by the security services, or their hired hands, we can either assume that these services are no longer controlled by the civilian administration, and to this extent the system cannot be called free, or that the civilian administration actually approves of the actions. In cases where the terror stems from parties or cliques outside of this structure, which to some degree has been the case in El Salvador, then the judgment has to be based on a finer balance of considerations.

(18-20) Democracies require freedom of organization that goes far beyond the right to organize political parties. The right of individuals to organize trade unions, or to organize cooperatives, or business enterprises, are certainly basic rights that may be limited only with great care in a free society. The right of union or peasant organization has been particularly significant because it allows large groups of ordinary people in many societies to balance through numbers the ability of the wealthy to concentrate power. However, in some societies, such as those of western Africa, the ability of medical, bar, and academic associations to mobilize or maintain alternatives to ruling groups has been of equal importance. Democracies require freedom of organization because there must be organized, countervailing power centers in a society—which is one definition of pluralism—if a society is going to maintain free institutions against the natural tendency of governments to aggregate power.

(21) It is for this reason that religious freedom, in belief and in organization, has been particularly important for the defense of freedom in a more general sense. Religious institutions have been able to maintain opposition strength in societies as different as those of Poland and Chile. A strong religious institution can build a wall around the individual dissident that a government will be loathe to breach for the sake of imposing its order. In countries such as Argentina or Poland, in recent years the organized church and organized unions have gone a long way toward insuring a society able to resist the encroachments of government. The question is not whether a particular established organization, such as the church, is itself favorable toward democracy. It is rather whether there are organizational structures willing and able to exist independently of government direction. Without such countervailing organizational power, it is unlikely that significant civil liberties can be maintained against government pressure.

(22) Civil liberties also include personal and individual social rights, particularly those that are likely to most directly affect the ability of people to withstand the pressures of the state. Especially important are those to property, travel (including emigration), and to an independent family life. The right to property does not necessarily mean the right to productive property,

but it does mean the right to property that can provide a cushion against government pressures such as dismissal from a position, that will make possible private publications, or other activity that cannot be financed unless people have more than subsistence incomes. The ability of an individual to travel, particularly to leave the country, is of great importance to dissidents or potential dissidents. It allows them additional sources of support and an additional refuge should the effort to improve conditions in their own country fail. An independent family offers another type of emotional haven that makes possible independent thinking and action. Opposition to Mao during the 1960s in China became almost impossible when individuals could no longer trust even spouses and children not to inform on their activities. The complete isolation of the individual, even in the midst of a crowded life, is the ultimate goal of oppressors.

(23-24) Civil liberty requires, then, that most people are relatively independent in both their lives and thoughts. It implies socioeconomic rights that include freedom from dependency on landlords, on bosses, on union leaders, or on bureaucrats. The kind of dependencies that the socioeconomic system imposes on individuals will vary from society to society, but widespread dependencies of these kinds are incompatible with democratic freedoms. This implies that there should be freedom from gross socioeconomic inequality. It should be noted that we are not saying that democracy requires that incomes or living standards be equalized. But we are saying that if inequalities are too great, if a small group of very wealthy lives in the midst of a large number of very poor individuals, it is likely that relations of dependency will develop that will make impossible the unfettered expression of opinion or a free and uncoerced vote.

(25) Finally, there would seem to be an indirect requirement that the civil liberties of a democracy include freedom from the extremes of government indifference and corruption. These conditions make it impossible for the people affected to feel that they are in any important sense the sponsors of their political system. Such indifference and corruption also implies that the mechanisms of democracy in the state are simply not working. If there is a continued record of disregard for the interests of the people, and

yet the representatives of the people are not replaced by the electoral or judicial process, the system is not working. Such indirect tests are necessary for a rating system that is based in large part on regular monitoring of press reports from around the world.

Status of Freedom

After countries are rated on seven-point scales for levels of political rights and civil liberties, these ratings are summarized in terms of overall assessments as free, partly free, and not free. This categorization is interpreted to mean that the list of operating democracies in the world is made up of those countries given the summary status of "free." Terms such as "free" and "not free" are only to be understood as relative expressions of the degree of political and civil liberties in a country. Use of the Status of Freedom rating necessarily places in the same category countries that are actually quite far apart in terms of their democratic practices—such as Hungary or South Africa at the less-free edge of partly free and Thailand or or Mexico at the more free.

The Survey is based on library research, updated by a more or less continuous flow of publications across the author's desk. Once the basic nature of the political system and its respect for civil liberties is established, following the flow of information either confirms or disconfirms this general picture, as well as recording any changes that may occur. It also has had the effect since the beginning of the Survey in 1972 of refining the author's sensitivity to those conditions and indicators that go with different levels of democratic rights.

The use of general descriptions and a flow of information is particularly useful because the Survey is based on evidence of democratic or nondemocratic **behavior** by the governments of countries in regard to their own peoples. Because interest in human rights and democracy is often centered in the legal community, many students or analysts in this area concentrate their attention on changes in laws or legal structures. Even Amnesty International takes the position that the numbers imprisoned or executed in a country is a less important indicator of change than change in the law in regard to these practices.[17]

The criticism is often made that the Survey ignores many "human rights," such as the right to adequate nutrition. This criticism can be addressed on several levels. Most appropriate is the remark that the Survey is of political and civil freedoms and not of human rights. (In philosophical terms neither freedom nor democracy are properly understood as including all "goods" and only goods.") The Survey is seriously concerned with some of the social and economic group of "rights." Clearly, some social and economic rights, such as the right to the freedom of workers or of businessmen to organize, are considered basic rights by the Survey. It is our feeling that some of the other proposed rights, including some of those implied by the Universal Declaration of Human Rights, involve social priorities that societies have a right to decide for themselves through the political process. In order to give people maximum freedom to develop their societies in terms of their needs and desires as they understand them, it is important that the list of rights be reduced to the minimum that allows them to make this determination.

The objection that the Survey should take more seriously "economic rights" in the narrower sense of economic freedom has been addressed in the 1982 and 1983-84 Freedom in the World volumes. As was mentioned in the beginning of this Chapter, the conclusion was that the basic economic right of all democracies was for the people to have an authentic and repeated opportunity to choose the economic system they desired. Their choice might range from libertarian to any one of a number of forms of socialist. To this we added that to be effective this economic freedom of choice must be based on some relative equalities in power; the absence of dependency that is included in the checklist above as a requisite civil liberty in a democracy must be generally present for economic freedom to be meaningful.

If more resources were available for assistance and on-site investigations, the Surveys could be greatly improved. They began, and have continued to be, a generalized attempt to improve the informed public's picture of the world. In spite of their limitations, some political scientists, economists, and sociologists have used the yearly Surveys as a source of data for correlation analyses of related variables. They are useful simply because they represent the only annual attempt to compare the level of democratic rights in all the countries in the world. (For further discussion of the Survey see the discussion below "The Comparative Survey: Criticisms and Comparisons.")

NOTES

1. See R. D. Gastil, Freedom in the World: 1982 (Westport: Greenwood Press, 1982), especially the article by Lindsay Wright, and Freedom in the World: 1983-84. For further discussions of the definitions of freedom and democracy from the viewpoint of the Survey see the relevant discussions in Freedom in the World 1978 and 1984-85.

2. James Bryce, Viscount, Modern Democracies 2 vols. (Macmillan, 1924).

3. Arthur Banks and Robert Textor, A Cross-Polity Survey (Cambridge: MIT Press, 1963).

4. Robert Dahl, Polyarchy: Participation and Opposition (New Haven: Yale University Press, 1971), pages 231-49.

5. Dankwart A. Rustow, A World of Nations (Washington: Brookings Institution, 1967).

6. Charles Humana, World Human Rights Guide (London: Hutchinson, 1983).

7. For example, United States Department of State, Country Reports on Human Rights Practices for 1985, Department of State (Washington, 1986).

8. Amnesty International Report, 1983 (London: Amnesty International, 1983).

9. On Senegal see Africa Research Bulletin, December 1983, page 7050; on Egypt, Middle East, July 1984, page 22.

10. See Keesing's Contemporary Archives 1982 and 1983, pages 31339-40, 33096.

11. Keesing's Contemporary Archives, 1984, pages 32782-85; Far Eastern Economic Review, September 20, 1984, pages 40ff. Compare also the discussion by Leonard Sussman, pages 99-131 below.

12. William Rugh, The Arab Press: News Media and Political Process in the Arab World (Syracuse: Syracuse University Press, 1979).

13. For an attempt to suggest the relatively greater importance of sub-cultural as opposed to class or other interests in determining the opinions of people in our society see R. D. Gastil, "'Selling Out' and the Sociology of Knowledge," Policy Sciences, 1971, 2, pages 271-277.

14. Amnesty Action, January 1985.

15. See, for example, **Far Eastern Economic Review**, August 23, 1984.

16. Alfred Kuhn, The **Logic of Social Systems** (San Francisco: Jossey-Bass, 1975), pages 330-61.

17. **Amnesty Action** January 1, 1985, page 7. Here it is suggested that improvement in human rights is not seen less in changes in the numbers imprisoned or killed as in changes in the laws of a country, such as the outlawing of torture or changing a policy that permits unjust imprisonment.

Survey Ratings and Tables for 1986

The past year will be best remembered by many readers as a year of fiery struggles for freedom in South Africa, South Korea, Philippines, Chile, and Afghanistan. In most cases the headlines of events in these countries reflected more continuity than change. But the struggles were an indication of a growing realization among many peoples that they no longer need to suffer the oppressions and limitations of the past. From this perspective, it is not surprising that many more countries expanded than contracted freedom in 1986.

The Tabulated Ratings

The accompanying Table 1 (Independent States) and Table 2 (Related Territories) rate each state or territory on seven-point scales for political and civil freedoms, and then provide an overall judgment of each as "free," "partly free," or "not free." In each scale, a rating of (1) is freest and (7) least free. Instead of using absolute standards, standards are comparative. The goal is to have ratings such that, for example, most observers would be likely to judge states rated (1) as freer than those rated (2). No state, of course, is absolutely free or unfree, but the degree of freedom does make a great deal of difference to the quality of life.[1]

In political rights, states rated (1) have a fully competitive electoral process, and those elected clearly rule. Most West European democracies belong here. Relatively free states may receive a (2) because, although the electoral process works and the elected rule, there are factors that cause us to lower our rating of the effective equality of the process. These factors may include extreme economic inequality, illiteracy, or intimidating violence. They also include the weakening of effective competition that is implied by the absence of periodic shifts in rule from one group or party to another.

Table 1

Independent States: Comparative Measures of Freedom

	Political Rights[1]	Civil Liberties[1]	Status of Freedom[2]
Afghanistan	7	7	NF
Albania	7	7	NF
Algeria	6	6	NF
Angola	7	7	NF
Antigua & Barbuda	2	3	F
Argentina	2	1 +	F
Australia	1	1	F
Austria	1	1	F
Bahamas	2	2	F
Bahrain	5	5	PF
Bangladesh	4 +	5	PF
Barbados	1	1 .+	F
Belgium	1	1	F
Belize	1	1	F
Benin	7	7	NF
Bhutan	5	5	PF
Bolivia	2	3	F
Botswana	2	3	F
Brazil	2 +	2	F
Brunei	6	5	PF
Bulgaria	7	7	NF
Burkina Faso[4]	7	6	NF
Burma	7	7	NF
Burundi	7	6	NF
Cambodia[3]	7	7	NF
Cameroon	6	6 +	NF
Canada	1	1	F
Cape Verde Islands	6	6 .+	NF
Central African Rep.	7	6	NF
Chad	7	7	NF
Chile	6	5	PF
China(Mainland)	6	6	NF
China(Taiwan)	5	5	PF
Colombia	2	3	F
Comoros	6	6	NF

	Political Rights[1]	Civil Liberties[1]	Status of Freedom[2]
Congo	7	6	NF
Costa Rica	1	1	F
Cuba	6	6	NF
Cyprus(G)	1	2	F
Cyprus(T)	2 ·	3	F ·
Czechoslovakia	7	6	NF
Denmark	1	1	F
Djibouti	6	6	NF
Dominica	2	2	F
Dominican Republic	1	3	F
Ecuador	2	3	F
Egypt	5 ·	4	PF
El Salvador	3 ·	4	PF
Equatorial Guinea	7	7	NF
Ethiopia	7	7	NF
European Community	2	1	F
Fiji	2	2	F
Finland	2	2	F
France	1	2	F
Gabon	6	6	NF
Gambia	3	4	PF
Germany(E)	7	6	NF
Germany(W)	1	2	F
Ghana	7	6	NF
Greece	2	2	F
Grenada	2	2 · +	F
Guatemala	3 +	3 +	PF
Guinea	7	5	NF
Guinea-Bissau	6	7 · –	NF
Guyana	5	5	PF
Haiti	5 +	4 +	PF +
Honduras	2	3	F
Hungary	5	5	PF
Iceland	1	1	F
India	2	3	F
Indonesia	5	6	PF

31

Survey: 1986

	Political Rights[1]	Civil Liberties[1]	Status of Freedom[2]
Iran	5	6	PF
Iraq	7	7	NF
Ireland	1	1	F
Israel	2	2	F
Italy	1	1	F
Ivory Coast	6	5	PF
Jamaica	2	3	F
Japan	1	1	F
Jordan	5	5	PF
Kenya	6	5	PF
Kiribati	1	2	F
Korea(N)	7	7	NF
Korea(S)	4	5	PF
Kuwait	6 –	5 –	PF
Laos	7	7	NF
Lebanon	5	4	PF
Lesotho	5	5	PF
Liberia	5	5	PF
Libya	6	6	NF
Luxembourg	1	1	F
Madagascar	5	5 ·	PF
Malawi	6	7	NF
Malaysia	3	5	PF
Maldives	5	6 ·	PF
Mali	7	6	NF
Malta	2	4	PF
Mauritania	7	6	NF
Mauritius	2	2	F
Mexico	4	4	PF
Mongolia	7	7	NF
Morocco	4	5	PF
Mozambique	6	7	NF
Nauru	2	2	F
Nepal	3	4	PF
Netherlands	1	1	F

	Political Rights[1]	Civil Liberties[1]	Status of Freedom[2]
New Zealand	1	1	F
Nicaragua	5	6 –	PF
Niger	7	6	NF
Nigeria	7	5	NF
Norway	1	1	F
Oman	6	6	NF
Pakistan	4	5	PF
Panama	6	3	PF
Papua New Guinea	2	2	F
Paraguay	5	6 –	PF
Peru	2	3	F
Philippines	4	2 +	PF
Poland	6	5	PF
Portugal	1	2	F
Qatar	5	5	PF
Romania	7	7	NF
Rwanda	6	6	NF
St. Kitts-Nevis	1	1	F
St. Lucia	1	2	F
St. Vincent	2	2	F
Sao Tome & Principe	7	7	NF
Saudi Arabia	6	7	NF
Senegal	3	4	PF
Seychelles	6	6	NF
Sierra Leone	5	5	PF
Singapore	4	5	PF
Solomon Islands	2	2 ·	F
Somalia	7	7	NF
South Africa	5	6	PF
Spain	1	2	F
Sri Lanka	3	4	PF
Sudan	4 +	5 +	PF +
Suriname	6	6	NF
Swaziland	5	6	PF
Sweden	1	1	F

	Political Rights[1]	Civil Liberties[1]	Status of Freedom[2]
Switzerland	1	1	F
Syria	6	7	NF
Tanzania	6	6	NF
Thailand	3	3 . +	PF
Togo	6	6	NF
Tonga	5	3	PF
Transkei	5	6	PF
Trinidad & Tobago	1	2	F
Tunisia	6 –	5	PF
Turkey	3	4 +	PF
Tuvalu	1	1 .	F
Uganda	5	4	PF
USSR	7	7	NF
United Arab Emirates	5	5	PF
United Kingdom	1	1	F
United States	1	1	F
Uruguay	2	2	F
Vanuatu	2	4	PF
Venezuela	1	2	F
Vietnam	7	7	NF
Western Samoa	4	3	PF
Yemen(N)	5	5	PF
Yemen(S)	6	7	NF
Yugoslavia	6	5	PF
Zaire	7	7	NF
Zambia	5	5	PF
Zimbabwe	4	6	PF

Notes to the Table

1. The scales use the numbers 1-7, with 1 comparatively offering the highest level of political or civil rights and 7 the lowest. A plus or minus following a rating indicates an improvement or decline since the last yearbook. A rating marked with a raised period (.) has been reevaluated by the author in this time; there may have been little change in the country.

2. F designates "free," PF "partly free," NF "not free."

3. Also known as Kampuchea.

4. Formerly Upper Volta.

Below this level, political ratings of (3) through (5) represent successively less effective implementation of democratic processes. Mexico, for example, has periodic elections and limited opposition, but for many years its governments have been selected outside the public view by the leaders of factions within the one dominant Mexican party. Governments of states rated (5) sometimes have no effective voting processes at all, but strive for consensus among a variety of groups in society in a way weakly analogous to those of the democracies. States at (6) do not allow competitive electoral processes that would give the people a chance to voice their desire for a new ruling party or for a change in policy. The rulers of states at this level assume that one person or a small group has the right to decide what is best for the nation, and that no one should be allowed to challenge that right. Such rulers do respond, however, to popular desire in some areas, or respect (and therefore are constrained by) belief systems (for example, Islam) that are the property of the society as a whole. At (7) the political despots at the top appear by their actions to feel little constraint from either public opinion or popular tradition.

Turning to the scale for civil liberties, in countries rated (1) publications are not closed because of the expression of rational political opinion, especially when the intent of the expression is to affect the legitimate political process. No major media are simply conduits for government propaganda. The courts protect the individual; persons are not imprisoned for their opinions; private rights and desires in education, occupation, religion, and residence are generally respected; and law-abiding persons do not fear for their lives because of their rational political activities. States at this level include most traditional democracies. There are, of course, flaws in the liberties of all of these states, and these flaws are significant when measured against the standards these states set themselves.

Movement down from (2) to (7) represents a steady loss of the civil freedoms we have detailed. Compared to (1), the police and courts of states at (2) have more authoritarian traditions. In some cases they may simply have a less institutionalized or secure set of liberties, such as in Portugal or Greece. Those rated (3) or below may have political prisoners and generally varying forms of censorship. Too often their security services practice torture. States rated (6) almost always have political prisoners; usually the

Table 2

Related Territories: Comparative Measures of Freedom

	Political Rights[1]	Civil Liberties[1]	Status of Freedom[2]
Australia			
Christmas Island	4	2	PF
Cocos Island	4	2	PF
Norfolk Island	4	2	PF
Chile			
Easter Island	5 +	5	PF
Denmark			
Faroe Islands	1	1	F
Greenland	1	1	F
France			
French Guiana	3	2	PF
French Polynesia	3	2	PF
Guadeloupe	3	2	PF
Martinique	3	2	PF
Mahore (Mayotte)	2	2	F
Monaco[4]	4	2	PF
New Caledonia	3	2	F
Reunion	3	2	PF
St. Pierre & Miq.			
Wallis and Futuna	2	2	F
	4	3	PF
Israel			
Occupied Territs.	5	5	PF
Italy			
San Marino[3]	1	1	F
Vatican City[3]	6	4	PF
Netherlands			
Aruba	1 +	1	F
Neth. Antilles	1 +	1	F
New Zealand			
Cook Islands	2	2	F
Niue	2	2	F
Tokelau Islands	4	2	PF
Portugal			
Azores	2	2	F
Macao	3	4	PF
Madeira	2	2	F

	Political Rights[1]	Civil Liberties[1]	Status of Freedom[2]
South Africa			
Bophuthatswana[4]	6	5	PF
Ciskei[4]	6	6	NF
SW Africa (Namibia)	6	5	PF
Venda[4]	6	6	NF
Spain			
Canary Islands	1	2	F
Ceuta	2	3	F
Melilla	2	3	F
Switzerland			
Liechtenstein	3	1	F
United Kingdom			
Anguilla	2	2	F
Bermuda	2	1	F
B. Virgin Islands	2	1	F
Cayman Islands	2	2	F
Channel Islands	2	1	F
Falkland Islands	2	2	F
Gibraltar	1	2	F
Hong Kong	4	2	PF
Isle of Man	1	1	F
Montserrat	2	2	F
St. Helena	2	2	F
Turks and Caicos	2	2	F
United States			
American Samoa	2	2	F
Belau[5]	2	2	F
Guam	3	2	PF
Marshall Islands[5]	2	2	F
Micronesia (F.S.M.)[5]	2	2	F
Northern Marianas	1 +	2	F
Puerto Rico	2	1	F
Virgin Islands	2	3	F
France-Spain (Con.)			
Andorra[3]	3	3	PF

Notes to the Table

1, 2. See Notes, Table of Independent States.

3. Nominally independent, these states are legally dependent on another country (or countries in Andorra's case) in such areas as foreign affairs, defense, customs, or services.

4. The geography and history of these newly independent "homelands" cause us to consider them dependencies.

5. Now in transition; high degree of self-determination.

37

legitimate media are completely under government supervision; there is no right of assembly; and, often, travel, residence, and occupation are narrowly restricted. However, at (6) there still may be relative freedom in private conversation, especially in the home; illegal demonstrations do take place; and underground literature is published. At (7) there is pervading fear, little independent expression takes place even in private, almost no public expressions of opposition emerge in the police-state environment, and imprisonment or execution is often swift and sure.

Political terror is an attempt by a government or private group to get its way through the use of murder, torture, exile, prevention of departure, police controls, or threats against the family. These weapons are usually directed against the expression of civil liberties. To this extent they surely are a part of the civil liberty "score." Unfortunately, because of their dramatic and newsworthy nature, such denials of civil liberties often become identified in the minds of informed persons with the whole of civil liberties.

Political terror is a tool of revolutionary repression of the right or left. When that repression is no longer necessary to achieve the suppression of civil liberties, political terror is replaced by implacable and well-organized but often less general and newsworthy controls. Of course, there is a certain unfathomable terror in the sealed totalitarian state, yet life can be lived with a normality in these states that is impossible in the more dramatically terrorized. It would be a mistake to dismiss this apparent anomaly as an expression of a Survey bias. For there is, with all the blood, a much wider range of organized and personal expression of political opinion and judgment in states such as Lebanon and Guatemala than in more peaceful states such as Czechoslovakia.

In making the distinction between political terror and civil liberties as a whole we do not imply that the United States should not be urgently concerned with all violations of human rights and perhaps most urgently with those of political terror. Again it must be emphasized that the Survey is not a rating of the relative desirability of societies—but of certain explicit freedoms.

A cumulative judgment of "free," "partly free," or "not free" is made on the basis of the foregoing seven-point ratings, and an understanding of how they were derived. Generally, states rated (1) and (2) will be "free"; those at (3), (4), and (5), "partly free";

and those at (6) and (7), "not free." A rating of (2),(3) places an independent country in the "free" category; a rating of (6),(5) places it in the "partly free."

It has long been felt that the Survey has paid too little attention to the material correlates, conditions, or context of freedom or non-freedom. While we have argued elsewhere that there is no one-to-one relation between wealth and freedom, and that history has diffused freedom along with economic wealth more than one has produced the other, the relationship remains an important one to ponder.

The reporting period covered by this Survey (November 1985 to November 1986) does not correspond with the calendar of short-term events in the countries rated. For this reason the yearly Survey may mask or play down events that occur at the end of the year.

The Survey is aware that many of its judgments of what is or is not an independent country are questioned. The principle that we have used is a pragmatic one that combines several criteria. A country exists independently to the extent that persons from a central core of people identified with that country more than any other country rule in the name of their country through control of its territory, or at least what they define as the central area of that territory. It helps if a country, in the modern world, has some historical and geographical continuity. But historical existence in the past, such as that of Lithuania or Georgia in the USSR, or Tibet in China, is not enough to make the Survey's list. Whether a country's leaders are actually in control, or "rule" is also defined loosely. Many doubt, for example, the existence of a separate country of Transkei—and for good reason. However, the Survey believes that the independence or separateness of Transkei is comparable to that of Swaziland, Lesotho, Mongolia, Laos, or, in a different sense, Afghanistan or Lebanon. The separateness of the other homeland states is less clear, if only marginally.

The 1986 Survey adds for the first time the European Community (EC) as a separate country. Of course, for many purposes the EC cannot be treated the same as other countries. Yet its democratic and juridical political reality deserves to be recognized. For some purposes its law is held to be superior to its member states. The EC has a directly elected Parliament, Court of Justice, and executive institutions that offer it political power

Table 3

RATING COUNTRIES BY POLITICAL RIGHTS

Most Free 1	Australia Austria Barbados Belgium Belize Canada Costa Rica Cyprus (G) Denmark	Dominican Rep. France Germany (W) Iceland Ireland Italy Japan Kiribati Luxembourg	Netherlands New Zealand Norway Portugal St. Kitts-Nevis St. Lucia Spain Sweden Switzerland	Trinidad & Tobago Tuvalu United Kingdom United States Venezuela
2	Antigua & Barb. Argentina Bahamas Bolivia Botswana Brazil Colombia	Cyprus (T) Dominica Ecuador Fiji Finland Greece Grenada	Honduras India Israel Jamaica Malta Mauritius Nauru	Papua New Guinea Peru St. Vincent Solomons Uruguay Vanuatu
3	El Salvador Gambia Guatemala	Malaysia Nepal	Senegal Sri Lanka	Thailand Turkey
4	Bangladesh Korea (S) Mexico	Morocco Pakistan Philippines	Singapore Sudan Western Samoa	Zimbabwe
5	Bahrain Bhutan China (Taiwan) Egypt Guyana Haiti Hungary	Indonesia Iran Jordan Lebanon Lesotho Liberia Madagascar	Maldives Nicaragua Paraguay Qatar Sierra Leone South Africa Swaziland	Tonga Transkei Uganda United Arab Emirates Yemen (N) Zambia

6	Algeria
	Brunei
	Cameroon
	Cape Verde
	  Islands
	Chile
	China
	  (Mainland)
		Comoros
		Cuba
		Djibouti
		Gabon
		Guinea-Bissau
		Ivory Coast
		Kenya
		Kuwait
			Libya
			Malawi
			Mozambique
			Oman
			Panama
			Poland
			Rwanda
			Saudi Arabia
				Seychelles
				Suriname
				Syria
				Tanzania
				Togo
				Tunisia
				Yemen (S)
				Yugoslavia

7 Least Free	Afghanistan
	Albania
	Angola
	Benin
	Bulgaria
	Burkina Faso
	Burma
	Burundi
	Cambodia
		Central
		  African Rep.
		Chad
		Congo
		Czechoslovakia
		Equatorial
		  Guinea
		Ethiopia
		Germany (E)
			Ghana
			Guinea
			Iraq
			Korea (N)
			Laos
			Mali
			Mauritania
			Mongolia
			Niger
				Nigeria
				Romania
				Sao Tome &
				  Principe
				Somalia
				USSR
				Vietnam
				Zaire

Table 4

RATING COUNTRIES BY CIVIL LIBERTIES

Most Free 1	Argentina Australia Austria Barbados Belgium Belize	Canada Costa Rica Denmark Iceland Ireland Italy	Japan Luxembourg Netherlands New Zealand Norway St. Kitts-Nevis	Sweden Switzerland Tuvalu United Kingdom United States

2	Bahamas
	Brazil
	Cyprus (G)
	Dominica
	Fiji
	Finland
	France
		Germany (W)
		Greece
		Grenada
		Israel
		Kiribati
		Mauritius
		Nauru
			Papua
			  New Guinea
			Philippines
			Portugal
			St. Lucia
			St. Vincent
			Solomons
				Spain
				Trinidad &
				  Tobago
				Uruguay
				Venezuela

3	Antigua & Barb. Bolivia Botswana Colombia	Cyprus (T) Dominican Rep. Ecuador Guatemala	Honduras India Jamaica Panama	Peru Thailand Tonga Western Samoa
4	Egypt El Salvador Gambia Haiti	Lebanon Malta Mexico Nepal	Senegal Sri Lanka Turkey Uganda	Vanuatu
5	Bahrain Bangladesh Bhutan Brunei Chile China (T) Guinea Guyana	Hungary Ivory Coast Jordan Kenya Korea (S) Kuwait Lesotho Liberia	Madagascar Malaysia Morocco Nigeria Pakistan Poland Qatar Sierra Leone	Singapore Sudan Tunisia United Arab Emirates Yemen (N) Yugoslavia Zambia
6	Algeria Burkina Faso Burundi Cameroon Cape Verde Is. Central African Rep. China (M) Comoros	Congo Cuba Czechoslovakia Djibouti Gabon Germany (E) Ghana Indonesia Iran	Libya Maldives Mali Mauritania Nicaragua Niger Oman Paraguay Rwanda	Seychelles South Africa Suriname Swaziland Tanzania Togo Transkei Zimbabwe

7
 	
Least
Free
	Afghanistan
	Albania
	Angola
	Benin
	Bulgaria
	Burma
	Cambodia
		Chad
		Equatorial
		  Guinea
		Ethiopia
		Guinea-Bissau
		Iraq
		Korea (N)
			Laos
			Malawi
			Mongolia
			Mozambique
			Romania
			Sao Tome &
			  Principe
				Saudi Arabia
				Somalia
				Syria
				USSR
				Vietnam
				Yemen (S)
				Zaire

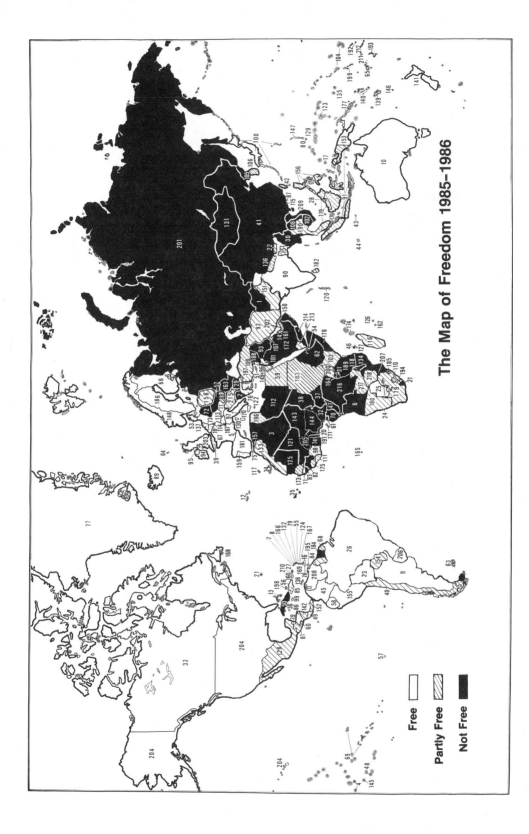

The Map of Freedom 1985–1986

Free

Partly Free

Not Free

Free States

8	Antigua & Barbuda
9	Argentina
10	Australia
11	Austria
13	Bahamas
16	Barbados
18	Belgium
19	Belize
23	Bolivia
25	Botswana
26	Brazil
33	Canada
45	Colombia
49	Costa Rica
51a	Cyprus (G)
51b	Cyprus (T)
53	Denmark
55	Dominica
56	Dominican Republic
58	Ecuador
65	Fiji
66	Finland
67	France
73	Germany (W)
76	Greece
78	Grenada
86	Honduras
89	Iceland
90	India
94	Ireland
96	Israel
97	Italy
99	Jamaica
100	Japan
104	Kiribati
114	Luxembourg
126	Mauritius
135	Nauru
137	Netherlands
141	New Zealand
148	Norway
153	Papua New Guinea
155	Peru
159	Portugal
166	St. Kitts–Nevis
167	St. Lucia
169	St. Vincent
177	Solomons
181	Spain
186	Sweden
187	Switzerland
195	Trinidad & Tob.
199	Tuvalu
203	United Kingdom
204	United States
206	Uruguay
208	Venezuela

Related Territories

4	Amer. Samoa (US)
7	Anguilla (UK)
138a	Aruba (Ne)
12	Azores (Port)
17	Belau (US)
21	Bermuda (UK)
27	Br. Vir. Is. (UK)
34	Canary Isls. (Sp)
36	Cayman Isls. (UK)
157a	Ceuta (Sp)
39	Channel Isls. (UK)
48	Cook Isls. (NZ)
63	Falkland Is. (UK)
64	Faroe Isls. (Den)
75	Gibraltar (UK)
77	Greenland (Den)
95	Isle of Man (UK)
113	Liechtenstein (Sw)
117	Madeira (Port)
123	Marshall Isls. (US)
127	Mayotte (Fr)
157b	Melilla (Sp)
129	Micronesia (US)
132	Montserrat (UK)
138	Ne. Antilles (Ne)
139	New Caledonia (Fr)
145	Niue (N.Z)
147	No. Marianas (US)
160	Puerto Rico (US)
165	St. Helena (UK)
168	St. Pierre-Mq. (Fr)
170	San Marino (It)
198	Turks & C. (UK)
210	Virgin Isls. (US)

Partly Free States

14	Bahrain
15	Bangladesh
22	Bhutan
28	Brunei
40	Chile
42	China (Taiwan)
59	Egypt
60	El Salvador
71	Gambia
81	Guatemala
84	Guyana
85	Haiti
88	Hungary
91	Indonesia
92	Iran
98	Ivory Coast
101	Jordan
103	Kenya
106	Korea (S)
107	Kuwait
109	Lebanon
110	Lesotho
111	Liberia
116	Madagascar
119	Malaysia
120	Maldives
122	Malta
128	Mexico
133	Morocco
136	Nepal
142	Nicaragua
151	Pakistan
152	Panama
154	Paraguay
156	Philippines
158	Poland
161	Qatar
173	Senegal
175	Sierra Leone
176	Singapore
179	So. Africa
182	Sri Lanka
183	Sudan
185	Swaziland
190	Thailand
193	Tonga
194	Transkei
196	Tunisia
197	Turkey
200	Uganda
202	United Arab Emirates
140	Vanuatu
212	W. Samoa
213	Yemen (N)
215	Yugoslavia
217	Zambia
218	Zimbabwe

Related Territories

5	Andorra (Fr–Sp)
24	Bophuthatswana (South Aff)
43	Christmas Is. (Austral)
44	Cocos Isls. (Austral)
57	Easter Is. (Ch)
68	French Guiana (Fr)
69	French Polynesia (Fr)
79	Guadeloupe (Fr)
80	Guam (US)
87	Hong Kong (UK)
115	Macao (Port)
124	Martinique (Fr)
130	Monaco (Fr)
146	Norfolk Is. (Aus)
149	Occupied Trs. (Isr)
162	Reunion (Fr)
180	SW Africa (Namibia) (SA)
192	Tokelau Isls. (NZ)
211	Vatican (It)
	Wallis and Futuna (Fr)

Not Free States

1	Afghanistan
2	Albania
3	Algeria
6	Angola
20	Benin
29	Bulgaria
205	Burkina Faso
30	Burma
31	Burundi
102	Cambodia
32	Cameroon
35	Cape Verde Is.
37	Central African Republic
38	Chad
41	China (Mainland)
46	Comoros
47	Congo
50	Cuba
52	Czechoslovakia
54	Djibouti
61	Equatorial Guinea
62	Ethiopia
70	Gabon
72	Germany (E)
74	Ghana
82	Guinea
83	Guinea-Bissau
93	Iraq
105	Korea (N)
108	Laos
112	Libya
118	Malawi
121	Mali
125	Mauritania
131	Mongolia
134	Mozambique
143	Niger
144	Nigeria
150	Oman
163	Romania
164	Rwanda
171	Sao Tome & Principe
172	Saudi Arabia
174	Seychelles
178	Somalia
184	Suriname
188	Syria
189	Tanzania
191	Togo
201	USSR
209	Vietnam
214	Yemen (S)
216	Zaire

Related Territories

219	Ciskei (SA)
207	Venda (SA)

over the members of the community far beyond that attained by other intergovernmental structures in modern times.

Declines in Freedom in 1986

No country had a major decline in its freedom rating or status in 1986. A distinct setback occurred in **Kuwait** when the parliament was dissolved, and closer controls were placed on the press. This was especially unfortunate in the Gulf region where leaders had observed with interest Kuwait's experiments in liberalization. Elsewhere in the Middle East the modest degree of freedom in **Tunisia** was undermined by the increasing authoritarianism of its ruler, both within the dominant party and in relation to opponents struggling for expression outside that party. Union and press activity has been further restricted. In November 1986, these conditions led to an opposition boycott of the general election.

In the Americas, freedom slipped a degree in **Nicaragua** as the last remaining generally available critical voice, the newspaper La Prensa, was closed. Other minor publications were suspended, as well as the broadcasting station of the Catholic Church. **Paraguay**'s last major critical voice, a radio station, was closed down, and religious publications forced to publish outside the country. In both cases these developments were continuations of trends well underway in the previous year.

Advances in Freedom

In spite of continuing problems throughout the region, significant improvement occurred in a number of countries in the Americas. **Argentina** further institutionalized its democratic forms as it overcame the spectre of past military intervention to develop a free and open society in all media, and to extend its democracy in regional form. The same spirit animated the further institutional-ization of democracy in **Brazil**. Local and national elections during the year were open, contested by a wide range of parties, and their outcome served to confirm the mandate of the president (who had arrived at the position partially through chance and spe-cial transitional regulations). **Barbados**'s strong democracy was reenforced by a decisive win by the opposition; there were no further instances of the negative reaction to criticism that had previously caused pressures on the media.

The most dramatic gains in the Americas were in Guatemala and Haiti. In **Guatemala,** 1986 saw the consolidation of the return to electoral democracy—a process already well underway in the electoral campaigns and results of late 1985. However, because of the continuing insurgency and the entrenched power of the military, particularly in rural areas, the civilian leadership moved slowly. The disappearances and cruelty that have marked recent years were reduced but not brought to an end. Rights of assembly, demonstration, and organization are again commonly expressed.

In **Haiti,** a tyrannical regime was brought to an end by a genuine, if unfocused, popular uprising. The army, which had remained relatively untarred by the regime, stepped in to fill the vacuum. But progress has been slow, and by the end of the year the freedoms that flourished in the media and on the streets in the aftermath of revolution remained insecure, caught between the lawlessness of a disorganized population and the danger of repression from the security services. A poorly organized constituent assembly election attracted few substantial candidates and very few voters.

The best-known advance of freedom in 1986 was in the **Philippines** where authoritarian rule crumpled in the face of a united middle class and Washington's ultimate support of change. The change was almost universally welcomed, and was certainly a necessary step back to democracy. However, the new government did not move quickly to establish its legitimacy either through a new election or a careful reanalysis of the one that made the change possible. The new government seemed to imitate its predecessor in its high-handed removal of thousands of local officials. In a continuing crisis atmosphere, military leaders maintained and may even have increased their role in government. The press and radio of the country were now freer than they had been in many years, and the judicial system was beginning to be revived.

Thailand passed through another electoral period with a growing respect for diversity of opinion and participation. The country's steady development of democratic institutions from a more traditional base has been one of the most promising in

Southeast Asia. Nevertheless, in late 1986 there was again talk of military restiveness. Elections in **Bangladesh** and the ending of martial law were an advance. But they were so marred by violence, repressions, boycotts, and probable vote miscounting, that the country's democratic advance was only marginal. In spite of continuing inability to recognize the rights of the large Kurdish minority, **Turkey** has improved its human rights record in other respects, particularly in the openness of the press.

In Africa, progress was made in **Sudan** where a a fair election brought back parliamentary government. To the extent Sudan should be considered a part of the Arab Muslim world, it now has the best functioning democracy in that world. Unfortunately, in the southern third of the country the election could not be held sucessfully because of the continuing civil war. At least in the capital, the new regime brought a much broadened and more open media. **Cameroon** is far from democratic, but the year saw an improvement in the degree of democracy through elections within the single ruling party.

Several related territories have also improved their ratings. The peaceful division of the **Netherlands Antilles** with the creation of the new territory of **Aruba** improved the self-determination of the area. Chile's **Easter Island** has developed a notable degree of self-determination in local affairs in the last two years. The people of the **Northern Marianas** have at last achieved their goal of formally becoming a Commonwealth of the United States.

Other Changes and Trends

Many countries were characterized by continuing struggle for or against the expansion of freedom, without that struggle eventuating in changes in the ratings of the Survey. Sometimes this is because the only changes that could be made in a rating would place the country in company with countries that show a distinctively different level of freedom. Sometimes the changes of interest are more potential than realized. In other cases, significant changes in one direction seem to have been balanced by changes in the other.

Poland saw an institutionalization of its mixed system. On the one hand, the dissidents were let out of prison; on the other, the enthusiasm of the Polish opposition seemed to have ebbed. The rebel movement of **Uganda** succeeded in finally winning its long struggle against an oppressive regime. However popular the result in much of the country, this did not bring the immediate restoration of democracy, nor the thorough acceptance of the right to free expression. A coup brought an end to an unpopular regime in **Lesotho,** but the new rule of military leader and monarch offered little advance in freedom.

It was a disappointing year for democracy in some areas. Although Guatemala was a bright spot in **Central America,** there was little progress in Honduras, Nicaragua, El Salvador, or Panama beyond the military-dominated patterns of the past. Major countries such as **Kenya** and **Indonesia** seem slowly to be sliding into institutionalized tyranny, although the extent of the change is not quite enough yet for these to be considered "not free." In both, the ability to express opinions other than those sanctioned by the system has been progressively narrowed, and fear has replaced argument.

Violence continued to characterize the democratic struggle in **South Africa, Chile,** and **South Korea.** Yet the fact that the democratic opposition in these struggles still preserved its organization and voice continued to distinguish these societies from "not free" societies in which there is no organized opposition, and little if any public criticism of the system. In Chile and South Africa the courts showed a continuing ability to resist, or at least publicly question, the system. A quick comparison of these countries with "not free" regimes rated immediately below them, such as Libya, Oman, or mainland China, suggests that they do not belong in such company. Chile and South Africa seem more comparable to Iran, Nicaragua, or Paraguay, countries ruled often arbitrarily by a small clique, but countries with well-organized and vocal groups that within limits offer alternative views to their peoples differing substantially from government positions. South Korea's rating remains higher than this cluster, closer perhaps to countries such as Morocco or Malaysia. Its opposition parties play a major role in the legislature, and the government is closer to accepting the right of the opposition to rule in the near future.

In the longer term, the most promising trend continuing in 1986 was in the liberalization of discussion and mode of life in the People's Republic of **China.** All reports suggest that at every level, including that of national congresses, the Chinese discuss their problems and alternatives more openly than in any other "not free" Marxist-Leninist country. Chinese now have more choices than formerly in their daily lives. The repression in fringe areas such as Tibet has also greatly eased. Of course, the system remains ostensibly Marxist-Leninist and those who would question the control mechanisms of the system face jail. Although the opposition media have been suppressed more than ever in **Nationalist China** in 1986, toward the year's end the government announced that it was planning to end martial law and allow the establishment of political parties other than the governing Kuomintang. This was particularly significant as it followed a direct challenge by the opposition through its establishment of a new party in defiance of regulations. An election in December came too late to test the sincerity of this opening; preliminary reports suggested substantial opposition gains.

The Record of Gains and Losses: 1973-1986

Table 5 relates the most important of this year's changes in country ratings to the recent record of the countries involved. In this regard "important" must be a partly subjective judgment, but it certainly excludes those changes in ratings that resulted from the analyst's judgment or method of rating.

Table 6 allows the reader to roughly trace the course of freedom since the Survey began. It should be noted that changes in information and judgment since 1973 make many ratings not strictly comparable from year to year. Nevertheless, the table reflects the direction of trends in each country.

Since the Survey began, the world has experienced a number of gains and losses of freedom, either immediate or prospective. Most generally, there has been an advance of Soviet communism in Southeast Asia after the fall of South Vietnam, and at least its partial institutionalization in South Yemen, Ethiopia, and the former Portuguese colonies of Africa. In the Americas an imminent danger of the spread of communism has arisen in Nicaragua, and an erstwhile danger in Grenada. Perhaps equally significant has been the amelioration of communism in many areas. While mainland China is still a repressive society, it has increased freedom through

Table 5

MOST SIGNIFICANT CHANGES: 1985 to 1986

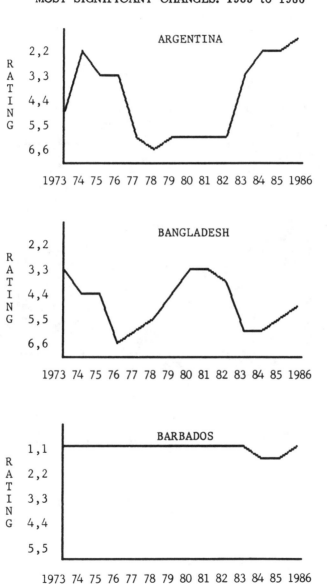

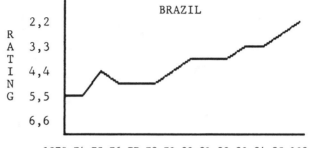

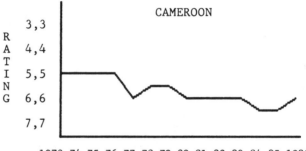

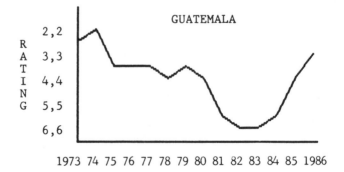

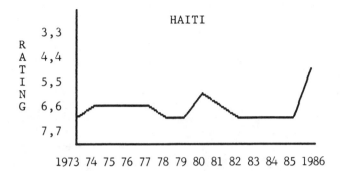

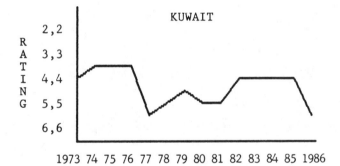

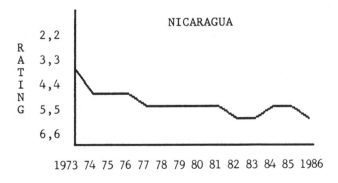

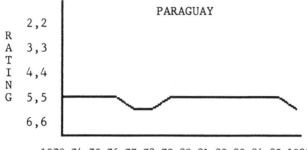

PARAGUAY

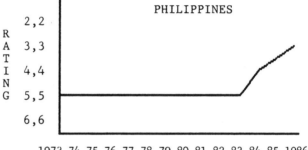

PHILIPPINES

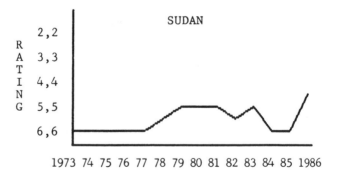

SUDAN

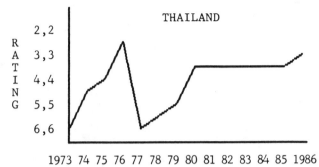

THAILAND

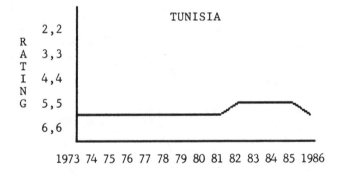

TUNISIA

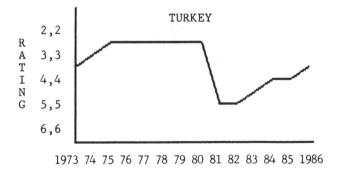

TURKEY

Table 6

RATINGS OF COUNTRIES SINCE 1973

Country	73	75	76	77	78	79	80	81	82	83	84	85	86
Afghan-	4	7	7	7	7	7	7	7	7	7	7	7	7
istan	5	6	6	6	6	7	7	7	7	7	7	7	7
	PF	NF	NF	NF	NF	NF	NF	NF	NF	NF	NF	NF	NF
Albania	7	7	7	7	7	7	7	7	7	7	7	7	7
	7	7	7	7	7	7	7	7	7	7	7	7	7
	NF	NF	NF	NF	NF	NF	NF	NF	NF	NF	NF	NF	NF
Algeria	6	6	7	6	6	6	6	6	6	6	6	6	6
	6	6	6	6	6	6	6	6	6	6	6	6	6
	NF	NF	NF	NF	NF	NF	NF	NF	NF	NF	NF	NF	NF
Angola3	7	6	6	6	7	7	7	7	7	7	7	7	7
	6	4	6	6	7	7	7	7	7	7	7	7	7
	NF	PF	NF*	NF	NF	NF	NF	NF	NF	NF	NF	NF	NF
Antigua &	2	2	2	2	2	2	2	2	2	2	2	2	2
Barbuda3	3	3	3	3	2	2	2	2	2	3	3	3	3
	F	F	F	F	F	F	F	F	F*	F	F	F	F
Argentina	6	2	2	6	6	6	6	6	6	3	2	2	2
	3	4	4	5	6	5	5	5	5	3	2	2	1
	PF	PF	PF	NF	NF	NF	NF	NF	NF	PF	F	F	F
Australia	1	1	1	1	1	1	1	1	1	1	1	1	1
	1	1	1	1	1	1	1	1	1	1	1	1	1
	F	F	F	F	F	F	F	F	F	F	F	F	F
Austria	1	1	1	1	1	1	1	1	1	1	1	1	1
	1	1	1	1	1	1	1	1	1	1	1	1	1
	F	F	F	F	F	F	F	F	F	F	F	F	F

Notes to the Table

*. Indicates year of independence.

1. Ratings are from the Jan/Feb issues of Freedom at Issue through 1982. The ratings for 1983, 1984, and 1985 are based on 1983-84 and subsequent yearbooks. The three lines are political rights, civil liberties, and status of freedom.

2. Ratings for 1974 may be obtained from Table 6, 1985-86 yearbook.

3. Until 1975 Angola, Mozambique, and Guinea-Bissau (formerly Portuguese Guinea) were evaluated together as Portugal Colonies (A), while Sao Tome and Cape Verde were Portugal (B). Until 1978 Antigua, Dominica, and St. Lucia were considered together as the West Indies Associated States (and Grenada until 1975). The Comoros and Djibouti (Territory of the Afars and Issas) were considered as "France: Overseas Territories" until 1975. Until 1975 Kiribati and Tuvalu were considered together as the Gilbert and Ellice Islands. Cyprus was regarded as a unit until 1981.

4. 1973 ratings for South Africa were white: 2,3,F and black: 5,6,NF.

5. Ratings for North Vietnam for 1973-1976 were 7,7,NF; those for South Vietnam were 4,5,PF for 1973-75, 7,7,NF for 1976.

Table 6 (continued)

Country	73	75	76	77	78	79	80	81	82	83	84	85	86
Bahamas	2	1	1	1	1	1	1	1	1	2	2	2	2
	2	2	2	2	2	2	2	2	2	2	2	2	2
	F	F	F	F	F	F	F	F	F	F	F	F	F
Bahrain	6	4	6	6	6	6	6	5	5	5	5	5	5
	5	4	4	4	4	4	4	4	5	5	5	5	5
	NF	PF	PF	PF	PF	PF	PF	PF	PF	PF	PF	PF	PF
Bangla- desh	2	4	7	7	6	4	3	3	3	6	6	5	4
	4	4	5	4	4	4	3	3	4	5	5	5	5
	PF	PF	NF	PF	PF	PF	PF	PF	PF	PF	PF	PF	PF
Barbados	1	1	1	1	1	1	1	1	1	1	1	1	1
	1	1	1	1	1	1	1	1	1	1	2	2	1
	F	F	F	F	F	F	F	F	F	F	F	F	F
Belgium	1	1	1	1	1	1	1	1	1	1	1	1	1
	1	1	1	1	1	1	1	1	1	1	1	1	1
	F	F	F	F	F	F	F	F	F	F	F	F	F
Belize	2	1	1	1	1	1	1	1	1	1	2	1	1
	2	2	2	2	2	2	2	2	2	2	1	1	1
	F	F	F	F	F	F	F	F	F	F	F	F	F
Benin (Dahomey)	7	7	7	7	7	7	7	7	7	7	7	7	7
	5	6	7	7	7	7	6	6	6	6	7	7	7
	NF	NF	NF	NF	NF	NF	NF	NF	NF	NF	NF	NF	NF
Bhutan	4	4	4	4	4	4	5	5	5	5	5	5	5
	4	4	4	4	4	4	5	5	5	5	5	5	5
	PF	PF	PF	PF	PF	PF	PF	PF	PF	PF	PF	PF	PF
Bolivia	5	6	6	6	6	5	3	7	7	2	2	2	2
	4	5	5	4	4	3	5	5	5	3	3	3	3
	PF	NF	NF	PF	PF	PF	PF	NF	NF	F	F	F	F
Botswana	3	2	2	2	2	2	2	2	2	2	2	2	2
	4	3	3	3	3	3	3	3	3	3	3	3	3
	PF	F	F	F	F	F	F	F	F	F	F	F	F
Brazil	5	4	4	4	4	4	4	4	4	3	3	3	2
	5	4	5	5	5	4	3	3	3	3	3	2	2
	PF	PF	PF	PF	PF	PF	PF	PF	PF	PF	PF	F	F
Brunei	6	6	6	6	6	6	6	6	6	6	6	6	6
	5	5	5	5	5	5	5	5	5	5	6	5	5
	NF	NF	NF	NF	NF	NF	NF	NF	NF	NF	NF	PF	PF
Bulgaria	7	7	7	7	7	7	7	7	7	7	7	7	7
	7	7	7	7	7	7	7	7	7	7	7	7	7
	NF	NF	NF	NF	NF	NF	NF	NF	NF	NF	NF	NF	NF
Burkina Faso	3	6	6	5	5	2	2	6	6	6	7	7	7
	4	4	4	5	4	3	3	5	5	5	5	6	6
	PF	PF	PF	PF	PF	F	F	PF	PF	PF	NF	NF	NF
Burma	7	7	6	6	7	7	7	7	7	7	7	7	7
	5	5	6	6	6	6	6	6	6	7	7	7	7
	NF	NF	NF	NF	NF	NF	NF	NF	NF	NF	NF	NF	NF

Table 6 (continued)

Country	73	75	76	77	78	79	80	81	82	83	84	85	86
Burundi	7	7	7	7	7	7	7	7	7	6	7	7	7
	7	7	6	6	6	6	7	6	6	6	6	6	6
	NF	NF	NF	NF	NF	NF	NF	NF	NF	NF	NF	NF	NF
Cambodia	6	6	7	7	7	7	7	7	7	7	7	7	7
	5	6	7	7	7	7	7	7	7	7	7	7	7
	NF	NF	NF	NF	NF	NF	NF	NF	NF	NF	NF	NF	NF
Cameroon	6	6	6	7	6	6	6	6	6	6	6	6	6
	4	4	4	5	5	5	6	6	6	6	7	7	6
	PF	PF	PF	NF	NF	NF	NF	NF	NF	NF	NF	NF	NF
Canada	1	1	1	1	1	1	1	1	1	1	1	1	1
	1	1	1	1	1	1	1	1	1	1	1	1	1
	F	F	F	F	F	F	F	F	F	F	F	F	F
Cape Verde Isls.3	5	5	5	6	6	6	6	6	6	6	6	6	6
	6	5	6	6	6	6	6	6	6	6	7	7	6
	NF	PF*	PF	NF	NF	NF	NF	NF	NF	NF	NF	NF	NF
Central Afr. Rp.	7	7	7	7	7	7	7	7	7	7	7	7	7
	7	7	7	7	7	7	6	6	5	5	6	6	6
	NF	NF	NF	NF	NF	NF	NF	NF	NF	NF	NF	NF	NF
Chad	6	6	7	7	7	6	7	6	7	7	7	7	7
	7	7	6	6	6	6	6	6	6	6	7	7	7
	NF	NF	NF	NF	NF	NF	NF	NF	NF	NF	NF	NF	NF
Chile	1	7	7	7	7	6	6	6	6	6	6	6	6
	2	5	5	5	5	5	5	5	5	5	5	5	5
	F	NF	NF	NF	NF	NF	PF	PF	PF	PF	PF	PF	PF
China (M)	7	7	7	7	6	6	6	6	6	6	6	6	6
	7	7	7	7	6	6	5	6	6	6	6	6	6
	NF	NF	NF	NF	NF	NF	NF	NF	NF	NF	NF	NF	NF
China (T)	6	6	6	5	5	5	5	5	5	5	5	5	5
	5	5	5	5	4	4	5	6	5	5	5	5	5
	NF	NF	NF	PF	PF	PF	PF	PF	PF	PF	PF	PF	PF
Colombia	2	2	2	2	2	2	2	2	2	2	2	2	2
	2	2	3	3	3	3	3	3	3	3	3	3	3
	F	F	F	F	F	F	F	F	F	F	F	F	F
Comoros3	4	2	5	5	4	5	4	4	4	4	5	6	6
	4	2	2	3	3	4	4	5	5	4	5	6	6
	PF	F	PF*	PF	PF	PF	PF	PF	PF	PF	PF	NF	NF
Congo	7	5	5	5	7	7	7	7	7	7	7	7	7
	7	6	6	6	6	6	7	7	6	6	6	6	6
	NF	PF	PF	PF	NF	NF	NF	NF	NF	NF	NF	NF	NF
Costa Rica	1	1	1	1	1	1	1	1	1	1	1	1	1
	1	1	1	1	1	1	1	1	1	1	1	1	1
	F	F	F	F	F	F	F	F	F	F	F	F	F
Cuba	7	7	7	7	7	6	6	6	6	6	6	6	6
	7	7	7	6	6	6	6	6	6	6	6	6	6
	NF	NF	NF	NF	NF	NF	NF	NF	NF	NF	NF	NF	NF

Table 6 (continued)

Country	73	75	76	77	78	79	80	81	82	83	84	85	86
Cyprus(G)4	2	4	4	3	3	3	3	3	1	1	1	1	1
	3	4	4	4	4	4	4	3	2	2	2	2	2
	F	PF	PF	PF	PF	PF	PF	PF	F	F	F	F	F
Cyprus(T)4									4	4	4	3	2
									3	3	3	3	3
									PF	PF	PF	PF	F
Czecho-slovakia	7	7	7	7	7	7	7	7	7	7	7	7	7
	7	7	6	6	6	6	6	6	6	6	6	6	6
	NF	NF	NF	NF	NF	NF	NF	NF	NF	NF	NF	NF	F
Denmark	1	1	1	1	1	1	1	1	1	1	1	1	1
	1	1	1	1	1	1	1	1	1	1	1	1	1
	F	F	F	F	F	F	F	F	F	F	F	F	F
Djibouti3	4	4	4	3	2	2	3	3	3	5	5	6	6
	4	3	3	2	2	3	4	4	5	6	6	6	6
	PF	PF	PF	PF	F*	F	PF	PF	PF	NF	PF	NF	NF
Dominica3	2	2	2	2	2	2	2	2	2	2	2	2	2
	3	3	3	3	2	3	2	2	2	2	2	2	2
	F	F	F	F	F	F*	F	F	F	F	F	F	F
Dominican Republic	3	4	4	4	4	2	2	2	2	1	1	1	1
	2	2	2	3	2	2	3	3	3	2	3	3	3
	F	PF	PF	PF	PF	F	F	F	F	F	F	F	F
Ecuador	7	7	7	6	6	5	2	2	2	2	2	2	2
	3	5	5	5	5	3	2	2	2	2	2	3	3
	PF	NF	NF	PF	PF	PF	F	F	F	F	F	F	F
Egypt	6	6	6	5	5	5	5	5	5	5	4	4	5
	6	4	4	4	4	5	5	5	6	5	4	4	4
	NF	PF	PF	PF	PF	PF	PF	PF	PF	PF	PF	PF	PF
El Salvador	2	2	2	3	3	4	5	6	5	4	3	2	3
	3	3	3	3	3	4	3	4	5	5	5	4	4
	F	F	F	PF	PF	PF	PF	PF	PF	PF	PF	PF	PF
Eq. Guinea	6	6	6	6	7	7	7	7	7	7	7	7	7
	6	6	7	7	7	7	6	6	6	6	6	7	7
	NF	NF	NF	NF	NF	NF	NF	NF	NF	NF	NF	NF	NF
Ethiopia	5	6	7	7	7	7	7	7	7	7	7	7	7
	6	5	6	6	7	7	7	7	7	7	7	7	7
	NF	NF	NF	NF	NF	NF	NF	NF	NF	NF	NF	NF	NF
Fiji	2	2	2	2	2	2	2	2	2	2	2	2	2
	2	2	2	2	2	2	2	2	2	2	2	2	2
	F	F	F	F	F	F	F	F	F	F	F	F	F
Finland	2	2	2	2	2	2	2	2	2	2	2	2	2
	2	2	2	2	2	2	2	2	2	2	2	2	2
	F	F	F	F	F	F	F	F	F	F	F	F	F
France	1	1	1	1	1	1	1	1	1	1	1	1	1
	2	2	2	1	1	2	2	2	2	2	2	2	2
	F	F	F	F	F	F	F	F	F	F	F	F	F

Table 6 (continued)

Country	73	75	76	77	78	79	80	81	82	83	84	85	86
Gabon	6	6	6	6	6	6	6	6	6	6	6	6	6
	6	6	6	6	6	6	6	6	6	6	6	6	6
	NF	NF	NF	NF	NF	NF	NF	NF	NF	NF	NF	NF	NF
Gambia	2	2	2	2	2	2	2	2	3	3	3	3	3
	2	2	2	2	2	2	2	2	4	4	4	4	4
	F	F	F	F	F	F	F	F	PF	PF	PF	PF	PF
Germany (East)	7	7	7	7	7	7	7	7	7	7	7	7	7
	7	7	7	7	7	6	7	6	7	7	6	6	6
	NF	NF	NF	NF	NF	NF	NF	NF	NF	NF	NF	NF	NF
Germany (West)	1	1	1	1	1	1	1	1	1	1	1	1	1
	1	1	1	1	1	2	2	2	2	2	2	2	2
	F	F	F	F	F	F	F	F	F	F	F	F	F
Ghana	6	7	7	7	6	6	4	2	2	6	7	7	7
	6	5	5	5	5	4	4	3	3	5	6	6	6
	NF	NF	NF	NF	PF	PF	PF	F	F	NF	NF	NF	NF
Greece	6	2	2	2	2	2	2	2	1	1	1	2	2
	6	2	2	2	2	2	2	2	2	2	2	2	2
	NF	F	F	F	F	F	F	F	F	F	F	F	F
Grenada	2	2	2	2	2	2	4	5	6	7	5	2	2
	3	4	4	4	3	3	5	5	5	6	3	3	2
	F	PF*	PF	PF	F	F	PF	PF	NF	NF	PF	F	F
Guatemala	2	4	4	4	4	3	3	5	6	6	5	4	3
	3	3	3	3	4	4	5	6	6	6	6	4	3
	F	PF	PF	PF	PF	PF	PF	PF	NF	NF	PF	PF	PF
Guinea	7	7	7	7	7	7	7	7	7	7	7	7	7
	7	7	7	7	7	7	7	7	7	7	5	5	5
	NF	NF	NF	NF	NF	NF	NF	NF	NF	NF	NF	NF	NF
Guinea- Bissau	7	6	6	6	6	6	6	6	6	7	6	6	6
	6	6	6	6	6	6	6	6	6	6	6	6	7
	NF	NF*	NF	NF	NF	NF	NF	NF	NF	NF	NF	NF	NF
Guyana	2	4	4	3	3	4	4	4	5	5	5	5	5
	2	3	3	3	3	3	4	4	4	5	5	5	5
	F	PF	PF	PF	PF	PF	PF	PF	PF	PF	PF	PF	PF
Haiti	7	6	6	6	7	7	6	6	7	7	7	7	5
	6	6	6	6	6	6	5	6	6	6	6	6	4
	NF	NF	NF	NF	NF	NF	NF	NF	NF	NF	NF	NF	PF
Honduras	7	6	6	6	6	6	6	4	3	3	2	2	2
	3	3	3	3	3	3	3	3	3	3	3	3	3
	PF	PF	PF	PF	PF	PF	PF	PF	PF	PF	F	F	F
Hungary	6	6	6	6	6	6	6	6	6	6	6	5	5
	6	6	6	6	5	5	5	5	5	5	5	5	5
	NF	NF	NF	NF	NF	NF	NF	NF	NF	NF	PF	PF	PF
Iceland	1	1	1	1	1	1	1	1	1	1	1	1	1
	1	1	1	1	1	1	1	1	1	1	1	1	1
	F	F	F	F	F	F	F	F	F	F	F	F	F

Table 6 (continued)

Country	73	75	76	77	78	79	80	81	82	83	84	85	86
India	2	2	2	2	2	2	2	2	2	2	2	2	2
	3	3	5	5	2	2	2	3	3	3	3	3	3
	F	F	PF	PF	F	F	F	F	F	F	F	F	F
Indonesia	5	5	5	5	5	5	5	5	5	5	5	5	5
	5	5	5	5	5	5	5	5	5	5	6	6	6
	PF	PF	PF	PF	PF	PF	PF	PF	PF	PF	PF	PF	PF
Iran	5	5	6	6	6	6	5	5	6	6	5	5	5
	6	6	6	6	5	5	6	5	6	6	6	6	6
	NF	NF	NF	NF	NF	PF	PF	PF	NF	NF	PF	PF	PF
Iraq	7	7	7	7	7	7	7	6	6	6	7	7	7
	7	7	7	7	7	6	7	7	7	7	7	7	7
	NF	NF	NF	NF	NF	NF	NF	NF	NF	NF	NF	NF	NF
Ireland	1	1	1	1	1	1	1	1	1	1	1	1	1
	2	2	2	1	1	1	1	1	1	1	1	1	1
	F	F	F	F	F	F	F	F	F	F	F	F	F
Israel	2	2	2	2	2	2	2	2	2	2	2	2	2
	3	3	3	3	3	2	2	2	2	2	2	2	2
	F	F	F	F	F	F	F	F	F	F	F	F	F
Italy	1	1	1	2	2	2	2	1	1	1	1	1	1
	2	2	2	1	1	2	2	2	2	2	1	1	1
	F	F	F	F	F	F	F	F	F	F	F	F	F
Ivory Coast	6	6	6	6	6	6	6	6	5	5	6	6	6
	6	6	5	5	5	5	5	5	5	5	5	5	5
	NF	NF	NF	NF	NF	NF	PF	PF	PF	PF	PF	PF	PF
Jamaica	1	1	1	1	2	2	2	2	2	2	2	2	2
	2	2	2	3	3	3	3	3	3	3	3	3	3
	F	F	F	F	F	F	F	F	F	F	F	F	F
Japan	2	2	2	2	2	2	2	1	1	1	1	1	1
	1	1	1	1	1	1	1	1	1	1	1	1	1
	F	F	F	F	F	F	F	F	F	F	F	F	F
Jordan	6	6	6	6	6	6	6	6	6	6	5	5	5
	6	6	6	6	6	6	6	6	6	6	5	5	5
	NF	NF	NF	NF	NF	NF	NF	NF	NF	NF	PF	PF	PF
Kenya	5	5	5	5	5	5	5	5	5	5	6	6	6
	4	4	5	5	5	5	4	4	4	5	5	5	5
	PF	PF	PF	PF	PF	PF	PF	PF	PF	PF	PF	PF	PF
Kiribati	2	2	2	2	2	2	2	2	2	1	1	1	1
	2	2	2	2	2	2	2	2	2	2	2	2	2
	F	F	F	F	F	F*	F	F	F	F	F	F	F
Korea (N)	7	7	7	7	7	7	7	7	7	7	7	7	7
	7	7	7	7	7	7	7	7	7	7	7	7	7
	NF	NF	NF	NF	NF	NF	NF	NF	NF	NF	NF	NF	NF
Korea (S)	5	5	5	5	5	5	4	5	5	5	5	4	4
	6	6	5	6	5	5	5	6	6	6	5	5	5
	NF	PF	PF	NF	PF	PF	PF	PF	PF	PF	PF	PF	PF

Table 6 (continued)

Country	73	75	76	77	78	79	80	81	82	83	84	85	86
Kuwait	4	4	4	6	6	6	6	6	4	4	4	4	6
	4	3	3	5	4	3	4	4	4	4	4	4	5
	PF	PF	PF	NF	PF	PF	PF	PF	PF	PF	PF	PF	PF
Laos	5	5	6	7	7	7	7	7	7	7	7	7	7
	5	5	6	7	7	7	7	7	7	7	7	7	7
	PF	PF	NF	NF	NF	NF	NF	NF	NF	NF	NF	NF	NF
Lebanon	2	2	4 -	4	4	4	4	4	4	5	5	5	5
	2	2	4	4	4	4	4	4	4	4	4	4	4
	F	F	PF	PF	PF	PF	PF	PF	PF	PF	PF	PF	PF
Lesotho	7	5	5	5	5	5	5	5	5	5	5	5	5
	4	4	4	4	4	4	5	5	5	5	5	5	5
	NF	PF	PF	PF	PF	PF	PF	PF	PF	PF	PF	PF	PF
Liberia	6	6	6	6	6	6	6	6	6	5	6	5	5
	6	3	4	4	4	4	5	6	6	5	5	5	5
	NF	PF	PF	PF	PF	PF	PF	NF	NF	PF	PF	PF	PF
Libya	7	7	7	7	7	6	6	6	6	6	6	6	6
	6	7	6	6	6	6	6	6	7	6	6	6	6
	NF	NF	NF	NF	NF	NF	NF	NF	NF	NF	NF	NF	NF
Luxem- bourg	2	2	2	2	1	1	1	1	1	1	1	1	1
	1	1	1	1	1	1	1	1	1	1	1	1	1
	F	F	F	F	F	F	F	F	F	F	F	F	F
Madagascar (Malagasy Rep.)	5	5	5	6	5	5	6	6	6	5	5	5	5
	3	4	5	5	5	5	6	6	6	6	6	6	5
	PF	PF	PF	NF	PF	PF	NF	NF	NF	PF	PF	PF	PF
Malawi	7	7	7	7	7	6	6	6	6	6	6	6	6
	6	6	6	6	6	6	7	7	7	7	7	7	7
	NF	NF	NF	NF	NF	NF	NF	NF	NF	NF	NF	NF	NF
Malaysia	2	3	3	3	3	3	3	3	3	3	3	3	3
	3	3	4	4	4	3	4	4	4	4	5	5	5
	F	PF	PF	PF	PF	PF	PF	PF	PF	PF	PF	PF	PF
Maldives	3	3	4	4	4	5	5	5	5	5	5	5	5
	2	2	4	4	4	5	5	5	5	5	5	5	6
	PF	PF	PF	PF	PF	PF	PF	PF	PF	PF	PF	PF	PF
Mali	7	7	7	7	7	7	7	7	7	7	7	7	7
	6	6	7	7	7	7	6	6	6	6	6	6	6
	NF	NF	NF	NF	NF	NF	NF	NF	NF	NF	NF	NF	NF
Malta	1	1	1	1	2	2	2	2	2	2	2	2	2
	2	1	1	2	2	2	2	3	3	4	4	4	4
	F	F	F	F	F	F	F	F	F	PF	PF	PF	PF
Mauri- tania	6	5	6	6	6	6	6	7	7	7	7	7	7
	6	6	6	6	6	6	6	6	6	6	6	6	6
	NF	NF	NF	NF	NF	NF	NF	NF	NF	NF	NF	NF	NF
Mauritius	3	3	2	2	2	2	2	2	2	2	2	2	2
	2	2	2	2	2	4	4	4	3	2	2	2	2
	F	F	F	F	F	PF	PF	PF	F	F	F	F	F

60

Table 6 (continued)

Country	73	75	76	77	78	79	80	81	82	83	84	85	86
Mexico	5	4	4	4	4	4	3	3	3	3	3	4	4
	3	3	3	4	4	4	3	4	4	4	4	4	4
	PF	PF	PF	PF	PF	PF	PF	PF	PF	PF	PF	PF	PF
Mongolia	7	7	7	7	7	7	7	7	7	7	7	7	7
	7	7	7	7	7	7	7	7	7	7	7	7	7
	NF	NF	NF	NF	NF	NF	NF	NF	NF	NF	NF	NF	NF
Morocco	5	5	5	5	4	3	3	4	4	4	4	4	4
	4	5	5	5	3	4	4	4	5	5	5	5	5
	PF	PF	PF	PF	PF	PF	PF	PF	PF	PF	PF	PF	PF
Mozam-bique3	7	6	6	7	7	7	7	7	7	7	6	6	6
	6	6	6	7	7	7	7	7	7	6	7	7	7
	NF	NF	NF*	NF	NF	NF	NF	NF	NF	NF	NF	NF	NF
Nauru	2	2	2	2	2	2	2	2	2	2	2	2	2
	2	2	2	2	2	2	2	2	2	2	2	2	2
	F	F	F	F	F	F	F	F	F	F	F	F	F
Nepal	6	6	6	6	6	6	5	3	3	3	3	3	3
	5	5	5	5	5	5	4	4	4	4	4	4	4
	NF	NF	NF	NF	NF	NF	PF	PF	PF	PF	PF	PF	PF
Nether-lands	1	1	1	1	1	1	1	1	1	1	1	1	1
	1	1	1	1	1	1	1	1	1	1	1	1	1
	F	F	F	F	F	F	F	F	F	F	F	F	F
New Zealand	1	1	1	1	1	1	1	1	1	1	1	1	1
	1	1	1	1	1	1	1	1	1	1	1	1	1
	F	F	F	F	F	F	F	F	F	F	F	F	F
Nicaragua	4	5	5	5	5	5	5	5	6	6	5	5	5
	3	4	4	5	5	5	5	5	5	5	5	5	6
	PF	PF	PF	PF	PF	PF	PF	PF	PF	PF	PF	PF	PF
Niger	6	7	7	7	7	7	7	7	7	7	7	7	7
	6	6	6	6	6	6	6	6	6	6	6	6	6
	NF	NF	NF	NF	NF	NF	NF	NF	NF	NF	NF	NF	NF
Nigeria	6	6	6	6	5	5	2	2	2	2	7	7	7
	4	4	5	4	4	3	3	3	3	3	5	5	5
	PF	PF	PF	PF	PF	PF	F	F	F	F	NF	NF	NF
Norway	1	1	1	1	1	1	1	1	1	1	1	1	1
	1	1	1	1	1	1	1	1	1	1	1	1	1
	F	F	F	F	F	F	F	F	F	F	F	F	F
Oman	7	7	7	6	6	6	6	6	6	6	6	6	6
	6	6	6	6	6	6	6	6	6	6	6	6	6
	NF	NF	NF	NF	NF	NF	NF	NF	NF	NF	NF	NF	NF
Pakistan	3	3	5	4	6	6	6	7	7	7	7	4	4
	5	5	5	5	4	5	5	6	5	5	5	5	5
	PF	PF	PF	PF	PF	PF	NF	NF	NF	NF	NF	PF	PF
Panama	7	7	7	7	6	5	5	4	4	5	4	6	6
	6	6	6	6	5	5	5	4	4	4	3	3	3
	NF	NF	NF	NF	NF	NF	PF	PF	PF	PF	PF	PF	PF

Table 6 (continued)

Country	73	75	76	77	78	79	80	81	82	83	84	85	86
Papua New Guinea	4 2 PF	3 2 PF	3 2 PF*	2 2 F	2 2 F	2 2 F	2 2 F	2 2 F	2 2 F	2 2 F	2 2 F	2 2 F	2 2 F
Paraguay	4 6 PF	5 5 PF	5 5 PF	5 6 NF	5 6 NF	5 5 PF	5 5 PF	5 5 PF	5 5 PF	5 5 PF	5 5 PF	5 5 PF	5 6 PF
Peru	7 5 NF	6 6 NF	6 4 PF	6 4 PF	6 4 PF	5 4 PF	5 4 PF	2 3 F	2 3 F	2 3 F	2 3 F	2 3 F	2 3 F
Philip-pines	4 6 PF	5 5 PF	5 5 PF	5 5 PF	5 5 PF	5 5 PF	5 5 PF	5 5 PF	5 5 PF	5 5 PF	4 4 PF	4 3 PF	4 2 PF
Poland	6 6 NF	6 6 NF	6 6 NF	6 6 NF	6 5 NF	6 5 PF	6 5 PF	6 4 PF	5 4 PF	6 5 PF	6 5 PF	6 5 PF	6 5 PF
Portugal	5 6 NF	5 3 PF	5 3 PF	2 2 F	2 2 F	2 2 F	2 2 F	2 2 F	2 2 F	1 2 F	1 2 F	1 2 F	1 2 F
Qatar	6 5 NF	6 5 NF	6 5 NF	5 5 PF	5 5 PF	5 5 PF	5 5 PF	5 5 PF	5 5 PF	5 5 PF	5 5 PF	5 5 PF	5 5 PF
Romania	7 6 NF	7 6 NF	7 6 NF	7 6 NF	7 6 NF	7 6 NF	7 6 NF	7 6 NF	7 6 NF	7 6 NF	7 7 NF	7 7 NF	7 7 NF
Rwanda	7 6 NF	7 5 NF	7 5 NF	7 5 NF	7 5 NF	6 5 NF	6 6 NF	6 6 NF	6 6 NF	6 6 NF	6 6 NF	6 6 NF	6 6 NF
St.Kitts-Nevis3	2 3 F	2 3 F	2 3 F	2 3 F	2 3 F	2 3 F	2 3 F	2 3 F	2 3 F	2 3 F*	1 1 F	1 1 F	1 1 F
St.Lucia3	2 3 F	2 3 F	2 3 F	2 3 F	2 3 F	2 3 F	2 3 F*	2 3 F	2 2 F	2 2 F	1 2 F	1 2 F	1 2 F
St.Vincent	2 2 F	2 2 F	2 2 F	2 2 F	2 2 F	2 2 F	2 2 F*	2 2 F	2 2 F	2 2 F	2 2 F	2 2 F	2 2 F
Sao Tome & Principe3	5 6 NF	5 5 PF	5 5 PF	5 5 PF	6 5 NF	6 5 NF	6 6 NF	6 6 NF	6 6 NF	7 7 NF	7 7 NF	7 7 NF	7 7 NF
Saudi Arabia	6 6 NF	6 6 NF	6 6 NF	6 6 NF	6 6 NF	6 6 NF	6 6 NF	6 6 NF	6 6 NF	6 7 NF	6 7 NF	6 7 NF	6 7 NF
Senegal	6 6 NF	6 5 NF	6 4 PF	6 4 PF	5 3 PF	4 3 PF	4 3 PF	4 4 PF	4 4 PF	4 4 PF	3 4 PF	3 4 PF	3 4 PF

Table 6 (continued)

Country	73	75	76	77	78	79	80	81	82	83	84	85	86
Sey-chelles3	3	2	2	1	6	6	6	6	6	6	6	6	6
	2	2	2	2	3	4	5	6	6	6	6	6	6
	PF	F	F	F*	PF	PF	PF	NF	NF	NF	NF	NF	NF
Sierra Leone	4	6	6	6	5	6	5	5	5	5	4	5	5
	5	5	5	5	5	5	5	5	5	5	5	5	5
	PF	PF	PF	PF	PF	PF	PF	PF	PF	PF	PF	PF	PF
Singapore	5	5	5	5	5	5	5	5	4	4	4	4	4
	5	5	5	5	5	5	5	5	5	5	5	5	5
	PF	PF	PF	PF	PF	PF	PF	PF	PF	PF	PF	PF	PF
Solomons	4	4	3	2	2	2	2	2	2	2	2	2	2
	2	2	2	2	2	2	2	2	2	2	3	3	2
	PF	PF	F	F	F	F*	F	F	F	F	F	F	F
Somalia	7	7	7	7	7	7	7	7	7	7	7	7	7
	6	6	6	7	7	7	7	7	7	7	7	7	7
	NF	NF	NF	NF	NF	NF	NF	NF	NF	NF	NF	NF	NF
South Africa4		4	4	4	5	5	5	5	5	5	5	5	5
		5	5	5	6	6	6	6	6	6	6	6	6
		PF	PF	PF	PF	PF	PF	PF	NF	PF	PF	PF	PF
Spain	5	5	5	5	2	2	2	2	2	1	1	1	1
	6	5	5	3	2	3	2	3	3	2	2	2	2
	NF	PF	PF	PF	F	F	F	F	F	F	F	F	F
Sri Lanka	2	2	2	2	2	2	2	2	2	3	3	3	3
	3	3	4	3	2	3	3	3	3	4	4	4	4
	F	F	PF	F	F	F	F	F	F	PF	PF	PF	PF
Sudan	6	6	6	6	6	5	5	5	5	5	6	6	4
	6	6	6	6	5	5	5	5	6	6	6	6	5
	NF	NF	NF	NF	NF	PF	PF	PF	PF	PF	NF	NF	PF
Suriname	2	2	2	2	2	2	2	7	7	7	7	6	6
	2	2	2	2	2	2	2	5	5	6	6	6	6
	F	F	F*	F	F	F	F	NF	NF	NF	NF	NF	NF
Swaziland	4	6	6	6	6	6	5	5	5	5	5	5	5
	2	4	4	4	4	5	5	5	5	5	6	6	6
	PF	PF	PF	PF	PF	PF	PF	PF	PF	PF	PF	PF	PF
Sweden	1	1	2	1	1	1	1	1	1	1	1	1	1
	1	1	1	1	1	1	1	1	1	1	1	1	1
	F	F	F	F	F	F	F	F	F	F	F	F	F
Switzer-land	1	1	1	1	1	1	1	1	1	1	1	1	1
	1	1	1	1	1	1	1	1	1	1	1	1	1
	F	F	F	F	F	F	F	F	F	F	F	F	F
Syria	7	6	6	6	5	5	5	5	5	6	6	6	6
	7	7	7	6	6	6	6	6	6	7	7	7	7
	NF	NF	NF	NF	PF	PF	PF	NF	NF	NF	NF	NF	NF
Tanzania	6	6	6	6	6	6	6	6	6	6	6	6	6
	6	6	6	6	6	6	6	6	6	6	6	6	6
	NF	NF	NF	NF	NF	NF	NF	NF	NF	NF	NF	NF	NF

Table 6 (continued)

Country	73	75	76	77	78	79	80	81	82	83	84	85	86
Thailand	7	5	2	6	6	6	4	3	3	3	3	3	3
	5	3	3	6	5	4	3	4	4	4	4	4	3
	NF	PF	F	NF	NF	PF	PF	PF	PF	PF	PF	PF	PF
Togo	7	7	7	7	7	7	7	7	7	7	6	6	6
	5	6	6	6	6	6	6	6	6	6	6	6	6
	NF	NF	NF	NF	NF	NF	NF	NF	NF	NF	NF	NF	NF
Tonga	4	5	5	5	5	5	5	5	5	5	5	5	5
	2	3	3	3	3	3	3	3	3	3	3	3	3
	PF	PF	PF	PF	PF	PF	PF	PF	PF	PF	PF	PF	PF
Transkei				6	6	5	5	5	5	5	5	5	5
				5	5	5	6	6	6	6	6	6	6
				NF*	NF	PF	PF	PF	PF	PF	PF	PF	PF
Trinidad & Tobago	2	2	2	2	2	2	2	2	2	1	1	1	1
	3	2	2	2	2	2	2	2	2	2	2	2	2
	F	F	F	F	F	F	F	F	F	F	F	F	F
Tunisia	6	6	6	6	6	6	6	6	5	5	5	5	6
	5	5	5	5	5	5	5	5	5	5	5	5	5
	NF	NF	NF	NF	NF	NF	PF	PF	PF	PF	PF	PF	PF
Turkey	3	2	2	2	2	2	2	5	5	4	3	3	3
	4	3	3	3	3	3	3	5	5	5	5	5	4
	PF	F	F	F	F	F	F	PF	PF	PF	PF	PF	PF
Tuvalu3	2	2	2	2	2	2	2	2	2	1	1	1	1
	2	2	2	2	2	2	2	2	2	2	2	2	1
	F	F	F	F	F	F*	F	F	F	F	F	F	F
Uganda	7	7	7	7	7	7	6	5	5	4	4	5	5
	7	7	7	7	7	7	6	5	5	5	5	4	4
	NF	NF	NF	NF	NF	NF	NF	PF	PF	PF	PF	PF	PF
USSR	6	6	7	7	7	7	6	6	6	6	7	7	7
	6	6	6	6	6	6	6	7	7	7	7	7	7
	NF	NF	NF	NF	NF	NF	NF	NF	NF	NF	NF	NF	NF
United Arab Emirates	7	6	6	5	5	5	5	5	5	5	5	5	5
	5	5	5	5	5	5	5	5	5	5	5	5	5
	NF	NF	NF	PF	PF	PF	PF	PF	PF	PF	PF	PF	PF
United Kingdom	1	1	1	1	1	1	1	1	1	1	1	1	1
	1	1	1	1	1	1	1	1	1	1	1	1	1
	F	F	F	F	F	F	F	F	F	F	F	F	F
United States	1	1	1	1	1	1	1	1	1	1	1	1	1
	1	1	1	1	1	1	1	1	1	1	1	1	1
	F	F	F	F	F	F	F	F	F	F	F	F	F
Uruguay	3	5	5	6	6	6	6	5	5	5	5	2	2
	4	5	5	6	6	6	6	5	5	4	4	2	2
	PF	PF	PF	NF	NF	NF	NF	PF	PF	PF	PF	F	F
Vanuatu	4	4	4	3	3	3	3	2	2	2	2	2	2
	3	3	3	3	3	3	3	3	3	4	4	4	4
	PF	PF	PF	PF	PF	PF	PF	F*	F	PF	PF	PF	PF

Table 6 (continued)

Country	73	75	76	77	78	79	80	81	82	83	84	85	86
Venezuela	2	2	2	1	1	1	1	1	1	1	1	1	1
	2	2	2	2	2	2	2	2	2	2	2	2	2
	F	F	F	F	F	F	F	F	F	F	F	F	F
Vietnam[5]				7	7	7	7	7	7	7	7	7	7
				7	7	7	7	7	7	6	6	7	7
				NF	NF	NF	NF	NF	NF	NF	NF	NF	NF
Western Samoa	4	4	4	4	4	4	4	4	4	4	4	4	4
	2	2	2	2	2	2	2	3	3	3	3	3	3
	PF	PF	PF	PF	PF	PF	PF	PF	PF	PF	PF	PF	PF
Yemen (N)	4	5	6	6	6	6	6	6	6	6	5	5	5
	4	4	4	5	5	5	5	5	5	5	5	5	5
	PF	PF	NF	NF	NF	NF	NF	NF	NF	NF	NF	PF	PF
Yemen (S)	7	7	7	7	7	7	6	6	6	6	6	6	6
	7	7	7	7	7	7	7	7	7	7	7	7	7
	NF	NF	NF	NF	NF	NF	NF	NF	NF	NF	NF	NF	NF
Yugoslavia	6	6	6	6	6	6	6	6	6	6	6	6	6
	6	6	6	6	5	5	5	5	5	5	5	5	5
	NF	NF	NF	NF	NF	NF	NF	NF	NF	PF	PF	PF	PF
Zaire	7	7	7	7	7	7	6	6	6	6	6	7	7
	6	6	6	6	6	6	6	6	6	6	7	7	7
	NF	NF	NF	NF	NF	NF	NF	NF	NF	NF	NF	NF	NF
Zambia	5	5	5	5	5	5	5	5	5	5	5	5	5
	5	4	5	5	5	5	5	6	6	6	5	5	5
	PF	PF	PF	PF	PF	PF	PF	PF	PF	PF	PF	PF	PF
Zimbabwe	6	6	6	6	6	5	4	3	3	4	4	4	4
	5	5	5	5	5	5	5	4	5	5	5	6	6
	NF	NF	NF	NF	NF	PF	PF	PF	PF	PF	PF	PF	PF

the support of private initiative, through more open discussion in some areas, and through the sending of thousands of students overseas. While Poland suggests the immediate limits of change, nearly every country in Eastern Europe is freer today than it was at the beginning of the 1970s. Unfortunately, the same cannot be said of the Soviet Union.

In Western Europe gains for democracy in Spain, Portugal, and Greece were critical to its continual advancement everywhere. After the setback in Chile, gains have been achieved in many parts of Latin America. Argentina, Bolivia, Brazil, Dominican Republic, Ecuador, Honduras, Peru, and Uruguay reestablished democratic institutions. Several countries that the Survey listed as "free" at the beginning may now be more authentically free. Colombia is an example. (El Salvador and Guatemala probably should not have been listed as free in 1973. El Salvador may be as free today.)

African democracy has not fared well during these years. In many areas there has been a noticeable decline, especially in countries such as Ghana, Nigeria, Burkina Faso (Upper Volta), and Kenya in which great hopes were placed in the 1970s. In sub-Saharan Africa only Senegal seems to have made progress. Recently we have seen a modest resurgence of free institutions in the Middle East. The destruction of Lebanon will be hard to make up. Further to the east there has been remarkably little advance. The people of Sri Lanka have lost freedoms; those of Thailand and Nepal have made some hopeful progress.

During this period many new democratic states successfully emerged—in the South Pacific from Papua New Guinea to the east, and among the islands of the Caribbean.

Elections and Referendums

Evidence for political freedom is primarily found in the occurrence and nature of elections or referendums. Therefore, as a supplement to our ratings we summarize in the accompanying Table 7 the national elections that we recorded for independent countries since late 1985. One or more elections from earlier in 1985 are included because they were overlooked in last year's annual. The reader should assume that the electoral process appeared comparatively open, fair, and competitive, unless our remarks suggest otherwise;

Table 7

NATIONAL ELECTIONS AND REFERENDUMS

Country Date	Type of Election	Results and Remarks
Algeria 1/16/86	referendum on national charter	reported 96% turnout, 98% approval is questioned; casual polls, not secret
Austria 5/4/; 6/8/86	presidential (two rounds)	well contested, intense contest
11/23/86	parliamentary	gains on right and left lead to "grand coalition" of two major parties
Bangladesh 5/7/86	parliamentary	partial boycott, violence, and probable fraud; but many parties win seats
10/30/86	presidential	opposition boycott, and continued martial law led to minimal competition
Barbados 5/28/86	parliamentary	opposition wins decisively
Brazil 11/15/86	parliamentary	open competition; government parties win parliament and many regional governorships
Bulgaria 6/8/86	parliamentary	single list, but not all party members
Burma 10/6–20/85	assembly	virtually no opposition; little public interest

Survey: 1986

Country Date	Type of Election	Results and Remarks
Cape Verde Islands 12/7/85	parliamentary	essentially one party, but some democracy in process; many did not vote
Central African Republic 11/21/86	referendum	doubtful process; 91% said to accept one-party constitution that keeps president in power
China (Taiwan) 12/6/86	parliamentary	first multiparty; opposition does well (too late to affect Survey ratings)
Colombia 3/10/86	parliamentary	opposition wins; far left enters process
5/25/86	presidential	well contested; Conservative replaced by Liberal
Costa Rica 2/2/86	general	very fair; high turnout; government party wins (unusual in Costa Rica)
Cyprus (G) 12/14/85	parliamentary	well contested; government does well; Greece accused of interference
Czechoslovakia 5/23-24/86	parliamentary	99% vote and 99% support national front candidates
Denmark 2/27/86	referendum	people approve increase in power of European Community

Country Date	Type of Election	Results and Remarks
Dominican Rep. 5/16/86	general	vigorous campaign; results accepted after serious dispute; larger party loses because of split in ranks
Ecuador 6/1/86	parliamentary referendum	government decisisvely defeated in both areas
Egypt 10/1/86	senatorial	advisory upper house elected; opposition boycotts for cause
France 3/16/86	parliamentary	opposition wins narrowly; also important regional assembly relections
Germany (East) 6/8/86	parliamentary	one list, little choice, 99% participation and support
Gabon 11/9/86	presidential	unopposed exercise
Guatemala 12/8/86	presidential (run-off)	easily won by popular civilian candidate
Guyana 12/9/86	parliamentary	government wins decisively; but evidence of widespread violence and fraud
Haiti 10/19/86	constituent assembly	lack of popular interest; poor preparation; most politicians boycott
Ireland 6/16/86	referendum	government's divorce proposal fails

Survey: 1986

Country Date	Type of Election	Results and Remarks
Japan 7/7/86	parliamentary	government wins decisively; socialists decline
Malaysia 8/2–3/86	parliamentary	government wins handily against hamstrung opposition; Chinese speakers shifting to opposition
Nepal 5/12/86	parliamentary	nonparty, but opposition groups attain a large proportion of seats
Netherlands 5/21/86	parliamentary	low key; televised debates; government maintains position as extremes lose
Philippines 2/7/86	presidential	marked by violence, fraud, and disputed count; led to turnover of government
Portugal 1/26/; 2/16/86	presidential	social democratic leader in surprising win
Romania 11/23/86	referendum	only 228 fail to vote and vote correctly; compulsory exercise
Sierra Leone 5/30/86	parliamentary	one party; apathetic; many candidates excluded
Spain 3/12/86	referendum	government's NATO initiative wins in spite of polls
6/22/86	parliamentary	government wins with reduced majority; regional parties advance

Country Date	Type of Election	Results and Remarks
Sudan 4/1–12/86	parliamentary	competitive multiparty; election difficult or impossible in third of country
Switzerland 12/1/85	referendum	ban on vivisection defeated
3/16/86	referendum	government supported proposal to join UN decisively defeated
Syria 2/10–11/86	parliamentary	mostly one-party, but independents and small parties win some seats
Thailand 7/27/86	parliamentary	multiparty; well-contested; increased turnout; party growth
Tunisia 11/2/86	parliamentary	After numerous disqualifications, opposition parties decide to boycott
Tuvalu 9/12/86	parliamentary	nonparty; fair and open; most incumbents reelected
United States 11/4/86	congressional	low turnout; government loses majority in senate

extremely one-sided outcomes also imply an unacceptable electoral process. Voter participation figures have been omitted this year because they are often unobtainable, and when obtainable, highly questionable. Many states compel their citizens to vote, in others it is unclear whether voter participation figures refer to a percentage of those registered or of those of voting age.

Although we seldom include non-national elections, they are occasionally more significant than national elections. Recent regional elections in India, France, and Italy come to mind. The reader's attention should also be drawn to the number of referendums that occurred during the year. There seems to be a definite tendency toward letting citizens more directly influence their government through this means.

Political-Economic Systems and Freedom

The accompanying Table 8 (Political and Economic Systems) fills two needs. It offers the reader additional information about the countries we have rated. For example, readers with libertarian views may wish to raise the relative ratings of capitalist countries, while those who place more value on redistributive systems may wish to raise the ratings of countries toward the socialist end of the spectrum. The table also makes possible an analysis of the relation between political and economic forms and the freedom ratings of the Survey. Perusal of the table will show that freedom is directly related to the existence of multiparty systems: the further a country is from such systems, the less freedom it is likely to have. This could be considered a trivial result, since a publicly competitive political system is one of the criteria of freedom, and political parties are considered evidence for such competition. However, the result is not simply determined by our definitions: we searched for evidence of authentic public competition in countries without competitive parties, and seldom found the search rewarded. Both theoretical and empirical studies indicate the difficulty of effective public political opposition in one-party systems.

The relation between economic systems and freedom is more complicated and, because of our lack of emphasis on economic systems in devising our ratings of freedom, is not predetermined by

72

our methods. Historically, the table suggests that there are three types of societies competing for acceptance in the world. The first, or traditional type, is marginal and in retreat, but its adherents have borrowed political and economic bits and pieces from both the other types. The second and third, the Euro-American and Sino-Soviet types, are strongest near their points of origin, but have spread by diffusion and active propagation all over the world. The Leninist-socialist style of political organization was exported along with the socialist concept of economic organization, just as constitutional democracy had been exported along with capitalist economic concepts. In this interpretation, the relation of economic systems to freedom found in the table may be an expression of historical chance rather than necessary relationships. Clearly, capitalism does not cause nations to be politically free, nor does socialism cause them to be politically unfree.[2] Still, socialists must be concerned by the empirical relationship between the rating of "not free" and socialism that is found in tables such as this.

The table shows economies roughly grouped in categories from "capitalist" to "socialist." Labeling economies as capitalist or socialist has a fairly clear significance in the developed world, but its usefulness may be doubted in labeling the mostly poor and largely agrarian societies of the third world in this manner. However, third world states with dual economies, that is, with a modern sector and a preindustrial sector, have economic policies or goals that can be placed along the continuum from socialist to capitalist. A socialist third world state usually has nationalized all of the modern sector—except possibly some foreign investment—and claims central government jurisdiction over the land and its products, with only temporary assignment of land to individuals or cooperatives. The capitalist third world state has a capitalist modern sector and a traditionalist agricultural sector, combined in some cases with new agricultural projects either on family farm or agribusiness models. Third world economies that fall between capitalist and socialist do not have the high taxes of their industrialized equivalents, but they have major nationalized industries (for example, oil) in the modern sector, and their agricultural world may include emphasis on cooperatives or large-scale land reform, as well as more traditional forms.

TABLE 8

TABLE 8

POLITICAL SYSTEM:							
	Multiparty					Dominant-Party	
	centralized				decentralized		

ECONOMIC SYSTEM:

Capitalist — inclusive

centralized				decentralized		Dominant-Party	
Antigua & Bar.	F	Iceland	F	Australia	F	Malaysia	PF
Bahamas	F	Ireland	F	Belgium	F		
Barbados	F	Japan	F	Canada	F		
Belize	F	Korea (S)[1]	PF	Germany(W)[3]	F		
Colombia[4]	F	Luxembourg	F	Lebanon	PF		
Costa Rica	F	Mauritius	F	Switzerland	F		
Cyprus (G)	F	New Zealand[3]	F	United States	F		
Cyprus (T)	F	St.Kitts-Nevis	F				
Dominica	F	St.Lucia[3]	F				
Dom. Rep.[4]	F	St. Vincent[3]	F				
El Salvador[1/3]	PF	Spain	F				

non-inclusive

centralized				decentralized		Dominant-Party	
Ecuador	F	Thailand[1]	PF	Botswana	F	Liberia[1]	PF
Fiji[4]	F			Papua New Guinea	F	Transkei	PF
Gambia[4]	PF			Solomons[2]	F		
Guatemala[1]	PF						
Honduras[1/4]	F						

Capitalist-Statist — inclusive

centralized				decentralized		Dominant-Party	
Argentina	F	Sri Lanka	PF	Brazil[3/4]	F	China(Taiwan)	PF
Grenada	F	Turkey[1/4]	PF	Trinidad & Tobago	F	Mexico	PF
Italy	F	Venezuela	F				
Jamaica[3]	F	Panama[1]	PF				
South Africa	PF						

non-inclusive

centralized				decentralized		Dominant-Party	
Bolivia	F			India	F	Bangladesh[1]	PF
Morocco[3]	PF			Vanuatu	PF	Indonesia[1/4]	PF
Pakistan[1/2]	PF					Iran[2/4]	PF
Peru[4]	F					Paraguay[1/3/4]	PF
						Philippines	PF

Mixed Capitalist — inclusive

centralized				decentralized		Dominant-Party	
Austria	F	Netherlands	F			Egypt[1/3/4]	PF
Denmark	F	Norway	F			Nicaragua	PF
Finland	F	Portugal	F			Senegal[3/4]	PF
France	F	Sudan[5]	PF			Singapore	PF
Greece	F	Sweden	F			Tunisia[4]	PF
Israel	F	U.K.[3]	F			Zimbabwe[5]	PF
Malta	PF	Uruguay	F				

Mixed Socialist — inclusive

						Dominant-Party	
						Guyana	PF
						Syria[1/4]	NF

non-inclusive

						Dominant-Party	
						Madagascar[1/2]	PF

Socialist

inclusive

non-inclusive

Notes to the Table

1. Under heavy military influence or domination.   (All countries in the Nonparty Military column are military dominated.)
2. Party relationships anomalous.
3. Close decision along capitalist-to-socialist continuum.
4. Close decision on inclusive/noninclusive dimension.
5. Noninclusive.

POLITICAL-ECONOMIC SYSTEMS

| One-Party | | Non-Party | | |
socialist	communist	nationalist	military	nonmilitary
		Djibouti NF	Chile[3] PF Suriname NF	Jordan[2/3/4] PF Western Samoa[2/4] PF
Sierra Leone[1] PF		Cameroon[3] NF Comoros NF Gabon NF Ivory Coast[4] PF Kenya PF Malawi NF	Chad NF Haiti PF Lesotho PF Niger NF Yemen (N) PF	Bhutan[3] PF Maldives PF Nepal[3] PF Swaziland PF Tonga PF Tuvalu F
			Ghana NF Nigeria[3/4] NF	Bahrain PF Brunei PF Kuwait PF Nauru F Qatar PF Saudi Arabia NF Un. Arab Emirs PF
		Zaire[1] NF	Cent. African Republic[3] NF Eq. Guinea[3] NF Mauritania NF Uganda[3] PF	Kiribati F Oman NF
Burundi[1/5] NF			Guinea[5] NF	
Libya[1/2/3] NF Seychelles[3] NF	China (M)[3] NF Poland[1] PF Yugoslavia[3] PF			
Burma[1] NF Cape V.I.[3/4] NF Congo[1/3] NF Somalia[1/3] NF Zambia[3] PF		Mali[1] NF Rwanda[1/3] NF Togo[1] NF	Burkina Faso NF	
Algeria[1] NF Sao Tome & Prin.[3/4] NF	Albania NF Bulgaria NF Cuba NF Czecho-slovakia NF Germany(E) NF	Hungary[3] PF Korea (N) NF Mongolia NF Romania NF USSR NF Vietnam NF		
Angola NF Benin[1/3] NF Guinea-Bissau[1/3] NF Iraq[3/4] NF Mozambique NF Tanzania NF Yemen (S)[1] NF	Afghanistan NF Cambodia NF Ethiopia[1] NF Laos NF			

The terms inclusive and noninclusive are used to distinguish between societies in which the economic activities of most people are organized in accordance with the dominant system and those dual societies in which fifty percent or more of the population remain largely outside.

States with inclusive capitalist forms are generally developed states that rely on the operation of the market and private provision for industrial welfare. Taxes may be high, but they are not confiscatory, while government interference is generally limited to subsidy and regulation. States classified as noninclusive capitalist, such as Liberia or Thailand, have not over fifty percent of the population included in a capitalist modern economy, with the remainder of the population still living traditionally. In these the traditional economy may be individual, communal, or feudal, but the direction of change as development proceeds is capitalistic.

Capitalist states grade over into capitalist-statist or mixed capitalist-states. Capitalist-statist countries are those, such as Brazil, Turkey, or Saudi Arabia, that have very large government productive enterprises, either because of an elitist development philosophy or major dependence on a key resource such as oil. Government interferes in the economy in a major way in such states, but not primarily because of egalitarian motives. Mixed capitalist systems, such as those in Israel, the Netherlands, or Sweden, provide social services on a large scale through governmental or other nonprofit institutions, with the result that private control over property is sacrificed to egalitarian purposes. These nations still see capitalism as legitimate, but its legitimacy is accepted grudgingly by many in government. Mixed socialist states, such as Syria or Poland, proclaim themselves to be socialist but in fact allow rather large portions of the economy to remain in the private domain.

Socialist economies, on the other hand, strive programmatically to place an entire national economy under direct or indirect government control. States such as the USSR or Cuba may allow some modest private productive property, but this is only by exception, and rights to such property can be revoked at any time. The leaders of noninclusive socialist states have the same goals as the leaders of inclusive socialist states, but their relatively primitive economies or peoples have not yet been effectively included in the socialist system. Such states generally have a small socialized modern economy and a large preindustrial economy in which the organization of production and trade is still largely traditional. It should be understood that the characterizations in the table are impressionistic; the continuum between capitalist and socialist economies is necessarily cut arbitrarily into categories for this presentation.

Political systems range from democratic multiparty to absolutist one-party systems. Theoretically, the most democratic countries should be those with decentralized multiparty systems, for here important powers are held by the people at two or more levels of the political system, and dissent is legitimated and mobilized by opposition parties. More common are centralized multiparty systems, such as France or Japan, in which the central government organizes lower levels of government primarily for reasons of efficiency. Dominant-party systems allow the forms of democracy, but structure the political process so that opposition groups do not have a realistic chance of achieving power. They often face censorship, vote fraud, imprisonment, or other impediments.

The now classical form of one-party rule is that in states such as the USSR or Vietnam that proclaim themselves to be communist. The slightly larger group of socialist one-party states are ruled by elites that use Marxist-Leninist rhetoric, organize ruling parties very much along communist lines, but either do not have the disciplined organization of communist states or have explicitly rejected one or another aspect of communism. A final group of nationalist one-party states adopts the political form popularized by the communists (and the fascists in the last generation), but the leaders generally reject the revolutionary ideologies of socialist or communist states and fail to develop the totalitarian controls that characterize these states. There are several borderline states that might be switched between socialist and nationalist categories (for example, Libya). "Socialist" is used here to designate a political rather than economic system. A socialist "vanguard party" established along Marxist-Leninist lines will almost surely develop a socialist economy, but a state with a socialist economy need not be ruled by a vanguard party. It should be pointed out that the totalitarian-libertarian continuum is not directly reflected by the categorization in this table.

Nonparty systems can be democratic, as in the small island of Nauru, but generally they are not. Nepal's nonparty system is one of the most democratic of attempts to establish such systems. Other nonparty systems may be nonmilitary nonparty systems such as Tonga or Saudi Arabia, or military nonparty systems, such as that in Niger.

Conclusion

The trend toward democracy continues. There were several decisive moves toward greater freedom in 1986; there were no important retreats. The areas of struggle were primarily areas in which there was much freedom to gain, but relatively little to lose. China is an area of particular note. Nothing is more encouraging than the possibility that the two Chinese governments are making an effort to become a part of the modern, and necessarily more democratic, world.

Yet in much of the world the freedom that did exist was fragile and insecure. We should not be surprised that the openings to freedom made during the year in countries such as Haiti, Philippines, Sudan, Guatemala, or Uganda did not immediately produce democratic societies. These events illustrated once again that for many countries the primary problem in the struggle for democracy is not that of devising a strategy for overthrowing the tyrants. Often enough the people themselves will do this. The problem is to help lay a basis in policies and programs before revolution or crisis that will help the new society once it has destroyed the old. Without effective post-revolutionary help, struggles for freedom, in many countries, will prove to produce little more than the sacrifice of the participants. Even with this help, and massive two-way contact with the democratic world, democracy will come to much of the world only with the passage of time.

NOTES

1. For further details on the methods and criteria used in the Survey see the foregoing section on definitions and criteria.

2. See Lindsay M. Wright, "A Comparative Survey of Economic Freedoms," in R. D. Gastil, **Freedom in the World: Political Rights and Civil Liberties, 1982** (Westport, Connecticut: Greenwood Press, 1982), pp. 51-90.

The Comparative Survey:
Criticisms and Comparisons

The Survey of Freedom has gained critics as well as admirers.[1] Often the criticisms have been directed at a different survey than we have attempted, or have been guided by incorrect assumptions about the purpose of the survey. To avoid misinterpretation by future readers, a discussion of these criticisms may be useful. After this discussion, we will go on to examine comparable surveys that address more directly the concerns of Survey critics.

Two species of criticisms should be identified: ideological and methodological. Although there are instances of overlap, these generally can be discussed separately.

The ideological argument is made on two levels. The first is an argument by association. It is claimed that since Freedom House sponsors the Survey, or apparently in the minds of some "designed" the Survey, it is obviously a tool of the assumed right-of-center leanings of the Freedom House Board.[2] Taking this tack, two critics assumed it was relevant to describe at length members of the Board, and the positions they had held in government and other organizations. This was offered as evidence that the Survey was biased.

That this line of argument hardly belongs in a scholarly endeavor is suggested by its leading either deliberately, or through extreme carelessness, to misstatement of fact. For example, Scoble and Wiseberg offer the following as proof of the ideological stance of Freedom House and the Survey:

> These allies and satellites of the United States (El Salvador, Guatemala, Indonesia, Iran, Namibia, Rhodesia, and South Africa), no matter how repressive the regime, nonetheless are consistently ranked "freer" than any neutralist nations, any Black African nations (e.g. Tanzania), or any socialist nations (e.g. revisionist Yugoslavia).[3]

Faced with such a statement one hardly knows where to start. During the period they studied (1973-79), most of the "satellites and allies" were not rated as free, while neutralist India was rated "free", except for the two-year "emergency." The small black African states of Gambia and Botswana were consistently rated "free", as well as the somewhat marginal Mauritius. The ratings of "allies or satellites"—Rhodesia, South Africa, and Namibia—were consistently in the 5-6 range, while that of Black African Nigeria had moved up to 5,4 and 5,3 and Senegal to 5,3 and 4,3 by 1978-1979. During this period the ratings of Kenya averaged better than those of Indonesia, and much better than those of Iran.

Similarly, Lars Schoultz, argues in a review of the 1978 year-book that the Survey is essentially a defense of capitalism; he then proceeds to read and quote only those passages that fit his impression.[4] He writes that according to the Survey "If a nation is liberal in the classical sense, capitalist, and (generally) wealthy, then it is free." Or he says that the book's position is that "socialist states must either change their economic system or face the continued opprobrium of Freedom House . . ." He says this in the course of discussing a section in the 1978 yearbook that explicitly refutes this suggestion. After discussing the possible advantages and disadvantages of capitalism and socialism for freedom, I conclude: "The best economic systems for the expression of civil and political freedom are modern limited capitalism under multiparty control or multiparty socialism."[5] One wonders why Lars Schoultz failed to notice that Chile, Malawi, and Ivory Coast, three of the outstanding "capitalist" states of the third world in 1978, were all rated "not free."

The attacks on the Survey are, in part, attacks on Freedom House. This is not the place to defend Freedom House, except to say that its Board and its products have since before the inception of the Survey represented a much wider range of ideological positions and interests than its critics evidently assume.

What is most irritating in these criticisms of the Survey is the assumption that their author has been spending the last few years doing a Survey to serve ideological masters, or that what purports to be a Survey of Freedom is really a propagandistic attempt to generate support for American foreign policy, or the capitalist economic system. The author would like to take this opportunity to assure readers that he serves no such masters, and that his judgments can be as unpalatable to many within the Freedom House organization as to these critics. The Board has considered that the Survey is sufficiently valuable for the organization and the cause of freedom, that they can overlook ideological disagreements. That the decision to give partly free status to Chile, Poland, South Africa, and Yugoslavia in one year led to some strong reservations can be inferred from a note to Table 1 and an unusual paragraph in the Preface of **Freedom in the World: 1983-84.** Rating Iran as "partly free" may not rest well with either the general American public or some members of the Board. Nevertheless, to its credit the Board has never directly or indirectly determined a rating.

The second category of criticism relates to the Survey's standards and methodology. These criticisms are often based on the misapprehension that the Survey is meant to be a survey of human rights instead of a survey of certain related political and civil liberties. However, it is by no means as narrowly focused on political issues as some critics believe.[6] Many economic and social rights, such as those to trade union or business organization, or to association or demonstration for any other nonviolent purpose are explicitly a part of the rating system. The emphasis on the right of self-determination either within or without a political framework certainly includes "cultural rights," and belies the idea of an exclusive concern with individual rights. They are necessary civil liberties for the formation of effective alternatives to any current system or law. Incidentally, the critics should understand that while environmental conditions, such as low literacy rates, might make the attainment of the highest ratings for civil liberties difficult, high literacy rates do not improve a country's rating without evidence that literacy is freely enjoyed. Literacy and feudal employee-employer relations, are not "scored" as civil liberties; they suggest conditions that raise questions about the full effectiveness of a range of civil liberties (such as a free press).

Critics are unwilling to accept that the ratings (and **not** "rankings" as in the quotation above) are not meant arithmetically. If 1-7 were A-G, the results would be the same. This does not mean that there cannot be high A's and low A's or high and low G's; nor does it conflict with the assumption that in most cases one can average an A and a C to get a B.

There are not, and never have been, subratings that are somehow added up to make the reported ratings. As discussed below, an organized checklist is not used in this fashion because of lack of data, and because in comparing apples and oranges the overall determination must depend on holistic judgment.

McCamant's often-quoted discussion of the problem with "operationalizing" the Survey rating system is particularly unconvincing.[7] He took the seven levels of civil liberties "conditions" that explanations of the Survey have used as a shorthand means of suggesting how conditions should be expected to vary from the top to the bottom of the civil liberties scale. He then scrambled the statements and found that five students were unable to place them in order. Since in the text each statement refers to the statements that go before and after it, and these relational aspects must have been removed in his scrambling, and since each level is given meaning primarily through the examples of countries that fit the category (which are omitted from McCamant's quotation of my presentation), it would have been patently impossible to scramble them and find out anything from their ordering by students.

It is true that "area experts" would be likely to disagree with some of the comparative ratings. But as McCamant points out in criticizing Schoultz's work, what such tests do is to give us a measure of a country's "reputation" rather than actual behavior.[8] Today China and Yugoslavia have relatively good reputations with westerners, while Czechoslovakia and East Germany do not. Yet differences in levels of freedom are actually slight. For reasons that have little to do with the actual state of political and civil liberties, and much to do with their relationship to the United States, Mexico and Cuba are particularly likely to be forgiven their relative lack of freedom by Latin Americanists.

Contrary to the beliefs of its critics, the Survey is not based on an a priori assumption that multiparty systems are superior. We have been careful not to ignore experiments with other forms of political participation. We have specifically said that there is no concept suggesting that any society "ought immediately upon independence to generate a U.S.- or European style party system."[9] It is also not true that we assume that all countries can or should become "1,1's" tomorrow. From the first we have pointed out that other values may have precedence, particularly in emergency situations. Worker-management methods in Yugoslavia, and similar efforts in Libya have engaged our attention, as has the development of the **Mitbestimmungsrecht** in West Germany. But we doubt that such arrangements will be able to offer workers a form of power capable of substituting for effective choice in a broader political system. These experiments, as well as the example of Migros in Switzerland, have many analogies in cooperatives and worker-controlled enterprises in the last century in both the United States and Europe. In the long run, they do not seem to have been more than a partial replacement of entrenched political power. It is probable that the growth of regional power in the Yugoslav republics represents more of a diffusion of power from tight central government control than does worker control at the factory level. We have also not assumed an invariant one-party system. Many one-party systems, such as those in Ivory Coast and Kenya, exist in capitalist, pro-western societies. But we have yet to see an example of such systems actually guaranteeing the freedom of choice, the competition of ideas, or the revolution in power that multiparty systems sometimes afford.

Human Rights Indicators

The Comparative Survey is not, and never was proposed as, an exercise in developing a new level of social indicators. At the time the Survey was developed the author was in the midst of work on social indicators,[10] and would both then and now be the first to deny that it was a great methodological contribution to their development. At the very beginning of this work he laid down as a cardinal principle: "Generally avoid merging statistics into abstract indices."[11] He has often pointed out that the Survey is neither a human rights survey, nor a "goodness" survey, although there is surely much overlap with what such surveys might include. Let us consider for a moment these two propositions.

Social indicators are most useful if they are statistical measures of measurable quantities. The more doubtful the basis of the measurement, the less useful the indicator. Thus, the author's scientific work in the early 1970s had to do with homicide rather than other crime statistics, because homicide statistics were likely to be more reliable. Similarly, while there are always definitional problems, it is surely easy to see the distinction between infantile mortality rates and infantile morbidity rates. Indicators that combine a number of basic statistics into a higher level "statistic" generally confuse more than they enlighten, and the more so to the degree that the statistics brought together are themselves of doubtful validity. The PQLI of the Overseas Development Council combines infant mortality, life expectancy, and literacy rates.[12] This a fairly simple effort, yet the difficulty of achieving uniform standards on such rates, particularly for literacy, makes me feel that as much could be learned or communicated, and with more precision and verifiability, if selected rates were reported separately.

Another cardinal principle for social indicators was to use output instead of input measures. In terms of a Survey of Freedom, we are relatively uninterested in how much a country spends on elections, or how many candidates participate or vote in elections; we are equally uninterested in whether a country's laws prohibit censorship. What we are interested in is the degree to which a people is offered a choice between different policies or emphases in elections, achieve change through them, or have available uncensored literature. These are the appropriate outputs for understanding freedoms. Other measures, such as equality of incomes or living standards might be the output measures for studies examining economic equality, but not for political equality.

The first task of the social indicator analyst becomes choosing which types of reasonably available data are most critical for establishing significant differences among populations, selecting out those that seem most likely to be comparable across these populations at different times, and then establishing and continually improving the most rigorous data base that he can for the area of interest. The second becomes establishing trend lines, and areal, class, or other group variations. Finally, he should relate the indicators so mapped to broader social issues or hypotheses.

The second proposition, that the Survey is not a human rights survey, highlights the fact that it was developed for Freedom House, an organization with a particular interest in political and civil freedoms. In this context it was possible to establish a simple, traditional definition of freedom, and to base an orienting survey on it. Human rights, on the other hand, has no such clear definition, in spite of the many claims of the "human rights community" that it does. As generally understood by the media and Congress, human rights has a fairly narrow meaning. Amnesty

International narrows that meaning even further, and then adds on a right against execution that does not exist in international agreements.

The diffuseness of the definitions in international documents and the lack of international respect for these documents in practice combine with the impossibility of fixing the responsibility for observance for many of the rights. While Amnesty and others can generally fix the responsibility for a political execution on a government, fixing the responsibility of malnutrition in many or even most countries is much harder. "Measuring" the extent of "good faith" efforts might be even more daunting.

Another common criticism has been that the Survey is not suffi-ciently quantitative and rigorous. It has been pointed out that it would be possible to take the checklist variables, such as those found in the Checklist for Freedom ratings above (pages 9-10), and assign values to each, such that the results could be cumulated to yield more objective ratings. Aside from making a number of experiments along this line, the author has answered this criticism by pointing to the problems that others have had in applying such schemes to this data. Robert Dahl used such a scheme in developing his list of democracies. Yet he notes that in at least one case he had to adjust the results to obtain the relationships that he intuitively "knew" were correct in spite of the quantitative apparatus.[13]

Two more objections to more quantification may be mentioned. First, all such systems assign definite values to each area of the problem, so that when there is a particularly good or bad showing in an area the scoring system cannot flexibly record this special quality of a country's democracy or lack of it. Only a very few points could be accorded, for example, to religious freedom, and yet in a particular instance the denial of religious freedom might be the outstanding fact in judging a country's civil liberties. Second, we simply do not have adequate information to make possible assigning scores to the wide variety of individual variables that would be involved.

There has been neither adequate nor comparable information to fill all the "boxes" that analytically go into the Survey; nor has there been a way to a priori weight the boxes. The problem is exacerbated by the lack of comparable statistics for the most obvious data. For example, I am often asked how many countries imprison people for reasons of conscience, how many torture them, what the numbers are, and how they have changed over the years. Some want to know specific things, such as how many have been killed off the battlefield in El Salvador, or in communist countries. It is surprising how few times we can give adequate answers to such simple requests. A few years ago James Seymour published a short statistical survey on political imprisonment in the world.[14] It had many lacunae, but it remains one of the very few comprehensive efforts of its kind. The very fact that the Comparative Survey, and even the political terror scale that the author casually developed for one yearbook, is used repeatedly by social scientists for statistical analyses[15] indicates how little real information there is out there—in spite of a great deal of general philosophizing in academic journals in the last fifteen years about human rights and the causes of their sorry state.

My suggestion is that the greatest contribution that social scientists interested in indicators might make to elucidating the state of human rights, and to discovering the etiology of problems in this area, would be to develop and keep current adequate statistics on hard indicators of performance or lack of performance in those areas most amenable to counting. Only when we can look at much improved year-by-year statistics for imprisonment for reasons of conscience, torture, prison brutality, incidents of political censorship, and so on, will we begin to have the basis for the introduction of a little science into the field. Of course, an investigator is unlikely to get the information from "worst offender" countries such as North Korea or (for entirely different reasons) Chad, and this must be remembered in the generalizations that are drawn, but it would be a start. Whether this would ever allow causative generalizations to be developed is questionable, but even the presentation and communication of the information—as well as the effort to develop the criteria of assignment that this would require—would be a contribution.

Comparison With Other Surveys

Charles Humana's **World Human Rights Guide,** a comprehensive attempt to review the state of human rights in the world, is now in its second edition.[16]   Although Humana focuses on a broader and rather different set of values than the Survey, there is a remarkable similarity in the results.

Humana's selection of forty rights for detailed country-by-country examination is buttressed by citations of the international human rights documents that support each. These citations fail to erase the suspicion that many "rights" reflect the values of the liberal western community, and offer little evidence for universal acceptance. For example, among the seven rights to which Humana gives particularly heavy weighting, the right to be free from capital punishment is supported by reference to Article 6 of the Covenant on Political and Civil Rights: "Nothing in this article shall be invoked to delay or prevent the abolition of capital punishment by any state party to the present Covenant." Humana's assumption of a universal right to practice homosexuality or take contraceptive pills is supported only indirectly by reference to international instruments.

The author's courage in selecting rights of interest to him reflects the more general fact, mentioned above, that the international human rights referred to in international documents are not rights that the people of the world from widely differing backgrounds and cultures have openly and freely agreed to abide by.[17] They are rights decided on by small elites; indeed the Universal Declaration was decided on by a United Nations that included less than half of the countries in the UN today. Even today the elites that run most countries have been educated directly or indirectly by Western universities; they have not consulted with their peoples on such rights.

More important than the particular rights chosen or not chosen is the weight of the choices, and what these add up to. Humana's seven major rights are all "freedom from" rights; Humana gives these three times the weighting of the remaining thirty-three rights. The seven are freedom from: slavery, extrajudicial disappearances or killings, torture (including brutal prison conditions), compulsory work arrangements or work conscription, capital punishment, court sentences of corporal punishment, or indefinite detention without trial. This weighting was decided on the basis of personal pain, or as the author says, "An individual screaming while subjected to torture or locked for years in an unlit cell because of his or her opinions is enduring a degree of physical or mental suffering greater than the denial of a vote or of having his or her newspapers censored."[18]

This is, then, a survey of human rights as these are understood commonly by the popular press, or in the work of Amnesty International. Among the forty rights, only two, the right to "peaceful political opposition" (a vague category) and "multi-party elections by secret and universal ballot" are concerned with political rights. In this calculation two related minor civil rights, such as "to travel in country," "to travel outside country," or "to monitor human rights violations" are the equal of all political rights taken together.

The occasional differences between the **Guide** and the Survey are largely due to this difference in emphasis. But since civil and political rights are generally closely correlated the differences in the final judgements of nations are seldom significant.

More significant is the difference between the methodology for human rights reporting employed by Humana and the Survey's methods. Most human rights reporting is based on a "negative case method." Using this method a country's performance is graded according to the number of cases of human rights abuses reported for that country in a particular time period. Interestingly, even efforts with some statistical pretensions, such as Humana's, seldom relate the number of cases to the size of a country's population. But the significance of this failure is outweighed by the widely varying availability of information about human rights abuses. Most human rights abuses are never reported.

The difficulty with the negative case method is not only its concentration on discrete cases rather than the more general political-civil environment. The problem is that the human rights picture that emerges from examining "violations" is quite different from that which comes from examining both the positive and negative records of human rights observance in a country.

Although it is hard to gather positive "cases," especially where the positive case is considered the norm, we have found in the Survey that positive data can be decisive. For example, evidence that the government sometimes fails to win politically-relevant court cases is an important indicator of the rule of law. The existence of independent newspapers, and examples of their expression of opinion criticizing government policy (not minor officials), indicates a considerable level of freedom of expression. The same is true of the broadcast media. The existence of functioning human rights organizations reporting government abuses is often a critical indicator of rights—sometimes as much as the cases they report serve as negative indicators. The ability of groups to organize demonstrations in opposition to government policy, even where such demonstrations are "illegal" is a critical indicator of civil liberties.

It has become a standard Survey rule of thumb that no country for which such evidence is regularly received should be considered "not free" unless there are no operating popular political institutions at all. It will be noted that it is often the case that significant positive evidence can exist alongside political imprisonment, journal censorship and confiscation, and even political torture or execution. Using his negative case method, Humana gives a very low rating, for example, to South Africa. Its rating of 22% places it just below Libya and just above the USSR and Romania. The Survey places South Africa much higher than the latter states. The Survey notes that while few if any positive indicators were reported from the latter states in the last few years, they have all been regularly reported from South Africa— alongside the massive repressions of 1986. Similarly the very low rating Humana gives Iran is based on "massive" human rights violations;[19] his rating gives no credit to the intense and public policy discussion that goes on in that country. The Survey finds it significant that in the last Iranian presidential election a potential candidate was denied the right to compete, evidently because he had announced his intention to campaign against the war. Anti-war demonstrations have also been held in the last few years. Imprisonment for the crime of public opposition to the war on the scale of the Iran-Iraq war would have been automatic in countries with 6's or 7's for civil liberties. It certainly would have been automatic in Iraq.

Unlike civil liberties, political rights are expressed primarily through a series of positive expressions of rights. Their presence tends to be what is reported rather than their absence. Perhaps this is one reason that human rights surveys such as Humana's, based on the negative case method, find it harder to deal with this aspect of rights. Those who consider elections must be alert to the danger of noticing the extent to which elections fall short of certain ideals rather than the degree to which they express an important measure of political liberty. No elections anywhere are perfect in the sense that all potential positions are offered equally to the public, or in the sense that all citizens are actually equal in their ability to affect the election process. However, over the years the inequalities have tended to be reduced in the most effective democracies; the entrenched powers and rights of the few have been successfully challenged at the ballot box. In countries without this level of political freedom, the election process may still be used as a means of expressing popular dissatisfaction, or even viewpoints that otherwise would not get a hearing. Certainly both of these functions have been well served in Iran and South Africa in the last few years in spite of the limits on the range of discussion (especially Iran) and the limits on who can participate (especially South Africa).

Most of the differences between the Survey and the **Guide** can be explained by reference to the different goals and methodologies of these efforts. However, consideration of particular countries might serve to further illuminate these differences, and lead to the discovery of some apparent mistakes in judgment or information in the Humana work.

The Survey gives the United States and most traditional democracies its highest ratings. Although the United States is given a favorable rating in Humana's work, its 90% rating places it below the traditional democracies—even below recent newcomers such as Greece and Portugal. The United States ranks just below Papua New Guinea. The major cause for Humana's relatively low rating for the United States is its continued use of capital punishment, as well as minor problems in such areas as ethnic and gender equality, or the acceptance of homosexuals. It is significant that the right to be free of capital punishment is not actually an international standard in more than the eyes of its advocates. Aside from this major "blot" on the American record, Humana's placing of Papua New Guinea above the United States would seem to indicate more serious problems with his methodology. Humana fails to note the questionable operation of Papua New Guinea's political system. While the forms of democracy do function in Papua New Guinea, the willingness of those elected to change political parties and policy positions for personal advantage, irrespective of the basis of their election should be taken seriously. With all its remarkable progress, it is fair to say that there is not yet a truly national electorate in Papua New Guinea that uses elections to express positions on national problems. Humana should also in his own terms have noted the inability of Papua New Guinea's government to control continued tribal warfare, and the meaning of this warfare for effective individual rights of any kind.

As in many human rights discussions, European countries are treated much too gently in the Humana overview. The excessive rights of the Swedish state against the individual have often been noted, particularly in regard to the right of parents over their children. The weakness of the Swedish parliament vis-à-vis the bureaucracy is also a continuing problem. Humana notes that Finland has had continuing self-censorship, often with government encouragement, of public expression concerning the USSR, but fails to note the necessity to select a president acceptable to Moscow. (If Mexico or Canada had such restrictions in relation to the United States might they not be taken more seriously?) Yet Sweden and Finland are at the top of Humana's ratings. In rating France, Humana fails to note the ability of the government to ban books that displease its allies, or even on occasion the government. Finally, Greece has experienced a variety of problems with misuse of the state controlled media, and abuses of government power. In spite of the seizure of newspapers for insulting the president, and a ban on books offensive to either the president or religion, Greece scores a respectable 94%.

Perhaps the most obvious example of the difference between the Survey's ratings and that of the **Guide** is India. Although a fully functioning federal democracy, rated 2-3 or "free" in the Survey, Humana gives India a 60% rating, one point below Tunisia and one above South Korea. Humana's marginal interest in political rights is only part of the reason for the discrepancy. More important is his focus on negative human rights problems rather than the broader picture of negative and positive human rights conditions. India has highly varied print media, thousands of independent organizations, and continual demonstrations and campaigns for every conceivable cause. India's business and labor organizations are quite independent of the government. By contrast independent organizations or publications with policy content in South Korea or Tunisia must continually struggle to maintain even their right to exist. The crushing of any attempt by Muslim fundamentalists to put forward their position politically contrasts with the many successful efforts by comparable groups in India. None of this is to deny that socially the lives of Tunisians and South Koreans are smoother and generally easier than those of Indians. It is true that India's security forces often resort to unnecessary violence, but it is also true that its security forces have seldom if ever been used to put down the majority of the urban population, as is repeatedly done in South Korea, or to destroy the independence of the labor unions, as in Tunisia. It is true that whereas the UK has one continually disturbed and occasionally "repressed" Ulster, India at any one time has many Ulsters. But India also has fourteen times the population of the UK.

A system of positive indicators, and one with more weight given to the right of people to rule themselves, would have brought more balance to such cases. But until there is a reasonable way to solve the difficult problem of using such indicators, the necessarily "subjective" weighing of the rights balance will remain less convincing than studies based on dramatic rights violations.

Yet with all this, the ratings that Humana produces and those of the Survey are highly correlated. This suggest that the differences that stem from different ideologies, methodologies, or emphases can easily be overrated as long as the common flow of information on the world is fairly evaluated.[20]

Finally, it may be useful to consider briefly another attempt at the rating of countries that has received publicity recently. Richard Estes, **The Social Progress of Nations,** rates, and in essence ranks, 107 independent countries in terms of variables representing differential achievement in human welfare.[21] Estes includes a number of human rights or freedom variables, but these are not as central to his study as more material welfare indices. His purposes are to show change over time, to highlight particular areas of progress as well as stagnation and decline, and to point up the seriousness of the problems of the poorest states. Much more in the tradition of recent social science than either the Survey or Humana's work, Estes relies primarily on the relating and statistical manipulation of "hard data" rather than on qualitative judgments—although qualitative rating scales, including the Comparative Survey, are included in his statistics. In line with his emphasis on change, he compares results for 1970(1969) and 1980(1979) wherever possible.

Estes has eleven subindexes: education, health, status of women, defense effort, economic, demography, geography, political stability, political participation, cultural diversity, and welfare effort. The attempt, as in many similar studies, is then to find a few simple measures that will produce a figure that somehow represents the area of interest. Some of these are useful "output" measures such as economic growth rate, some are highly unreliable outputs, such as "number of political strikes," and others are next-to-meaningless "measures" of input or intent. For example the index for "welfare effort" consists entirely of "years since first law" for items such as old age benefits, unemployment benefits etc. It is surprising that the area with which Estes is most acquainted (he is a professor of social work) is the one with the least significant measures.

For purposes far different from ours, Estes includes a strange "geography" measure based on percent arable land mass (+), number of major natural disasters (-), and lives lost in major natural diasasters per thousand (-). It is primarily because of the very poor "performance" of the United States on this measure that in his Index of Social Progress the United States fell far below the rating of the USSR in 1970 and barely equaled it in 1980. According to Estes' statistics, during the period 1947 to 1979 the Soviet Union had 1.8 natural disasters and United States 326—with the result that the Soviet Union had 0.4 lives lost per million while the United States suffered 46. Even if this were true, its meaning would be hard to fathom, since there is no measure offered reflecting the ability of a society to react to disaster. But remember Estes is not interested only in performance, he wants to know how bad things are for the purpose of understanding the social welfare task. This is legitimate; the author's uncritical willingness to accept a statistic "because it is there" is not. Fortunately, Estes sees a problem with the geography statistic, and presents a "Net Social Progress Index" that ignores the geography subindex. In this index the United States still falls below the USSR in 1970 by a small margin, but is well above it in 1980.

Restricting our attention to the comparison of the United States and the Soviet Union in the rest of the subindexes, the United States falls below the Soviet Union in 1970 primarily because of the protests, riots and strikes in our country versus the placid USSR, and because of our military effort in Vietnam. By 1980 Afghanistan has in large part reversed the ratings on this score.[22]   Looking at political participation, Estes rates both systems as having fully functioning parliaments. The Soviet Union falls below the U.S. in having only one party and the military having more influence in politics; but it is ahead of us in having had national elections in both years (1969 and 1979), while we had none! In other indices the USSR is ahead of the United States in education and "welfare effort," while it lags in health, the economy, political participation (in spite of the above), and cultural diversity. The distance of Estes' work from standard human rights concerns is suggested by the ratings in the latter category—for example, the more homogeneous the language and culture of a country is, the higher the rating. This suggests that in some respects his approach may measure problems with perhaps a clearer eye than is offered by the human rights focus.

Estes' survey suggests some of the pitfalls of a more methodologically sophisticated and less judgmental approach. But it also is directed to different purposes. We may think that his comparisons of the developed West with the Warsaw Pact states (he finds them approximately equal) is deficient, but when he goes on to compare these states taken together with the developing and not developing parts of the world, the picture becomes more believable, and the parts fall together. His method also is more able to show trends than a relativized year-by-year approach such as we use.

NOTES

1. For a positive review see Kenneth Thompson, **Human Rights Quarterly**, 4,4 (November, 1982), pages 539-40. For the negative see below.

2. See Harry Scoble and Laurie Wiseberg, "Problems of Comparative Research on Human Rights," in V. P. Nanda, J. R. Scarritt, and G. W. Shepherd, **Global Human Rights: Public Policies, Comparative Measures, and NGO Strategies** (Boulder: Westview Press, 1981), pages 147-172. For references to more recent criticisms of this nature, see Kenneth Bollen, "Political rights and Political Liberties in Nations: An Evaluation of Human Rights Measures, 1950 to 1984," **Human Rights Quarterly**, 8,4, November, 1986, page 585, as well as other discussions in this issue.

3. Scoble and Wiseberg, page 160.

4. Lars Schoultz, "Freedom in the World: Political and Civil Liberties," (Review), **Universal Human Rights**, 1,2, January-March, 1980, pages 94-96.

5. Gastil, **Freedom in the World: 1978,** page 175. The reader might also be interested in the more extended discussion of the relation of economic and political freedoms in the 1982 and 1983-84 yearbooks. Of course, in no case does degree of capitalism figure in our political or civil liberties.

6. Scoble and Wiseberg, page 155 and passim. This point was made in the first survey (1973), page 22, and subsequently in other forms. For our interests in the relation of worker participation schemes to political and civil liberties, one might note the relevant country descriptions.

7. John F. McCamant, "A Critique of Present Measures of 'Human Rights Development' and an Alternative," in Nanda, Scarritt, and Shepherd, op. cit., pages 123-146., especially pages 131-2.

8. Ibid., page 130. Parenthetically it is interesting that McCamant mentions in criticism of another study the tendency of Latin American academics to underrate Brazil's freedom in the 1970s. On the basis of just such an underrating, Scoble and Wiseberg had attacked our rating of Brazil in this period.

9. Scoble and Wiseberg, page 154.

10. See for example, R. D. Gastil, "Social Indicators and Quality of Life," **Public Administration Review,** November/December, 1970, pages 596-601. "Social Accounting Versus Social Responsibility" in Meinolf Dierkes and Raymond Bauer, **Corporate Social Accounting** (New York: Praeger, 1973), pages 93-106. "Homicide and a Regional Culture of Violence," **American Sociological Review,** 1971, pages 412-427. This latter line of effort is included in R. D. Gastil, **Cultural Regions of the United States** (Seattle: University of Washington Press, 1975), Chapter 3, "Regional Variations in Common Social Indicators," pages 92-135.

11. Gastil, "Social Indicators and Quality of Life," page 600.

12. See John P. Lewis and Valeriana Kallab, eds. **U. S. Foreign Policy and the Third World: Agenda, 1983** (New York: Overseas Development Council, 1983), pages 206-222 and references cited.

13. Robert Dahl, **Polyarchy: Participation and Opposition** (New Haven: Yale University Press, 1971), pages 243-245.

14. James D. Seymour, "Indices of Political Improvement," **Universal Human Rights,** 1,1 January/March, 1979, pages 99-103.

15. Most recently, David Banks, The Analysis of Human Rights Data over Time," **Human Rights Quarterly,** 8,4, November 1986, pages 654-680.

16. Charles Humana, **World Human Rights Guide,** (New York: Facts on File, 1986). See also Charles Humana **World Human Rights Guide** (London: Hutchinson, 1983).

17. Joshua Muravchik **The Uncertain Crusade** (Lanham, Md.: Hamilton Press, 1986), pages 75ff.

18. Humana, 1986, pages 3-4.

19. Humana, 1986, page 131.

20. See Bollen, "Political Rights and Political Liberties in Nations," page 588 for a discussion of Banks' correlation of 0.9 of the two surveys is discussed.

21. Richard J. Estes **The Social Progress of Nations** (New York: Praeger, 1984).

22. Estes, 1984, pages 93-102, 200-201.

PART II

Current Issues

Communications: Revising
the Limits of Disclosure

Leonard R. Sussman

As long as a country has no civil liberty, no freedom of information, and no independent press, then there exists no effective body of public opinion to control the conduct of the government and its functionaries. Such a situation is not just a misfortune for citizens unprotected against tyranny and lawlessness; it is a menace to international security.

Andrey Sakharov

The United States and the Soviet Union had difficulty in 1986 coordinating domestic and international communications with overall national policy. Both superpowers managed to confuse the world's perception of their disparate societies. The Soviets embraced the Western public relations style, but belied their "openness" with the entrapment of an American journalist, used as a pawn to release a Soviet spy caught in the United States. That month-long incident also clouded the American denial that a Soviet spy was exchanged for a U.S. journalist. To be sure, the spy had been convicted and the journalist not tried, but the release of both simultaneously made a denial of a "swap" implausible.

The United States also tried clumsily after bombing Libya to generate fear of another attack: an effort to destabilize Muammar Qadafi. And months earlier through similar leaks the White House hinted that Libyan hitmen would soon try to assassinate President Reagan. The U.S. press regarded both efforts as "disinformation," the old technique of psychological warfare used increasingly by the Soviet Union. The press claimed, without the possibility of proof, that the incidents confused the U.S. public more than Qadafi.

The facts were not all in favor of the journalists. The Administration was split over whether to attack Libya for the second

99

time, an unidentified official told two major newspapers in August. Other newspapers carried the leaked report, but questioned its accuracy. Close readers of the press were hardly "disinformed." There can be no defense, however, for the National Security Adviser to the President putting on paper a memorandum authorizing the use of "real and illusionary events . . . through a disinformation program," even though directed at Qadafi. The negotiations among U.S. representatives, personages in Iran, and Israeli middlemen—revealed eighteen months after arms went to embargoed Iran and dollars to rebels in Nicaragua—proved again how difficult it is to employ secret methods and communications cover-ups, while maintaining a free and independent press.

The basic failure may not be the loss of credibility for an Administration that loudly chided other nations for negotiating with terrorists, while itself ransoming three hostages through third-country deals. Nor may the worst loss be the aborted, inept effort to persuade successors to the Ayatollah Khomeini that relations can be improved between the United States and the strategically important Islamic state.

The most serious setback for the United States may be its clear failure to conduct the competition of ideas successfully over Libya, Iran, the Icelandic summit, and to a lesser extent, the exchange of the American journalist Nicholas Daniloff for the Soviet spy Genaddy Zakharov. The loss in credibility of both the U.S. presidency and the American press is shown in one poll taken soon after Daniloff was arrested. Some sixty-six percent of American respondents believed it possible that he was, indeed, a spy as Moscow had charged.[1] Similar polls also show a low regard for the credibility of the press. This reflects a grave lack of trust in both the independent news media and the government that the media particularly criticize.

Diplomatic failures this year were all linked to the inability of Washington to devise a successful method of conducting policies abroad under restrictions set by law, and under the no less demanding restraint of open news media. That is not to argue for an Official Secrets Act to foreclose press reporting of certain top-secret activities abroad, even those intended to serve vital national interests. But the year's frustrations in Washington are real, and not entirely the result of inept handling of secret acts in an open society: the dilemma is endemic, and should be faced without bitterness or naivete by government officials, journalists, and the public.

The obverse of that dilemma was no less real in Moscow: how can the closed, centralized Soviet society secure greater credibility in the West and the Third World when there is no free access to officials or their deliberations, or to the vast Soviet population, or its territory? This dilemma was formally recognized by Mikhail Gorbachev on coming to office. He announced a policy of glasnost.

The word itself has two meanings. One, "openness," has been widely welcomed in the West, as was "detente" when first floated by the Kremlin, and for similar reasons: citizens and governments in the West want to negotiate life and death issues with Soviet leaders, but cannot trust deals with a regime that has yet to prove its legitimacy by open decision of its population, and operates in perpetual secrecy. The closedness of that society was most crudely reflected in the old Soviet press policy. It completely ignored negative news: earthquakes, plane crashes, disasters at sea, and the like were never reported to the Soviet public or the foreign press.

This year, under glasnost, the Soviets promptly announced the sinking of one of their nuclear submarines, a train crash that took many lives, and a collision of ships at sea. Each of these announcements was greeted with observations in the West that glasnost was working. Indeed, Gorbachev and other high-level officials also conducted press conferences in Moscow and at the Iceland summit, and used U.S. television opportunities repeatedly to imply a great opening of Soviet society and fundamental changes in its policies. This new PR approach was clearly evident at the October "pre-Summit" in Iceland. Gorbachev caught Americans off guard by making sweeping proposals for reduction of arms. Then in the midst of closed-session bargaining his aides went on U.S. television, live, to leak their proposals and suggest the Americans were about to approve an historic agreement. U.S. television reporters rushed to carry the Soviet propaganda ploy. It took center stage while Americans held to the closed-session agreement, and dealt with a surprise package of substantive proposals when only a concept-session had been anticipated. Americans, consequently, appeared defensive and stalling. The propaganda game carried over into post-Reykjavik superpower debates, further increasing the international confusion.

101

Glasnost, as presently practiced, displays no real lessening of centralized information controls. The openness itself is cleverly manipulated so that any small deviation from the traditional blackout is hailed as further liberalization. Disparagement of low-level inefficiencies and reporting errors in bureaucratic implementation are encouraged. Such "dissent" is used by the central authority to correct minor abuses, and advance the "openness" of glasnost. Yet the system is no less organized to destroy whoever tries to dissent on fundamental issues.

But little noted in the United States is another translation for glasnost: publicity. The conveying of propaganda while giving the appearance of greater openness is itself a tactic in the battle of ideas, just as was "detente." Both, as employed by the USSR seek a one-way softening of ideology and the use of ideas in international diplomacy. Glasnost is the Soviet term for public diplomacy, which in turn means psychological warfare. Glasnost, like detente, is friendly sounding, but no less burdened with ideological, political, and even military baggage.

Since Lenin's day, agitation and propaganda are the twin aspects of domestic and foreign affairs in the Soviet Union. The latest techniques of printing and radio, first exploited nearly seventy years ago by the Bolsheviks, have been supplemented by television and high-speed press and photo capabilities tied to satellites. But perhaps most important is the sophistication of ideas and ideology. After thorough market surveys of the yearnings and objectives of citizens in the West, Soviet responses are often dressed in Western colloquialisms that advance Moscow's policies.

The Soviet use of American journalism was eminently more adroit this year than in the past, with the glaring exception of the handling of the nuclear disaster of Chernobyl. There, as in the Daniloff case, the Soviets had trouble with glasnost—probably because of the merging interests of the Communist Party, army, and state security apparatus. It would seem in that clash of interests, on both occasions, the needs of the KGB, state security, predominated.

The arrest of Nicholas Daniloff, the American journalist with Russian antecedents and fluency in the language, told more about the harsh strictures of Soviet society than the incidental swap for a spying Soviet physicist in the U.S. The Soviet Union regards all information—economic, political, scientific, social, religious, military—as fully under centralized governmental control. No citizen, certainly none with informational responsibilities, has the right to seek or disseminate information that has not been approved for release by the central authority. Any citizen may be severely penalized as subversive for trying to secure, let alone reveal, unauthorized information. That ban may include statistics on births/deaths, crop production, unemployment, industrial growth rates, and other data which in the United States can be secured from libraries and government agencies. Since privacy is not permitted the Soviet citizen, meeting with a reporter must be subversive. And any citizen can be asked to provide information, that is, serve as a spy. That was the function served by the man who helped trap Daniloff.

In the Soviet system, a Western journalist is constantly suspect. His mission, in Soviet eyes, is more adversarial: subversive. Yet an American reporter, if he is conscientious, will accept an official statement and still try to convey the deeper meaning. Since he cannot find "officials" who will speak off the record or "for background," he will seek those few courageous Soviet citizens who risk meeting a foreigner. Under a three-year-old law, such meetings can bring harsh penalties for a Soviet citizen. That often limits the journalist's contacts to dissidents who are already under penalty.

This harsh system has had clear advantages for the Kremlin. Yet the turn toward glasnost provided a challenge and an opportunity. While seeming to practice greater openness, the Soviets can still capitalize on the actual control they maintain over the foreign journalist. It has become more important, therefore, to manipulate foreign correspondents stationed in Moscow.

The arrest of Daniloff, in addition to providing a pawn for the spy trade, served to warn the journalists against becoming too proficient and independent. Daniloff was one of the few American journalists who could speak directly to Soviet citizens. Some correspondents use translators provided by the KGB to interview Soviet officials and other citizens. Such ties to the security forces intimidate the interviewers and interviewees, and provide the Kremlin with accurate word about the interests of U.S. journalism, and the flow of information out of the country (even though stories may leave in the U.S. diplomatic pouch).

Daniloff, on leaving Moscow, read his colleagues in Russian this 1840 verse by a poet exiled to the Caucasus by the Czar:

> Farewell to you, unwashed Russia
> Land of slaves, land of gentry
> And to you, the blue uniforms
> And to you, the people who obey
> them.
>
> Maybe behind a Caucasian ridge
> I will hide from your pashas,
> From their all-seeing eyes,
> From their all-hearing ears.
>   Mikhail Lermontov

The Daniloff case also revealed something about the Soviet's misunderstanding of the United States. Moscow has never accepted that the American news media act independently of the U.S. government. The Soviets have stated categorically in UNESCO draft resolutions that all news media are, in fact, the responsibility of the governments within whose jurisdiction the media operate.[2] Those drafts never were approved, but the Soviets continue to act as though the U.S. media/government relationship is a mirror image of the fully centralized Soviet media system. Consequently, the regularized Soviet attacks on American news media, and the U.S. government are far stronger and more consistent than any anti-Soviet statements eminating either from the U.S. media or the Reagan Administration. In that context the role Daniloff was presumed to be playing is thoroughly in keeping with the historic employment of Soviet journalists at home and abroad.

The treatment of Daniloff, while shocking to American journalists, generated some ambiguity in the U. S. public. Its desire for peace with the Soviets, its inclination to go halfway to secure it, its lack of trust in American officials and journalists, the handful of what Lenin regarded as "useful fools"—all produced some contradictory reactions visible even in the Daniloff affair, but especially in the Iran and Libyan incidents.

These incidents emphasized that a free society is constantly subjected to the exploitation of its own messages by authoritarians abroad in their continuing campaign of psychological warfare. That

104

free society is further disadvantaged if it is seen to use, even briefly and limitedly overseas, some of the weapons of idea-warfare. This dilemma cannot be easily resolved. Psychological warfare, though a nasty-sounding term, will not disappear by the will of free societies. Indeed, psychological combat is eminently more desirable than the bloody kind, which can follow if more peaceful adversarial efforts fail.

Public diplomacy, the nicer term, should be rapidly and sophisticatedly supported. This includes broader uses of Radio Free Europe/Radio Liberty, the Voice of America, overseas book programs, academic and cultural exchanges, and other diverse activities of the U.S. Information Agency. The new National Endowment for Democracy should be far better supported. All of these open transmissions from the American culture to adversaries abroad will be only as successful as the understanding of the U.S. news media and the public that the war of ideas has been magnified and made more complex by Soviet glasnost. And the U.S. government must be expected—without waiving the First Amendment at home, or engaging in crude propaganda abroad—to provide an effective counter to the psychological warfare presently targeted on the United States.

At the Reykjavik summit, Soviet jamming of the Voice of America was also discussed. The Soviets would stop interference, Gorbachev told the President, if he would help Moscow gain access to U.S. domestic radio broadcasts. No mention was made of the vast Soviet jamming apparatus aimed at Radio Free Europe/Radio Liberty, the U.S. shortwave radios beamed to Eastern Europe and the Soviet Union. Ending the jamming of the VOA could release Soviet power to blot out RFE/RL entirely. And once U.S. domestic radios carried Moscow's leased broadcasts there is no assurance that jamming might not be renewed in a crisis. Private U.S. radios might not discontinue broadcasting Moscow's programs. Once again, a democratic society that says it would not barter its values to end illegal activities would have betrayed its principles, and disappointed its friends. For the USSR has more than one hundred jamming transmitters, and spends more on jamming than the United States spends on open broadcasting overseas. Yet the USSR, along with all other countries in the International Telecommunications Union (ITU), has pledged to desist from jamming. The U.S. planned to call this year for an ITU study of interference with its radio

signals.   The ITU's International Frequency Regulation Board
(IFRB), meanwhile, confirmed that jamming by the USSR, Poland,
and Czechoslovakia is interfering with American broadcasts.   This
was unprecedented recognition of widespread Soviet jamming.   The
ITU's regulations clearly prohibit such interference.   The IFRB has
formally notified the jamming countries, but by year-end they had
not ceased interference.   That notification may have triggered
Gorbachev's offer of an "equal" trade: ending of the minor jamming
of VOA for access to regular domestic radio programming in the
U.S.   If instead, equal time for uncensored American programming
over domestic Soviet channels is proposed, the deal might be a
significant sign of glasnost.   And Soviet citizens might approve:
for Pravda, the communist party newspaper, complained in May that
Soviet television coverage of the West was dull.   "Journalistic
cliches migrate from broadcast to broadcast," wrote Dmitri
Lynbosvetov.   Film clips from the West "show mainly meetings,
demonstrations and protests," he wrote.   "They rarely tell about
the achievements of science and technology, about what effect
these have on the ordinary worker in the conditions of
capitalism."[3]

This two-edged comment suggests some hazard to "the ordinary
worker" under capitalism.   Information technology poses quite a
different threat to the centralized controllers under Soviet
socialism.   Gorbachev has promised to heighten industrial and agricultural productivity, and provide more consumer goods as well.
Computerization of the means of production and distribution implies
an opening to information far beyond the present domestic glasnost.
The new technologies would break the Kremlin's monopoly on information.   Moscow restricts the use of copying machines as Poland
licenses typewriters.   Both are used to produce samizdat (self-
published, unofficial writing).   Moscow in 1982 pulled the plug on
direct-dial, long-distance telephone service.   It was too much for
KGB surveillance.   The great jump in American technological skills
may be traced to the million or more computer mainframes now in
use, with about ten percent that number permitted by the USSR.
Access in computers is severely restricted.   In Poland, meanwhile,
computers are commonplace among producers of underground books
and magazines.   Widespread, unofficial use of computers in Eastern
Europe may presage an eventual opening in the USSR.   Now,
Western cassettes are surreptitiously used on expensive Soviet

videocassette recorders (VCR's). When personal computers arrive in Moscow, **glasnost** may truly begin.

Meanwhile, to assume that a cosmetic opening is real can mislead Western citizens. "Socialist realism" is what it has always been: describing as true not what is, but what should be, to meet Leninist objectives. Anti-American films produced in the USSR have sharply increased in number over the past two years.[4] This is part of a scheduled campaign. Although greater sophistication is shown in these films, the depicting of Americans as villains and the Soviets as heroes having moral superiority comes through clearly. A 1984 decree of the Central Committee of the Communist Party called for films that would "propagate the Leninist foreign policy of the USSR, . . . take more accurately into account the peculiarities of the contemporary ideological struggle in the international arena, increase the vigilance of the Soviet people and its armed forces, and actively contribute to military-patriotic education." This is far more ideology than Rambo. A Soviet film critic, examining the new wave of anti-American films, notes that in one story "the leader of the Freemasons can only be an American, or CIA agent, for such is the logic of life and the natural development of the plot." Another film deals with the deployment of cruise missiles in a North European country. If one candidate for mayor wins an election, the film says, the missiles will not be deployed in that town, but if the winner is "the neo-fascist Olden, a puppet of the industrialist and of American resident spies," the missiles will be put in place.

Recently, for the first time, such Soviet films were sent to foreign audiences. At the 1985 Cannes International Film Festival a Soviet film portrayed President Truman and Prime Minister Churchill as horrific creatures resembling vampires, compared with the majestic Stalin, the diplomat. An honest Soviet journalist was contrasted with a craven and mercenary American counterpart.[5]

Yet the confusion is heightened when Soviet spokesmen appear on American television, as they did with greater frequency in 1986 than before. Network talk shows featured Vladimir Pozner, a sophisticated progagandist who cleverly employs American colloquialisms, and mixes truths with half-truths about both societies. Two TV bridges were shown between U.S. and Soviet citizens featuring Pozner and Phil Donahue. The limited opening to new information for Soviet viewers was more than compensated by the reemphasis in the United States on a new openness in the USSR—a boon to the larger Soviet purpose in this country. In addition, ABC, CBS, NBC, and PBS networks carried their own programs on life in the Soviet Union. In the main, these tended to be favorable views of the USSR, allowing for traditional differences, and a still-not-open society. The "freshness" of the new Politburo, for example, was described by CBS as "remarkable," a "sweeping generational change from the days of Leonid Brezhnev." Such an analysis of a still-closed society is difficult to verify, and both the Politburo and U.S. journalists bear watching.

It is instructive to examine how the Soviet Union lost credibility at Chernobyl. At 1:23 a.m. Saturday, April 26, fire broke out in a nuclear reactor. At noon, an investigation committee was appointed in Moscow. No warning was made public. At 4:00 p.m. there were two explosions, the roof blew off, and debris shot one-half mile into the air. Still no warning. By 7:00 a.m. Sunday a radioactive cloud appeared over Sweden. No news yet. At 10:00 a.m. Monday the Swedes called Moscow and said they assumed there had been a nuclear disaster in the USSR. At 6:00 p.m., eight hours after the Swedes called, and two and one-half days after the first fire, the Soviets denied on television any knowledge of an accident. At 9:00 p.m. Sunday—more than three days later—the Soviets announced the nuclear reactor catastrophe. Five days later they still had not acknowledged publicly exactly what had happened or the extent of the casualties. To deepen the silence, Western journalists and diplomats were promptly barred from traveling to Kiev.

The six-day delay in evacuating one major city near the disaster may ultimately cost thousands of lives and produce many deformed bodies. Other reports, not possible to confirm, tell of death and contamination among ethnic Estonians forced to work at the Chernobyl disaster site. Some 4,000 Estonians were forced to labor in the radioactive debris, according to an Associated Press report from an Estonian emigre group in Sweden. Doctors among those forced by soldiers to work at Chernobyl were said to have performed mass abortions of all pregnant women within thirty miles of the disaster site. At a hastily called international nuclear-development meeting in the fall, the Soviets began to release technical information about the accident, if not about the full impact on Soviet citizens. And by year-end, the Soviets activated another reactor at Chernobyl of the same design as the one that blew.

There was another international fallout from the Chernobyl disaster. Comments from Soviet citizens and recent emigrants from the USSR suggest that more Soviet citizens first learned about the nuclear accident from Western radio broadcasts than from any other source, Soviet or foreign. Nearly half the survey group learned about Chernobyl from Western radio, as a first or subsequent choice. Of 521 persons interviewed, 36 percent first learned of the disaster from Western radio, 28 percent from Soviet television, 15 percent word of mouth, 10 percent Soviet radio, 8 percent Soviet press, and 3 percent, other sources. Of those surveyed, 28 percent relied predominantly on the Voice of America, 18 percent on the U.S. freedom radios, 16 percent on the BBC, and the remaining 20 percent almost equally on the Swedish, West German, and Canadian radios. One Russian journalist in his thirties was quoted:

> Information began to trickle into the editorial office on the second day after the accident. We began to get all sorts of alarming reports. I don't know what their source was. We weren't allowed to use any of it. All we were allowed to print was official TASS reports, even though we knew that the extent of the accident was much more serious.[7]

In the absence of credible information, unofficial, unverifiable reports circulated—the bane of a closed society. One such is this from a blue-collar worker from Belgorod who emigrated the month after the disaster:

> A man who had fled a village near Chernobyl on 5 or 6 May told me that the explosion had killed many people in the area of the power station, including some who were on boats on the reservoir next to the reactor, and on a steamship which was passing nearby. Already on the day of the explosion, people were passing through his village from Chernobyl. They said there were bodies lying on the roads, and that people were

109

generally in a state of panic. The authorities were the first to flee, followed by everyone who could run. In the town of Chernobyl itself, the bank was robbed, and the militia station was burned down. Stores which had been abandoned were openly looted. When this man left, official evacuation orders had still not been given, and neither had people been instructed to avoid drinking water or milk and eating vegetables.[8]

All governments require some secrecy for the most sensitive, usually national security matters. The hard cases arise in a free society when journalists uncover, or are privately given, information that could reveal a crucial national secret. One this year was partly exposed at the trial of an American convicted of spying for the Soviet Union. The Washington Post learned that certain U.S. communications intelligence capabilities were at stake in the trial. The information involved locations of American signal collection agencies and evidence that the National Security Agency had penetrated the highest level of Soviet military connections. Still more was at risk. The Post had much of this information, and held it pending discussions with U.S. officials. President Reagan phoned Katherine Graham, publisher of the Post, to indicate the sensitive nature of some of the information. At one point William J. Casey, director of the Central Intelligence Agency, warned the Post, "I'm not threatening you, but you've got to know that if you publish this, I would recommend that you be prosecuted under the intelligence statute."[9] Casey cited an explicit 36-year-old law that provides ten years imprisonment and a fine of $10,000 for publishing classified information about intelligence communications intercepts.

Journalists regarded Casey's warning as intimidation. He later urged cooperation in handling highly sensitive information. Many journalists welcomed that step provided it did not result in official "clearance" for such reports. Lou Boccardi, the president of the Associated Press, said it well: "I don't think you can avoid the essential conflict in what they do and what we do." He added, "Like any journalist, I am opposed to government intervention, threats, and control, but I also think that a journalist has the responsibility to listen to legitimate security concerns." And, one expects, to act responsibly as a citizen as well as a journalist.

Danger also arises when either journalists or officials believe each has a constitutional right to determine the proper course in all instances involving the release of sensitive information. In only a few situations is secrecy desirable and necessary. But bureaucrats instinctively broaden the area to be placed under the blanket of secrecy, and journalists have a no less burning desire to reveal everything they choose. Official protectiveness this year has extended to repeated use of the McCarran-Walter Immigration Act (1952) to bar the entry of foreign journalists who hold offensive views of the United States.

A Colombian journalist who flew to New York in October to attend an award ceremony at Columbia University was barred from entry, detained for four days, and expelled. No explanation for the expulsion was given at the time, and the law, promulgated during the Joseph McCarthy era, requires none. The journalist, Patricia Lara, was regarded as the "distinguished" reporter for a popular Colombian newspaper. The Assistant Secretary of State, Elliott Abrams, under prodding from CBS' network show "60 Minutes," called Lara "a member of the M-19 terrorist organization" and an "active liaison" between "that terrorist organization, which is in the business of murdering people, and the Cuban secret police." The United States had years of intelligence reports on Lara, Abrams said. She denied she advocates violence, and said she had never been a member of M-19, or the communist party, or is a Cuban agent. She explained her contacts with M-19 and the Cubans by saying she wrote a book on the subject. Her editor and the Colombian government denied Lara is a foreign agent. The most appropriate course would have been to allow the visitor to enter, release verifiable information—if such exists—on her terrorist associations, and permit her to confront her accusers.

Americans need not be "protected" by denying a foreigner freedom to speak or write. Written from abroad, the same words may readily appear under her signature in an American publication. And among the millions of illegal immigrants who will be entitled to amnesty and citizenship next year are doubtless some who harbor no less negative views of the U.S. than Lara. The real loss for expelling a journalist is to America's prestige in those minority corners of the world where freedom is practiced, and in credible charges of American hypocrisy in places where freedom is absent.

The other side of the coin was also visible this year:

111

Does press freedom extend to interviewing the world's foremost terrorist on network television, and not revealing his whereabouts to the appropriate authorities? NBC interviewed Mohammed Abbas in Algeria while he faced murder and kidnapping charges in the hijacking of the Achille Lauro cruise ship in October 1985. NBC promised and provided secrecy for Abbas whose alleged hijacking ended with the murder of a crippled American.

Does press responsibility encompass interviewing the American shot down while flying arms to the rebels in Nicaragua, an interview conducted under the eyes of the captors when the trial was to start the next day? Copies of such interviews, arranged through the Interior Ministry, were used in evidence against the flier.

Does press freedom include the restriction by monopoly-sale of coverage of events surrounding the celebration of the refurbished Statue of Liberty? The event, mostly on government property, was restricted on the July 4th weekend to licensed extravaganzas on the ABC-TV network.

Is press freedom enhanced when a broadcast network (CBS) tries to intimidate a book publisher, and prevent the appearance of a volume critical of the network? Renato Adler, first in the New Yorker magazine and now in a Knopf-published book, critically analyzed the libel trials involving CBS and General Westmoreland, and Time magazine and General Sharon. Adler described the CBS documentary as "factually false and intellectually trivial," and its thesis "preposterous." The general had claimed he was libeled when CBS charged his command conspired to underreport enemy troop strength before the 1968 Tet offensive in Vietnam. In February 1986, after eighteen weeks of trial, the General dropped the suit. Adler also criticized Time, which said in a letter to her publisher that her writing was one-sided. CBS, however, prepared a lengthy reply, hired a press agent to attack the book before publication, and generally implied the publisher might be sued. The publisher delayed releasing the book—one may suspect a victim at least temporarily of CBS, which is generally active as a defender and invoker of press freedom. Most often, libel litigation can be avoided by less arrogance, and prompt admitting and correcting of error.

Is press freedom threatened when ownership of a major television network comes under the domination of a foreign government? The Mexican government has increased its influence over the Spanish International Network (SIN) headquartered in the United States. SIN's news programs originating in Miami serve some seventeen million Spanish-speaking viewers in the U.S. The network is said to reach eighty-two percent of Spanish-speaking viewers in the United States. The news division is being absorbed by a new agency headed by a Mexican television anchor who is closely identified with the government of Mexico. Another Mexican entrepreneur closely associated with his government also took full ownership of SIN. Earlier, the ownership of United Press International, the second most important U.S. news service, also passed to a Mexican. The issue of foreign control of domestic broadcasts, interestingly, has been raised by Third World critics who say U.S. news media dominate their news channels. Now the pattern is being reversed.

Not unrelated are activities at the United Nations and UNESCO where communications are perennially a controversial topic.

In December the UN General Assembly approved an omnibus information resolution that included support for "a new world information and communication order" (NWICO). Only the United States voted against the resolution, which was approved by 148 countries with 4 abstaining. A separate vote on the NWICO section (already included in the omnibus) drew 128 yes votes, 2 no (U.S. and Israel), and 22 abstentions. The omnibus resolution as approved was greatly modified from the earlier hard-line drafts. The diverse aspects of this still-undefined "order" have been argued for a decade in the United Nations Educational, Scientific and Cultural Organization (UNESCO). Since 1983, the UNESCO forum has been quieter. Consensual agreements on communications issues by Western, Third World, and Soviet representatives have generally mollified Western delegates. Communications controversies, however, helped fire attacks that led to the withdrawal of the United States (1975) and the United Kingdom (1976) from UNESCO. Hard-line supporters of NWICO turned to the UN General Assembly (GA) to resume the debate, generally taking stronger anti-Western positions.

TASS summarized the intention of the developing countries in the UN discussions as "aimed at countering the policy of information imperialism, and putting an end to the arbitrariness of a handful of the Western 'word monopolies' which is a threat to their sovereignty and independence."

It is unlikely most Third World countries would state the controversy in such terms. In the end, the Group of 77 (G-77) eliminated several controversial elements in the draft that had been debated for eight months. The objective of the resolution was cast in the UNESCO-approved formula: a NWICO "seen as an evolving and continuous process." This was absent in the early debates, and produced far more negative votes and abstentions. The final draft also called on states to cooperate in "establishing" a "new order" that would be "based on the free circulation, and wider and better balanced dissemination of information, guaranteeing diversity of sources . . . and free access to information." The United States applauded the G-77 for accepting the UNESCO formula, but regarded other formulations as "anti-free press prescriptions." The U.S. opposed what it termed "highly selective political recommendations" in the resolution for promoting peace, covering the Middle East and the Palestine question, and opposing apartheid (A/SPC/41.1.31).

The U.S. delegate at the opening of the November debates recognized the existence of "an information and communications imbalance, particularly in the impediments some members continue to impose on the free passage of ideas." He urged "practical measures to ensure the free flow of information within and between nations," and decried "endless incantations of the meaningless catch phrases." He denied the United States and other Western nations seek "a new colonial age of communications based on monopolistic control of the global information system." He added that calls for "free flow" and "press freedom" are not "a subterfuge for perpetuating Western economic dominance." Those who make such charges, he said, often seek to place information under the exclusive charge of the State, and impose internal monopolies on all incoming and outgoing information.

There is, however, diversity among developing countries as among the developed. Some are as free as the freest nations, and some as totalitarian as any in either the industrialized or the developing camps. All Third World nations, however, support the cry for a new information "order." And without charging "monopolistic" or "colonial" intentions, it is easily demonstrable that Western news media, international message carriers, and hardware manufacturers dominate the markets and the flow of information around the world. This is not likely to change because of a resolution in the UN, but such a statement would provide the moral authority for censors in all countries—developed and developing—to act without need for rationalizations, which even the most censorious now feel it necessary to employ.

The latest debate began in the UN Committee on Information and in the fall continued in the Special Political Committee, and then concluded in the General Assembly. When informal discussions began June 20, the United States and thirteen other Western countries decided for the first time to submit their own draft recommendations. The two previous years, the developing countries' G-77 had provided the only draft. Both years, no consensus was achieved and Third World proposals were passed by large votes. This year, the West was admonished in a closed session for "institutionalizing discord" by including an alternate statement reflecting Western views on news media issues. The G-77 paper was called the only basis for negotiation, and any other must lead to failure. The West regarded this as "outlandish" in a committee on information. Hastily, the Soviet bloc submitted a third draft. A recommendation to "cluster" similar ideas in all three drafts was contemptuously rejected by the G-77.

The closed meetings then turned to procedural rather than substantive discussions. The Western group offered to accept four recommendations of the G-77, and asked whether G-77 was willing to accept any Western proposals. The G-77 said it had not considered the Western draft. There could be no "fourth paper," the G-77 stated categorically. With an attempt at diktat and tones of menace from the G-77, the debate moved out of the closed session onto the floor of the committee.

The basic differences were clear, and familiar. The language and objectives of the G-77, now supported by the Soviet draft in still more menacing language, had reverted to the harshest tones and most threatening objections set forth in the debate at UNESCO some ten years earlier. Clearly, the hard-liners on the G-77 and the Soviet bloc had concluded that UNESCO since 1983 had gone soft on communications issues, and was no longer the lead forum for "new order" communications actions.

The G-77 draft headlined the "promotion" of the "establishment" of "the" new order. This language would support the imposition of a particular—"the"—order set forth, implicitly by governmental decisions. The fourteen-page resolution included specific tasks that the General Assembly should assign to the UN information office with regard to Namibia, South Africa, women, the Middle East, external debt adjustments, and other political and economic issues.

After days of speechmaking, bilateral consultations were held around the July 4th holiday between the Western group (represented by the U.S., Netherlands, Spain, Finland, West Germany, Japan, and briefly Denmark and Greece) and the G-77 (represented by Yugoslavia, Egypt, Mexico, and briefly Algeria). Some fifty-seven different changes were listed for discussion. No agreement was reached or found possible on six points.

Some single-word or phrase changes were tentatively accepted, and there was agreement to rewrite other passages. But the main differences represented yawning gaps; for example, refusal by the G-77 to accept the UNESCO compromise over the basic and only formally UNESCO-approved definition of the NWICO—a new order "seen as an evolving and continuous process," not a suddenly imposed "order" presumably to provide journalistic output with a stipulated agenda. Later, after consensus failed and the vote for the G-77 went 41 in favor, 11 against, and 5 abstaining, a G-77 speaker suggested erroneously that the West had accepted all but six of the fifty-seven talking points. The six points of difference were regarded by the West as nonnegotiable, and the full draft not acceptable unless the changes were accepted. For example, the G-77 proposed that "all countries" should collaborate to "change the dependent status" of developing countries in the field of information and communication, and support the principle of "sovereign equality." The dependency issue assures that governments, particularly in the West, can diminish the dominance of commercial news and information media, and also officially recognize "information sovereignty"—the right of governments to have access to international news media, implicitly as an enforceable "right of reply."

The American delegate, former CBS radio correspondent Richard C. Hottelet, expressed the U.S. position more in sorrow than anger. "Let's set aside the unproductive debate over the hypothetical NWICO," urged Hottelet. "It's time to give (communication) power to the people, enabling informed societies to come to grips with economic, social, technical and political problems of today's world"—directly and without "the jamming of radio broadcasts, the censorship of news, either directly or indirectly through the denial of access to news sources, pressures for self-censorship, (or) administrative measures such as denial of newsprint to prevent or intimidate free expression."

Hottelet also provided a list of scores of programs recently initiated in the United States to train journalists and communications technicians for developing countries. The list has been compiled by the newly created Center for Foreign Journalists in Reston, Virginia. At the Center's conference earlier many groups which provide training and communications hardware met for the first time. This is an effort to fulfill the often-repeated U.S. promise to assist Third World communications development.

Hottelet also mentioned the effort of a congressman to prove that political bias permeates the publications of the UN Department of Public Information. The General Accounting Office, at the congressman's request, conducted a content analysis of several subjects covered by the DPI in which the United States was said to have a particular interest. These subjects were mainly those in which the U.S. predictably found itself in the minority in UN voting. The GAO report, consequently, showed a high percentage of anti-U.S. statements in DPI reports on those subjects. Hottelet nevertheless called for "scrupulous staff adherence to a policy of balance and objectivity" in DPI materials.

There is irony in the U.S. position at the UN debates on NWICO. The United States repeatedly sought to invoke the UNESCO formula (NWICO "seen as an evolving and continuous process") despite having withdrawn from UNESCO partly because of decade-long dissatisfaction over the NWICO debates in UNESCO. To be sure, there were other U.S. complaints, but the news media controversies had embittered U.S. journalists, and made withdrawal easier to accomplish. Earlier in 1986, at a UN-UNESCO sponsored symposium in Copenhagen on the NWICO, the UNESCO secretariat produced a working paper that amply expressed Western attitudes toward the controversial issues. The meeting itself was mainly unobjectionable from the Western viewpoint. Clearly this reflected a change in the climate. Several UNESCO programs slated for 1988-89 would cover some contentious ground, though in low-level research formats.[10] Yet the directive for all communications programs reaffirms "the importance UNESCO attaches to the freedom of the press" and stipulates that studies of

117

NWICO mainly disseminate "the results of previous work." It refers to NWICO as "seen as an evolving and continuous process," the seven magic words of Western construction. Perhaps the most controversial project looming in 1987 is the first attempt to assemble a regular statistical summary of many national and international communications issues. This will be produced by the International Program for the Development of Communication (IPDC), a semi-autonomous division of UNESCO.

IPDC was created in 1980 largely at the urging of the United States. To date, the IPDC has provided $9,238,000 for 212 projects. They support national and regional news agencies, television and film projects, and diverse communication development programs. IPDC funds, with one small exception, have been dispersed through government bureaus, though associations of Western news media have urged that some support be given to independent news services in the Third World.

China, all year, pursued its "glasnost" policy with far more diversity than the Soviet Union. China sent waves of young journalists to the United States and elsewhere in the West to learn the latest reporting and production techniques. Since 1978 the number of such visits has grown. Chinese journalists are more willing to discuss the uses of diverse sources and different ideas, but still within the context of communist party discipline. Far more questioning of established procedures, if not official doctrine, is apparent in the Chinese press than appeared eight years ago, or than is now seen in the Soviet news media.

Zhang Bran, writing in China Daily, correctly stated that "probably no Chinese have experienced so many changes in a lifetime than our generation."[11] And, he said, "few people have been fully prepared to adapt to all these changes." He partly blamed the mass media that are, he added, "as much confused as the less informed." He complained that newspapers are too ready to publicize either policy successes or corruption, without more analysis of "development economics." There are, he said, "too few simple, creditable and insightful reports and analyses." One may explain this timidity by the recollection that shifts toward greater openness in the recent past were followed by reversals of policy, and the penalizing of those who most exercised Chinese "glasnost."

All year, the number of newspapers and magazines increased markedly. The People's Daily noted that from "1980 until 1985 a newspaper was born every 36 hours," in China.[12] There are now said to be 202 copies of newspapers for every thousand Chinese, 3.3 times as many as in 1978. Now, seventeen percent of the papers are Communist Party organs. Before 1978, almost all were party-owned. They all follow Beijing policy with variations to meet the age, literacy, or occupational level of their readers.

The papers now report low-level corruption and inefficiency. Several criticized a minister of the government for taking small bribes. Slowly, some papers are dropping the tradition of including editorial comment in news reports, and are holding opinion for the editorial page. The party encourages some criticism and the freer flow of ideas as necessary for modernization. The journalists respond cautiously, however, saying that present policies are generally good for China, so why speak against them? There was no domestic criticism, for example, when John Burns, the New York Times correspondent in China, was detained by the Public Security Bureau in Beijing in July. Burns' "crime" was visiting Shaanxi province, closed to foreigners, during a 1,000-mile motorcycle trip. Burns was accused (as Daniloff in the Soviet Union later) of "spying and intelligence gathering." China noted that by releasing Burns after several days it "acted with the utmost restraint." By Soviet KGB standards, the Chinese were indeed restrained.

Scholars were also engaged this year in encouraging the reform of China's press, according to the newspaper, Chinese Press Report.[13] A meeting of communications scholars called for a national press divided between a party and a non-party press. The papers were urged to carry "political opinion, even objections, before decisions are made." One or two non-party political journals were called for "to provide a forum for free discussion."

With the steady influx of tourists and businessmen working on China's industrial development, the receptivity for foreign cultural forms is obvious. There has been public criticism of the "negative aspects of the open policy," and a call to "guard against all foreign cultures." However, the Party's Twelfth National Congress, noted the Economic Daily, declared that China's culture will progress "by exchanging with other cultures while staying true to its traditions."[14] Said the Economic Daily, "competition becomes increasingly acceptable, the public's sense of democracy is improving, . . . changes have taken place in lifestyles, communications and social attitudes."

The mass media in China have been particularly urged to cover economic information. Yet, said Economic Information, there are still many obstacles to the flow of information.[15] Many "hidebound" governmental units restrict economic information "on the pretext of official secrecy," thereby blocking the flow of economic statistics. The commentary called for reform of the press and strengthening the coverage of economic issues in Chinese papers.

Media reform has been heatedly debated in the press, the deputy director of the Communist Party's Propaganda Department noted in August. Media reform was lagging behind economic and political reforms, the newspaper Unity said.[16] The papers, he added, bear some responsibility for "deplorable" events of the cultural revolution. Nonparty newspapers should become more independent, the paper said, "while following the lead of the party in essential matters." The key to reform, said the editor being quoted, "is that each newspaper should have adequate decision-making power. The party and the government should keep interference to a minimum." For, said the writer, "freedom of speech and publication is the basic condition for political democracy, which is the ultimate goal of China's political reform." He called for laws to protect the media. So long as they do not violate the law, he said, intervention in the work of an editor or editorial board "should be taken as infringing upon civil rights." He concluded that a free press can ensure people their right to criticize and persuade the government and to voice their ideas.

These heady ideas could have been heard at a press meeting in the United States, though the real modifier in China is government "interference" at crucial points. The Journalism Institute of the Chinese Academy of Social Sciences provided a fresh view of editorial judgment—one that moves away from the current Third World criterion for emphasizing "development news" and comes closer to what is presumed to be the American hard news criterion: "The lead story on the front page need not always be politically important," said the journalism scholars, "but can be about an international or socially significant event or news of major disasters."

Other headlines in a month's (November) time in China Daily reflect the intensity of the discussion of press reform:

More Debates on Press Will Encourage Democracy
Press Must Defend Its Role as Critic
Editorials Are a Must

China's press has come a long way from its "deplorable" function during the Cultural Revolution. Yet it has a long way to go before it can be regarded as a watchdog or fourth estate.

In Taiwan, meanwhile, a year-long intensive campaign of the Republic of China forced the opposition tangwai press underground. In previous years, the tangwai magazines would appear openly, and often risk banning for carrying particular articles. The publications would reappear shortly thereafter with a new name and slightly changed format. The heightened, blanket banning may have been planned to correspond with elections scheduled for December. Even underground circulation of openly oppositionist publications provides a more diverse offering of views, however, than is presently found in mainland China where the reforming of the news media and the freer flow of information is being widely discussed in a press completely under government and party control.

On another continent, international as well as domestic flows of information were sharply restricted. On June 12, the day South Africa imposed a nationwide state of emergency, the government also issued broad censorship and self-censorship instructions. The emergency was declared in anticipation of widespread protests by blacks on the tenth anniversary of the Soweto uprisings. The press restrictions were applied just as the fourth edition appeared of The Newspaperman's Guide to the Law.[17] This 332-page book is the detailed map of the numerous laws and regulations that guide every reporter and editor. The Byzantine press laws became infinitely more difficult for the journalist, foreign or domestic, after these elaborate new restrictions were applied.

Journalists are barred from describing actions by security forces without permission, identifying people detained under the emergency decree, or reporting a wide range of statements regarded as "subversive" (for example, promoting an unlawful organization, inciting participation in an unlawful strike, supporting boycott action, participation in any unlawful demonstration, taking part in civil disobedience, discrediting compulsory military service). Television has additional difficulty: it cannot transmit live reports. Television crews drive through embattled areas without mounting a camera. They get stoned for seeming to be officials, but cannot respond with coverage. "We could sit here and watch them killing people and couldn't do a thing," said one cameraman. The Weekly Mail, a newspaper critical of the government, noted on its front page June 20: "Our lawyers tell us we can say almost nothing critical about the emergency. But we'll try." Six phrases in the editorial were eliminated. The page carried the line: "Restricted. Reports on these pages have been censored to comply with emergency regulations." Several days later, the government barred this form of enterprise.

"There are only two versions of the truth" in South Africa today, said Frontline, the country's still-critical magazine published in English with some Afrikaans. The two versions: "the official version and the subversion. How do you tell the difference? Easy. You read between the blank spaces." Frontline scoffed satirically at another paper's declaration that "press freedom in South Africa (on June 12) has ceased to exist." Said Frontline: "What nonsense . . . (The press) is free to report whatever the Bureau of Information tells it to. It is free to wash its hands of the bothersome criterion of 'newsworthiness.' . . . It is free to publish and be banned. It is free to disregard the human tragedy behind the robotic daily roll call of death and destruction. It is free from taking on the almighty burden of investigative journalism at a time when history is bursting to be recorded."[18]

Two emergency decrees used by the South African government were later invalidated in the National Supreme Court because they had not been properly promulgated. Press lawyers were seeking to overturn another six press regulations. If past experience is a guide, the regulations would be reimposed in a form deemed legal under the emergency laws. Meanwhile, virtually all information on the details of the emergency are released by the Bureau of Information.

With the passage of sanctions against South Africa by the United States, the opposition white newspapers were more vulnerable than ever. These English-language papers received a veiled warning in August from President Botha. The papers must decide, he said, whether they will "throw their weight" on the side of "a developing South Africa" or "on the side of those who have eventually brought about the destruction of civilization as well as the media." Slowly, the remaining limited freedoms of the white press are being reduced to the level of the black press in South Africa (no longer as free as several black presses elsewhere on the continent).

The government press agency controls most of the news of the major story: the emergency. But who will believe even the truthful information the agency releases? That is the inherent handicap of all government-controlled news agencies (the accompanying Table 9 lists the world's government-controlled news systems).

ASEAN governments, except for Thailand and the Philippines, made journalism a more difficult profession this year in their territories: Brunei, Indonesia, Malaysia, and Singapore.

The newspapers of Thailand have been relatively free. Some would say freewheeling. Yet the licenses of some Thai papers were temporarily revoked until new editors were appointed. Radio and television are under greater government control. Increasingly this year, Thai broadcasters carried alternative views, including footage of an anti-government demonstration. Thai television is sending its own correspondents abroad for the first time, and generally improving the quality of radio and television programs. Opposition parties appear occasionally on the air. There is a sign that programming is borrowing too heavily from U.S. newscasting—moving too far toward combining show business with newsreporting.

The Philippines, meanwhile, had removed the heavy burden of Marcos' oligarchical journalism. The press is bolder and more diverse than ever. Manila by mid-year had twenty-one daily newspapers, though the number was later reduced. Three papers allowed to publish during the eight years of martial law continued to appear under President Corazon Aquino. Two changed their names, and neither has taken a pro-Marcos editorial position since the deposed leader fled the country in February. Newspapers which Marcos or his friends acquired are now being investigated to determine whether the property should be returned to the previous owners. The freewheeling Philippine press that was reined in and controlled by Marcos is again unleashed.

Table 9

NEWS MEDIA CONTROL BY COUNTRIES

	Generally Free[1]	Partly Free[1]	Generally Not Free[1]	Gov't News Agency[2]	Civil Liberties[3]
Afghanistan			PB	X	7
Albania			PB	X	7
Algeria			PB	X	6
Angola			PB	X	7
Antigua & Barbuda		PB			3
Argentina	PB			X	1
Australia	PB				1
Austria	PB				1
Bahamas	P	B			2
Bahrain			PB	X	5
Bangladesh		PB		X	5
Barbados	P	B			1
Belgium	PB				1
Belize	P	B			1
Benin			PB	X	7
Bhutan			P		5
Bolivia	P	B		X	3
Botswana	P	B			3
Brazil	PB				2
Brunei			PB		5
Bulgaria			PB	X	7
Burkina Faso			PB	X	6
Burma			PB	X	7
Burundi			PB	X	6
Cameroon			PB	X	7
Canada	PB				1
Cape Verde Is.			PB		6
Cambodia (Kampuchea)			PB	X	7
Central Afr. Rep.			PB	X	6
Chad			PB	X	7
Chile		PB		X	5
China (Mainland)			PB	X	6
China (Taiwan)		PB			5
Colombia	PB				3
Congo			PB	X	6
Costa Rica	PB				1
Cuba			PB	X	6
Cyprus (G)	P	B		X	2
Cyprus (T)	P	B		X	3
Czechoslovakia			PB	X	6

Notes to the Table

1. P designates print media; B designates broadcast (radio and TV) media. Print media refers primarily to domestic newspapers and news magazines. Countries with undeveloped media or for which there is insufficient information include: Comoros, Djibouti, Kiribati, Rwanda, Solomons, Tuvalu, and Western Samoa.

2. X designates the presence of a government news agency, with or without the availability of private news services.

3. See Table 1, above.

Table 9 (continued)

	Generally Free[1]	Partly Free[1]	Generally Not Free[1]	Gov't News Agency[2]	Civil Liberties[3]
Denmark	PB				1
Dominica	PB				2
Dominican Rep.	P	B			3
Ecuador	PB (?)				3
Egypt		PB		X	4
El Salvador		PB			4
Equatorial Guinea			PB		7
Ethiopia			PB	X	7
Fiji	PB				2
Finland	P	B			2
France	P	B		X	2
Gabon			PB	X	6
Gambia	PB				4
Germany (E)			PB	X	6
Germany (W)	PB				2
Ghana			PB	X	6
Greece	P (?)	B		X	2
Grenada	P	B			2
Guatemala		PB			3
Guinea			PB		5
Guinea-Bissau			PB		6
Guyana		P	B	X	5
Haiti	PB (?)				4
Honduras	PB				3
Hungary			PB	X	5
Iceland	PB				1
India	P	B		X	3
Indonesia		P	B	X	6
Iran			PB	X	6
Iraq			PB	X	7
Ireland	PB				1
Israel	PB				2
Italy	PB			X	1
Ivory Coast		P	B	X	5
Jamaica	P	B			3
Japan	PB				1
Jordan			PB	X	5
Kenya		P	B	X	5
Korea (N)			PB	X	7
Korea (S)		P	B	X	5
Kuwait		P	B	X	5
Laos			PB	X	7
Lebanon		PB		X	4
Lesotho		PB			5
Liberia	P		B		5
Libya			PB	X	6
Luxembourg	PB				1
Madagascar			PB	X	5
Malawi			PB	X	7
Malaysia		P	B	X	5

Table 9 (continued)

	Generally Free[1]	Partly Free[1]	Generally Not Free[1]	Gov't News Agency[2]	Civil Liberties[3]
Maldives		P	B		6
Mali			PB	X	6
Malta	P		B		4
Mauritania			PB	X	6
Mauritius	P	B			2
Mexico		PB		X	4
Mongolia			PB	X	7
Morocco		P	B	X	5
Mozambique			PB	X	7
Nauru	PB				2
Nepal		P	B	X	4
Netherlands	PB				1
New Zealand	PB				1
Nicaragua			PB	X	6
Niger			PB		6
Nigeria		PB		X	5
Norway	PB				1
Oman			PB		6
Pakistan		P	B	X	5
Panama		PB			3
Papua New Guinea	PB			X	2
Paraguay			PB		6
Peru	PB				3
Philippines	PB			X	2
Poland		P	B	X	5
Portugal	PB			X	2
Qatar			PB	X	5
Romania			PB	X	7
St.Kitts-Nevis	PB				1
St.Lucia	PB				2
St.Vincent	P	B			2
Sao Tome & Prin.			PB		7
Saudi Arabia			PB	X	7
Senegal		PB			4
Seychelles			PB	X	6
Sierra Leone		P	B	X	5
Singapore		P	B	X	5
Somalia			PB	X	7
South Africa		P	B		6
Spain	PB			X	2
Sri Lanka		PB		X	4
Sudan		P	B	X	5
Suriname			PB		6
Swaziland			PB		6
Sweden	PB				1
Switzerland	PB				1
Syria			PB	X	7
Tanzania			PB	X	6
Thailand		PB			3
Togo			PB	X	6

Table 9 (continued)

	Generally Free[1]	Partly Free[1]	Generally Not Free[1]	Gov't News Agency[2]	Civil Liberties[3]
Tonga		PB			3
Transkei			PB		6
Trinidad & Tobago	PB				2
Tunisia		P (?)	B	X	5
Turkey		P	B	X	4
Uganda		P	B	X	4
USSR			PB	X	7
United Arab Emirs.		P	B	X	5
United Kingdom	PB				1
United States	PB				1
Uruguay	PB				2
Vanuatu		PB			4
Venezuela	PB				2
Vietnam			PB	X	7
Yemen (N)			PB	X	5
Yemen (S)			PB	X	7
Yugoslavia			PB	X	5
Zaire			PB	X	7
Zambia		P	B	X	5
Zimbabwe			PB	X	6

Table Summary for Countries

	General Rating		Print Media		Broadcast Media	
	No.	%	No.	%	No.	%
Free	53	33	57	36	40	25
Partly free	55	34	39	24	33	21
Not free	52	33	64	40	86	54

Governments in three-fourths of the world have a significant or dominant voice in determining what does and what does not appear in the media. This definition of control does not include regulation such as that practiced by the FCC: it means control over newspaper or broadcast content. In some countries particular media (often broadcasting) may be government financed and indirectly government managed like the BBC, but are still largely free of government control of content.

In only one-fourth of the countries are both the print and broadcast media generally free: the press is generally free in one-third. Newspapers tend to be freer than radio or TV.

While this table concentrates on the status of the domestic news media, foreign journalists' access to sources and freedom to transmit news generally reflects the government's treatment of domestic journalists.

Nearly a half century ago there were thirty-nine national news services in twenty-eight countries. Seventy percent of these were at least nominally independent of government (Robert Desmond, The Press and World Affairs, Appleton-Century, 1937). Today there are eighty-eight. The number of government-operated news services has increased rapidly, partly in consequence of recommendations made at UNESCO. Fifty-six percent of the countries have a government news agency: seventy-six percent of the "not free," sixty-four percent of the "partly free," and twenty percent of the "free" countries. Of nations with the lowest civil liberties rating (7), eighty-eight percent operate government news agencies. National news agencies often use the world news services of the transnational Western media or TASS. They may then decide what world news may be distributed inside the country. Some national news agencies assign themselves the sole right to secure domestic news for distribution inside or outside the country.

Singapore resorted to intimidation and then indirect censorship of the foreign press in the country. On August 1 the Parliament amended the Newspaper and Printing Press Act (1974). The law now allows the government to restrict the sale or distribution of foreign publications "engaged in the domestic politics of Singapore." The law restricts the number of copies of the designated publication that may be circulated locally. The authorized copies of a "gazetted" publication are stamped, and other copies seized and the distributor jailed for two years or fined. The Minister of Information revealed that the government had made a study of adverse reporting. He said some foreign publications "cast aspersions on our established institutions," or engage in "campaigns to manipulate local public opinion."

In mid-October Time magazine became the first casualty of the new law. Time was declared in the government gazette to be a "newspaper engaging in the domestic politics of Singapore." The government decided that Time carried an article on Singapore that contained several factual errors, and then refused to publish in full and unaltered a letter of correction from the Prime Minister's press secretary. The government released the text of its letter and Time's reply. But the government also restricted by fifty percent the number of copies Time could sell from October 19, and further limited the number as of January 1, 1987, cutting the sale from 18,000 to 2,000 copies. Almost immediately, Time lost significant advertising revenue as its circulation dropped. Time publishes an Asia edition in Singapore, as do many other foreign publications. The new law is, therefore, a serious form of indirect censorship.

Neighboring Malaysia acted strongly against both domestic and foreign journalists. All year, the government threatened to amend the Official Secrets Act (1972) that had been fashioned after the British law. In December the parliament amended the act to provide a mandatory prison sentence for journalists who convey a "secret." The act still did not define the term "secret," or the particular subjects that may not be made public. Early in the year a foreign and a domestic journalist were convicted of publishing "secrets," and fined.

The Confederation of ASEAN Journalists strongly opposed the amendment. "The Official Secrets Act," said Bob Teoh, secretary-general of the Confederation, "is a fine example of abuse of the law. Originally, it was meant to safeguard the nation against spies and enemies. Later, it was used to rope in difficult journalists. Now that the press has been effectively shackled, other sectors of society are being targeted for silencing."

With tight censorship or self-censorship, said one critic of the amendment, "tne people will be kept in the dark about abuses in high places. Corruption will become more rampant and rumor-mongering become the order of the day."

Malaysia in September sent a chill through the foreign corps by banning the Asian Wall Street Journal and expelling two of its veteran reporters in Kuala Lumpur. The unspecified charge was related by the Deputy Prime Minister to his government's need for "people who write things which are fair and good, to contribute to stability." The Journal said it had suffered years of government-ordered periodic disruption of the paper's distribution in Malaysia. Prime Minister Mahathir, said the Journal, has claimed the paper is Jewish-controlled. He mentioned a Zionist plot involving the foreign press to topple his government.

The Journal, however, had just published a series of articles by both of its expelled writers that reported Malaysia's "disastrous attempt to corner tne tin market," a new economic policy that favors the Malay population (which discouraged foreign investment), and the crisis in Malaysia's uninsured Cooperative Central Bank (with bad loans to state officials). A Journal editorial referred to "the popular Third World notion that demo-cratic values just don't translate well to developing countries because they are fragile societies that need a guiding authoritarian hand. But if you look at what's been going on in Malaysia," said the Journal, "it's not the press that's the problem. It's the guiding hand."

Prime Minister Mahathir, arrived in New York hours after the editorial appeared to seek new investment for Malaysia. Two weeks later the government lifted the ban on the Journal, and expulsion orders against its two reporters. The reversal came after the government admitted to the presiding judge that it had not given the newspaper a chance to defend itself before issuing the order. The National Union of Journalists, which still opposed tne government on the Official Secrets question, commended the government for withdrawing the suspension of the Journal.

No such reversal was made by the government of Indonesia that gradually expelled most foreign correspondents by refusing to grant or renew work permits. Sensitive subjects in foreign journals such as references to the Chinese minority and President Sukarto were blacked out.

A 172-page book published this year by the Institute of Southeast Asean Studies reports on the flow of news in ASEAN countries.[19] It is based on media surveys and interviews with seventy news executives. "(ASEAN) newspapers and news agencies exist by government sufferance and supervision. As a result, journalists working for them are under severe environmental constraints. . . . Even though in statements each government has encouraged constructive criticism, the experience of newspapers is that it is much safer to refrain from criticizing if one is allowed to continue publishing."

The indefinite, insecure fate of journalists and other writers in most of the world this year may be best described by China's Culture Minister who said, "When a writer, whether a party member or not, writes, he has actually one God, that is the god of himself, and no one should tell him what to write." But if a writer, particularly one writing for a general audience, did not conform to Marxism, said Wang, he would "offer him a cup of coffee and give him some friendly advice, or let him go his way and I'd go mine."[20] Thus the censor addresses the self-censor; in Sakharov's words, this is "a misfortune for citizens," if not yet "a menace to international security."

NOTES

1. Report of a Gallup poll in Editor and Publisher, October 4, 1986, page 19.

2. Draft Article XII, 18 C/35, for the 19th General Conference of UNESCO, Nairobi, October-November, 1976.

3. New York Times, "Pravda Says TV Uses Cliches About West," May 20, 1986.

4. Radio Liberty Research, "Anti-American Films in the USSR," Vladimir Matusevich, RL 305/86, August 18, 1986.

5. Ibid., page 6.

6. Soviet Area Archives and Opinion Research, Radio Free Europe/Radio Liberty, "The Chernobyl Disaster: Sources of Information and Reactions," AR 4-86, October 1986.

7. Ibid., page 4.

8. Ibid., page 9.

9. Editor and Publisher, May 31, 1986, p. 6.

10. Efforts continue, particularly by the Soviet bloc, to cast as an element of international law, the 1978 News Media Declaration of UNESCO. This with similar steps would appear to give normative support to the objectives in the declaration that are hortatory. See Leonard R. Sussman and David W. Sussman, "Mass News Media and International Law," International Political Science Review, vol. 7, no. 3 (1986): 344-360.

11. China Daily, May 22, 1986.

12. Ibid., June 30, 1986.

13. Ibid., August 10, 1986.

14. Ibid., September 24, 1986.

15. Ibid., September 26, 1986.

16. Ibid., September 29, 1986.

17. Kelsey W. Stuart, The Newspaperman's Guide to the Law, fourth edition by William Lane et al. (Durban: Buttworths, 1986).

18. Gus Silber, "State of Submergency," Frontline, August 1986, p. 17.

19. Andrew Szende, From Torrent to Trickle (Singapore: Institute of Southeast Asian Studies, 1986).

20. Associated Press, Peking, November 26, 1986 (W396).

Election in the Philippines

From February 3 to 10, 1986, the National Democratic and National Republican Institutes for International Affairs sent a large team of "International Observers" to the Philippines to observe the "snap" presidential election called by President Marcos to quiet the claim by his opposition within and without the country that he ruled without an adequate mandate from the people. The author was a member of this team. This group of observers should not be confused with the official American observer team under the direction of Senator Lugar, as well as observers sent officially and unofficially by other countries. Both teams relied extensively on previous investigations of the situation by the Center for Democracy and a group sent by the Institutes to lay the basis for the mission. The American interest that led in part to the elections, as well as the decision to send such extensive observer groups, developed after the murder of Benigno Aquino in 1983 at the Manila airport, and the highly vocal opposition that emerged as a result of this event.

Background

The Philippine Islands did not exist as a country prior to the coming of the Spanish in the sixteenth century. Small Muslim states were at the time rapidly expanding over a still largely pre-Muslim population. Most of the islands' peoples spoke one or another of several closely related Malay languages—languages that remain the primary languages for daily discourse for most Filipinos today. Chinese merchants had already played a part in the life of the people, and their role was to continue.[1]

The Spanish generally ruled the Philippines indirectly and casually; they never attempted the detailed occupation and exploitation that occurred in Latin America. This had two results. First, the Spanish population, and the percentage of people speaking Spanish, were never numerous. A small number of Spaniards and native upper class Filipinos and their entourages, however, did look to the Spanish language and Spain for western culture, an attitude they preserve to this day. Secondly, the Catholic Church developed as the main western influence, creating a Philippine Church with a large native component, and with priests speaking the languages of the several islands.

In making these generalizations, it should not be forgotten that although the Spanish managed to reduce the Islamicized area, and this Christian expansion continues to this day, small areas in the south and west remained defiantly Muslim. Similarly, non-Christian animists have managed to maintain their way of life in some areas. The Spanish period also saw an expansion of Chinese influence, especially through the development of an influential part-Chinese, or "mestizo", population.

In the latter part of the nineteenth century an increasingly westernized and educated segment of the population became acquainted with the nationalistic concepts of the day, and began pressing Spain for more self-determination and ultimately independence. In the eighteen nineties this movement led to revolution. Fortuitously, the revolution was continuing at the time of the Spanish-American War. At first American interference in the Philippines was welcomed, for it made possible victory over the Spanish. But our forces then turned around and denied independence to the Filipino rebels and the interim government they had established. The resulting bloody colonial war served little purpose. It ended with American victory, but by the time this victory was complete we had in effect made an agreement to incorporate elements of the Filipino ruling class into the new administrative system. The highly pragmatic Filipino elite had maintained relations with both sides during the struggle with the Spanish, and subsequently with the Americans. As a result it was well placed to achieve an accommodation that would preserve its standing under American suzerainty. Thus, although a tiny Spanish elite was replaced at the pinnacle of power by American officials and educators, the power of the Filipino elite was considerably greater in 1910 than it had been in 1890.

The American period was characterized by rapid increase in education, population, and production. The Philippine people became quickly acquainted with the forms of American style democracy, but they managed the system in an oligarchical and feudal form found in the United States primarily in parts of the American South—or a few large cities at the height of the wave of foreign immigration. Political parties were formed very early. However, the growing familiarity of Filipinos with American political forms obscured the largely personalist and familialist nature of political activity. By the 1930s the country was already well on its way to independence.

World War II witnessed a typically Filipino obscuring of relationships. While on the one hand many Filipinos aided a sporadic guerrilla effort against the Japanese, many Filipino leaders took part in the Japanese-sponsored puppet government. There may have been cooperation between these two groups under the Japanese.[2] In any event, remarkably little recrimination took place after the war when the country achieved independence. In part, this was due to the rise of the "Huk" movement, a communist guerrilla force that had fought the Japanese and now attempted to preserve and extend its power within an independent Philippines. The Philippine establishment quickly united against this new menace.

Politics in the independent republic was generally considered a success. Political power alternated regularly between two major parties. The communist guerrillas were defeated, the economy was reconstructed, and reforms undertaken in many areas. However, the essentially personalistic and anarchical style of Filipino politics was maintained. Families and family connections remained more important than ideologies or policies. Politicians often changed parties. Politics was violent and dangerous; political murders were frequent, especially at election times. Corruption was endemic: in nearly every election credible accusations of corruption were a major means by which the "ins" managed to defeat the "outs." Election spending, including the widespread buying of votes both directly and indirectly, steadily escalated.[3]

With the coming to power of President Marcos the nature of the game changed. Elected in 1965, he was reelected to an unprecedented second term in 1969 amid charges of extravagent election spending and violence (107 killed and 117 wounded). The off-year election in 1971 suggested a political tide running against Marcos. Violence increased: twice as many were murdered as in the election of 1969. In any event, Marcos faced mandatory retirement

135

in 1973. Instead he proceeded in 1972 to declare martial law and suspend the constitution. Leading members of the opposition were imprisoned; many soon became temporary exiles. The fortunes of major families were confiscated or transferred to others, and the major newspapers were forced out of existence, to be replaced by papers controlled by friends of the President.

At first many welcomed the Marcos intervention. They feared the escalating violence and corruption that he pledged to address. Marcos called for a restructuring of the society along less feudalistic lines, and to this end promoted an initially effective land reform. He destroyed the power of many local bosses by confiscating the arms of their private armies. The communist New People's Army (NPA) had revived the communist threat, but the threat hardly carried the weight Marcos made it bear. More serious was the threat from the Moro, or Muslim movement, demanding enhanced self-determination or independence. The Muslims had serious grievances due to the continued pressure from Catholic settlers on their areas, and were traditionally well-organized and militant.

Politics in Marcos' 1970s' authoritarian state centered around referendums in a highly controlled atmosphere. The issues were local government, the continuation of Marcos' rule, and a new constitution. For these staged events the opposition was not allowed sufficient political organization or media outlets to affect the results. Television stations were all supportive of the government, although a few independent radio stations and independent mayors still functioned.

Gradually the Marcos world crumbled in the early 1980s. The New People's Army became steadily more powerful, and came to control many rural areas of the country. Imelda Marcos' spending on show projects while millions remained in starvation, as well as her highly visible and excessive personal spending enflamed opposition. Security forces grew rapidly and seemed increasingly out of control. Private armies, now controlled by Marcos supporters, reappeared stronger than ever, and their murderous oppression was widely resented.

Characteristic of Filipino politics, a major opposition leader, Benigno Aquino, was imprisoned in the 1970s for murder—a charge that was never proved. (Marcos himself had first come to public notice in the 1930s when he was accused of murdering his father's political rival—a charge he managed to talk himself out of on a technicality.) Aquino returned to the country in 1983, with the charges still outstanding. He was gunned down as he got off his plane, either on Marcos' orders or the orders of persons unknown who most Filipinos believed were supporters of Marcos. By 1983 Aquino had become the man most likely to be able to lead a movement that would unseat the president. It should be noted that millions of Filipinos evidently support Marcos in spite of his suspected involvement in this blatant political killing. This is simply a matter of different attitudes and values: history suggests that in the reverse situation many members of Marcos' opposition would take an analogous position.

Yet by forcing nearly everyone in the educated classes to take sides, the murder hastened the expansion of the anti-Marcos forces. The Marcos controlled newspapers became noticeably less one-sided, new publications appeared opposing the president, more radio stations or radio announcers talked against Marcos. The church became increasingly involved in opposition. The opposition apparently had so thoroughly penetrated the system that the report of the commission established by Marcos to investigate the Aquino murder led to an indictment of leading members of the military, including General Ver, head of the army general staff and intelligence. A subsequent trial, however, led to the dismissal of all charges.

The 1984 legislative election marked a partial return to electoral politics. Many campaigned for a boycott, with some success, on the basis that the fairness of the process, was not adequately guaranteed. An effective organization, NAMFREL, became an important force for election fairness, by overseeing the process. In the end, and in spite of the removal of much of the opposition by its boycott, anti-Marcos forces managed to elect nearly one-third of the members of parliament. Many accusations of cheating were leveled against the process by both NAMFREL and the opposition parties. Particularly important charges were those of double registration, overspending, and intimidation.[4]

The 1986 Presidential Election

The election called in late 1985 for February 7, 1986, was insti-
gated to defuse mounting opposition at home and abroad by proving
that President Marcos retained the support of the people. The
election's legal status was dubious, but the courts allowed it to
proceed on the grounds of public interest. (Law is very flexible in
Philippine society.)[5]

President Marcos campaigned as the candidate of the KBL, the
political organization he personally organized to support his rule,
although it was in part a reorganization of the Nacionalista party.
He chose as his running mate Arturo Tolentino, an older popular
figure who earlier in the year Marcos dismissed from his cabinet
post, apparently for disloyalty. Before this anomalous choice,
Tolentino had publicly said he would not support Marcos for reelection.

Mrs. Corazon Aquino became the emotional choice of the Laban
coalition, and Salvador Laurel of the UNIDO coalition. At the last
minute they agreed to join forces under the UNIDO banner with
Aquino as the presidential candidate and Laurel as the vice-presi-
dential. It is significant that the Laurel and Marcos families have
been close and mutually supportive political groupings since the
1930s when Laurel's father (who later headed the puppet government under the Japanese) dismissed the murder charges against the
young Marcos. Laurel had been in the KBL party until 1983, when
he had left to found UNIDO. Both opposition candidates were from
wealthy landowning families with strong support in their home
areas. Although there were other candidates for president and
vice-president, this was essentially a two-party contest.

All potentially eligible voters who had not voted in the
previous election, for whatever reason, were required to register.
Registration took place on two days at the end of December, 1985.
Pictures were required of the registrants, and many did not have,
or could not attain, the required pictures. In some places those
without pictures registered anyhow; their registration would be
finalized if they presented a picture in January. Many people
petitioned for the right to register after the January closing, and
the courts granted many of these petitions on the days immediately
before the election—some of these registrants could have been
authorized to vote as late as the voting day itself. The extent to

which such petitions were made, and then carried through to an actual vote seemed to vary widely; they may well have been exceptional.

Both sides campaigned vigorously. The complete government control of television, directly or indirectly, gave a very unfair advantage to the Marcos ticket in spite of the campaign time given the opposition. The exact division of support for the two sides among radio stations is unclear—both sides claimed the other had overwhelming radio support.[6] The major newspapers were all Marcos supporters; press releases and advertisements of the opposition were printed, although generally in less conspicuous spots. There were small opposition papers, however, both in Manila and the provinces. The opposition protested at the shortness of the campaign, which was little more than seven weeks after the opposition decided on its ticket.

On February 7 voting took place between seven and three o'clock. The polls were closed as early as three o'clock to prevent the interruptions and stealing of ballot boxes that occurred in 1984 as soon as it became dark. Polling places were generally at public schools. Each polling place might have from one to fifty or more precincts; each precinct had about 300 registered voters, and was located in a separate room. Each precinct had a chairman, clerk, one representative of the government party (KBL) and one representative of the official opposition party (UNIDO). The chairman was generally a public school teacher. NAMFREL was also officially designated as an independent citizen's group having a right to have a representative within the voting area. Not more than twenty voters were allowed to be in the room at any one time.

The voters must be on the registration list for the precinct. Considerable discretion was in the hands of the precinct chairman as to challenges, or accepting last minute petitions, but practically this generally made little difference in the outcome. Each voter had their index nail marked with a special ink. Their name was placed next to a number, and a thumb print placed on the ballot stub, which was then separated to make sure the ballot could not be traced. Stubs were placed separately in the ballot box. Voters used booths to write out the names of their selections—ballots this time having no names on them, although any version of a candidate's name was to be accepted. The ballot boxes were delivered to the precinct sealed, and had a plastic area through which all could see if the box was empty.

At three o'clock the polls were closed; anyone in line at that time was allowed to vote. The counting occurred immediately after at the precinct level, and within reason anyone who wished could observe the counting. The tallies were then sent to city or provincial centers where the votes were "canvassed" or collated from the precincts of the area. These results are then forwarded to the National Assembly for a final decision. The precinct committee also produced a number of other copies of its results. One was put in the ballot box (which was also forwarded to the provincial center), one was given to the KBL representative, one to the UNIDO representative, and one to the NAMFREL representative (as the result of a last-minute decision), and one was forwarded to the provincial canvas and one to the national election commission, COMELEC. Counting of the forwarded tally sheets at the provincial center was also open to the general public. It was officially attended by representatives of the same organizations as at the precinct level.

Since in accordance with past experience the official results of the election would be received slowly, and tallied slowly, and since there was legitimate fear that slowdowns or interruptions in the count could indicate interference with the election through deliberate changes in the results, the NAMFREL organization decided to make a "quick count" similar to one they had tried in the 1984 election. After a great deal of discussion, NAMFREL and COMELEC decided to make separate quick counts, with complete exchange of information. In both cases the quick counts were to be based on NAMFREL copies of the precinct tallies. Meanwhile, the newspapers and television stations put together organizations to give their own quick counts based on phoned in results from their representatives from around the country who would have access to results in a number of different ways.

Criticisms of the Election Process

Among the many criticisms of the conduct of the election, one of the most serious was the accusation that names were deliberately left off registration lists at the last minute, or that persons were added to the lists that should not have been, through, for example, the use of petitions. A subsidiary objection was that although the master lists in the hands of the precinct chairmen were complete, posted lists by which voters initially guided themselves at the polling stations deliberately left off names, or misplaced them to confuse voters. In evaluating this claim, certainly the relatively insignificant number of people registered in December (1,300,000) would seem to support the allegation that registration was deliberately made difficult—certainly the requirement for photographs had an inhibiting effect. The government election commission admitted that there were many, perhaps 100,000 excess, or double, registrations that it would not have time to annul. Nevertheless, the fact there were 26,000,000 registered voters out of a population of about 55,000,000 suggested that a very large segment of the population could vote, and vote fairly.[7] The accusation that, in particular areas of opposition strength, large numbers were unable to vote because of deliberate non=inscription on the rolls could be checked by a careful analysis.

It was alleged that several hundred thousand people in Manila were denied the vote by being arbitrarily excluded from the rolls. In this connection two points must be mentioned. First, persons who did not vote in the two previous elections, or perhaps just the 1984 election, were taken off the rolls legally.[8] Since there was a more active boycott campaign in 1984, particularly in Manila, than in 1986, there should have been quite a few persons who did not register in 1984, or who had their names removed as the result of not voting at that time. The relatively small number registering in December, 1985,[9] suggests that many potential voters overlooked the requirement for reregistering. Secondly, the opposition claimed that there were more than 500,000 persons who voted more than once in the Manila area in 1984.[10] If so, then a legitimate voting total, or numbered registered, could be considerably less than in 1984. But these remain hypothetical relationships.

Evidence was brought forward that people were coerced in a variety of ways to vote, not to vote, or to vote for particular candidates. This might be enforced by murders of those who opposed the local power system, by threats of dismissal from scarce jobs, by the brandishing of arms, or the stealing of ballot boxes. One factory owner was said to have told his workers the plant would shut if Marcos was defeated. In certain communities it

141

might become impossible to live safely if it was known that a particular leader had been defied by a voter—or a whole community might fear repercussions if it was found to have voted against the candidate desired by such a leader. Certainly, in NPA country voters were coerced in one way or another—either not to vote if the army was not powerful enough, or to vote for Marcos where it was sufficiently powerful and feared that villagers would find a pro-Marcos vote in their interest. Some precincts had no voters and others may have had 100% Marcos votes from such pressures. In other areas, 100% or near 100% votes for one or another candidate, combined with the obvious presence of private armies, or security forces used by local strong men as though they were private armies, give a prima facie case for such coercion. More subtle coercion is, of course, always present in elections.

The next most common accusation was that the votes were bought, Payment might be in the form of pre-election campaign "jobs," much as in some American campaigns, the holding of expensive parties for the people, the promise, direct or implied, of future benefits for oneself or one's family, or the distribution of free food. The most flagrant form of payment, and one that had become almost institutionalized before the Marcos regime, was the direct payment of a certain number of pesos to each voter, or a larger amount to members of the precinct committees (such as the NAMFREL or UNIDO representative). The amount in Negros was said to be fifty pesos. (UNIDO was said at times to spread rumors of a higher base payment in order to cause resentment in those who got less.) Buying votes and intimidation may not be unconnected: in many communities it may be considered both ungrateful and a direct challenge to the local system for a voter to refuse to accept what he is offered for his vote. Fearing such buying on a massive scale, the opposition tried to popularize the idea that it was all right to take the money, but then vote any way one wanted. This presumed the theory that an illegal bargain is no bargain at all. However, this argument may have had little affect on villagers used to the idea of reciprocal obligations.

Coercion or bribery was sometimes to get a specific vote, and sometimes to keep the voter away from the poll altogether. For example, the payment might include painting the finger nail with the indelible ink to achieve the latter result. Ways in which the bargain was said to be enforced were numerous. One that observers from our mission saw in common evidence in one area was the use of small carbon paper that could be slipped under the ballot to prove that the vote was for a certain candidate. Another method said to be observed was the crowding into booths in such a way that an observer could see the vote of the one before. In other cases voters were said to be voting deliberately out in the open so that everyone could see how one voted. Certainly some of the voting booths would have been easy to peer into. A common previous practice, "lanzadera," was to stagger the voting so that the ballots put into the box were filled out before the voter actually entered the polling area—although supposedly there would be ways to prevent this. It is more generally my impression that a poor person in a highly controlled area would not want to have to lie about whom he voted for. The danger of being discovered, even if he did not know how his vote would be discovered, might well make it in his interest to vote as he was told, or as he had been paid to vote.

Significantly, several observation teams from our mission reported direct experience of some of the problems recited above. They found areas where 100% votes for Marcos were incredible, due to the presence of voters who claimed they personally had voted for Aquino. They saw numerous examples of the carbon papers used to prove how one voted, and even of people showing the carbons and exchanging money. They were present where UNIDO people were directly gunned down for attempting to interfere with vote buying. They saw public voting. In my experience, for observation teams actually to see or be in the vicinity of such practices is unusual. It was also significant that several areas were found in which there seemed to be real fear of the authorities; in such areas it was often impossible for credible opposition or NAMFREL representatives to monitor the process adequately. Many of the foregoing problems were reported by members of the press, publicly and privately. Most teams reported instances of the ink not being successfully used to prevent double voting. Several teams met many people who said their registrations had been lost.

Beyond the level of directly influencing voter behavior, manipulating the results would require that persons in authority in the voting system be directly paid off, or placed under pressure. Such persons must be paid a good deal more, or given more reason to

143

fear repercussions. Such potential targets of electoral chicanery are much better educated, and politically conscious, people who will have to live in a larger community of persons less likely to accept gracefully dereliction of duty by their fellows. It appears that on the bottom rungs, payoffs to party representatives and precinct chairmen did happen. In totally controlled areas there may be no really independent persons to act in these positions. However, in very few provinces was it likely case that from the provincial level upward deliberate interference with the results was possible.

At the level of the National Assembly it was possible for the majority party, the KBL, to achieve the result it wanted by arbitrarily allowing or denying objections to results from certain precincts or provinces in accordance with party interests.

On the evening of February 7 and subsequently, the election outcome was placed in doubt by confusion in the reporting of election results to the public. The newspaper and television systems reported much faster than the other systems. They reported Marcos ahead from the beginning, and yet, because of the pro-Marcos political tendency of both, their results were generally not considered credible. Of the two slower "quick counts," those of COMELEC and NAMFREL, the former was much the slower. The reason was that COMELEC had expected to rely on the NAMFREL count, but had required that NAMFREL have the counts submitted by precinct to be independently authenticated by voting registrars before being sent further. Where this was possible, NAMFREL sent the results to both its system and COMELEC's. Where this was not possible, it sent the results only to its own system "because it understood COMELEC only wanted those that the registrar had authenticated." When COMELEC realized it was receiving only a portion of what NAMFREL was, it started using other sources of more official information—but then had to deal with the complications of using several sources of information.

As the unofficial count proceeded, COMELEC generally showed Marcos ahead while NAMFREL showed him behind. Both sides ascribed this to a political preference to hold up certain results while including others. This practice would, of course, only affect interim results, and since neither was actually an official count, such a practice could not be regarded as a major crime. It did have, however, the affect of making both sides feel they had won,

144

and claim that their opponents were merely slowing things down in order to shift the real contest into a different arena.

Evidence suggests that if there was fraud, it was primarily at the precinct, or "retail" level that it occurred. A deliberate denial of voting rights to hundreds of thousands in the Manila area may have occurred. While a few provincial centers might have supplied false returns, even in NAMFREL tallies Aquino was not developing the early lead that might have been required to win. Rural tallies were generally slower in coming in, and most admitted that the opposition was much stronger in cities than villages—except for a few locales. It was also true that in those few areas from which NAMFREL was wholly or partially excluded, or did not have representatives, NAMFREL would either not have the results, or would be likely—with some reason—to contest the results without publishing them. These would in most cases be overwhelmingly Marcos areas.

In judging the unfairness of the election, the analysis must begin with the fact that many, if not most, military officers were open supporters of the regime. In rural areas, and areas of conflict, this could not help but be determinative. Government control over television was pervasive and very biased. (The few days of television reporting of election controversies outraged observers.) Television sets are not, however, widely owned by Filipinos outside of the Manila area, but interested persons in the cities and larger towns have access to television sets. (The feeling that the mass media were against them must have alienated many Filipinos.) Support of the major newspapers for Marcos was less blatant, but of great importance in a largely literate country. Unfairness also existed in the excessive use of "pork barrel" projects to reward local and provincial leaders who committed themselves to bringing in the votes for the Marcos regime. In Negros Occidentale, for example, a new province had just been created for a leader promising to deliver his area to Marcos; another province was in the process of being carved out of the southern part of the province for yet another supporter. The Marcos system was a gigantic countrywide machine comparable to Mexico's. Overcoming the strength of this "feudal" or paternalistic structure of society was the key to the problem of insuring fairness in the electoral system.

NAMFREL

The present National Citizens' Movement for Free Elections was ostensibly established to bring more fairness to the 1984 legislative elections. Praised for its work then, it expanded its activities and membership to play a major role in the 1986 election. However, no matter how well intentioned its membership, it had come to be so identified with the opposition that it was no longer a credible group for anyone who did not believe in its opposition politics. The observation mission did not meet anyone in NAMFREL who belonged to KBL or supported President Marcos. There may, of course, be isolated individuals. Nor did we encounter any criticisms of electoral malpractices by the opposition that came to us through NAMFREL—in spite of the fact that many in the opposition were seasoned political actors, quite able to practice the tricks of Philippine politics. For this reason, it is hard to doubt that those local provincial or poll authorities that excluded or expelled NAMFREL representatives from the process because of perceived bias had, or were likely to have had, good reason. The original COMELEC certification said, for example, that accreditation of NAMFREL may be revoked at any time if the organization or any of its chapters or officials are found to be "partisan."[11] To many in the observer mission the wonder was that NAMFREL was allowed to play the major role that it did in most of the country as a semi-official arm of the government.

Certainly, the aid that NAMFREL gave to the election observers was deeply appreciated, but perhaps we were as much the victims as the benefactors of this assistance.

Who Supported UNIDO?

UNIDO united nearly all the opposition elements in the country aside from the hard-line communists of the NPA. As such, it brought together the remnants of the party structures that had been effectively neutralized by the rise of Marcos and the KBL. In social terms, the Marcos regime destroyed or demoted much of the old political-economic aristocracy and replaced it with a new, often nouveaux-riches aristocracy that was deeply resented by most of the older landowning families, as well as many in the educated and middle-class families. We were told confidentially that many in the extreme-left Bayan party that officially opposed the election as a trick, and even some in the communist party itself, also supported the Aquino candidacy.

The strongest alternative institution in the Philippines, the Catholic Church, seemed in our experience to contain few if any supporters of the Marcos regime. It made little difference whether the priests were Filipino or foreign. Most priests supported the Aquino candidacy; a few supported the boycott campaign. The NAMFREL organization was almost entirely supported by the Catholic Church in some areas--often it was run out of their buildings. Namfrel slogans were commonly displayed outside churches—even over the altar. The Bishop of Negros, co-chairman of NAMFREL, and said to be a member of a wealthy land-owning family, certainly made no secret of his political preference, or of his left-leaning ideology.

The NPA and the Election

The New People's Army has taken the place of the earlier Huk movement in the Philippines. Loosely related originally to Maoist China, Philippine communism is now largely cut adrift from international communism. It may also be internally divided into many subgroups. But with all its problems, the economic decline of much of the country has combined with the sense of injustice of the educated young to create an expanding and widely supported movement. In many of the forested or mountainous areas of the country movement had become unsafe without an armed escort, and in some battalion strength units would be necessary for penetration. Industries such as mines or forestry are likely to pay-off the NPA regularly, while landowners and village officials on surrounding plains may either make payments or move their residences to major cities. This abandonment of the countryside, for example in the southern part of Negros Occidentale leaves a vacuum that is likely to be filled by the NPA and its civilian cadres. One cannot help but believe that one reason the church has become so favorably disposed to their movement is the necessity of the priests to live among the people in often very exposed localities. This situation is also responsible for the rapid redevelopment of the private armies of the landowners and "big men" in many locales. Such people have few options if they are to maintain their position. They must fight or leave. The contest does not, of course, lessen the burden on the peasant caught in between.

Many Filipinos felt that the election of Aquino was critical to controlling the growth of the NPA. It is certainly true that many young people have joined the guerrilas out of disgust with the system. However, the average NPA volunteer is more likely to be an unemployed peasant in an economically declining region. To him the NPA is a way of making a living, and his behavior is rather comparable to the gangs that have always infested China in times of trouble. For such people a variety of programs, including enough force to show that the guerrilla life does not "pay," and economic revival will be required to make a turn-around.

Conclusions and Recommendations

On February 15, the National Assembly announced that Marcos had won the election with 54% of the ballots, or 1,500,000 votes. This claim raised many issues. First, should this be considered a legitimate or illegitimate outcome? Second, what practically did this mean for the country? Third, what American policies would be most useful under the circumstances? Fourth, what should the opposition and government be urged to do under the circumstances? Fifth, what might in-country voter observation groups such as NAMFREL do to improve their performance in the future? Sixth, what might foreign observer groups do to improve their future performance? These issues will be addressed briefly, and primarily from the perspective of February, 1986. It seems useful to look back on the decisions of February, for Americans are likely to find themselves in many similar situations in the future.

The evidence suggests that the problems in the electoral process that may have produced an unfair and illegitimate outcome were in the registration, campaign, voter manipulation, and pre-cinct tabulation stages rather than in the later canvassing and determination of results. Although the evidence has not been sufficiently quantified, there is sufficient reason to believe that the combination of violent and financial pressures exerted on the voters against a background of intimidation in many provinces over a period of years is likely to have accounted for the margin of victory for the Marcos administration.

Given the evidence of serious problems in procedure in certain parts of the country, and the problems of registration, two main cases could be made against the legitimacy of the announced outcome. First, even if the voting process had been essentially fair in ninety percent of the country, which appears overly optimistic, the ability of the Marcos regime to decisively influence by unacceptable means the votes in the remaining ten percent of the country (over 2,000,000 voters) would be sufficient for Marcos to win. (Given the structure of the country, it is not necessary to assume that ex-President Marcos himself ordered exceptional pressures be used to achieve his victory in such areas.) In addition, it must be remembered that the lack of a balanced press and a completely one-sided television service made the campaign of the opposition much more difficult than in democratic systems with which Americans are familiar.

The second argument is based on the active exclusion of voters. Voters participated in this election at a much lower than predicted rate. If the rate in the 1984 election had been sustained, there would have been 2.2 million additional votes.[12] The dimensions of the shortfall could be substantially increased, perhaps to 3.0 million, since by all accounts the boycott campaign in 1984 was much more successful than in 1986. Many politicians that supported boycott in 1984 did not in 1986; in 1986 only part of the communist fringe opposed the process. While it is impossible to determine what mixture of methods was used to reduce the participation of pro-Aquino voters, there is good evidence many were excluded, particularly through omission from registry rolls. Against this, we have heard little or no evidence or argument that significant numbers of Marcos supporters were deprived of the vote. The inference is that the great majority of those who failed to vote were Aquino supporters. If more than 75% of the missing voters supported Mrs. Aquino she would have won.

On the basis of available evidence, the case for the first argument was stronger than that for the second. It is important to note that the cases did not greatly overlap, and so might be considered additive. The first case was based primarily on information from some of the most rural parts of the country; much of the second case was based on reports from urban areas, particularly the greater Manila area. Admittedly, the evidence for neither case was decisive.

For then-President Marcos to have claimed victory and resumed office on this basis of a doubtful win would not have necessarily meant disaster. It should be remembered that Salvador Laurel claimed that the 1984 legislative election was the last chance for democracy[13]—and yet we had this election. Other partly free countries, such as Mexico, consistently fail to allow honest electoral processes, and yet the people carry on. Marcos' apparent ability to win this election at the local level, whatever the means used, indicated that Marcos had continued to have considerable support in the country.

However, it was the experience of the observation team that the middle classes were overwhelmingly in favor of political change, and it is the wider experience of political analysts that the support of the middle classes is necessary for a democratic system of government to develop, or indeed any system protective of human rights. Specifically, the failure of the Philippine system to accommodate the strongly felt need for change could have given the growing antidemocratic forces, represented by the New People's Army, many more recruits. If a democratic choice ultimately is unavailable to the Filipino people, they may be led to choose an alternative despotism—or at least go too far down that road to turn back. In a land of glaring contrasts, the NPA holds out at least the chance of greater equality.

To maintain its control the Marcos regime would have been forced to stronger and stronger measures to resist the forces arrayed against it. The outlook for human rights and democratic evolution under these circumstances would not have been encouraging. The murders of opposition leaders and workers in the immediate aftermath of the election gave a hint of what might occur, while at the time making the legitimation of a Marcos victory even more difficult.

American leaders, under these circumstances, were unwilling to prop up a government that was ever more disliked by a large segment of its population, and regularly excoriated in the court of world opinion. It was judged that maintaining support for Marcos would hamper American ability to support the development of democracy elsewhere. Such support would diminish the credibility of the United States both with authoritarian rulers and their oppositions, particularly in East and Southeast Asia.

Aside from political considerations, certain recommendations should be made stemming directly from the experience of the observer mission.

The NAMFREL organization illustrates a type of movement that should be supported in the Philippines and other democracies of the first and third world. However, to be able to play its role more effectively, NAMFREL should be encouraged to restructure its cadres so that it becomes more of a watchdog organization and less of a political instrument. While the objectives of those involved were laudable, the organization as we found it could not be viewed by the KBL as legitimate, and this surely laid the basis for occasionally excluding the organization from polling areas. A more professional or disciplined approach might also support a greater effort by NAMFREL to do its homework. It should be able to analyze election districts and registration figures before elections to determine exactly what the problems are, and to have a data base against which it can instantaneously compare voting results as they come in for probability of malpractice. The tendency of the organization and its representatives always to speak in terms of generalities, and to not provide observers with documented demographic and voter data reduced its credibility, and its ability to communicate with observers.

Observer missions, such as our own, should plan to devote significant time to the development of demographic and election statistics so that they can adequately compare registration and voting statistics with what is probable. A model, no matter how crude, of what the number of registrants and voters should look like nationally and locally should be prepared beforehand for any observed election. Before, during, and after the election a small team should be assigned exclusively to this work. Observers wander too long in a wilderness of assertions. Only adequate statistics are likely to make possible pinning down a fraction of these.

Observer missions cannot operate in isolation. To a degree they must establish dependency relations with local groups. However, in so doing they must strive to develop dependencies on a variety of organizations and individuals representing the main political forces in the country observed. Members of the mission should plan to switch back and forth between dependency on different groups, accompanying, for example, representatives of

151

opposing groups into the field on successive site visits. It may be useful for Americans, on occasion, to support some political forces to the exclusion of others. In this case, human rights and democratic support organizations should develop a different designation for such missions, even when in connection with an election.

Postscript

In the event Mrs. Aquino and her followers were able so to move American and Filipino opinion that the military leaders decided to cast their lot with her movement. After this, Marcos' position rapidly crumbled, and Aquino took over, and decreed a temporary constitutional order on the strength of her "winning" the election. On this basis, the government arbitrarily removed thousands of local leaders from elective positions throughout the country.

It is significant that the new administration neither moved to have a new election in the succeeding months nor attempted to make a new and more adequate "count." Given that they controlled all of the levers of power this count might also have appeared questionable to disinterested observers. But at least it would have demonstrated a concern for legitimacy that was thrown away by leaders who appeared to feel that declaring an electoral victory should be enough.

Without a government effort to establish electoral victory, it has been easier for the enemies of the Aquino government to gather to both right and left, and to invoke once again the argument of illegitimacy. The problem was exacerbated by the administration writing a new constitution for popular approval that would avoid another test of Aquino's popularity until 1992. As this is written (November 1986) the threat of a military coup was hanging over the society, a coup that would surely be based, in part, on the argument that Aquino did not rule legitimately. Even without a coup, the military threat has already greatly limited the room for maneuver, and thus for reform, of the new government.

Democracy has not yet been established in the Philippines. The removal of President Marcos opened a door that can make possible its institutionalization—but only if democratic Filipinos and their foreign supporters maintain their momentum, and work steadily toward the establishment of a firm foundation in legal and constitutional norms, and consistently avoid autocratic and arbitrary short-cuts.

NOTES

1. The background discussion is based primarily on Nena Vreeland, et al. **Area Handbook for the Philippines,** second edition (Washington: Superintendent of Documents, 1976).

2. See also Fred Poole and Max Vanzi, **Revolution in the Philippines: The United States in a Hall of Cracked Mirrors** (New York: McGraw-Hill, 1984), pages 114-115.

3. See **Area Handbook for the Philippines,** pages 209-230.

4. **Keesing's Contemporary Archives,** 1984, pages 32914, 33101-3.

5. On the election see **Resource Book: Philippine Elections, 1986** (Evidently produced at Manila, 1986, by the Philippine government); National Democratic Institute for International Affairs and National Republican Institute for International Affairs, "Report on the Feasibility of an International Delegation to Observe the February 7 Election," (Washington: 1986); and Center for Democracy, "The Presidential Election Process in the Philippines," A Report to the Committee on Foreign Relations United States Senate" (Washington: January, 1986).

6. Center for Democracy, "The Presidential Election process in the Philippines," A Report to the Committee on Foreign Relations United States Senate (Washington: January 1986), page 20.

7. Statement of Comelec Commissioner Bankuyan to International Observers, February 5, 1986.

8. **Omnibus Election Code of the Philippines** (Manila: Commission on Elections, 1985), Sections 123,125.

9. 1,300,000 according to the statement of Comelec Commissioner Bankuyan to the International Observers, February 5, 1986.

10. **Keesing's Contemporary Archives,** 1984, page 33102.

11. **Resource Book: Philippine Elections, 1986,** Comelec Resolution No. 1729, Article V.

12. **The New York Times,** February 16, 1986, pages 1, 14-15.

13. **Keesing's Contemporary Archives,** op.cit.

PART III

Democracies: Issues and Comparisons

Criticisms of the Liberal Concept of Democracy

In terms of the Comparative Survey a free society is a liberal democratic society. A liberal, modern democracy is defined as:

> a politically organized community that places primary value on enhancing the effectiveness of the sponsorship[1] of the political system by its people, and in so doing extends sponsorship to the whole adult population; that gives this population a variety of means of directly and indirectly expressing this sponsorship, including the election of representatives that enact and administer its laws; that is committed to the rational discussion of political issues and the right of all persons to express any rational position on these issues, and to compete for political office, so that within the broad limits required by the maintenance of a democratic system, minorities may become majorities on any issue; that regulates those matters and only those matters the people or their representatives wish to be politically determined; that respects guarantees for ideological or ethnic minorities, and in other ways strives to balance the interests of majorities and minorities; and that with few exceptions is made up of citizens that consider themselves a part of the same democratic political community.

However, there are many on the left or right of the political spectrum that both oppose this concept of political society and see themselves as advocates of political freedom. Many find unacceptable the institutionalization of conflict that characterizes modern democracy, particularly that of a large multiparty state. Along with representatives in lieu of direct participation, the multiparty system in lieu of unfettered individual choice has become an apparently inescapable requirement for large-scale democracy.

Nevertheless, this is a requirement that many find so abhorrent that they continue to espouse a Rousseauian doctrine of consensus that in practice becomes rule by the few. For example, recently the British editor of the **Far Eastern Economic Review** warned his fellow citizens of Hong Kong against copying western democracy:

> The shortcomings of democracy as it has evolved in Europe and the United States are becoming increasingly evident—the wooing of votes by promises politicians know they can never keep; the wearisome mouthing of cliches of irrelevant ideologies; the Hobson's choice presented to an electorate by a two-party system and the zigs and zags in national policy (as with nationalization, denationalization, renationalization, followed by privatization); the emergence of unworkable coalitions which results from proportional representation; the enormous amounts of money expended in campaigns which owe more and more to show business as politicians play to the audiences provided by the media; the distortions to the system wrought by special-interest groups, and the resulting refusal of the best brains and personalities to enter politics.
>
> One would have thought that, surrounded by the various examples East Asia supplies of new forms of representational government emerging, and with the prospect of 1997 looming, those most actively involved in the debate on the way Hong Kong people will run Hong Kong would lay the greatest stress on finding a system which would first create and then implement a consensus.[2]

The democracy that we have been defining and whose history we have sketched is often described in a more neutral political science as pluralist democracy, and the institutional setting in which it occurs as "pluralism." Modern democracy is also often referred to as "liberal democracy," and by the Marxists as "bourgeois democracy." To American ears this identification may seem strangely off-key, for in our popular political discussion "liberal" has little to do with the class associations of the term "bourgeois."

Most Americans are used to the label "liberal" being applied vaguely to anyone whose views of politics or social behavior are "left of center"; earlier the term also included the concept of breadth and generality, as in "liberal education."

The term "liberal" in British or European usage, however, has come to be applied to those who believe in capitalistic or market economies, and who see the economic role of government as primarily that of an umpire regulating the operation of a "free economy." Historically, the European liberal that supported the free economy in the nineteenth century was a supporter of change, of broader ideas, and thus the antithesis of the "conservative" who was opposed to change in any sphere, who saw the government's role as much more general if need be, and who was suspicious of the destruction of traditional structures that often accompanies the operation of a liberal economy.

Therefore, as democracy developed in the nineteenth century along with increasingly free and explosive economic growth, the two aspects of change were frequently considered as aspects of the same ideology, by both proponents and opponents.

This would matter little to Americans except that in the last few years an increasing number of American academics, particularly political scientists and sociologists, have come increasingly under the influence of Marxist thinking. Since Marxism in America has been very much an imported European product, it is natural that they should come to link "liberalism" with capitalism in the European manner—and if the terms do not seem to quite fit, to make them fit anyhow.

"Liberal democracy," in the sense that Americans naturally use the word liberal, is a useful phrase, because it points to the ever-evolving sense of what democracy has been about in our country, and ideally should be about in all countries. To me a liberal is a person who educates himself and thinks about the problems of society in an open and inquiring manner. Without being a strong activist, or overly sure of himself, the liberal continually presses for the amelioration of the condition of others and the gradual improvement of the institutions of society. The primary weakness of a liberal is that he does not have a sufficiently strong core of belief. Always changing, and always willing to see other viewpoints, he may find it hard to support consistent and strong actions when these are required. But it is the liberal who established the intellectual basis for progressive change in institutions and beliefs, and when those sections of society demanded their rights, it was the liberal--and liberal beliefs—that prevented the rulers, including eventually themselves, from crushing the demands.

Liberal democracy has always had its enemies. The first enemies of democracy were, of course, those whose interests were directly challenged by the developing breadth and range of democratic institutions. The nobility and the higher clergy and their intellectual defenders, as well as the defenders of older ways of life for their own sake, were the enemies. However, with the complete victory of liberal democracy, in the sense used here, among countries representing Western Civilization, the critics of democracy have tended to come from rather different directions.

Today, the critics of liberal democracy include on the right libertarians and traditionalists, and on the left Marxists. The libertarians believe that there is too much government in general, the traditionalists that the government has its priorities confused, and the Marxists that there should be a shift in the control of government. Although there are important differences in their critiques, particularly in the values that each group holds most dearly, there are more similarities than differences among these critics—they are essentially reacting to the same difficult but sadly inevitable problem of the liberal polity.

This is the problem that has become central to the work of Robert Dahl: democracy is rule by the people and yet the people cannot rule.[3] To Dahl the central problem is one of size. Many problems cannot be successfully addressed by small, face-to-face groups. Yet as larger and larger political units are devised to handle such problems, the role of the individual is necessarily diminished. Except on the simplest level, most individuals cannot be direct participants in the running of their political life.

Equally serious is the fact that those who staff a democratic administration, whether through representative institutions, or through delegated power from such institutions, inevitably tend to accumulate more than their share of political power, and come among themselves to form a ruling elite. This elite will, in turn, have more than average contact with the other elites of the society—professional, spiritual, business, or simply of wealth—than ordinary citizens. The leaders of these groups, together with the political elites, will form governing strata that will serve the interests of one another more than the interests of the people at large. Democracies have as their task reducing the injustices this situation engenders. Because they are open societies they do much better in controlling the accumulation of power by the governing strata than other systems, whether traditional and feudal or radical and communist. But they succeed only partially and always will.

Most people in most societies, and the governing strata in all societies, will oppose those who violently threaten to change the system, and they will resist those whose criticisms of the system are most radical and thoroughgoing. Those who have the most to lose by change will oppose it most strongly. More prosaically, all governments will exact sacrifices from their citizens in the form of taxes and aggravation, in the form of regulations and restrictions that will be resented as wrong by many, and will be unjust for some. Governments will use a variety of means, including their control over violence, to preserve the peace, to preserve the system, and to enforce their regulations and exactions. In this sense all societies do have a repressive apparatus, and practice some forms of repression.

How an analyst responds to the expression of these facts in real-world democratic polities varies widely. The liberal analyst emphasizes the qualitative and quantitative distinctions between the forms and frequency of repression in democracies and nondemocracies. He examines the degree and type of repression practiced in democracies in order to see how repression might be reduced or government and administration made fairer. The radical critic emphasizes that repression exists in liberal democracies, although in a more sophisticated fashion than in nondemocracies. He then points out that liberal democracy requires repression (ignoring both theoretical and empirical argument that any political system requires repression). To him proving that repression exists in democracies offers cause enough to press for fundamental change in the socio-political system.[4]

The radical critics' indiscriminate lumping of democracies and nondemocracies together as repressive finds broad support among Western intellectuals. In 1982, **Index on Censorship** published a series of short descriptions on the problems of censorship of the media in a range of countries from nondemocratic to democratic. At the liberal democratic end of the spectrum Nicholas Garn was asked to comment on the freedom of the BBC in the United Kingdom. Evidently rejecting the idea that the BBC was somehow freer than many of the other systems discussed, Garn asserted instead that it was ridiculous to expect freedom in broadcasting. Any radio station will merely represent the viewpoints, or acceptable range of viewpoints, of those in charge of the station. It was impossible to fight racism, sexism, and other repressions unless those in charge really wanted to use the media to fight them. To Garn the very wide range of viewpoints aired on BBC (or American public radio) merely reflected just another oppressive system.[5]

Elections

The central technical criticism of liberal democracy is that elections are necessarily "insignificant," in that they offer little opportunity for average citizens to influence who rules them or to what end. This critique has two aspects that should concern Americans: the extent to which elections in liberal democracies generally are insignificant, and the extent to which elections in the United States are particularly insignificant.

The first aspect suggests either that people are unable by the nature of the case to control a society through the ballot box, or that modern liberal societies are constructed so as to make it impossible for most people to effectively use the ballot box to express their wishes. In either case, these arguments leave readers with doubt as to the implications of the argument, particularly the implication that there is a better alternative for expressing the sponsorship of the majority over a political system.

The argument for the general impossibility of popular control through elections rests on reasonable propositions and much empirical evidence. The most neutral proposition is that in a large, modern society it is never in an individual's interest to vote in an election. The chance of an individual's vote having an affect on the outcome, leave alone an affect on the desired policies that will eventuate from the election is vanishingly low—so low that taking the trouble to go the polls, or even more, the trouble to inform oneself so that an intelligent vote may be made, is a very poor investment for all those who do not see such processes as rewarding forms of recreation.[6] For the average person, contributing to a political campaign is equally hard to defend on rational grounds.[7] In general, the plausible case for nonparticipation is irrefutable empirically.

Another line of argument, that elections have in any event no affect on policy, is more open to empirical consideration. It can be shown that the victories of one or another party or individual often has much less affect on policy trends than is claimed at the time by the participants. In many countries taxes and government involvement in the economies of democracies has grown rather steadily over a period of years in spite of elections that alternate control between parties from the right or left of the spectrum. Trends in military expenditure in recent years in the United States have often risen or fallen in cycles that seem to be "out of synch" with the election of particular administrations, including the last.[8] However, it can be shown that political parties try in many cases to live up to their campaign slogans, and that the expectations of voters of parties on the left and right are reflected in some measurable differences in policy: for example, those of the left show more attention to reducing unemployment, while those of the right pay more attention to holding down inflation.[9]

The inability of voters to affect outcomes is remarked on most often in regard to the United States. A review of electoral participation rates in the leading democracies in recent years points to the poor performance of American voters. A recent study shows, for example, that the United States, Switzerland, Colombia, and India had the lowest participation rates of major democracies.[10] Many technical arguments are advanced to explain these figures. It is often suggested that the relative difficulty of registering in the United States, one of the few democracies that puts the responsibility primarily on the individual, is responsible for much of the shortfall. Easier or more automatic registration would help. Certainly, countries at the other extreme that compel (although not vigorously) voters to vote, such as the Netherlands and Australia, have some of the highest participation rates.

However, that there is more to it than regulations is suggested by the fact that all four low-participation countries are characterized by systems that greatly reduce the level of effective political competition. Relatively low electoral turnouts in Colombia and India surely stem from the low levels of development and education. The politics of such countries are necessarily closer to the elite politics of traditional societies. Switzerland and the United States, on the other hand, have not developed party systems that allow voters to relate their electoral decisions to policy change.

Swiss lack of interest in their elections, in which participation has been steadily declining, can be attributed partly to the now long-standing control of the system by a "grand coalition" of all the major parties, a coalition that divides the legislative and administrative functions among its members in carefully graded shares by party, religion, and language. Switzerland has also experienced declining participation in referendums, as well as local and cantonal elections. One reason may simply be too many elections. But the decline in voting on referendums may also be ascribed to the lack of interest, or lack of contest, in many of them. Some are on narrow topics or obviously have little support. But the fact that the system taken as a whole emphatically does give voters a chance to control the system is suggested by the 1986 referendum on a government proposal, supported by all parties, to join the United Nations. Fifty percent of Swiss voters participated (an unusually high percentage on an individual question) and decisively defeated the proposal in every canton.[11]

Low voter participation in the United States has somewhat different causes. While in most democracies there is a fairly clear development of party lines, and the parties are often arranged on a perceivable left-right spectrum, this is far from the case in the United States.[12] U.S. politics began with nonparty elections and fear of "faction," developed rather quickly into strong party affiliations if not strong parties—affiliations that often had a more regional than ideological cast—and then, under the pressure of many well-meaning reforms, has become increasingly personalist and anarchical. Most Americans now vote for, and expect to vote for, a candidate rather than a party. Since the probability of a candidate receiving a vote is directly related to the probability that a voter recognizes who the candidate is, incumbents have an overwhelming and increasing advantage. For example, between 1956 and 1976 over ninety-two percent of incumbents in the House of Representatives seeking reelection were successful.[13] There is very little pressure for representatives to conform with party or presidential positions on either domestic or foreign issues because few voters are acquainted with their representatives' positions on issues. Voting for or against such representatives does not appear to be a very meaningful exercise for most voters in most districts.

With evidence such as this, some analysts have concluded that the real politics is still elite politics, in which the economic interests of the few determine policies irrespective of which individuals or parties attain office.[14] A less ideological case can be made that voters in America, and to a lesser extent in all democracies, vote essentially as a means of reaffirming their attachment to the political, economic, and social system of which they are a part. Voting is, then, a rational act for that half of the population that participates in the United States, for it strengthens or upholds the system that sustains them and from which they benefit. According to this analysis, most of those who do not vote decide not to vote (or are not motivated to vote) because they do not feel that they have sufficient stake in the system to make it worthwhile to participate in its support.[15]

At first glance this seems to be supported by the evidence. Economic level and propensity to vote are strongly correlated. The young and very old vote less, according to this analysis, because their interests are less regularly taken into account by the system. But there are also reasons to doubt this analysis. The young and very old are also likely to find voting more "costly" in terms of acquiring information, or travel to registration and polling places, than is the bulk of the population. The fact that education is more important than any other variable in predicting likelihood of voting casts doubt on the idea that people refrain from voting for reasons of relative satisfaction or ideology, as does the lack of a significant distinction between the party or policy preferences of voters and nonvoters.[16] Studies of what causes high turnout in elections suggest that "dissatisfaction" with an individual or policy rather than satisfaction causes relatively high turnouts.[17] This supports the plausible assumption that voter nonparticipation reflects the general satisfaction of most nonvoters, rather than their judgment against the system.

Elections are not the only, or even major, means of directly affecting policy in democratic countries, particularly in the United States. Other means include legislative hearings, scientific studies, journalistic exposes, scholarly treatises, juridical decisions, and a broad proliferation of activities by pressure groups ranging from the Audubon Society to the American Medical Association. Much of this effort over a period of years is summarized for politicians in public opinion polls, which are a major output of the communication system. One cannot read an account of presidential elections without noting the extent to which the acceptability of candidates, and beyond that, the acceptability of the positions of candidates, is determined primarily by the extent to which their thinking and positions are in tune with the thinking of at least three publics: the elite educated community, the backers of particular individuals or parties, and the general attitudes of the public at large. The latter is decisive on all issues that are sufficiently developed in the popular mind to be salient.[18]

The common claim that money determines elections in democracies cannot be made for democracies such as Britain in which elections consume very little private money, or campaigns are largely subsidized. Even where the size and source of campaign chests seems to play an inordinate role both in campaigns and the subsequent behavior of elected officials, it is still unclear what the alternative to unrestricted contribution should be. Restricting campaign contributions may reduce the competitiveness of elections. A recent American study suggests that only the ability to raise campaign funds easily makes possible a successful challenge to an incumbent, whose position is the more unassailable the more his potential opponents are unable to raise funds to overcome his natural lead.[19] Most money that is raised in campaigns is raised, however, not because a candidate is willing to follow the preferred policy of the giver, but because the candidate is likely to win. Convincing potential contributors that one can win, and thus that one has the qualities that voters want, or the opponent has negative qualities that can be exploited, is the surest way to contributions. If this process cannot be started, incumbents will have less reason than ever to worry about what voters think.

The meaning of elections in new or third-world democracies is that they are concrete opportunities to involve ever-widening circles of the people in participation in the governmental system. The enthusiasm of many voters stems from the hope that the system will at last have to take them into account. To a degree they are right. For example, politicians in such countries include many who are willing and able to promote policies that will have redistributive effects favoring a larger percentage of people than in the past. This has been the experience in the development of European and Commonwealth social democracies. This phase has been passed by the more established democracies. There is no longer a substantial public left in the audience. Representatives of innumerable groups, large and small, struggle for their separate interests through institutionalized leaders and channels of communication. In established democracies, the greatest threat to the people's ability to actually control the staffs of their government is the tendency of all members of elites who become involved in government—whether from the bureaucracy, labor, education, business, science, or the military—to come to consider the government to be theirs. Elections are the primary means, if too often a feeble means, for the people to remind such ruling circles that they are accountable to a force beyond their charmed circle.

Philosophical Alternatives

Critics of liberal democracy, right or left, essentially accept a Rousseauian view of the nature of man and the possibilities of society. They agree that people have, or can without coercion come to have, sufficient interests in common that the political structures of modern society will not be necessary. Beyond this, they argue that the structures of liberal democracy fundamentally destroy the ability of people to perceive their true interests.

The libertarians come to their position through a radical cri-tique of the concept of "public interest." To a true libertarian there is no "public interest." There may be common interests—such as the common interest to work for a libertarian society—and the cumulative interest of all individuals when added together.[20] To radical libertarians the concept of public interest is merely a smoke screen thrown up by a few members of the elite in order to cover their expropriation of the rights of others. Most taxation, whether for large defense establishments or public schools, serves to enhance the power of the few at the expense of the many. There is no "public interest" in controlling the drugs people take, the drinks they purchase, or the safety of the foods they eat. While libertarians vary in their radicalism from those who would merely reduce somewhat the interventions of government and recognize the needs of national defense to those who would reduce society to an anarchical series of contractual arrangements among individuals—even to the extent of requiring payment from each driver for the use of privatized highways.

From the libertarian perspective, the rights of the individual are always (or nearly always) paramount. Aggression is defined as any attempt to invade the person or property of the individual when the individual has not freely consented to this particular invasion. It makes little difference whether the leviathan of government has the democratic vote of a majority behind it or the selfish interests of a single dictator. Regardless of the public sanction, to the libertarian, "War is Mass Murder, Conscription is Slavery, and Taxation is Robbery."

Libertarians view liberal democracy as it exists in the last part of the twentieth century as a cover for the progressive socialization of economic systems and the imposition of the values of the few on the many. In this sense they see representative democracy as only somewhat less repressive than communist states. Both embody the assumption that governments have a right to take away the property of citizens for objectives that serve only governmental interests.

In their rejection of any sort of positive function for government, libertarians would return society to the moment of—or before—the "signing" of the social contract of the political theorists. They would have us review and largely reject the provisions of such a contract. Curiously, they seem to expect that the interests of individuals, in the absence of a public interest, will be sufficiently in harmony to support the complex maze of contractual arrangements that such a society would demand. The great inequalities inevitably produced by such a system are thoroughly accepted by libertarian theoreticians—indeed, their acceptance is one of the reasons for denying the validity of the oppressive governments we have today. But their faith that in the absence of coercive police establishments such spiraling inequalities would not come to be regarded as unjust and illegitimate, and thus any contractual arrangements insupportable, seems bizarre.

The Marxist critique of liberal democracy has not changed greatly since the nineteenth century. But here we shall be concerned primarily by how it has been developed recently.[21] For those readers who have been through this before I apologize, yet it is useful to have even a brief sketch of the central ideas as a background to the general survey of approximations to the ideals of liberal democracy that will be presented below. The most common criticisms in this country and abroad of liberal democracy will come out of this intellectual tradition.

The Marxist begins with the proposition that all history is the struggle of social classes, and that political institutions merely represent control mechanisms for the dominant social class at any one time. Therefore, everything else that is done or said in the political arena, or relative to it, is an expression, however veiled, of this struggle. If there seems to have been a steady increase in the size of the electorate since the eighteenth century in many countries, or if there seems to have been a decrease in punishments for the expression of dissenting opinion, this is viewed as the result either of the successful struggle of the poor for their rights, or of the crafty ability of the ruling classes to legitimate their continued rule by making superficial concessions to those they oppress. Democracy is a facade, then, that makes over and makes more acceptable the expression of naked power by rulers.

A critical aspect of the Marxist critique that should be mentioned, though it is irrelevant for our purposes—and I would argue harmful to theirs—is the assumption that economic factors are primary in the definition of social classes, and that the rulers necessarily represent an economic class. Therefore, the rise of liberalism has been seen as the tool of a rising capitalist class to destroy the feudal elite and their privileges, replacing it with a new regime dedicated to the interests of their "new class." From this perspective the identification of liberalism with a fixed class interest became a fixation of the Marxist analysis.

What the bourgeoisie has taken by force can be taken from them by force. For the classical Marxist the solution to continued class domination becomes the capture of the state by the "workers," that is by the largest class, the subsequent use of the state to destroy the other classes, and finally the elimination of the need for the state in a classless society. Since such a society has never been created, the Marxist defends the repressive nature of actual communist states by pointing to the need to destroy the other classes and weld out of often recalcitrant material a one-class society. Since most people in most societies are brainwashed

169

by the cultural products of the social systems they live under, or have lived under, and therefore have a "false consciousness" of their own interests, actual communist societies must repress the expression of survivals of previous noncommunist education. This leads to a transitory period of apparent oppression, even of some members of the proletariat.

The argument of the superior "freedom" of the communist press over the bourgeois press is well illustrated by a recent speech by Hu Yaobang to the Central Committee of the Chinese Communist Party. He argues that the Chinese press is freer than the Western because it is owned by the government. Since by definition the government, the Party, and the people have the same interests, the freedom of the people is expressed by the Chinese press that acts as the mouthpiece of the government. Owned by special interests the press of the West can never be as free.[22] This is the application to the question of the press of the more general Marxist argument that since freedoms in any society are only freedoms for the dominant class, and since in pre-Marxist societies the owners of productive property make up a smaller percentage of the population than the workers and peasants, it follows that there is more freedom in a Marxist society.[23]

Many Marxist critics of liberal democracy today, however, no longer accept this approach. Thoroughly aware of the repressive nature of real-world communist systems, these "soft Marxists" are apologists for such systems only to the extent that they may see them as little different from democratic governments in the degree of repression, or to the degree that they find more exciting than most westerners such experiments as that in Yugoslavia with worker management.

The solutions advanced by these modern Marxists (outside of Marxist societies) often stress the establishment of a network of participatory face-to-face institutions only loosely controlled by larger governmental structures. Rather than the "adversarial democracy" that these Marxists see as leading to the repressions of liberal democracy, where majorities are manipulated to repress the rights of minorities, such Marxists propose an emphasis on unitary or consensus democracy, which they increasingly recognize is only possible in small groups. The home, the workplace, the television station, the school, all are to be run democratically by the participants. Yet there is more than a little hint that the people in these examples of direct democracy are to have their minds opened up in the Marxist manner by the right "guides," as Rousseau would have said. Since in the Marxist view only they know the true direction of history, the people will always need the enlightened of the Party to lead them.[24] A swimmer is free only if he has been taught how to swim.

How this grass-roots socialism translates into an effective political system for millions is not always clear. But surely one of the thoughts is that the experience of true equality on the community level will help to develop a true sense of public interest, in which creativity rather than competition, self-sacrifice rather than self-interest, are the values. On the basis of such a cultural transformation it may be possible to have nonexploitative and nonrepressive politics on a national plane—or at least a much better approximation of it than we have today.

The traditionalist believes that the value-free doctrines of liberal democracy, dedicated to the defense of the rights of the individual instead of the rights of the society, have progressively destroyed the inherited moral traditions that made possible past successes. In Europe or America the traditionalist would add "in the West"; in contemporary Iran he would add "in the East." Fascism has sometimes been seen as a traditionalist reaction to liberal democracy: certainly, fascism exploited for the benefit of a few leaders a yearning that many have felt and feel for a society with less neutral values, for something that will stem what liberalism seems determined to create—a world where "anything goes." It is reasonable to assume that if everyone, whatever the race, religion, or culture, is to be treated equally, and if all ideas are to be accepted as having an equal right to compete in the intellectual marketplace, then there are no values that can be taken seriously.

The traditionalist is likely to see democratic rights as historically given rights that only have meaning and sense within the confines of inherited Western tradition. Democracy becomes frightening when it seems to be a rudderless ship led by the rabble, or, worse, by "liberal intellectuals" that would be willing and able to toss out the historical underpinnings of the civil order in the name of majority rule. To the conservative the danger may be that the democracy has not been hedged about with sufficient controls over the extension of government into spheres where it has no business. On the other hand, his concept of sacrosanct areas that should not be "invaded" is less individualistic than the libertarian. He emphasizes units such as the family or church standing above the individual and separately from the state. Indeed, the state may have a role to play in expressing the values of the society in these areas. This is the argument of the "moral majority," and yet in the hands of many conservatives it is certainly not majority desire that makes something right. In this sense the conservative is likely to feel the need for a guide and a censor to assist the majority in the manner of the Marxists and Rousseau.[25]

Like libertarianism and Marxism, conservatism represents a fundamental abhorrence of twentieth century society. Conservatives also agree with the other two lines of criticism in rejecting the importance placed upon modern politics. The real life is elsewhere, just as the real community is elsewhere. They also see leviathan as producing alienation through the imposition of an incomprehensible social order.[26] Conservatives differ on the value to be placed on inherited values, but their reaction to these dangers separates them fundamentally from the majority of modern businessmen, who might better be regarded as liberal capitalists.

The core of similarity in these critiques of liberal democracy is in the feeling that modern democracy has imposed alien rulers on peoples whose real interests would lead them to govern themselves more directly in terms of their own values. The people are being exploited, and the system is using educational and communications media to falsely convince them of the justice and legitimacy of their predicament. All three critiques stem from concern over the cultural future of societies governed as liberal democracies.

The primary distinction in the critiques is in their attitude toward the public interest. The libertarian claims to see nothing but atomism; thus he takes what the other critics see as a primary deficiency of liberal democracy and raises it to a still higher level. Rejecting the individualism of liberal democracy, the traditionalist and Marxist would recreate a world, or worlds, of like-thinking communitarians. The traditionalist would base his world on the symbols and belief systems that his society has inherited from the past; the most liberal Marxists would have individual communities create out of their own experience the guiding values of their lives, the more traditional would require the guidance of Marxist thought, if not the Marxist-Leninist state, in this creation.

As prescriptions for the organization of complex societies, neither libertarianism nor communitarian Marxism has more than pious hopes to offer—and experience suggests that these approaches do not work for most, even on a small scale. The traditionalist could conceivably reorganize society in terms of more definite values than a liberal democracy allows. One doubts, however, that there is a way to have a progressive modern society that denies the flexibility that liberal democracy provides.

Aspects of all three critiques could be accommodated within the limits of liberal democracy. As long as their proponents do not insist that they are so right that they have a mission to impose their vision on their fellows—and in the democracies few advocates seem to be fanatic to this extent—then they can strive to incorporate their thoughts into operating democracies. Certain limits could not, however, be transgressed within the assumptions of a liberal democracy. A complex society that declared multiple parties illegal in the name of unity, or a society that declared that all citizens must ascribe to a particular religion, would fall outside the boundaries of liberal democracy. As long as the society kept its focus on the irreducible rights of people to democratic forms it should be able to avoid such extremes.

Many critics of modern democracy remain definitely within the liberal democratic fold while developing ideas that may be useful for further perfection of the liberal society. Friedrich Hayek is claimed by both libertarians and conservatives, but in fact he uses aspects of both traditions to propose some possibly useful changes to the pattern of liberal democracy. Hayek accepts emotionally much of the libertarian's thesis as to the absolute validity of individual rights, and also much of the capitalist belief in the pragmatic superiority of the market economy. But Hayek also appreciates the importance of the public interest and the claims of the whole on the part.

Hayek believes that a critical failure of the American Constitution's separation of powers, which was to defend natural rights against the momentary vote of the crowd, was that the legislative branch confused an assembly for the consideration of basic legislation with one for the promulgation of those transient "laws" that are necessary for the day-to-day operation of a society. His solution would be to augment the present legislatures by placing responsibility for more basic legislation as to the principles by which a society operates in the hands of a body of persons elected at age forty for one, non-repeatable, fifteen-year term. Such a group could decide, for example, on the degrees and forms of equality or inequality between the genders to be allowed by the system, free from day-to-day political pressures, such as those arising from the need for reelection. Placed between Congress and the Supreme Court, this constitutional legislature might come closer to standing for the general public interest than any elected body we have today.[27] Transferring to the national plane, Robert Dahl's advisory groups selected by lot—and chosen only once—might provide an alternative means of selecting legislative bodies such as Hayek proposes.[28]

Benjamin Barber contrasts the "thin" democracy he identifies as a necessary concomitant of liberal democracy with the "strong" democracy that he would prefer.[29] With a background in careful study of the evolution of Swiss democracy, and much attracted to the ideas of Rousseau (which also stemmed in part from Swiss experience), Barber describes liberal democracy as based on an anarchical denial of the social nature of man. To Barber the idea that people only cooperate out of concern for narrow personal interests, and that their relationships with one another can be reduced to transactions equivalent to those of the marketplace, demonstrates the poverty of the liberal democratic thinking.

Although propounded at length, what Barber's thesis comes down to is a belief that Rousseau's emphasis on emotional and consensual elements in community life, as expressed in his emphasis on the public will rather than majority rule, has been too easily dismissed by a succession of cynical theorists. Barber is uncomfortable with adversarial democracy, for he believes that it emphasizes differences in interests when the objective of democratic institutions should be to concert interests. From this standpoint Barber advances solutions that are at one and the same time conservative and tinged with an element of soft Marxism. Common to such critics, alienation is seen as the natural offspring of liberal democracy, and an unacceptable price to pay for freedom.

Barber's proposals for the creation of a strong democracy come, as so often, as an anticlimax to his critique; most are proposals that can, and often are, comfortably included within the broad limits of liberal democracy. They include primarily devices to increase the extent of participation in the political process,

through such measures as neighborhood assemblies, electronic bal-
loting, and selection to some offices by lottery. They also include
ideas borrowed from Swiss practice such as the initiative and
referendum and universal service (though not necessarily military),
as well as the old idea of more democratic workplaces.

Barber's critique suggests that he has seriously misunderstood
the history and temper of democratic society. In fact, the strong
New England tradition of American democracy, historically a major
determinant of our institutions, and with an influence still
spreading today, has been moralistic and community centered. In
this tradition service of the public interest is the goal of politics,
and politics is to be the responsibility of everyone, not just
professional politicians.[30] Certainly a tradition of public service
and an emphasis on the community rather than adversarial relations
has also characterized many other democratic societies, beginning
with the United Kingdom.

Jane Mansbridge's study of democratic alternatives begins with
concerns very similar to those of Barber.[31] But she properly notes
that much of what she desires already exists. In spite of the
theory of majority rule, most people at most times in assemblies,
especially face-to-face assemblies, value unitary (consensual)
outcomes over adversarial outcomes. Most people at most times do
not want majority rule; they want rule in the common interest in
which everyone agrees to the solution. Mansbridge believes that
we should more explicitly recognize such procedures, but **only
when they are appropriate.** When there is a real conflict of
interests, then reliance on consensus can become a denial of rights
instead of their expression. For when people disagree, a
requirement of consensus leads either to compulsion or a break-
down in the ability of the community to act at all.

As Mansbridge points out, attempts to base decision on unitary
processes on the national scale can take many forms. Marxist societies may attempt to create an emotional sense of community
among all citizens on the fascist model, or may simply resort to
defining all interests as identical through class analysis. Conservative states may see certain wise statesmen as able to define
the national interest separately from the political process (as does
also our Supreme Court). Japanese elites define interests as
unitary by proportionally dividing up the benefits of policies among
power groupings. (See the following discussion of Indian and

Japanese democracy.) Technocrats or administrative specialists may believe that there is only one correct way to solve an essentially political problem, and so remove it unfairly from the arena of adversary politics.   But if there is a real conflict of interests, all of these solutions, engineered from the top down, necessarily ignore most of the citizenry, by assuming for them that their interests are adequately represented by the national consensus.

She concludes that for large political units, such as the nation-state, attempts to express the unitary ideal may be damaging, for they are often based on a false claim to unitary interests. On the other hand, on a smaller scale, she believes in creating and expanding opportunities for group life in which unitary, cooperative relationships are realistic expectations.   She sees such opportunities as a necessary corrective for a society in which a sense of a public interest is often very weak.

NOTES

1. For the discussion of sponsorship in Kuhn's terms see earlier discussions in this series of Kuhn's work. (For example, R. D. Gastil, **Freedom in the World: 1978**, pages 118-119. The full reference is Alfred Kuhn, **The Logic of Social Systems** (San Francisco: Jossey-Bass, 1975), pages 330-361.

2. Far Eastern Economic Review, Feb. 14, 1985, p. 31.

3. Robert A. Dahl, **Polyarchy: Participation and Opposition** (New Haven: Yale University Press, 1971); and Robert A. Dahl, **After the Revolution** (New Haven: Yale University Press, 1971).

4. This is the position developed by Alan Wolfe, **The Seamy Side of Democracy: Repression in America,** 2nd edition (New York: Longman, 1978).

5. Nicholas Garn, in **Index on Censorship,** May, 1982, pages 26-27.

6. See Iain McLean, **Dealing in Votes** (New York: St. Martin's Press, 1982), pages 68-92.

7. Gary Jacobson, **Money in Congressional Elections** (New Haven: Yale University Press, 1980), pages 57-72.

8. In spite of differences in rhetoric, one notes, for example, the consistency in the rise of the military budget after 1979 under the Carter and Reagan administrations. See International Institute for Strategic Studies, **The Military Balance: 1985-86** (London, 1985).

9. See Anthony King, "What Do Elections Decide?" in David Butler, Howard Penniman, and Austin Ranney, editors, **Democracy at the Polls: A Comparative Study of Competitive National Elections** (Washington: American Enterprise Institute, 1981), pages 293-324.

10. Ivor Crewe, "Electoral Participation," in Butler, Penniman, and Ranney, **Democracy at the Polls,** pages 216-263.

11. **New York Times,** March 17, 1986, page A9.

12. Seymour Lipset and Stein Rokkan, editors, **Party Systems and Voter Alignments: Cross-National Perspectives** (New York: Free Press, 1967).

13. Jacobson, **Money in Congressional Elections,** page 1.

14. Thomas Ferguson and Joel Rogers, editors, **The Hidden Election: Politics and Economics in the 1980 Presidential Campaign** (New York: Pantheon, 1981).

15. Kim Ezra Shienbaum, **Beyond the Electoral Connection: A Reassessment of the Role of Voting in Contemporary American Politics** (Philadelphia: University of Pennsylvania Press, 1984).

16. Raymond Wolfinger and Steven Rosenstone, **Who Votes?** (New Haven: Yale University Press, 1980).

17. Jacobson, **Money in Congressional Elections,** page 29.

18. For example, Theodore H. White, **The Making of the President: 1960** (New York: Atheneum, 1961).

19. Jacobson, **Money in Congressional Elections.**

20. This discussion borrows heavily from Stephen L. Newman, **Liberalism at Wits' End: The Libertarian Revolt Against the Modern State** (Ithaca: Cornell University Press, 1984).

21. Herbert Aptheker provides a classical Marxist position in **The Nature of Democracy and Freedom** (New York: International Publishers, 1967); Alan Wolfe, **Seamy Side of Democracy,** provides the more modern American Marxist approach, one echoed by many affected at least in part by Marxist thinking.

22. **Far Eastern Economic Review,** April 25, 1985, page 45.

23. Aptheker, **Nature of Democracy and Freedom.**

24. C. B. Macpherson, **The Real World of Democracy** (New York: Oxford University Press, 1966); also Aptheker, pages 71-72.

25. Compare the writings of Russell Kirk, such as **Enemies of Permanent Things: Observations of Abnormality in Literature and Politics** (New Rochelle: Arlington House, 1969).

26. William R. Harbour, **The Foundations of Conservative Thought: An Anglo-American Tradition in Perspective** (Notre Dame: University of Notre Dame Press, 1982), especially pages 177-189.

27. As discussed in Newman, **Liberalism at Wits' End.** See also F. A. Hayek, **New Studies in Philosophy, Politics, Economics and the History of Ideas** (Chicago: University of Chicago Press, 1978), pages 71-162.

28. Dahl, **After the Revolution.**

29. Benjamin Barber, **Strong Democracy** (Berkeley: University of California Press, 1984).

30. Compare Daniel Elazar **American Federalism: A View from the States** (New York: Thomas Y. Crowell, 1972).

31. Jane J. Mansbridge, **Beyond Adversary Democracy,** (New York: Basic Books, 1980), especially pages 273 ff.

Democracy in the United States: A Comparative Evaluation

Although the Comparative Survey rates most Western democracies as approximately equal in the extent to which they offer their citizens a full spectrum of political and civil liberties, there are important differences in the institutions of these countries. On close examination these differences may be judged to result in distinctive advantages and disadvantages for these countries from the perspective of a freedom survey. But in this, and the following discussions, we will only touch on some of the more obvious differences, and the significance these may have for the achievement of a fully realized democracy. In making this comparison we will not be concerned with current issues as much as general institutional forms and practices.

An analysis of the traditional democracies suggests that government in the United States comes closer to representing the views of the citizenry as a whole than do the governments of most, if not all, other democracies.[1] All governments, and to a degree, all democracies are run by relatively small elites that define the issues for the rest of the population. Such elites rule in democracies by virtue of their higher education, greater access to money and other resources, greater energy and desire for political power, superior information on political and related matters, inherited position, and intra-group contacts embracing the news media, the bureaucracy, legal institutions, business, and labor, as well as the political community. The direct involvement of non-governmental institutions, particularly labor unions and religious establishments, with political parties or movements increases the concentration of power that falls into the hands of governing elites in many democracies.

Outside the United States the road to a place in the political elite of a democracy, if one is not "born to it" is to spend years working loyally for one of the larger political parties. Ultimate success will depend on the extent to which one has earned the confidence of party superiors as to loyalty and competence. Ordinarily, success will not depend on the ability of the individual aspirant to inspire voters by the extent to which he reflects or inspires voters by his ideas or "causes." For the causes that he supports, the measures for which he fights, will be defined by the party leadership. Only after achieving a position within this leadership will he have a determining influence on how he will vote and for what reasons. The result is that the leaders of most democracies are created by self-perpetuating boards of political trustees that often have much more in common with the views of one another than with the views of the majority of their citizens.

In the case of the United Kingdom studies have shown that the views of MPs in both parties and the British public differ markedly, with the opinions of Labour Party MPs differing more from those of their constituents than those of Conservative MPs, for example, on capital punishment or the nature of TV programming.[2] Of course, it is easy to overstate. If these boards fail in the longer term to satisfy their "customers," they will fail, and their parties will decline (as may be happening to Labour) and become extinct.

"Ruling elites" also exist in the United States. But their monopoly on the political process, their ability to determine the issues and candidates that are presented to the people, is much less than in party-dominated democratic systems. The resulting "populism" also affects civil liberties. In some cases it may foster aspects of the "tyranny of the majority" that critics of democracy have so often feared. But at least in modern conditions, and in a society the size of the United States, it serves to reduce the ability of the ruling elite to defend its special interests against those of the whole, for elite members of the judiciary, government, and the press are less likely to identify their interests with one another.

Turning first to **political rights,** most analyses of the American system spend little time on the fundamentals, such as the basic right to a fair election. Yet as has been mentioned, the United States has created a direct primary system for elections to Congress and other bodies that is rare, if not entirely absent, in other multiparty democracies. In the last few years this approach has even been extended to the presidential election, with open primaries in a few states having a determining role in the choice of the candidates that was formerly the right of national party conventions. On one level this would seem to increase the democratic nature of the system, for it adds another layer of popular participation. An additional result, however, has been the further weakening of the political party structure, and the consequent added difficulty in selecting candidates that would offer the voters a clear choice. In those states where a voter can vote in any primary he wishes, this effect is even more palpable.[3]

The history of the United States has been characterized by recurrent efforts to increase the direct power of the people. The setting aside of the indirect election of the president through the electoral college was followed later by the direct election of senators. At the turn of the century the introduction of the initiative, referendum, and recall (in local and state elections) served to increase the extent of direct democracy in most of the states of the union.

However, voting registration procedures have remained relatively restrictive, or at least individualistic. While in most democracies the government takes on the function of developing registration rolls, in the United States the individual has had to prove his qualifications, generally by fulfilling residency requirements at some time before an election, and making a special effort to register. Part of the reason for this approach was the very unsettled nature of the country throughout its first two hundred years. The first registration laws seem to have been occasioned by the continual movement of new people into the large cities, and the impossibility of keeping up with this influx. An additional reason was the reluctance of Americans to institute the close police control of movement common in many countries, including democracies. While in Europe the "authorities" may know where everyone is most of the time, this has not generally been true in this country.

Whatever the cause, one result of our more difficult requirement for personal registration has been generally lower participation in elections than in other countries, together with a tendency for the more settled and better off parts of the community to have relatively higher participation rates.

Another characteristic of the American electoral process has been the degree of local and state control over the system. It was on this basis that the southern states were able for many years to use registration procedures, literacy tests, poll taxes, all-white primaries, and threats of violence to deny the vote to blacks (similar measures were used to deny the vote to Mexican-Americans and Indians in some areas). In the last generation these restrictions have been largely removed by federal action. The Voting Rights Act allowed the federal government to directly intervene in cases where there was a presumption of unfair exclusion of minorities from the electoral process.[4]   In the 1980s the votes of blacks and Mexican-Americans were widely courted by politicians of all stripes; many people from minority groups have been elected in all states, particularly to local and state positions.

The United States meets the requirement of a multiparty system. Anyone can organize a political party that wishes to, and many parties have come and gone over the years.   But in practice the party system is anemic, and even closed.

The American party system has tended to loosely organize politics since the eighteenth century.   The parties have been both remarkably long-lived and weak.   The two-party structure has come to be institutionalized to the extent that voters are unlikely to feel that voting for a third party can be anything other than a wasted vote.   When the party structure in the South or major cities became a one-party structure, the party primaries preserved public policy choice within the system. Although weak nearly everywhere, today the two parties are alive and well throughout the country.   The size and complexity of the country as well as its cultural differences have combined with the inherent individualism of its elected representatives to produce a loose connection between policy positions and party affiliations.   This incoherence is mitigated to some extent by the tendency of presidential candidates to set the party agendas of their respective parties for at least brief periods (though the agendas of defeated candidates are almost immediately forgotten).

A noted political scientist has argued that the United States is the only major democracy in which the parties have not consistently represented ideological alternatives, even for a generation.   He argues that the major ideology of both parties has been a national ideology, and that the major issue of politics recurrently has been the extent to which the American system has lived up to that ideology.[5]

While parties allow many more persons to participate actively in politics than would otherwise be the case, only a very small number of persons are active in American parties. (The previous tendency of even this small number to be directed oligarchically by a few leaders has become less obvious.) Another source of party weakness, and even irrelevance, is the tendency of most of those involved in political campaigns to be primarily interested in, and loyal to, individuals, and to come and go politically in terms of the fortunes of individual candidates rather than any party.

The parties serve to organize fund raising, and to reduce the ability of wealthy individuals to "buy" positions through their private wealth or that of their friends. This party function also lessens the significance of the growing cost of American elections. On the other hand, the relative weakness of the parties requires that most fund raising be by individuals, and be spent on individual campaigns. Where most campaigning is party-directed, and nationwide, costs per voter should be lower.

Party weakness also reenforces the stability, or, from a more critical perspective, the lack of responsiveness of the system. Because of the emphasis on personalities, popular incumbents can almost never be defeated in an election, regardless of their party, or party positions. This fact of American political life leads to, and is reenforced by, the tendency of incumbent Congressmen to receive much larger campaign donations. For this reason, as well as the staggered elections of Senators, the landslides that occasionally defeat incumbent presidents seldom occur in congressional elections. This reenforces the potential for executive-legislative conflict, in that a winning presidential candidate may fail to carry his party to victory.

The role of violence and corruption in American politics has often been considered a major impediment to the full realization of true democracy.[4] This has been true at certain periods in our history, and in certain sections of the country. However, in recent years these aspects of our tradition have had little influence on the outcome of political campaigns and elections. Significantly, in the last generation the extremist killings that have ravaged Italy and other European countries have had surprisingly little echo in this country, in spite of the well-publicized murders of the Kennedys and Martin Luther King, Jr. While in Europe the attempt has been made to indict and threaten whole classes of people, similar efforts in the United States, certainly since 1970, have been primarily directed against isolated individuals (in spite of evidence of grandiose plans for widespread killing by groups such as the Aryan Nation).

To what extent are Americans able to use elections to control their political system? Many feel the division of powers, and the great personal visibility of the president, unremovable during a fixed term of office, takes the power out of the hands of the people.

The American presidency was a major historical innovation, and its model continues to find imitators. Unlike many democracies the American president combines both the ceremonial functions of head of state with that of chief executive. He serves for a fixed term of office. According to a recent amendment he can only be reelected once. Stemming essentially from a fear of quasi-dictatorship, an even more stringent ban on reelection is found in many states for the office of governor.[5]

A critical problem of the American system has been the lack of a clear definition of presidential power vis-a-vis the other branches of government. Over the years the presidency has tended to gather more and more power. First, he has become the acting head of the political party in power at any one time. Secondly, his office has become a major source of legislative proposals. Most important is the extent to which the president has come to dominate the military and international affairs of the country. While declarations of war must be made by Congress, and the Senate must ratify treaties, these limitations on presidential power were written for a more deliberate age. Today, the real powers of war or peace, initiated militarily or through the outcome of international political decisions, are in the hands of the president.

Although the strength of the American presidency has tended to grow over the years, it has severe limits, especially in the domestic arena. These limits are particularly apparent when the president is from a different party than the majority in either house of Congress, a situation almost unparalleled in the history of other democracies. The only reason it works in the United States at all is that the weak party allegiances and genuinely consensual approach of American politicians makes it unlikely that Congress will deliberately "gang up" on a president and force his resignation.

Nevertheless, most presidents tend to lose support as their presidencies age, and second term presidents who cannot be reelected tend to have different interests than congressmen even of their own party who can be.

The defeat of President Nixon in the Watergate controversy exemplified the limits on the presidency, or indeed the executive branch of government, in a way incomprehensible to many foreign observers. In this case the judiciary, the Congress, and the "fourth estate" (the press and television) responded effectively to a pattern of rather minor invasions of the privacy of individuals and organizations, uses of administrative power to support his reelection, and subsequent denials of his personal participation and that of his colleagues, and interference with the Office of the Attorney General in its investigative efforts. Part of the incomprehensibility of the actions against the administration of President Nixon stemmed from the fact that in no other country would it be expected that a duly elected government could be removed from office by other branches of government, with the partial support of that government's own party. No other democracy has the separation of powers, nor the weak top-down party structure characteristic of the United States.

The bicameral legislature adopted by the United States was originally meant to represent two very different assumptions about the nature of the country. To the extent that the country was a confederation of independent states, the Senate was to represent them each individually. To the extent that the country was a unitary republic of individually equal voters, the House of Representatives was to represent them. These are, of course, also the assumptions of other federal states such as West Germany or Switzerland. There has also been the assumption that the Senate would represent a somewhat different class of people than the more popularly elected House, or, even more generally, that it would protect the interests of minorities against the tyranny of the majority. These theoretical justifications for two houses were eroded by the change to the direct election of Senators. Still, the existence of two houses and the longer terms and broader views associated with the Senate have tended to make majority tyranny, or better, unconsidered and rash moves, less likely.

The two-year terms of members of the House keeps them in close touch with their constituencies. In earlier years, unequal district size tended to favor certain areas, particularly rural, in the allotment of House seats. But in recent years court decisions have mandated equal district sizes; today the representativeness of members of the House is perhaps more fully realized than at any time in our history. This is in marked contrast to the Senate, where the two Senators per state rule ensures that a small fraction of the U.S. population can dominate the choice of Senators.

The ability of the House to reflect the feelings and interests of constituents is reduced by the ignorance of most voters of the policy positions of their representatives on most, or even any, issues. Nevertheless, members of the House go to great efforts to try to mirror the opinions and attitudes of constituents, and on domestic issues they largely succeed. The change from the concept that a representative was chosen because the people trusted him to the concept that he was chosen to represent their views in Congress has been greatly affected by changes in communication and transportation that make conceivable a more accurate and timely relation of representative and constituent, and by public and private polls that make it easier for representatives to know what their constituents are thinking.

It is should be added that in this process representatives take into account both the strength of a position and its distribution. Since their objective is reelection, they may respond to small pressure groups that they feel will work hard for or against them more than the much larger but electorally more passive group of average voters. This ability to reflect intensity of positions as well as their nature should perhaps be accepted as a desirable aspect of democracy frequently missed in the one-man, one-vote analysis.

Compared to legislatures in other democracies the power of the American Congress is considerably greater. This power derives from the Constitutional powers granted Congress and from traditions that have developed around Congress and Congressmen. Congressional power is also the result of the size and competence of the staffs of individual Congressmen and Congressional committees. Only in the United States is the legislature adequately equipped to carry its legislative load vis-a-vis the executive.[6] The independence of Congressmen of whatever party has meant that their control by party leaders or an administration in power—even when of the same party—can never be taken for granted. Congress' ability to question and even refuse to confirm appointments for executive and judicial positions has denied many administrations the ability to sharply define its policy directions. Leading Congressmen frequently become public leaders on particular issues of interest to them, and may become so irrespective of party or the relation of their positions to those of the government. While in theory the veto power gives the President special powers to overcome the opposition of Congress, this power must be used sparingly. Most administrations would choose to avoid the danger of a veto being overriden by Congress; in addition, since the government will have to work with Congress on many pieces of legislation, using a veto to deny the will of Congress on one issue may turn out to be a Pyrrhic victory.

The Supreme Court is the pinnacle of a complex federal, state, and local court system. Although the system is not highly unified, and decisions of one court are not automatically reflected in all courts, there is still a sense in which the Supreme Court defines the system as a whole. The addition to the American Constitution of a Bill of Rights, and the later extension of its coverage to the acts of the states as well as the federal government, has given a special flavor to the sense that the Supreme Court stands as the ultimate guarantor of the rule of law and American liberties.

The ability of the Court to question and overturn laws in terms of their congruence with the basic rules of the Constitution as these have been interpreted by previous Courts has tended to diminish Congress' ability to legislate and the President's to administrate. This power of judicial review protects the rights of individuals that may be transgressed by the decisions of the majority or their representatives **and** reduces the extent to which the democracy represents the contemporary will of the people. In both ways the courts introduce another aspect of aristocratic or oligarchic rule into the system.

It is true that Supreme Court justices are appointed by popularly elected Presidents and are confirmed by popularly elected Congressmen. However, justices and other federal judges are appointed for life. Therefore, by the time a group of justices confer on a particular case they are far removed from public control and the sense of any public mandate. As the ancient Greeks thought that any elected system of representatives was aristocratic, they would surely see little in common between our Supreme Courts' right of judicial review and democracy. Athenian "judicial review" was by citizens chosen by lot.

The American concept of limited government, exemplified in the division of powers between the branches of government and the right of judicial review, suggests that our democracy is "democracy over time," and so represents the "will of the people" over time rather than the day-to-day beliefs and desires of majorities. In the long run court rulings are always reversible. If the people in their considered judgment elect representatives and presidents that are no longer in sympathy with past court rulings, then their appointments and confirmations should lead to a gradual and long-term shift in the character of court decisions.

The American system constitutionally grants residual powers to the constituent states of the union. The states, in turn, grant powers to the cities, towns, counties, townships, and other administrative districts. While these other units do not have separate rights to existence, as shown in recent years by some city-county mergers, many political units at local levels are so entrenched that neither state nor federal governments are likely to suppress them.

The powers of states and cities are considerable both because of law and because such units have representatives in Congress that will fight any attempts to infringe on their rights. This is one reason why the emphasis on geographical rather than ideological representation in our system serves to preserve the pluralistic nature of our institutions, with the dispersion of power that this entails.

Federal actions such as the Civil War, the pressure for conformity against Mormon Utah, the Voters Rights Act, and the mandated "busing" for many cities have proved the ability of the federal government to overcome the resistance of state and local authorities in certain instances. Nevertheless, in a broad area of social legislation, and recently in environmental legislation, a great deal of freedom has been achieved below the federal level. To a significant degree, the differences in the quality of state and local government, and in the nature of legislation at these levels, reflect real and enduring cultural differences within the country.[7]

While a federal and dispersed structure may protect the interests of minorities in so far as they are geographically able to dominate particular areas—as Mormons in Utah or Japanese in

Hawaii—it does less for the individual or powerless group that stands in danger of oppression by local or state authorities. In this case it is important that the federal government, through its administrative or judicial powers, can step in to defend these threatened rights. Certainly American Indians in South Dakota or blacks in Mississippi have had to look to the federal government for support against local majorities. The universal problem of the greater disinterestedness of power at a distance may be handled better in the United States than in most democracies because of its complex division of power.

Although there is no significant difference in the extent of citizens' participation on national and local levels, ordinary citizens may have a greater sense of competence when faced with local issues. In this sense the average voter may be more willing to think that his opinion is important, and therefore that his vote is well informed in this arena. One of the most discouraging aspects of American democracy is surely the size of the country and the complexity of its national and international affairs. This is one possible cause for the relatively low rate of participation by Americans in all politics. The strength of local democratic institutions must surely play a part in ameliorating this condition.

In **civil liberties** the United States has stood for very high standards. Although the practice has often not been up to its standards, American practice has generally been remarkably liberal. It has been many years since prior censorship was an issue in the United States. The **Pentagon Papers** case in 1971 illustrates the length to which the American courts will go in their attempt to protect freedom of the press.[8] In this case the government tried to prevent the **New York Times** from publishing selections from a voluminous Pentagon study of the history of the Vietnam War that had been classified <u>secret</u>. The Supreme Court ruled that the government had not proved that publishing the study would substantially hurt the national interest, thereby reenforcing the presumption that Pentagon classified papers could not automatically be considered to be legally secret in spite of their classification. Similarly, the Supreme Court has ruled unconstitutional attempts by the Post Office department to interfere in any way with the distribution of materials it considers offensive or subversive.

As might be expected, American courts are particularly concerned with defending the interests of the courts. They are restrictive when it involves holding back or publishing evidence relating to a crime or a trial, but quite willing to limit the rights of a journalist to withhold or reveal information. Still, these issues have not had serious implications for the restriction of policy or political discourse.

American courts have been much more reluctant than those of other democracies to convict people for libel, particularly when the offending statement has been directed toward public figures. While generally more liberal than the public at large, the courts have only in recent years become relatively unrestrictive in regard to obscenity as well. Even obscenity used as a part of political protest has tended to be considered a legitimate form of expression. While speech that incites a breach of the peace is not protected, the danger has to be very direct and obvious for a successful case to be made on this basis against free expression.[9]

American democracy accepts the right of demonstrators to directly or indirectly interfere with the rights of others. Blocking traffic, for example, can be costly and irritating. Permits for demonstrations are often required, but on public lands they are seldom denied. Arrests of demonstrators for which the police cannot produce adequate evidence of their breaking a law other than the police request to disperse can be costly—juries have awarded demonstrators as much as $12,000,000 for false arrest.[10]

The right of association has become an important subsidiary right to that of expression and demonstration. For many years it was assumed, that this right did not include the right for an organization to be formed for the purpose of overthrowing the government of the United States. On the basis of this exception the Communist Party, and parties with analogous objectives, were for a time outlawed. In this regard the American system became less tolerant than other traditional democracies. However, the Communist Party has for some years been readmitted to the American political spectrum, on condition, in effect, that its advocacy of violent revolution remains abstract. This does not exempt from sanctions groups, such as the Weathermen on the left or the Aryan Nation on the right, that have been explicitly involved in violence. Nor is there a constitutional right to organize a criminal organization such as the Mafia or Cosa Nostra.

American business and labor are freer to organize and manage their own affairs than is true in most democracies. However, this very freedom has led to internal hegemonies that deny freedom to the average worker within the units of American society. The monopoly power of some business and labor organizations or arrangements, separately or in tandem, may be used to deny other aspects of the democratic rights of individuals.

The separation of church and state was an American innovation. In terms of democracy its most important effect was perhaps that citizens who did not believe in an established religion supported by the state, as was the European practice, were freed of the use of their taxes for something they did not believe in. Much of the concern with the separation of church and state in the United States is otherwise unconnected with civil liberties, and may even be said to have unnecessarily restricted the right of majorities to use the state for their purposes.

The most onerous restrictions on civil liberties in the United States are those that relate to movement in and out of the country. While it is not a denial of American civil liberties to restrict entry into the country, it surely would be a denial of rights to prohibit citizens from leaving the country. In general this right has not been denied. But it has been infringed by the placing of specific prohibitions on visiting certain foreign countries, generally communist countries such as Cuba. Turning the same laws around to prevent particular individuals, again generally communists or communist sympathizers, from coming into the country has been used to deny American groups the right to hear particular individuals speak to them. Arguably, this is an indirect infringement of the right to Freedom of Speech of American citizens.

Many observers consider that the United States does not have the civil liberties of some other democracies because there is not the degree of equality in standards of living, levels of education, infant mortality, or other social statistics that would indicate that the several peoples or classes of the country are being given equal rights. However, with the removal of the more obvious legal disabilities, and without proof of specific discriminations, the subject has entered the realm of political decision and coalition politics that is no longer best dealt with by the application of the rights concepts of elite jurists. Comparative statistics by themselves do not prove lack of rights, for we do not know what the averages and ranges for individuals and groups would be in a population with equivalent characteristics but without the alleged discrimination.

NOTES

1. Arend Lijphart, **Democracies: Patterns of Majoritarian and Consensus Government in Twenty-One Countries** (New Haven: Yale University Press, 1984).

2. Richard Rose, **Politics in England: An Interpretation for the 1980s** (Boston: Little, Brown, 1980), pages 270-274 and passim.

3. Paul Kleppner, et al., **The Evolution of American Electoral Systems** (Westport: Greenwood Press, 1981), pages 165-169.

2. William Ebenstein, et al., **American Democracy in World Perspective** 4th edition (New York: Harper and Row, 1976), pages 176-177.

3. Samuel Huntington, **American Politics: The Promise of Disharmony** (Cambridge: Harvard University Press, 1981).

4. See Joseph LaPalombara, **Politics Within Nations** (Englewood Cliffs: Prentice-Hall, 1974), pages 370-419.

5. Much of the following discussion is based on Robert A. Dahl, **Democracy in the United States: Promise and Performance** 3rd. edition (Chicago: Rand McNally, 1976).

6. J. Blondel, **Comparative Legislatures** (Englewood Cliffs: Prentice-Hall, 1973).

7. See R. D. Gastil, **Cultural Regions of the United States** (Seattle: University of Washington Press, 1976).

8. Ebenstein et al., page 148.

9. See also Daniel C. Kramer, **Comparative Civil Rights and Liberties** (Washington: University Press of America, 1982), pages 33-38.

10. Ebenstein et al., page 161.

Comparing Democracy in India and Japan

Taken together, India and Japan form the key to understanding the possibilities for democracy in the nonwestern world. The fate of democracy in the next generation will be in large part dependent on what occurs in these countries. On the surface, India and Japan appear very different, yet in many ways their similarities are more important than people of either culture realize.

While both are democracies, their conditions of life, political cultures, and national values are strikingly different. India suffers from widespread poverty and illiteracy. While it has a large modern sector, the bulk of its population is traditional and "third-world." In many ways Japanese society and life are hypermodern, its people enjoy a relatively comfortable living standard, and are highly literate. Yet it is well to remember that the Buddhist culture that conquered Japan in the Middle Ages came from India, and the holy language for many Japanese priests remains Sanskrit. Japan is a highly unified, insular society. India, on the other hand, was until recently a geographical term covering a multitude of peoples from different races, ethnic backgrounds, and religions. It is perhaps symbolic of both the differences and the ties that bind the two societies that the only major caste division in Japan, that between the vast majority and the Burakimin, is based on downgrading people handling meat and dead carcasses, a prejudice that came to Japan with Buddhism.

A significant difference between these political systems is reflected in the different attitudes of governmental elites toward business and businessmen.[1] Since long before the war, Japanese governmental and business administrative classes have been closely interwoven, and the purposes and goals of both have been seen as almost indistinguishable. Whether government controls business or business controls government is a fine question: the personnel and purposes of both are not highly distinct. Such questions are unlikely to arise in India, where government has tended to see private business as existing only on suffrage. While Indian leaders may talk more socialism than they actually introduce, government elites do assume their superiority, morally and technically, over private businessmen. Indian politicians and bureaucrats are much more likely than Japanese to see the problem of society as the division of scarce resources rather than the rapid creation of new resources. The problems of India since World War II have been feeding, housing, and providing basic education and medical care for its citizens, while ensuring a fragile stability in the relations between hostile classes, castes, and tribes. Those of Japan have been promoting rapid economic progress through intensifying efficiency and trade without evoking foreign reprisals for its success.

The Indian political system is based on the long experience of the Indian people, and especially their educated elite, with the English parliamentary system (the Westminster model), and borrowings from Canadian, Irish, and American systems, as these have been adapted to the particular requirements of the Indian geographical and cultural situation.[2] The Indian parliamentary system reflects this mixed parentage. India's long, written constitution gives form to a federal republic, with the twenty-two major states enjoying reserved powers, and operating parliamentary systems modeled in most respects on the national system.

The two houses of parliament are the Council of States and the House of the People. The Council of States, analogous to our Senate, particularly before 1900, is not subject to dissolution. All but twelve of its members are elected proportionally by the state legislatures, with one-third elected every two years. The remaining Senators are nominated by the president. The House of the People is directly elected from single-member constituencies in the states and territories. The states are ruled analogously, although most have only unicameral legislatures. As chief executive the prime minister is chosen by parliament. The official head of state is a relatively powerless president elected for five years by an electoral college consisting of the houses of parliament and the state legislatures—in practice he is generally chosen by the prime minister. The Supreme Court functions much as in our country. However, the tenure of judges is not as secure: they serve to age 65, and it is easier for them to be removed.

The division of powers between the several states and the central government is in theory not too different from that in the

United States. There are both federal and state judicial systems, with priority given to the federal. As in the United States, control over police, public health, and education are primarily under state control. An important difference is that many of the twenty-two states represent important linguistic or other ethnic subdivisions of the country. As such, they are quite likely to insist on different cultural policies. Many are also very large, with populations greater than those of major European countries. Many must be considered as candidates for future independence in a sense that is true for few if any states in federal systems such as the United States or Australia. While separatism has remained a minor concern in regard to the major states, persistent attempts of smaller peoples at the fringes of Indian society to achieve independence, or at least separate statehood, has been met with a mixture of compromise and repression. Government reactions have reflected the persistent fear that the country might unravel if concessions to such peoples were too easily made or generous.

Federalism is diluted by two factors. First, the "union territories" and New Delhi itself are directly administered by the central government. More important, the central government has interfered repeatedly in the affairs of the constituent states. This interference may be merely that of a ruling prime minister changing the lineup of candidates nationally or locally within his own party. But it has also involved forcing new elections on recalcitrant states, and intervening to set aside the ruling state government in "emergencies" that on occasion have been partially of the government's own making. Some interventions, such as those in Assam and the Punjab have been justified to contain the violent political struggles that have occurred, but in other cases, such as Kashmir, they seem to have been simple power plays by the ruling Congress party.

Such threats to federalism have not gone unchallenged. Bengal, for example, has for many years managed to preserve an independent state government. In 1984 an attempt by the central government to overturn an opposition government in the southern state of Andhra Pradesh was successfully turned back. The new Prime Minister, Rajiv Gandhi, seems prepared to abandon some of the more high-handed efforts of past governments to assert the dominance of the federal government.

Perhaps the greatest achievement of the Indian democratic system has been its ability, in spite of a number of external and internal violent conflicts requiring military force, to maintain the tradition of civilian, and thus democratic, control over the armed services.

The party structure is both complex and simple. It is relatively simple in that one party, Congress, has formed all cabinets in post-independence India except for a few years in the 1970s. For nearly all of this period Congress has been under the control of members of the same family. It is complex in that there has long been a large number of significant parties, with regional, class, religious, or nationwide objectives, and varying degrees of cooperation among these parties and with Congress.

In spite of the apparent continuity of Congress rule, two periods of Congress rule should be distinguished. The first, lasting until about 1970, was based on an alliance of regional and ideological factions that came through the independence struggle together. Although national in scope, well-organized, and effective at all levels of society, the factions did not add up to a highly disciplined party in the British or European sense. In this they resembled the factions of the Liberal Party that ruled Japan during the same period. However, with the rise of Indira Gandhi, recurring defections of old party bosses and recurrent attempts by the prime minister to instill discipline led the factions to become different parties using the Congress label (such as Mrs. Gandhi's Congress[I]). The subsequent success of Mrs. Gandhi in overcoming these defections led to a much more tightly disciplined Congress Party in which state leaders can be changed almost at will. This is the Congress Party inherited by the current Prime Minister, Rajiv Gandhi.

Continued success of the Congress Party under the Gandhis did not mean that the Party received overwhelming endorsement at the polls. The typical outcome was for the Congress party to receive less than forty-five percent of the votes; because of the splintering of the opposition, this was sufficient to give it a comfortable majority of parliamentary seats. In December 1984, following an outpouring of national sympathy for the family in the wake of Mrs. Gandhi's murder, Congress received just over fifty percent of the votes, the largest total yet received—and one that subsequent state elections suggested would not be soon repeated.

Formed in 1885, the Congress Party of India is unmatched in the underdeveloped world in longevity, and probably in size and organization.[3] For this reason the single-member parliamentary districts of India have not produced a two-party system. The other parties have been too weak, and have appealed to too limited sectors of society (regionally or socially), to mount an effective challenge. When they were able to unite, in a common crusade against the arbitrary rule of Mrs. Gandhi in the mid-seventies, they won easily—only to fall apart quickly as the disparate elements of this coalition tried to rule together. Opposition party activity has been characterized by extreme fluidity, with individuals frequently changing their affiliations, often after elections. But certain main party groupings can be identified. Parties on the left have included moderate socialists, and at least two communist groupings. Communists have been particularly successful in Bengal, Kerala, and border areas. Most communists have not taken a revolutionary stance, and so have been at least the equivalent of Eurocommunists. On the right, Hindu parties, some with extremist tendencies, have attracted many votes, while more free enterprise and small farmer groups have been active toward the middle. Support or opposition to particular castes or religious groups has often characterized the appeal, or disappeal, of these parties. Congress' record of support for minorities of all kinds, including the Harijans (formerly untouchables) and Muslims has generally stood them in good stead with the majority of voters.

The most effective non-Congress parties often have been local parties with appeals to a particular linguistic or religious group. These parties have become especially strong in the Dravidian south, where they have not had the effect of supporting separatist tendencies as might be feared. The most recent example of such a party achieving success has been the Akali Dal Party, representing the Sikhs of the Punjab.

The ease with which the government was defeated in 1977, and the complexity of the results, would argue for an overall fairness in the election process. Nevertheless, there have been many accusations against the fairness of elections. Although in theory what can be spent in campaigns is strictly limited, restrictive laws are easily evaded. As in America many groups are said to give money to all sides, but particularly to winners, to preserve their special privileges. For example, the establishment of election rolls offers an opportunity for cheating. While election rolls have consistently shown an increase in the number eligible to vote in most districts, suspicious declines in some areas have remained unexplained. The polling process can be manipulated by those in charge to affect the results. This can be done by the location of the polling places, by slowing down the processing of voters in certain areas, by using supporters of one candidate to make abnormally long lines, or even by driving voters away, or "capturing" a polling station and forcing votes for a particular candidate to be inscribed. Young people may be given false identities and brought to vote before the real voters have a chance to vote. Candidates can be paid to run artificial campaigns in order to split a particular community's vote. More insidious is the mass hiring of campaign workers, a practice that can escalate to the point where in a very poor country people can be said to have been paid for their votes.[4]

Political scientists have commonly supposed that societies with great disparities in income, and with markedly depressed classes making up large proportions of the population would find it hard to make democracy function satisfactorily. It is generally assumed that apparently functioning democratic institutions in such an environment are actually a facade for continued oppression of the many by the few. However, studies of the development of Indian political parties and of elections occurring in India over the last generation should give pause to all who make such generalizations. Indians at all economic levels have become politically organized and politically conscious from an early date: compared to the generality of democratic countries, Indian voters are active and relatively knowledgeable participants in electoral processes.[5]

Many observers have commented on the extent to which Indian people of all classes reacted negatively to the imposition of emergency decrees in the mid-1970s by Mrs. Gandhi that took away civil liberties to which they had become accustomed. The result was a massive defeat for the Congress Party in the 1977 election, an election fought almost exclusively on the single issue of preserving democracy and rights (although for some the "rights" protected were social rights such as not to be sterilized).[6]

The 1980 parliamentary elections followed in many ways the script of previous elections. While national trends affected nearly every state and territory, there were regional and local explanations for the particular association of groups with one or another party. The most important determinants of the "boundaries" of these groups were class and caste, religious affiliation, or ethnic and linguistic identity. While ideology may have been particularly important only to elite party leaders, nevertheless, many groups can be clearly shown to have voted their interests as they understood them.[7]

The scheduled castes (Harijans), scheduled tribes (poor, largely non-Hindu peoples living at the fringes of society without states of their own), and Muslims make up about one-third of the electorate. In 1980 they shifted back to their traditional identification with the more secular and mildly leftist Congress(I), which they see as protecting them against both the excesses of religious Hindus and the greater emphasis on property of more propertied parties. The "backward castes" (those castes that most resent affirmative government action in favor of the "scheduled" groups) cemented their identification with the new Lok Dal party representing the interests of small, rural, landed farmers against both the poorer classes and the upper classes and castes.

In the December 1984 election these trends toward Congress were confirmed. There is also faith in the son's moderation and a more general tendency to abandon the strictly Hindu parties in favor of Congress(I). In the Punjab and Assam the election had to be postponed because of recent or threatened violence, but nevertheless 375,000,000 people voted (63 percent of the potential electorate) for 5,300 candidates. Repolling was ordered for 200 polling stations, mostly for booth capturing.[8] The state elections a few months later showed a resurgence of the strength of "regional parties"—or parties that performed especially well on the regional level.[9] This trend was continued later in the year when the Akali Dal, a Sikh communal party, took control of the Punjab handily in that state's much postponed elections.[10]

The federal system has gone some way toward satisfying the desire for self-determination of the peoples that make up India, but it has not satisfied, nor is it likely ever to satisfy, the desires of all Indian peoples. The State of Kashmir is populated by a Muslim majority that probably would vote to join Pakistan or secede, if ever given the choice. The people of Sikkim and Goa, small states more or less forcibly incorporated into India may, at least in part, desire to rule themselves. Mizo, Naga, and other tribal peoples of the Northeast have struggled to free themselves from Indian rule. Certainly some Sikhs desire a separate Khalistan. The fact that only about thirty percent of Indian people speak the most common language, Hindi, and the general lingua franca, English, is being replaced in many government schools by regional languages suggests the danger many Indians see in yielding further to fissiparous tendencies. (However, the demand for private-school English is increasing.) To this point, it would appear that India's imperfect but expanding federal system represents the best available compromise between meeting the demands for self-determination of its many peoples and the desire of most Indians to maintain the integrity of the country.

The level of **civil liberties** in India resembles that in the United States in its early years. The basis is a similar Bill of Rights, although in general the judiciary is not as independent as in the United States, a deficiency particularly apparent in the Emergency period.[11]

In theory Indians have freedom of speech. However, the complete control of radio and television by the government places a great burden on any who would rate India's media freedom highly, especially when a large proportion of the Indian electorate remains illiterate.[12] The broadcast media, operating as part of the Ministry of Information, have come to be seen as mouthpieces of the government. No doubt this control has a pro-government effect at election time.[13]

The Indian press, on the other hand, is free and varied, and has recently been augmented by a number of important journals of news and opinion. Often noted more for their passivity, the print media have begun to develop a more aggressive and investigative journalism. Papers and journalists have not been prosecuted for their expression of opinion, but fear of government sanctions has led to self-censorship. Government influence on the channels by which papers receive their news is also restrictive: aside from the news services, many small papers receive their news from readings on All India Radio.

As in most societies the government can limit speech in the interest of public order. Occasionally abused, this government option has generally been taken with great reluctance. The communist parties of India have tended to be relatively mild in their assertions of a right to revolution, and in turn they have been allowed to compete quite openly, as in most of western Europe. This has not been the case for the more violent Naxalites, or for peoples in the Northeast striving for independence, such as the Nagas. Reaction here is more in line with the common Indian practice of detention, usually for short periods, of anyone who threatens public order. Except during the "Emergency" this has generally been under judicial control.

Possibly because of the tradition of the independence movement and the fact that the printed word does not reach many Indians, political and policy struggles in India tend to be fought out in the streets through the organization of massive demonstrations. This is a treasured right, but one that is accompanied by the threat of violence, often ending in violent confrontation with the security forces and massive detentions of those involved, with numbers sometimes running into the tens of thousands. Acceptance of detention seems almost to be part of the demonstration in many cases.

However, in one period the Indian government clearly went too far. The Emergency, declared in June 1975, led to detention for thousands, the banning of twenty-six extremist groups, and stringent controls on the press. It became illegal to publish anything defamatory about a long list of government officials, even in parliament.[14] The Emergency legislation bears some analogy to the sedition law passed by the U.S. Congress in 1798. Although it was little used, the sedition law also reduced the ability of the opposition to criticize the system, and also helped the opposition to subsequent victory and the revocation of the law after 1800. But Indian law remains even today more like that of the United Kingdom or the European democracies in its restrictions on the right to attack public officials verbally, especially judges. Prosecutions for criticizing public officials are frequent.

India, especially in the guise of the Congress Party, prides itself on being a secular state; it has enshrined separation of church and state and freedom of religion in the political system. This is especially important where hundreds or more are killed every year in religious riots. But in the Indian form this has meant that the government has taken it upon itself to ban religious practices not according with its image of modern society, such as animal sacrifice and dedicating virgins to a temple. For a social religion such as Hinduism based on concepts of inherited purity and religious distinctions among castes, forbidding untouchability has required an important government-imposed change in religious practices and beliefs. The government requires accessibility by all Hindus to Hindu temples, except for a few occasions, and has given itself the right to interfere with the management of temple properties.

On the other hand, the fact that the overwhelming number of Indians are still Hindus, at least socially, and highly nationalist has led to restrictions on non-Hindu religions. In particular, Christian missionaries have been reduced in number and effectiveness over a number of years. In part this has been to satisfy those Hindu and Muslim conservatives who see them as a threat. The identification of Christian missionaries with marginal peoples, such as the Nagas in the Northeast, and the subsequent independence movements in these areas have led some Hindus to see missionary activity as little short of traitorous. Some states have passed laws, sustained by the Supreme Court, making it difficult to convert persons to any religion. (Hinduism is not a proselytizing religion in theory—in spite of what Americans may see at their airports.) In another direction, bans on the slaughter of cows, enacted because of the pressure of conservative Hindus, have been felt as onerous by Muslims for which such slaughter is traditional, particularly for certain ceremonies. At one time the government attempted to reduce the ability of Muslims to control "their" university, Aligarh, an effort supported by the Supreme Court on the basis of specious and biased logic.[15] This effort was later abandoned for political reasons. State governments, particularly the Communist government in Kerala, have interfered with running schools that were under religious auspices. Commonly, the approach has been similar to that in the United States: religious instruction is banned in schools supported wholly by the state; however, there has not been interference with nondenominational prayer.

The extreme disabilities of the Harijans in India have been greatly lessened by the government, although on a village level they continue to a considerable extent. Most important have been the reserved positions in universities and government services, as well as free books for Harijan students. This "affirmative action" has been extended to scheduled tribes as well. As a result the upper castes and the middle castes ("backward castes") have campaigned, sometimes violently, for curtailment or elimination of these privileges—or for compensating privileges for their own groups. In addition, these measures have led, as in the United States, to litigation, for while they may help some groups, they hurt others, and so deny justice in the search for justice.

In theory the Indian system guarantees a fair trial on much the same basis as American law—the accused is innocent until proven guilty, there is a right of habeas corpus, confessions are only accepted under strict conditions, and free lawyers are to be provided to the poor. However, practice is rather different: preventive detention is often found to be indefinitely extended—some individuals have been forgotten in the system. Even for the indicted, trials are often delayed indefinitely.

The behavior of the police has been a major civil liberties problem made more difficult by state control over police. In many cases the police have been justly accused of extreme cruelty, or of partiality toward or against certain groups, such as the Harijans, especially in Bihar. Suppression of the Naxalite rebellion also led to excesses by security forces. This problem is closely related to the problem of group hatred and communal violence between groups, whether religious sects or castes. Large numbers are killed annually by communal violence. As an example, thousands of Sikhs may have been killed after the murder of Mrs. Gandhi, while hundreds more Sikhs were killed in recent years in the Punjab as the result of fighting among rival factions. Near Bombay recently murderous clashes have again developed between Muslims and Hindus, while in Assam hundreds of Bengalis have been cut down by the local Assamese or tribal peoples that consider their lives or way of life threatened. From the viewpoint of political freedom, the major problem is the implanting of fear in the lives of many, making them unwilling to act in their own interest or express their opinions for fear of raising the hatreds of others.[16] In many ways some Indians live in a climate of hate and fear reminiscent of parts of the American South in earlier generations. This problem cannot be laid squarely at the feet of the national government, but it is a problem for the effective functioning of a democratic system.

Although **Japan** is today one of the largest and most powerful democracies in the world, its special culture and background cause analysts to be reserved in describing the country unequivocally as a democracy in the western sense. On the surface its institutions are democratic; they function efficiently and effectively. And yet the unchanging nature of the internal power balance in the post-war period, and its small, highly centralized elite structure lead many to question the depth of Japan's adherence to democracy.

Japan's history is one of change and continuity, of eager adoption of techniques and ideas from others without abandoning the special personality of the society. In modern times change was forced on Japan by western navies in the middle of the nineteenth century. Japanese leaders, sensing that the only way to preserve Japanese independence was to incorporate much of western culture, set out to transform the feudal society from the top down. The society was rapidly and thoroughly educated, and western institutions were rapidly adopted, including democratic forms of constitutional monarchy. By the 1920s Japan had a functioning democratic system comparable to many in the West. However, the changing spirit of the early thirties fostered a kind of fascism, based essentially on the unwillingness of military leaders to accept civilian leadership other than the Emperor.

Democracy was recreated by the United States in Japan after World War II much as it was recreated in West Germany—however, the continuing presence of the Emperor gave Japan a much greater sense of continuity. The system features a bicameral legislature. Although both houses are elected, the lower house is more powerful, as in most parliamentary systems. The state is essentially unitary: local and regional officials are elected, but power is not significantly diffused among the several levels of government. In theory there is a division of power among the branches of government: in fact the executive, made up of the leaders of the dominant party, has the dominant power. The courts have the power of judicial review, which they have exercised. However, their edicts (such as those on malapportionment or the illegality of the self-defense forces) have frequently not been accepted as binding, nor has the court been anxious that they should be so regarded.

Since the mid-1950s the political scene has been dominated by the Liberal Democratic Party (LDP), which in turn is an amalgam of factions of the center-right. The party strengths of Socialists, Social Democrats, Communists, and others to the left have fluctuated relatively little. These groups have never posed a threat.

The Komeito party of the Sokka Gakkai religious movement continues to gain adherents, but its sympathies are unlikely to lie with other parties of the opposition.

For these reasons, although the Liberals barely manage with the help of a few allies to maintain majorities in the two houses, the real political action in the country seems to lie in the power struggles among the personalist or clientelist factions of the Liberal Party. These struggles are often fought out at the polls as well—a result that has led the Liberals in the last few years to hold national primaries for the Liberal Democratic Party.

LDP factions operate in many ways like separate political parties. They campaign against one another for representation from the multimember districts—some as party endorsed candidates, and some as quasi-independents. Factions are not distinguished primarily by ideology or policy, but rather by fealty to the factional leader. The death or retirement of a factional leader leads necessarily to either the demise of the faction or the complete restructuring of the faction around another individual.[17]

In sharp contrast to India, in Japan businessmen are held in high esteem. Their influence on politics is often pictured as decisive—although it might be better to speak of a corporatist interweaving of business and government.[18] Shortly after the war there was a chance that worker organizations might be able to play a decisive part in the Japanese political system,[19] but this challenge was soon put aside; a powerful labor party, able to share power as in many democracies, has never emerged. Japanese businessmen exert their power through their domination of the Liberal Party.

One reason for the continued success of the business-bureaucrat-party structure in Japan is the importance of money in the operation of the political system. A political leader is expected to be able to care for his people, either through obtaining necessary government help or through direct and obvious contributions to their welfare. Therefore, campaign expenses, which include a great deal of partying at the expense of candidates, are only a part of the expense of proving to the voter that a candidate has the social and financial ability to care adequately for his constituency. At a higher level, the Japanese voter seems relatively unconcerned by major bribery scandals that would destroy the reputations of politicians in most democracies.

They accept as part of the natural order the need of politicians to amass large amounts of money to meet their responsibilities, and likewise the right of those with high position to use their position to obtain these resources.[20]

"Japan Incorporated" is best thought of as a giant conglomerate whose employees are content to allow the board members to reap great rewards and decide on policy as long as they are convinced that ultimately all are working for the company. This produces a different political atmosphere in which Euro-American or even Indian concepts of political right and wrong begin to seem irrelevant. Political equality and strict legality are less important than maintaining the confidence of followers in leaders, at a variety of levels. The continued economic success, and ability to spread the effects of that success over the bulk of the population account in this view for the unbroken success of the Liberal Party.

Even given this quite different context, a serious defect in the democratic system of Japan remains the malapportionment of voter districts, an issue particularly for the lower house. Some rural districts, where Liberals are strong, may have as few as one-fifth the number of voters that the largest districts have. The courts have ruled that the apportionment was manifestly unfair—but sanctions have not yet forced a change. When reapportionment comes, it is likely to still fall far short of one man, one vote.

The press and radio of Japan are not known for their harsh criticism. Yet the print media are perhaps the most informative, serious, and widely read in the world. Public and private broadcasting systems for both radio and television are highly developed. The Japanese people may well be the best informed in the world, which is certainly an important criterion for effective democracy. While a high percentage of Indians remain illiterate and underfed, very few in Japan suffer from either of these constraints on effective citizenship.

In contrast to the frequent accusations of cruelty and favoritism made against the Indian police, those of Japan are pictured as models of good and efficient behavior. Yet in the American sense the Japanese may not have the protection of the law that we enjoy (and pay for). The Japanese characteristically avoid turning to the courts to resolve disputes. With few lawyers, the Japanese believe that rights are better protected by recourse to mediation and consultation. While this seems more likely to preserve the public peace and to achieve a non-zero sum justice, it is also more likely than standard judicial processes to be open to behind-the-scenes pressures from current power holders in the community. In this sense it is subject to the same tendencies that have been alleged to characterize small-town justice in the United States.

NOTES

1. On this issue compare Chitoshi Yanaga, **Big Business in Japanese Politics** (New Haven: Yale University Press, 1968), and Stanley Kochanek, **Business and Politics in India** (Berkeley: University of California Press, 1974).

2. For a summary of the Indian political system see **Encyclopedia Britannica** (Chicago: Encyclopedia Britannica, 1985), pp. 19,18. More generally compare Vera Micheles Dean, **New Patterns of Democracy in India,** 2nd Edition (Cambridge: Harvard University Press, 1969), and Weiner cited below.

3. See Crawford Young, **The Politics of Cultural Pluralism** (Madison: University of Wisconsin Press, 1976), pages 308-326.

4. This discussion is based on Myron Weiner, **India at the Polls: A Study of the Parliamentary Elections** (Washington: American Enterprise Institute, 1983).

5. Compare Lloyd I. and Suzanne H. Rudolph, **The Modernity of Tradition: Political Development in India** (Chicago: University of Chicago Press, 1967). See also Myron Weiner, **Party Building in a New Nation: The Indian National Congress** (Chicago: University of Chicago Press, 1967), and Richard Sisson, **The Congress Party in Rajasthan** (Berkeley: University of California Press, 1972).

6. Weiner, **India at the Polls,** pages 3-12.

7. Weiner, **India at the Polls.**

8. **Keesing's Contemporary Archives,** 1985, pages 33460-33468.

9. **Economist** March 9, 1985; **Keesing's,** pages 33735-37.

10. **Economist,** October 5, 1985.

11. The following discussion is based largely on the relevant sections in Daniel C. Kramer, **Comparative Civil Rights and Liberties** (Washington: University Press of America, 1982). Kramer compares civil liberties in the United States, England, India, the Soviet Union, and France.

12. **Far Eastern Economic Review,** July 18, 1985, pages 36 forward presents a comprehensive review of the status of the Indian news and other media.

13. Compare the remarks on the December 1984 election in the **Far Eastern Economic Review,** January 10, 1985, page 22.

14. See Kramer, **Comparative Civil Rights and Liberties,** pp. 78-80.

15. Ibid., page 132.

16. Compare **Keesing's Contemporary Archives,** 1983-85.

17. See Nathaniel B. Thayer, **How the Conservatives Rule Japan** (Princeton: Princeton University Press, 1969).

18. See Yanaga, **Big Business in Japanese Politics.**

19. Joe Moore, **Japanese Workers and the Struggle for Power: 1945-47** (Madison: University of Wisconsin Press, 1983).

20. Thayer, **How the Conservatives Rule Japan.**

Mauritius: A Small
Third World Democracy

Political and civil liberties are weak in both the second and third
worlds. In the second world they are displaced by communist
ideology. In the third, their weakness results from a variety of
social, cultural, and economic factors.

Mauritius is the most democratic country in the African region.
The fact that the majority of its people are of non-African background, and its history quite different than that of the continental
states, makes the lessons of its democratic development less
applicable to Africa as a whole, but no less significant for understanding the problems of democracy in the developing world.

Lying well east of Madagascar, Mauritius has experienced the
isolation of many independent islands. An island entirely formed by
relatively recent volcanic activity, the topography of its 28-by-32
mile expanse is characterized by rolling plains interspersed by
steep, jagged, "young" mountains. Although rising barely over 2000
feet, many of these are bare and stark at their crests. The
climate varies from a moderately hot and humid coastal zone to a
somewhat cooler inland, with rainfall ranging from 40 inches to 200
in the wettest areas. Cyclones have always been a problem, and
even today restrict what agricultural crops may be successfully
grown.

When first encountered by European expeditions to the Indies,
Mauritius was entirely uninhabited, and its wildlife was both
special and quite limited. The flightless Dodo bird that could only
exist in the almost complete absence of mammals is, of course, the
best known. The island seemed anything but pleasant to its first
visitors. Sailors, they came of necessity; they quickly destroyed
much of the special fauna and decimated the forests. Aside from a
stop for food, water or wood, its chief virtue to the early visitors
was the absence of diseases, such as malaria or cholera, that
ravaged other tropical areas.[1]

The Dutch tried twice in the seventeenth century to build a
successful colony that would serve as a provisioning port on the

way to the Indies. Since by the early eighteenth century, the population had only reached 300, the colonists tried importing African slaves and growing sugar. They cut down most of the ebony. But convinced that settlements would never thrive, the island was abandoned in 1710. Twelve years later the French established a new colony, and after a desultory start began in the 1730s to develop the sugar and slave society that came to characterize the island. Even this was an an appendage of the French colonies in India, and its fortunes rose and fell with that of French India. The highly stratified and often cultured French colonial society quarreled with revolutionary France in the 1790s over its desire to suppress slavery. For a time almost independent, Mauritius was finally conquered by the British in 1810. The population of about 80,000 consisted overwhelmingly of African slaves.

The British conquest was marked by an agreement allowing the French to maintain their language and culture. As a result, although the official language became and remained English, and the public schools are taught in English, the most common language has been and remains French Creole; the language of culture and the newspapers is French. This entrenched bilingualism has stood the Mauritians in good stead in their effort to be accepted as a mediating people on the African continent.

Soon the British moved to suppress the slave trade, and finally slavery itself. By the late 1830s planters were forced to turn to importing indentured laborers from India. With the ending of slavery the African workers stayed in Mauritius, but preferred casual work and subsistence activities to continued work in the fields. Indians were brought in rapidly, and often worked in conditions little better than that of the slaves before them. By 1846 one-third of the population was Indian, and by 1870 two-thirds, a ratio maintained to this day. The elite French population stabilized at about 10,000, and has maintained its cultural and economic leadership without growth since. The island prospered in the middle of the nineteenth century, but subsequently the quality of life declined as tropical diseases such as malaria and cholera decimated the population.

Prosperity returned during World War I, and the development of the island was little interrupted by the worldwide depression of the 1930s.

Councils had been established as far back as the 1790s, and councils of the elite continued to play an important role throughout the nineteenth century. Early in the twentieth century Indian leaders brought the idea of popular rights to their large and by now stabilized communties. Followers of Gandhi started a newspaper, and pressed for improvements in living conditions. Indian workers achieved legal independence in the 1920s from the plantations on which they worked, and began to be paid by the day. Importation of indentured labour ceased. In reaction, some French colonialists pressed for the island's return to French control. Failure of this movement to attract support even in the French community confirmed the split between culture and politics that had characterized the society since 1810.

Educational and cultural movements among the Indians, and the general improvement in their position led to the first election of Indians to public office, and in the 1930s to the establishment of the Labour Party, largely supported by the Indian community. Education and working conditions continued to improve, but, as all communities became more conscious of their rights, demonstrations and riots also became more fequent.

The electorate remained small; national elections in 1945 were still open to only five percent of the population. The 1947 constitution extended suffrage to all those literate in any language, but the Legislative Council was still dominated by the colonial governor. The governor held most of the power, and, in addition, appointed many Council members.

New political parties were established in the fifties, representing the French and Creoles (Mauritian Social Democratic Party), as well as a Muslim bloc. The growing power of the Hindu majority to determine the future of the island led to general opposition by smaller groups both to universal suffrage and independence.

The mid-sixties witnessed an increasingly violent struggle between the opposing sides. But the British pressed ahead for full independence. The society they finally propelled into full independence in 1968 had deep ethnic divisions. But by now the country was also well on its way toward full literacy. Its nutritional and health standards were rapidly improving—which also meant at the time a very rapid rate of population increase. For a time population growth was seen as a critical problem. With little but sugar to sustain the economy, Mauritius during this period was often cited as an example of the demographic disaster that was overtaking much of the third world.

Although Mauritian society contained a wide variety of ethnic and religious communities, the primary division was along the lines of attachment to one of three imported cultural traditions—French, English, and Indian. Yet the overlap of the traditions was as important. Many Mauritians, including all of the better educated, were attached to more than one, if not all three, of these cultural worlds. Fortunately, the "homelands" for people ascribing to any of these three traditions had strong democratic traditions. The strength of these reenforcing attachments to democratic traditions, and the lack of a truly "native" tradition or culture set the problems and opportunities of Mauritius quite apart from those of much of the third world.

Each of the major ethnic divisions is again internally subdivided into quite different groups. Amounting to about thirty percent of the total, the "general population" includes the whites, primarily of French background, the coloureds, and the Africans (with the latter two groups collectively referred to as Creoles). The French maintain a high level of education and income, and still own the bulk of the sugar land on which the economy is based. The French government subsidizes an important high school, and a lively social life is maintained entirely within the 10,000 or so members of this community. Much larger is the mixed African-white, coloured, community. Many have become successful in professions such as teaching, the law, and the ministry, as well as the civil service. African Creoles tend to be darker, and to be commonly urban labourers or artisans. They are the most likely group to be monolingual in the Creole patois.

Representing about two-thirds of the population, people of Indian ancestry came as agricultural laborers, and still form the bulk of the agricultural and rural population. Some are Christians, but the majority of the population is either Hindu (three-fourths) or Muslim. The Indian community is further divided between non-Hindi speakers from the south of India (Tamil and Telegu) and the majority Hindi speakers, and between those of the different castes. While caste is less important in overseas Indian communities than at home, and the tight restrictions on contact characteristic of traditional India are not observed, there is conflict between the communities rhetorically and in politics. Differences between communities have also been exacerbated by the differentiation of Indians by occupation, with Muslims more likely to be urban merchants. In recent years the reluctance of the non-Hindu, non-Hindi-speaking groups to support the majority community has threatened to erase Indian dominance in politics. Indian dominance has also been diluted by the growth in the number of people with Indian background who now report that they speak Creole rather than an Indian language in the home.

There are about twice as many Chinese as Europeans, and they have traditionally dominated retail and wholesale trade, particularly in the capital city. Highly educated, they have also risen in the civil service and the professions, but remained outside of politics. To this older population should perhaps be added the small group of wealthy entrepreneurs and managers that have recently arrived from the Far East to establish textile industries.

Rural and urban populations are ethnically quite different, with the countryside overwhelmingly Hindu. But the smallness of the island, and the closeness of its interlocking urban areas, has combined with the absence of ethnic regionalism to create a country that is at once homogeneous and highly differentiated.

Politics has been played out in ethnic and ideological terms, and yet has been unable to offer clear alternatives to the voters beyond those of independence and democracy themselves. During the independence struggle the Labour Party under Indian leadership played the major role, along with Liberal London politicians. Since the 1950s it seems fair to say that the same group that brought Labour to predominance has remained in power even though Labour has splintered and broken in so many directions that it is no longer a major party.

Since independence Mauritius has played a curiously mixed role in the world. With an elite strongly attached to democratic traditions, the country has nevertheless come to see itself as an African country, and thereby to espouse the cause of increasingly nondemocratic countries. The issue of Diego Garcia has come to be a persistent irritant in its relation to the countries of the West, and to be a useful political ploy in the hands of any opposition leader.

The issue as seen from Mauritius is one of territorial loss and foreign duplicity. Diego Garcia, a sparsely inhabited island, was incorporated into the British Indian Ocean Territory before Mauritius' independence for a consideration of three million pounds. The British resettled its population in the Seychelles and Mauritius, and leased the island to the United States for a military base. Mauritius claims that such a use was not foreseen, but there is little evidence of what was discussed prior to the sale. Whatever may have been said, it is easy to make the argument that it was sold too cheaply, and at a time when Mauritius was preoccupied with the issue of independence for its home territory, and when its leaders were willing to agree to anything to achieve this objective.

The party structure of the 1960s that pitted a dominant, pro-independence Labour Party, based on an Indian elite and a majority of rural Indians, against everyone else, and particularly the Parti Mauricien, began to fall apart almost as soon as Independence was achieved. In 1969 the opposition leader joined the government to create a grand coalition on condition that elections planned for 1972 would be postponed. From the perspective of what was occurring in much of Africa, this move might have looked like the preliminary step toward a one-party state. But it was not.

At almost the same time as the coalition was established a new, radical left-wing movement under the leadership of a native Frenchman was also established. The Militant Movement (MMM) quickly captured the imagination of the younger generation, and particularly of the urban population. Although its urban base would seem to make it relatively isolated from the Indian population, its international political stance, and its anticommunalism gave it appeal in all communities.

The first post-independence election did not occur until 1976, at a time when the Parti Mauricien had returned to the opposition. Running as the Independence Party, with new coalition partners, the old Labour party hierarchy represented the struggles of the past. Economically they were centrist but establishment. The Independence Party's security legislation, detainment of dissidents, anti-labor measures, and introduction of foreign investment became the campaign issues. The Party Mauricien supported capitalist policies, while the MMM campaigned for the workers interests as a "class" party, although its leader, Paul Berenger, was certainly not from this background. The MMM was easily open to accusations of communism and inexperience. But the election was clearer than those before or after in the definition of parties and issues, and ninety percent of eligible voters participated.

The result of the election was a very narrow victory for the establishment. The largest winner was the MMM with 41 percent of the votes and 34 out of 70 seats. The losing parties, with a narrow majority between them, managed to put together the government.

Since this was a less complex election than most, and the unique "best loser" system's application was relatively uncomplicated, this is a good time to pause briefly to consider this Mauritian innovation. Through its use the electoral system of Mauritius has been carefully developed to defuse the problems of ethnic voting. The electors actually elected 30 MMM candidates, 25 Independence candidates, and 7 Parti Mauricien supporters. The eight remaining seats were then apportioned to best losers. These persons must have run as candidates and done relatively well in the election. The first four of the eight are those four persons from ethnic groups that have not achieved their proportional share of seats in the election of the 62, but did the best among persons from their ethnic group of those who lost. The next four are chosen to repair the damage to the party preferences that the people have shown in the election that might have occurred as a result of the choosing of the first four. In this case the result was the final total of 34, 28, and 8 respectively. The system may also be used for other purposes, as we shall see: it certainly is also used to bring back in particularly desirable persons who happened to have been defeated.

MMM quickly came back with victories in municipal elections. Soon their leaders were again involved in labor strife, and several were arrested. Their detentions, as in the early seventies, were for short periods.[2]

By the time of the 1982 general election, a socialist party (PSM) emerged as a splinter movement from the Independence (Labour) party. This time the PSM and MMM won all elective seats (in combination with a small regional party from the island of Rodriques). The two parties that had dominated politics in the mid-1960s (Parti Mauricien, now the "social democratic" PSDM, and the Labour Party, now Independence Party in alliance with an old Muslim grouping) had to be content with four of the "best loser" seats among them. (The other four best loser seats were apparently ignored as not needed.)

The winning coalition was under the direction of Aneerood Jugnauth, who had formerly been a political leader in the Independent Forward Bloc representing Hindu interests in the mid-1960s. In this capacity he had attended the independence negotiations in London and later joined the government. In the 1950s he joined the MMM and quickly became its leader. Boodhoo, the leader of the PSM, and Berenger were the other leaders of consequence. Jointly, they promised selective nationalization and the expansion of the welfare state.[3]

Within a few months the government collapsed when most of the MMM ministers resigned, leaving essentially the Prime Minister and the PSM ministers. Jugnauth was expelled from the MMM, of which he was the leader, but not from the prime ministership. The division made sense in ethnic terms, for the expansion of the MMM to include Jugnauth's leadership had always been in realization of the necessity of the party to escape its early Creole base. Yet, when this base pressed for making Creole a national language to replace English, the result was inevitably that the Indians, who have traditionally been supporters of English, would again leave the coalition. More confusing was the fact that financial disagreements, resulting from austerity measures promoted by Berenger that raised the prices of basic goods, also played a part in the split.

The outcome was a party realignment, which saw Jugnauth creating a new MSM (Militant Socialist Movement), with which Boodhoo's PSM immediately joined. Berenger again became leader of the MMM. However, when Jugnauth and his new government failed to attain a majority, new elections were held in 1983.[4]

In this election the new and supposedly radical MSM, the "capitalist" PMSD, and the resurrected centrist Labour Party campaigned as an "Alliance" against the MMM, and particularly against Berenger for his anti-populist measures as Finance Minister. This time the MMM received only seventeen of the elective seats, although forty-six percent of the popular vote.[5] The situation has been highly volatile since 1983, with a steady growth in the strength of the opposition and a fragmentation in that of the Alliance. By 1984 the long-time leader of the Labour Party, Sir Seewoosagur Ramgoolam, had become governor-general, and the Labour Party fell under the leadership of Sir Satcam Boolell, who opposed the apparent merging of the interests of the older party in the new Alliance. Boolell's continued independence led to his expulsion from the government. He countered by expelling all those from the party, "his party," that did not leave the government with him. He failed to take along any of the others who remained in the government; they now redesignated themselves the RTM, or Assembly of Mauritian Workers. Later others from this group also defected to the opposition. Shortly after Boolell's separation from the Alliance, Sylvio Michel, the former leader of the MSM quit the government to form his own party. In 1985 the Rodriguan regional party split, with its leader going to the opposition. In this same year five leading members of the parliament were also suspended from parliament for insulting the president of the assembly. They did not return until April 1986, after they had made a formal apology.[6]

The continuing struggle between the government and the highly partisan and "involved" community of journalists was renewed in 1984. The first blow, the rise in the cost of newsprint by nearly fifty percent was perhaps explicable in terms of economics. But the second, a new government requirement that large bonds be posted by all publications before they could be legitimized, led to a demonstration in front of the parliament and the subsequent detention of forty-four journalists. Although quickly released the journalists went international with their complaints, and held meetings throughout the society. Ultimately, the courts and a joint committee brought the dispute to an end by achieving the revocation of the government's bill.[7]

In January 1986 four government ministers resigned their posts, but did not leave the coalition. Another member of the (now) RTM joined the opposition. More serious perhaps was the split within MSM, with the party whip, Boodhoo, the old leader of the PSM, being dropped. He attained, however, control over the party-supported newspaper, Le Socialiste, which then led Jugnauth to found another paper, the Sun, in opposition to his own party's paper.

What led to all this activity is a little mysterious. In part, it reflects the difficulties of combining ethnic loyalties with coherent policies. In part, it reflects the lack of strong party loyalties within a new ruling class for which position is clearly more important than party. From a comparative, third-world perspective Mauritius is doing very well economically. The people are well-educated, literate, productive, and there is a lively freedom of activity in many spheres, including the political. The latest vital statistics on the country show a population of about one million, rising slowly to 1,250,000 in the year 2000. The death rate of the young population has fallen to 6.6, while the infant mortality rate is about 25 per 1000 live births. The people receive 119 percent of their minimum food requirement according to FAO standards. Eighty-five percent have at least a minimum level of literacy. Newspaper circulation is 75 per 1000 population (compared to 15 in Nigeria, 14 in Kenya, and 42 in South Africa). The GNP/Capita is $1000. Although an agricultural society, overwhelmingly dependent on sugar, only twenty-six percent of the population is actually engaged in agriculture.[8]

Nevertheless, to Mauritians, perhaps because they are so well-off, and so well-traveled as a people, and therefore so aware of the outside world, conditions do not seem good. Unemployment rates are very high. Many young people can neither afford a private high school, nor pass the examinations required to enjoy a free secondary education. Yet from the end of compulsory schooling at twelve until 16, young people cannot get a work permit. A great gulf exists between the ways of life of the old planter society, the foreign tourist society, and the new ruling class, on the one hand, and that of the majority of the people, on the other. Many do not see the older parties, or the "system" working for them. Against this general malaise—suggested already by opinion polls in the late 1970s that reported fifty percent of Mauritians would consider leaving, and three-fourth would advise their children to work elsewhere[9]—four ministers of government were arrested in Amsterdam for carrying drugs. Only one eventually was kept for trial, but the case served to blow up the dimensions of the drug problem, the drug trade, and corruption in the system. To American eyes this might appear a small problem; but in the small, compact island of Mauritius, an island emotionally and economically so dependent on the good opinion of the world, the issue threatened to bring down the government.[10]

Against this background local elections in the five municipalities in 1986 were won overwhelmingly by the MMM.

The process of political erosion reached a culmination in the demand for a vote of confidence in early May, 1986. The issues addressed in the motion were many; most important were the

Amsterdam scandal, the continuing housing shortage, and the repressive labour law. There was also a more diffuse allegation that the institutions of democracy, and particularly the parliament, were being by-passed by the government. A major purpose of the call for a vote was to discomfort the fence-sitters. The three members of the original Labour Party (Boodhoo), for example, were said to be split three ways by the call.[11] By the time for the debate, everyone agreed that the MMM had moved too early. It did not have the votes to bring down the government. The RTM, MSM-Jugnauth, and PSDM voted with the government, as did most of the other MSM members. Many abstained, including three ministers of the government. One walked out, and in the end the MMM was isolated in its vote for the resolution. The legislators had many reasons not to want another election at this time.

But some day, and some day soon, most observers are agreed tnat the MMM, the real MMM of Berenger, will come to power. Many fear this accession, and speak darkly of communism, and one-party Africa. Others see this as an outdated opinion of the "old Berenger," and believe they are now dealing with a more moderate movement. Certainly the party's newspaper **Le Militant** seems to be something less than a pro-Soviet mouthpiece.

Whichever it is, there is no doubt that the process of development that the government has pursued with the best of foreign and local advice has been successful, but at a price. Population growth has been brought down to manageable levels, except on the backward, Catholic island of Rodriques that exists on handouts from the main island. Industry nas been attracted, agriculture has been strengthened. Sugar is well financed and backstopped by scientific experiment. Diversification of agriculture is proceeding enthusiastically, if not as extensively as originally hoped. Textile exports have become increasingly important with the accession of a number of textile mills from the Far East in the last few years.

Stability and growth have been purchased at the cost of labor legislation that makes legal strikes so difficult that all major strikes since the early seventies have been "illegal." Consequently, strikes usually lead to arrests. Security laws have also allowed for detentions on a number of occasions. The "Public Order Act" allows for a near state of emergency even in normal times. Since independence, a National Intelligence Unit is said to have grown in power, facilities, and arrogance; opponents claim their phone lines are tapped and regularly monitored. A 1985 law against defamation of government ministers can be regarded as a severe curtailment of freedom of speech. Its terms include: "Any person who publishes or utters publicly any word or expression which imputes a fact which is injurious to or contemptuous or abusive of the government shall, unless he can substantiate such fact," be liable to a fine on first offense and up to ten years in prison for the second. This law specifically enjoins "imputations" of dishonesty, fraud, or corruption. A new law also states that the publication or diffusion of false information, even with reservations, or diffusion of true information to make its effect contemptuous, shall be subject to a fine.[11] Defenders of the system point out that actually no one has been detained under these laws. Critics point to frequent attacks on the press in the past, and other attempts to restrict its freedom.

In spite of the laws, an obviously vibrant and well-read press continues to express the views of every part of the political spectrum. Radio and television are government and public controlled, but have generally expressed a government viewpoint in the fashion of India. However, in 1986 government television was said to be giving a more neutral and fair presentation of news than formerly. This is a highly litigious society, top-heavy with professionals and powerful business leaders quite aware of their rights.

Mauritius has reached a point of "democratic takeoff" (in the Rustowian sense of a point from takeoff in economic development).[13] Whether this takeoff can be sustained in the near future depends on a variety of factors. Most important is the balance of influences that come upon the island from the outside. The fact that its main trading and intellectual connections are with Europe and India are certainly supportive of continued democratization. Yet the continued weakness of democratic attitudes, the inability of the democratic system to live up to a high level of behavior is threatening. The system will only be inoculated when it is possible to have a party leader in the government that represents the urban people and overcomes dependence on the ethnic politics of the past. Then a more organized political structure might develop truly responsible government.

NOTES

1. The following discussion is based primarily on Adele Smith Simmons, **Modern Mauritius: The Politics of Decolonization** (Bloomington: Indiana University Press, 1982), and A. R. Mannick, **Mauritius: The Development of a Plural Society** (London: Spokesman, 1979). Especially for the period after 1980 these have been supplemented by reference to **Keesing's Contemporary Archives** and similar sources, as well as the author's perusal of the current media and political discussions during a visit to Mauritius in May, 1986.

2. **Keesing's Contemporary Archives,** 1980, page 30030.

3. **Keesing's,** 1982, page 31763; See also **Maurice 85: Almanach d'information generale sur l'ile Maurice** (Port Louis: 1985), page 40.

4. **Keesing's,** 1983, pages 32297-8.

5. **Keesing's,** 1983, pages 32542-3.

6. For the expulsion of Boolell and formation of the Michel' party see **Maurice 85,** pages 37-38. **Africa Research Bulletin,** May 15, 1986, pages 8042-3.

7. **Maurice 85,** pages 96-97.

8. Encyclopedia Britannica, **1986 Britannica Book of the Year** (Chicago: 1986), especially page 735.

9. Simmons, **Modern Mauritius,** page 197.

10. **L'Express,** May 7, 1986, pages 5-6.

11. In addition to the above, see **Le Mauricien,** May 3, 1986, **Week-end,** May 4, 1986, and **Le Militant,** May 4, 1986, especially the interview with Anil Gayan, page 4.

12. Government Gazette of Mauritius, March 16, 1985, Legal Supplement No. 25.

13. W. W. Rustow, **The Stages of Economic Growth** (Cambridge: Cambridge University Press, 1961), especially pages 36-58.

PART IV

Country Summaries

Introduction

The following country descriptions summarize the evidence that lies behind our ratings for each country. They first bring together for each country most of the tabular material of Part I. Then, political rights are considered in terms of the extent to which a country is ruled by a government elected by the majority at the national level, the division of power among levels of government, and the possible denial of self-determination to major subnationalities, if any. While decentralization and the denial of group rights are deemphasized in our rating system, these questions should not be ignored. The summaries also contain consideration of civil liberties, especially as these include freedom of the media and other forms of political expression, freedom from political imprisonment, torture, and other forms of government reprisal, and freedom from interference in nonpublic group or personal life. Equality of access to politically relevant expression is also considered, as well as economic conditions and organization in their relation to freedom. In some cases the summaries will touch on the relative degree of freedom from oppression outside the government arena, for example, through slavery, labor bosses, capitalist exploitation, or private terrorism: this area of analysis is little developed at present.

At the beginning of each summary statement the country is characterized by the forms of its economy and polity. The meanings of the terms used in this classification may be found in the discussion of the relation of political-economic systems to freedom and its accompanying Table 8. The classification is highly simplified, but it serves our concern with the developmental forms and biases that affect political controls. As in Table 8, the terms inclusive and noninclusive are used to distinguish between societies in which the economic activities of most people are organized in accordance with the dominant system and those dual societies in which they remain largely outside. The system should be assumed to be inclusive unless otherwise indicated.

225

Each state is categorized according to the political positions of the national or ethnic groups it contains. Since the modern political form is the "nation-state," it is not surprising that many states have a relatively homogeneous population. The over-whelming majority in these states belong to roughly the same ethnic group; people from this group naturally form the dominant group in the state. In relatively homogeneous states there is no large subnationality (that is, with more than one million people or twenty percent of the population) residing in a defined territory within the country: Austria, Costa Rica, Somalia, and West Germany are good examples. States in this category may be ethni-cally diverse (for example, Cuba or Colombia), but there are no sharp ethnic lines between major groups. These states should be distinguished from ethnically complex states, such as Guyana or Singapore, that have several ethnic groups, but no major group that has its historic homeland in a particular part of the country. Complex states may have large minorities that have suffered social, political, or economic discrimination in the recent past, but today the governments of such states treat all peoples as equals as a matter of policy. In this regard complex states are distinguishable from ethnic states with major nonterritorial subnationalities, for the governments of such states have a deliberate policy of giving preference to the dominant ethnic group at the expense of other major groups. Examples are Burundi or China (Taiwan).

Another large category of states is labeled ethnic states with (a) major territorial subnationalities(y). As in the homogeneous states there is a definite ruling people (or Staatsvolk) residing on its historic national territory within the state. But the state also incorporates other territories with other historic peoples that are now either without a state, or the state dominated by their people lies beyond the new border. As explained in Freedom in the World 1978 (pp. 180-218), to be considered a subnationality a territorial minority must have enough cohesion and publicity that their right to nationhood is acknowledged in some quarters. Often recent events have forged a quasi-unity among quite distinct groups—as among the peoples of Southern Sudan. Typical countries in this category are Burma and the USSR. Ethnic states with major potential territorial subnationalities fall into a closely related category. In such states—for example, Ecuador or Bolivia—many individuals in pre-national ethnic groups have merged, with little

226

overt hostility, with the dominant ethnic strain. The assimilation process has gone on for centuries. Yet in these countries the new consciousness that accompanies the diffusion of nationalistic ideas through education may reverse the process of assimilation in the future, especially where the potential subnationality has preserved a more or less definable territorial base.

There are a few truly multinational states in which ethnic groups with territorial bases coexist in one state without an established ruling people. In such states the several "nations" normally have autonomous political rights, although these do not in law generally include the right to secession. India and Nigeria (when under civilian rule) are examples. One trinational and a few binational states complete the categories of those states in which several "nations" coexist.

The distinction between truly multinational states and ethnic states with territorial subnationalities may be made by comparing two major states that lie close to the margin between the categories—the ethnic Russian USSR and multinational India. In the USSR, Russian is in every way the dominant language. By contrast, in India Hindi speakers have not achieved dominance. English remains a unifying lingua franca, the languages of the several states have not been forced to change their script to accord with Hindi forms, and Hindi itself is not the distinctive language of a "ruling people"—it is a nationalized version of the popular language of a portion of the population of northern India. (The pre-British ruling class used a closely related language with Arabic, Persian, and Turkish infusions; it was generally written in Persian-Arabic script.) Unlike Russians in the non-Russian Soviet Republics, Hindi speakers from northern India do not have a special standing in their own eyes or those of other Indians. Calcutta, Bombay, and Madras are non-Hindi speaking cities, and their pride in their identities and cultures is an important aspect of Indian culture. By contrast, many Soviet Republics are dominated by Russian speakers, a situation developing even in Kiev, the largest non-Russian city.

Finally, transethnic heterogeneous states, primarily in Africa, are those in which independence found a large number of ethnically distinct peoples grouped more or less artificially within one political framework. The usual solution was for those taking over the reins of government to adopt the colonial approach of formally

227

treating all local peoples as equal, but with the new objective of integrating all equally into a new national framework (and new national identity) as and when this would be possible. Rulers of states such as Senegal or Zaire may come from relatively small tribes, and it is in their interest to deemphasize tribalism. In some cases the tribes are so scattered and localistic that there is no short-term likelihood of secession resulting from tribalism. However, in other cases portions of the country have histories of separate nationhood making the transethnic solution hard to implement. In a few countries recent events have placed certain ethnic groups in opposition to one another or to ruling circles in such a way that the transethnic state remains only the formal principle of rule, replaced in practice by an ethnic hierarchy, as in Congo, Sierra Leone, or Ghana.

The descriptive paragraphs for political and civil rights are largely self-explanatory. Subnationalities are generally discussed under a subheading for political rights, although the subject has obvious civil liberties aspects. Discussion of the existence or nonexistence of political parties may be arbitrarily placed in one or the other section. These paragraphs only touch on a few relevant issues, especially in the civil liberties discussion. An issue may be omitted for lack of information, because it does not seem important for the country addressed, or because a particular condition can be inferred from the general statement of a pattern. It should be noted that we have tried where possible to incorporate the distinction between a broad definition of political prisoners (including those detained for violent political crimes) and a narrow definition that includes those arrested only for nonviolent actions—often labeled "prisoners of conscience." Obviously we are primarily concerned with the latter.

Under civil liberties there is often a sentence or two on the economy. However, this is primarily a survey of politically relevant freedoms and not economic freedoms. In addition our view of economic freedom depends less on the economic system than the way in which it is adopted and maintained. (See Lindsay M. Wright, "A Comparative Survey of Economic Freedoms," in Freedom in the World 1982, pp. 51-90.)

At the end of each country summary we have included an overall comparative statement that places the country's ratings in relation to those of others. Countries chosen for comparison are often neighboring or similar ones, but juxtaposing very different countries is also necessary for tying together the system.

Human rights, in so far as they are not directly connected with political and civil liberties, are given little attention in the following summaries. Capital punishment, torture, denial of refugee status, or food and medical care are issues that are less emphasized in this treatment than they would be in a human rights report. The summaries take little account of the oppressions that occur within the social units of a society, such as family and religious groups, or that reflect variations in the nonpolitical aspects of culture. The reader will note few references in the following summaries to the relative freedom of women. Democracies today have almost universally opened political and civic participation to women on at least a formal basis of equality, while most nondemocratic societies that deny these equal rights to women also deny effective participation to most men. In such societies granting equal rights has limited meaning. There is little gain for political and most civil rights when women are granted equal participation in a totalitarian society.

A F G H A N I S T A N

Economy: noninclusive socialist
Polity: communist one-party
Population: 15,400,000*

Political Rights: 7
Civil Liberties: 7
Status: not free

An ethnic state with major territorial subnationalities

Political Rights. Afghanistan's ruling communist party is under the tutelage and direct control of the Soviet Union. The rule of this very small party has no electoral or traditional legitimization. Soviet forces control the major cities but their control is contested by a variety of resistance movements throughout the country. In many areas local administration is in the hands of traditional or ad hoc resistance leaders. Subnationalities: The largest minority is the Tajik (thirty percent), the dominant people of the cities and the western part of the country. Essentially lowland Persians, their language remains the lingua franca of the country. The Persian speaking Hazaras constitute five to ten percent of the population. Another ten percent belong to Uzbek and other Turkish groups in the north.

Civil Liberties. The media are primarily government owned and under rigid control. Antigovernment organization or expression is forbidden. Conversation is guarded and travel is restricted. In a condition of civil war and foreign occupation, political imprisonment, torture and execution are common, in addition to war deaths and massacres. Resources have been diverted to the Soviet Union as payment for its military "assistance." Economic, educational, and cultural programs may be laying the basis for incorporation into the USSR. The modern sectors of the economy are controlled; much of the agricultural economy has been destroyed. The objectives of the state are totalitarian; their achievement is limited by the continuing struggle for control.

Comparatively: Afghanistan is as free as Mongolia, less free than Iran.

---

* Population estimates generally are derived from the 1986 World Population Data Sheet of the Population Reference Bureau, Washington, DC. Many population totals, such as Afghanistan's, are very speculative. In this case, of the estimated total, several million Afghanistanis are refugees in Pakistan or Iran.

A L B A N I A

Economy: socialist
Polity: communist one-party
Population: 3,000,000

Political Rights: 7
Civil Liberties: 7
Status: not free

A relatively homogeneous population

Political Rights. Albania is a traditional Marxist-Leninist dictatorship. While there are a number of elected bodies, including an assembly, the parallel government of the communist party (4.5 percent of the people) is decisive at all levels; elections offer only one list of candidates. Candidates are officially designated by the Democratic Front, to which all Albanians are supposed to belong. In recent years extensive purges within the party have maintained the power of the top leaders.

Civil Liberties. Press, radio, and television are completely under government or party control, and communication with the outside world is minimal. Media are characterized by incessant propaganda, and open expression of opinion in private conversation may lead to long prison sentences. There is an explicit denial of the right to freedom of thought for those who disagree with the government. Imprisonment for reasons of conscience is common; torture is frequently reported, and execution is invoked for many reasons. All religious institutions were abolished in 1967; religion is outlawed; priests are regularly imprisoned. Apparently there are no private organizations independent of government or party. Only party leaders live well. Most people are required to work one month of each year in factories or on farms; there are no private cars. Attempting to leave the state is a major crime. Private economic choice is minimal.

Comparatively: Albania is as free as Cambodia, less free than Yugoslavia.

A L G E R I A

Economy: socialist
Polity: socialist one-party
Population: 22,200,000

Political Rights: 6
Civil Liberties: 6
Status: not free

An ethnic state with a potential subnationality

Political Rights. Algeria has combined military dictatorship with one-party socialist rule. Elections at both local and national levels are managed by the party; they allow little opposition to the system, although individual representatives and specific policies may be criticized. However, the pragmatic, puritanical military rulers may be supported by a fairly broad consensus. Subnationalities: Fifteen to twenty percent of the people are Berbers, who have demonstrated a desire for enhanced self-determination.

Civil Liberties. The media are governmental means for active indoctrination; opposition expression is controlled and foreign publications are closely watched. Private conversation appears relatively open. Although not fully independent, the regular judiciary has established a rule of law in some areas. Many prisoners of conscience are detained for short periods; a few for longer terms. There are no appeals from the decisions of special courts for state security and economic crimes. Land reform has transformed former French plantations into collectives. Although the government is socialist, the private sector has received increasing emphasis. Travel is generally free. Eighty percent of the people are illiterate; many are still very poor, but extremes of wealth have been reduced. Unions have slight freedom. Islam's continued strength provides a counterweight to governmental absolutism. There is freedom of religious worship.

Comparatively: Algeria is as free as Tanzania, freer than Iraq, less free than Morocco.

A N G O L A

Economy: noninclusive socialist
Polity: socialist one-party
Population: 8,200,000

Political Rights: 7
Civil Liberties: 7
Status: not free

A transethnic heterogeneous state with major subnationalities

Political Rights. Angola is ruled by a small, elitist, Marxist-Leninist party, relying heavily on Soviet equipment and Cuban troops to dominate the civil war and to stay in power. There is an elected parliament but essentially no choice in the elections. Subnationalities: The party is not tribalist, but is opposed by groups relying on particular tribes or regions—especially in Cabinda, the northeast, and the south-central areas. The UNITA movement, strongest among the Ovimbundu people, actively controls much of the south and east of the country.

Civil Liberties. The nation remains in a state of war, with power arbitrarily exercised, particularly in the countryside. The media in controlled areas are government owned and do not deviate from its line. Political imprisonment and execution are common; repression of religious activity has moderated, and church leaders speak out on political and social issues. Travel is tightly restricted. Private medical care has been abolished, as has much private property—especially in the modern sectors. Strikes are prohibited and unions tightly controlled. Agricultural production is held down by peasant opposition to socialization and lack of markets.

Comparatively: Angola is as free as Ethiopia, less free than Zambia.

A N T I G U A   A N D   B A R B U D A

Economy: capitalist
Polity: centralized multiparty
Population: 81,000

Political Rights: 2
Civil Liberties: 3
Status: free

A relatively homogeneous population

Political Rights. Antigua is a parliamentary democracy with an elected house and appointed senate. Allegedly, corruption and nepotism are problems of the government. The effectiveness of the rule of law is enhanced by an inter-island court of appeal for Antigua and five of the other small former British colonies in the Antilles. The secessionist island of Barbuda has achieved special rights to limited self-government.

Civil Liberties. Newspapers are published by opposing political parties, but an opposition paper has been repeatedly harassed, especially by libel cases. Radio and television are either owned by the state or the prime minister's family—both have been charged with favoritism. There is freedom of organization and demonstration. Unions are free, have the right to strike, and are politically influential.

Comparatively: Antigua and Barbuda is as free as Jamaica, freer than Malta, less free than Dominica.

A R G E N T I N A

Economy: capitalist-statist
Polity: centralized multiparty
Population: 31,200,000

Political Rights: 2
Civil Liberties: 1
Status: free

A relatively homogeneous population

Political Rights. Argentina has a functioning constitutional democracy under a strong president. The president is elected by electors, but it is essentially a process of direct election. Two successful elections and the well-publicized trials of the country's previous military junta leaders for murder and torture have exemplified democratic rule. Potentially, the military remains a threat to democracy. Elected provincial governments show increasing independence.

Civil Liberties. Private newspapers and both private and government broadcasting stations operate. The media freely express varying opinions. Political parties organize dissent, and public demonstrations are frequent. Courts are independent. The church and trade unions play a strong political role. Human rights organizations are active. The economy includes a large government sector.

Comparatively: Argentina is as free as Finland, freer than Bolivia, less free than Costa Rica.

AUSTRALIA

Economy: capitalist
Polity: decentralized multiparty
Population: 15,800,000

Political Rights: 1
Civil Liberties: 1
Status: free

A relatively homogeneous population with small aboriginal groups

Political Rights. Australia is a federal parliamentary democracy with strong powers retained by its component states. With equal representation from each state, the Senate provides a counterbalance to the House of Representatives. The British-appointed governor-general retains some power in constitutional deadlocks. Constitutional referendums add to the power of the voters. Trade unions (separately and through the Labour Party) and foreign investors have great economic weight. The states have separate parliaments and premiers, but appointed governors. The self-determination rights of the aborigines are recognized through limited self-administration and return of property.

Civil Liberties. All newspapers and most radio and television stations are privately owned. The Australian Broadcasting Commission operates government radio and television stations on a basis similar to BBC. Although Australia lacks many formal guarantees of civil liberties, the degree of protection of these liberties in the common law is similar to that in Britain and Canada. Freedom of assembly is generally respected, although it varies by region. Freedom of choice in education, travel, occupation, property, and private association are perhaps as complete as anywhere in the world. Relatively low taxes enhance this freedom.

Comparatively: Australia is as free as the United Kingdom, freer than India.

A U S T R I A

Economy: mixed capitalist
Polity: centralized multiparty
Population: 7,600,000

Political Rights: 1
Civil Liberties: 1
Status: free

A relatively homogeneous population

Political Rights. Austria's parliamentary system has a directly elected lower house and an upper (and less powerful) house elected by the provincial assemblies. The president is directly elected, but the chancellor (representing the majority party or parties in parliament) is the center of political power. The two major parties have alternated control since the 1950s, but the government often seeks broad consensus. The referendum is used on rare occasions. Provincial legislatures and governors are elective. Subnationalities: Fifty thousand Slovenes in the southern part of the country have rights to their own schools.

Civil Liberties. The press in Austria is free and varied, although foreign pressures have exceptionally led to interference. Radio and television are under a state-owned corporation that by law is supposed to be free of political control. Its geographical position and constitutionally defined neutral status places its media and government in a position analogous to Finland's, but the Soviets have put less pressure on Austria to conform to Soviet wishes than on Finland. The rule of law is secure, and there are no political prisoners. Banks and heavy industry are largely nationalized.

Comparatively: Austria is as free as Belgium, freer than Greece.

B A H A M A S

Economy: capitalist-statist
Polity: centralized multiparty
Population: 200,000

Political Rights: 2
Civil Liberties: 2
Status: free

A relatively homogeneous population

Political Rights. The Bahamas have a parliamentary system with a largely ceremonial British governor-general. The House is elective and the senate appointed. The ruling party has a large majority, but there is an opposition in parliament. Government power is maintained in part by discrimination in favor of supporters and control over the broadcast media. There has not been a change in government since independence. Most islands are administered by centrally appointed commissioners. There is no army.

Civil Liberties. There are independent and outspoken newspapers. The Speaker of the House has, on occasion, compelled the press not to print certain materials. Radio and television are government owned and interfere with the dissemination of opposition viewpoints. Labor and business organization are generally free; there is a right to strike. A program of Bahamianization is being promoted in several sectors of the economy. Rights of travel, occupation, education, and religion are secure. Corruption is widely alleged, and may reach the highest governmental levels.

Comparatively: Bahamas is as free as Fiji, freer than Honduras, less free than Barbados.

B A H R A I N

Economy: capitalist-statist
Polity: traditional nonparty
Population: 400,000

Political Rights: 5
Civil Liberties: 5
Status: partly free

The citizenry is relatively homogeneous

Political Rights. Bahrain is a traditional shaikhdom with a modernized administration. A former British police officer still directs the security services. Direct access to the ruler is encouraged. The legislature is dissolved, but powerful merchant and religious families place a check on royal power. There are local councils. Subnationalities: The primary ethnic problem has been the struggle between the Iranians who once ruled and the Arabs who now rule; in part this is reflected in the opposition of the Sunni and majority Shi'a Muslim sects.

Civil Liberties. The largely private press seldom criticizes government policy. Radio and television are government owned.

There is considerable freedom of expression in private, but informers are feared. Rights to assembly and demonstration are limited. The legal and educational systems are a mixture of traditional Islamic and British. Short-term arrest is used to discourage dissent, and there are long-term political prisoners. In security cases involving violence, fair and quick trials are delayed and torture occurs. Rights to travel, property, and religious choice are secured. There is a record of disturbances by worker groups, and union organization is restricted. Many free social services are provided. Citizenship is very hard to obtain; there is antipathy to foreign workers (but unlike neighboring shaikhdoms most people in the country are citizens).

Comparatively: Bahrain is as free as China (Taiwan), freer than Saudi Arabia, less free than India.

BANGLADESH

Economy: noninclusive
    capitalist-statist
Polity: centralized dominant-party
    (military dominated)
Population: 104,100,000

Political Rights: 4

Civil Liberties: 5

Status: partly free

An ethnically and religiously complex state

Political Rights. Bangladesh alternates between military and parliamentary rule. Political parties are active. Return to quasi-civilian rule through parliamentary and presidential elections in 1986 was seriously marred by violence, widespread abstention, and government interference. Local elective institutions are functioning, and have been expanded by well-contested subdistrict level elections. Subnationalities: Non-Muslim hill tribes have been driven from their lands, tortured, and killed.

Civil Liberties. The press is largely private and party. The papers are intermittently censored, and there is pervasive self-censorship through both government support and pressure. International news is closely controlled. Radio and television are government controlled, but are not actively used for mobilization. In a violent context, there have been recurrent executions and imprisonments, and considerable brutality. Opposition leaders are frequently detained, but there are few if any long-term prisoners of conscience. Political parties organize and mobilize the expression of opposition, and large rallies are frequently held—and as frequently banned. Civilian courts can decide against the government, but judicial tenure is insecure. In spite of considerable communal antipathy, religious freedom exists. Travel is generally unrestricted. Although they do not have the right to strike, labor unions are active and strikes occur. Over half of the rural population are laborers or tenant farmers; some illegal land confiscation by local groups has been reported. The country is plagued by continuing large-scale corruption and extreme poverty.

Comparatively: Bangladesh is as free as Jordan, freer than Burma, less free than Malaysia.

BARBADOS

Economy: mixed capitalist
Polity: centralized multiparty
Population: 300,000

Political Rights: 1
Civil Liberties: 1
Status: free

A relatively homogeneous population

Political Rights. Barbados is governed by a parliamentary system, with a ceremonial British governor-general. Elections have been fair and well administered. Power alternates between the two major parties. Public opinion has a direct and powerful effect on policy. Local governments are also elected.

Civil Liberties. Newspapers are private and free of censorship. Both the private and government radio stations are largely free; the only television station is organized on the BBC model. There is an independent judiciary, and general freedom from arbitrary government action. Travel, residence, and religion are free. Although both major parties rely on the support of labor, private property is fully accepted.

Comparatively: Barbados is as free as Costa Rica, freer than Jamaica.

BELGIUM

Economy: capitalist
Polity: decentralized multiparty
Population: 9,900,000

Political Rights: 1
Civil Liberties: 1
Status: free

A binational state

Political Rights. Belgium is a constitutional monarchy with a bicameral parliament. Elections lead to coalition governments, generally of the center. Continual instability due to linguistic controversies has enhanced the power of the bureaucracy. Subnationalities: The rise of nationalism among the two major peoples—Flemish and Walloon—has led to increasing transfer of control over cultural affairs to the communal groups. However, provincial governors are appointed by the national government.

Civil Liberties. Newspapers are free and uncensored. Radio and television are government owned, but independent boards are responsible for programming. The full spectrum of private rights is respected; voting is compulsory. Property rights, worker rights, and religious freedom are guaranteed.

Comparatively: Belgium is as free as Switzerland, freer than France.

BELIZE

Economy: capitalist
Polity: centralized multiparty
Population: 200,000

Political Rights: 1
Civil Liberties: 1
Status: free

An ethnically complex state

Political Rights. Belize is a parliamentary democracy with an elected house and indirectly elected senate. The governor-general retains considerable power. Elections are competitive and fair; a recent election transferred power to the opposition. Competitive local elections are also a part of the system. However, the increasing identification of parties with the two main ethnic groups is bringing new bitterness to the political system. A small British military force remains because of non-recognition by Guatemala.

Civil Liberties. The press is free and varied. Radio is government controlled but presents opposition viewpoints. Television is private and very diverse. Organization and assembly are guaranteed, as is the rule of law. The opposition is well organized, and can win in the courts. Private cooperatives have been formed in several agricultural industries. Unions are independent and diverse; strikes have been used to gain benefits.

Comparatively: Belize is as free as Costa Rica, freer than Honduras.

B E N I N

Economy: noninclusive socialist
Polity: socialist one-party
    (military dominated)
Population: 4,100,000

Political Rights: 7
Civil Liberties: 7

Status: not free

A transethnic heterogeneous state

Political Rights. Benin is a military dictatorship buttressed by a one-party organization. Regional and tribal loyalties may be stronger than national. Elections are single list, with no opposition. Local assemblies are closely controlled.

Civil Liberties. All media are rigidly censored; most are owned by the government. Opposition is not tolerated; criticism of the government often leads to a few days of reeducation in military camps. There are few long-term political prisoners, but the rule of law is very weak. Detainees are mistreated. Private schools have been closed. Although there is general freedom of religion, some sects have been forbidden. Independent labor unions are banned. Permission to leave the country is closely controlled. Economically, the government's interventions have been in cash crops and external trade, and industries have been nationalized; control over the largely subsistence and small entrepreneur economy remains incomplete. Widespread corruption aggravates already large income disparities.

Comparatively: Benin is as free as Iraq, less free than Burkina Faso.

B H U T A N

Economy: preindustrial
Polity: traditional nonparty
Population: 1,400,000

Political Rights: 5
Civil Liberties: 5
Status: partly free

An ethnic state with a significant subnationality

Political Rights. Bhutan is a hereditary monarchy in which the king rules with the aid of a council and an indirectly elected National Assembly. There are no legal political parties, and the Assembly does little more than approve government actions. Villages are traditionally ruled by their own headmen, but districts are directly ruled from the center. The Buddhist hierarchy is still very important in the affairs of the country. In foreign policy Bhutan's dependence on India has been partially renounced; it is still dependent for defense. **Subnationalities:** The main political party operates outside the country, agitating in favor of the Nepalese and democracy. Although they may now be a majority, the Nepalese are restricted to one part of the country.

Civil Liberties. The only papers are government and private weeklies. There are many small broadcasting stations. Outside media are freely available. There are few if any prisoners of conscience. No organized opposition exists within the country. The legal structure exhibits a mixture of traditional and British forms. There is religious freedom and freedom to travel. Traditional agriculture, crafts, and trade dominate the economy.

Comparatively: Bhutan is as free as Bahrain, freer than Swaziland, less free than Nepal.

B O L I V I A

Economy: noninclusive
            capitalist-statist
Polity: centralized multiparty
Population: 6,400,000

Political Rights: 2

Civil Liberties: 3
Status: free

An ethnic state with major potential subnationalities

Political Rights. Bolivia is a parliamentary democracy with a directly elected president. The traditional power of the military and security services has been curtailed, but not eliminated. Union power expressed through massive strikes has become a major challenge. Provincial and local government is controlled from the center. Subnationalities: Over sixty percent of the people are Indians speaking Aymara or Quechua; these languages have been given official status alongside Spanish. The Indian peoples remain, however, more potential than actual subnationalities. The Spanish-speaking minority still controls the political process.

Civil Liberties. The press and most radio stations are private and are now largely free. But fear remains in the presence of private security forces and mob action; torture has occurred. The Catholic Church retains a powerful and critical role. The people are overwhelmingly post-land-reform, subsistence agriculturists. The major mines and much of industry are nationalized; the workers have a generous social welfare program, given the country's poverty. While union leaders are frequently ousted, this results more from the often violent political struggle of union and government than from the simple repression of dissent.

Comparatively: Bolivia is as free as India, freer than Guyana, less free than Venezuela.

B O T S W A N A

Economy: noninclusive capitalist
Polity: decentralized multiparty
Population: 1,100,000

Political Rights: 2
Civil Liberties: 3
Status: free

A relatively homogeneous population

Political Rights. The republican system of Botswana combines traditional and modern principles. The assembly is elected for a fixed term and appoints the president who rules. There is also an advisory House of Chiefs. Nine district councils, led either by chiefs or elected leaders, have independent power of taxation, as well as traditional control over land and agriculture. Elections continue to be won overwhelmingly by the ruling party, as they were before independence, yet there are opposition members in

243

parliament and the opposition controls town councils. There is economic and political pressure from both black African and white neighbors. Subnationalities: The country is divided among several major tribes belonging to the Batswana people, as well as minor peoples on the margins. The latter include a few hundred relatively wealthy white farmers.

Civil Liberties. The radio and the daily paper are government owned; there are private and party papers. There is no censorship, and opposition party and foreign publications are available. Courts appear independent. Rights of assembly, religion, and travel are respected but regulated. Passport controls may be restrictive, and have been applied in the past to the opposition. Prisoners of conscience are not held. Unions are independent, but under pressure. In the modern society civil liberties appear to be guaranteed, but most people continue to live under traditional rules. (Government support is firmest in rural areas of great inequality.)

Comparatively: Botswana is as free as India, freer than Gambia, less free than Barbados.

B R A Z I L

Economy: capitalist-statist
Polity: decentralized multiparty
Population: 143,300,000

Political Rights: 2
Civil Liberties: 2
Status: free

A complex but relatively homogeneous population with many very small, territorial subnationalities

Political Rights. Although still in a transitional stage, in which the president has not been directly elected, the fully open process by which he came to power was effectively democratic. The legislature is popularly elected. The military remains politically powerful. Political party activity is free, but political power depends on individuals. There are independently organized elected governments at both state and local levels. Subnationalities: The many small Indian groups of the interior are under both private and governmental pressure on their lands, culture, and even lives.

censorship, however, government control of most industry, and thus advertising, limits freedom to criticize government. Radio and television are generally free. There is a right of assembly and organization, and no prisoners of conscience. Massive opposition demonstrations have become a recent feature of political life. Private violence against criminals, suspected communists, peasants, and Indians continues outside the law. The courts are beginning to move actively against officers and others accused of killing or corruption. Union organization is powerful and strikes are widespread, though sometimes repressed. There is considerable large-scale government industry, but rights to property, religious freedom, travel, and education of one's choice are respected. Extreme regional, class, and racial differences in living standards remains a major national issue.

Comparatively: Brazil is as free as Israel, freer than Bolivia, less free than Argentina.

B R U N E I

Economy: capitalist-statist	Political Rights: 6
Polity: monarchy	Civil Liberties: 5
Population: 200,000	Status: partly free

An ethnic state with a major nonterritorial subnationality

Political Rights. Brunei is ruled in the traditional manner as an absolute monarchy with little delegation of authority. Religious questions are decided by the government's religious department. Considerable reliance on the military forces and advice of the United Kingdom and Singapore continues.

Civil Liberties. Little or no dissent is allowed in the nation's media. Radio and television and a major paper are government owned. However, many students attend schools overseas, and foreign media of all kinds are widely available. Political parties calling for constitutional monarchy have been established. A few dissidents remain in jail. Formally the judicial system is patterned on the English model. The position of Chinese non-citizens (many long-term residents) has declined since independence. All land is government owned, as is most of the oil wealth.

Comparatively: Brunei is as free as Chile, freer than Burma, less free than Singapore.

BULGARIA

Economy: socialist	Political Rights: 7
Polity: communist one-party	Civil Liberties: 7
Population: 9,000,000	Status: not free

A relatively homogeneous population

Political Rights. Bulgaria is governed by its Communist Party, although the facade of a parallel government and two-party system is maintained. The same man has essentially ruled over the system since 1954; elections at both national and local levels have little meaning. Soviet influence in the security services is decisive. Subnationalities: The government has moved rigorously to destroy the cultural identity of Muslim minorities numbering about one million.

Civil Liberties. All media are under absolute control by the government or its Party branches. Citizens have few if any rights against the state. There are hundreds or thousands of prisoners of conscience, many living under severe conditions. Brutality and torture are common. Those accused of opposition to the system may also be banished to villages, denied their occupations, or confined in psychiatric hospitals. Believers are subject to discrimination. Hundreds have been killed in enforcing name changes. Citizens have little choice of occupation or residence. Political loyalty is required to secure many social benefits. The most common political crimes are illegally trying to leave the country, criticism of the government, and illegal contacts with foreigners. However, there have been openings through a new spirit of independence and attempts at deconcentration in the economic sphere.

Comparatively: Bulgaria is as free as Mongolia, less free than Hungary.

B U R K I N A   F A S O
(UPPER VOLTA)

Economy: noninclusive capitalist
Polity: military nonparty
Population: 7,100,000

Political Rights: 7
Civil Liberties: 6
Status: not free

A transethnic heterogeneous state

Political Rights. The anarchic and dictatorial military government appears to be modeled on Libya's. Traditional local government has been replaced by revolutionary committees.

Civil Liberties. Media are government-controlled means of
indoctrination. Censorship is the rule. Private criticism is
common. Prisoners of conscience are detained, although by late
1986 all were said to be released. Freedom of assembly or political organization is denied. Trade unions are under strong government pressure, and many leaders have been arrested for expressing
their opposition. External travel is restricted; internal movement
is free. The economy remains dependent on subsistence
agriculture, with the government playing the role of regulator and
promoter of development.

Comparatively: Burkina Faso is as free as Mali, freer than
Chad, less free than Sierra Leone.

B U R M A

Economy: noninclusive mixed
    socialist
Polity: socialist one-party
    (military dominated)
Population: 37,700,000

Political Rights: 7

Civil Liberties: 7

Status: not free

An ethnic state with major territorial subnationalities

Political Rights. Burma is governed by a small military elite as
a one-party socialist state. The government's dependence on the
army makes its strengths and weaknesses more those of a military
dictatorship than those of a Marxist-Leninist regime. Elections are

247

held at both national and local levels: the Party chooses the slate of candidates. **Subnationalities:** The government represents essentially the Burmese people that live in the heartland of the country. The Burmese are surrounded by millions of non-Burmese living in continuing disaffection or active revolt. Among the minorities on the periphery are the Karens, Shan, Kachins, Mon, and Chin. Many Muslims have been expelled, encouraged to leave, or imprisoned indefinitely.

Civil Liberties. All media are government owned, with alternative opinions expressed obliquely if at all; both domestic and foreign publications are censored. The media are expected to actively promote government policy. Organized dissent is forbidden; even private expression is dangerous. Massive arrests have brought the Buddhist hierarchy under control. Prisoners of conscience have been common, but few ethnic Burmans now seem to be detained for reasons of conscience. The regular court structure has been replaced by "people's courts." Racial discrimination has been incorporated in government policy. Emigration or even travel outside the country is very difficult. Living standards have progressively declined as the country falls into ruin. Although the eventual goal of the government is complete socialization, areas of private enterprise remain, subject to control by government marketing monopolies.

Comparatively: Burma is as free as Cambodia, less free than Bangladesh.

B U R U N D I

Economy: noninclusive mixed capitalist

Polity: socialist one-party (military dominated)

Population: 4,900,000

Political Rights: 7

Civil Liberties: 6

Status: not free

An ethnic state with a major, nonterritorial subnationality

Political Rights. Burundi is ruled by a self-appointed military president with the assistance of a Party Central Committee and Politburo. The assembly elections allow only the narrowest choice of pre-selected candidates from the one party; presidential elections allow no choice. **Subnationalities:** The rulers continue to be from the Tutsi ethnic group (fifteen percent) that has traditionally ruled; their dominance was reinforced by a massacre of Hutus (eighty-five percent) after an attempted revolt in the early 1970s.

Civil Liberties. The media are all government controlled and closely censored, as are often the foreign media. Lack of freedom of political speech or assembly is accompanied by political imprisonment and reports of brutality. Under current conditions there is little guarantee of individual rights, particularly for the Hutu majority. However, in recent years the exclusion of the Hutu from public services, the Party, and other advantages has been relaxed. There are no independent unions, but short wildcat strikes have been reported. Religion is closely regulated, especially in the areas of education and missionary activity; religious services are illegal on weekdays. Traditional group and individual rights persist on the village level: Burundi is not a highly structured modern society. Travel is relatively unrestricted. Although officially socialist, private or traditional economic forms predominate.

Comparatively: Burundi is as free as Czechoslovakia, freer than Somalia, less free than Kenya.

CAMBODIA

Economy: noninclusive socialist
Polity: communist one-party
Population: 6,400,000

Political Rights: 7
Civil Liberties: 7
Status: not free

A relatively homogeneous population

Political Rights. Cambodia is divided between the remnants of the Pol Pot tyranny and a less tyrannical, Marxist-Leninist regime imposed by the Vietnamese. Although the Vietnamese have reestablished a degree of civilized life, the people have little part in either regime. Other more democratic rebel groups are increasing in strength.

Civil Liberties. The media continue to be completely controlled in both areas; outside publications are rigorously controlled, and there are no daily papers. Political execution has been a common function of government. Reeducation for war captives is again practiced by the new government. There is no rule of law; private freedoms are not guaranteed. Cambodians continue to be one of the world's most tyrannized peoples. At least temporarily much of economic life has been decollectivized.

Comparatively: Cambodia is as free as Ethiopia, less free than Indonesia.

CAMEROON

Economy: noninclusive capitalist	Political Rights: 6
Polity: nationalist one-party	Civil Liberties: 6
Population: 10,000,000	Status: not free

A transethnic heterogeneous state with a major subnationality

Political Rights. Cameroon is a one-party state ruled by the same party since independence in 1960. The government has steadily centralized power. Referendums and other elections have little meaning; voters are given no alternatives, although a legislative candidate is occasionally rejected. Provincial governors are appointed by the central government. An attempt has been made to incorporate all elements in a government of broad consensus. A recent party election at several levels introduced a degree of democracy. Subnationalities: The most significant opposition has come from those opposing centralization. Politics is largely a struggle of regional and tribal factions.

Civil Liberties. The largely government-owned media are closely controlled; censorship and self-censorship are common; works of critical authors are prohibited, even university lectures are subject to censorship. A number of papers have been closed, and journalists arrested. Freedom of speech, assembly, and union organization are limited, but there is increasingly open discussion. Freedom of occupation, education, and property are respected. Prisoners of conscience are detained without trial and may be ill-treated. Many have recently been released. Internal travel and religious choice are relatively free; foreign travel may be difficult. Labor and business organizations are closely controlled. Although still relatively short on capital, private enterprise is encouraged wherever possible.

Comparatively: Cameroon is as free as Algeria, freer than Ethiopia, less free than South Africa.

C A N A D A

Economy: capitalist
Polity: decentralized multiparty
Population: 25,600,000

Political Rights: 1
Civil Liberties: 1
Status: free

A binational state

Political Rights. Canada is a parliamentary democracy with alternation of rule between leading parties. A great effort is made to register all eligible voters. The provinces have their own democratic institutions with a higher degree of autonomy than the American states. Subnationalities: French has linguistic equality, and French is the official language in Quebec. In addition, Quebec has been allowed to opt out of some national programs and maintains its own representatives abroad. Greater self-determination is being granted to Indian and Eskimo groups.

Civil Liberties. The media are free, although there is a government-related radio and television network. The full range of civil liberties is generally respected. The new Charter of Rights and Freedoms includes the right of judicial review. In Quebec rights to choose English education and language have been infringed. There has been evidence of the invasion of privacy by Canadian security forces in recent years, much as in the United States. Many judicial and legal structures have been borrowed from the United Kingdom or the United States, with consequent advantages and disadvantages. Some provinces limit employment opportunities for nonresidents.

Comparatively: Canada is as free as the United States of America, freer than France.

C A P E   V E R D E

Economy: noninclusive socialist
Polity: socialist one-party
Population: 300,000

Political Rights: 6
Civil Liberties: 6
Status: not free

An ethnically complex state

Political Rights. Although elections are closely controlled, choice is allowed, and there are extensive consultations. MPs have some independence. Abstention and negative votes are common.

Civil Liberties. The media are government owned; all are controlled to serve party purposes. Foreign print and broadcast media are freely available. Rights to organize opposition, assembly, or political expression are not respected, but discussion is relatively open, and there is little political imprisonment or mistreatment. The judiciary is weak. Drought and endemic unemployment continue to lead to emigration. Most professions, fishing, farming, and small enterprises are private. Land reform has emphasized land-to-the-tiller programs. Religion is relatively free, although under political pressure; labor unions are government controlled. Travel is relatively free.

Comparatively: Cape Verde is as free as Oman, freer than Equatorial Guinea, less free than Ivory Coast.

C E N T R A L   A F R I C A N   R E P U B L I C

Economy: noninclusive
     capitalist-statist
Polity: military nonparty
Population: 2,700,000

Political Rights: 7
Civil Liberties: 6
Status: not free

A transethnic heterogeneous state

Political Rights. The Central African Republic is a military dictatorship without representative institutions. Prefects are appointed by the central government in the French style. Heavily dependent on French economic and military aid, France has influenced or determined recent changes of government, and French forces are still present.

Civil Liberties. All media are government owned or closely controlled; the right to free expression is denied. There are prisoners of conscience. Religious freedom is generally respected. The judiciary is not independent. Movement is occasionally hampered by highway security checks. Most economic activity is private with limited government involvement; workers are not free to organize. Corruption is particularly widespread.

Comparatively: Central African Republic is as free as Mali, freer than Somalia, less free than Kenya.

C H A D

Economy: noninclusive capitalist
Polity: military decentralized
Population: 5,200,000

Political Rights: 7
Civil Liberties: 7
Status: not free

A transitional collection of semi-autonomous ethnic groups

Political Rights. The central government is under control of a military-factional leader. Much of the country remains governed by reprisals and counter-reprisals of warring groups. Massacres and pillaging are uncontrollable by government or opponent leaders. France's participation in the defense of the present government has seriously reduced its independence in inter-state relations. Subnationalities: Ethnic struggle pits the southern negroes (principally the Christian and animist Sara tribe) against a variety of northern Muslim groups (principally nomadic Arabs). Political factionalism is only partly ethnic.

Civil Liberties. Media are government owned and controlled. There is little chance for free expression. In recent years many have been killed or imprisoned without due process; mass killings continue to be reported. Labor and business organizations exist with some independence. Religion is relatively free. Not an ideological area, traditional law is still influential. The economy is predominantly subsistence agriculture with little protection of property rights.

Comparatively: Chad is as free as Ethiopia, less free than Tanzania.

C H I L E

Economy: capitalist
Polity: military nonparty
Population: 12,300,000

Political Rights: 6
Civil Liberties: 5
Status: partly free

A relatively homogeneous population

Political Rights. The government of Chile is led by a self-appointed military dictator assisted by a junta of military officers. Although a 1980 plebiscite confirming government policy allowed an opposition vote of thirty percent, all power is concentrated at the center; there are no elective positions. Popular support for the system has declined.

Civil Liberties. All media have both public and private outlets; newspapers are primarily private. The media, although censored and often suspended, express a considerable range of opinion, occasionally including direct criticism of government policy. Limited party activity is tacitly allowed, and human rights organizations operate under pressure. Students, church leaders, and former political leaders regularly express dissent, sometimes massively and in the face of violent government repression. While one can win against the government, the courts are under government pressure. Prisoners of conscience are still commonly taken for short periods; torture, political expulsion, internal exile, and assassination of government opponents continue. Violent confrontations lead repeatedly to repressions, only to be followed by new periods of relaxation. Unions are restricted but have some rights, including a limited right to strike and organize at plant levels. Many nationalized enterprises have been resold to private investors, with government intervention in the economy now being limited to copper and petroleum.

Comparatively: Chile is as free as Kenya, freer than Czechoslovakia, less free than Peru.

C H I N A (Mainland)

Economy: socialist
Polity: communist one-party
Population: 1,050,000,000

Political Rights: 6
Civil Liberties: 6
Status: not free

An ethnic state with peripheral subnationalities

Political Rights. China is a one-party communist state under the collective leadership of the Politburo. A National People's Congress is indirectly elected within party guidelines, but its discussions are now much more open and competitive than is common in Marxist-Leninist states. Still, national policy struggles are obscured by secrecy, and choices are sharply limited. Some local elections have had limited competition. Party administration is decentralized. Subnationalities: There are several subordinated peripheral peoples such as the Tibetans, Uygurs, Mongols, and the much acculturated Zhuang. These are granted a limited degree of separate cultural life. Amounting to not more than six percent of the population, non-Chinese ethnic groups have tended to be diluted and obscured by Chinese settlement or sinification. However, minority peoples have been given a special dispensation to have more than the single child allowed most Han Chinese.

Civil Liberties. The mass media remain closely controlled tools for mobilizing the population. While the underground and wall-poster literature of 1978-79 has been suppressed, there is limited non-political cultural freedom. Many local papers not entirely under government control have developed recently. Although there is movement toward "socialist legality" on the Soviet model, court cases are often decided in political terms. There are unknown thousands of political prisoners, including those in labor-reform camps; the government has forced millions to live indefinitely in undesirable areas. Political executions are still reported. Millions of Chinese have been systematically discriminated against because of "bad class background," but such discrimination has recently been curtailed. Political-social controls at work are pervasive.

Compared to other communist states popular opinions and pressures play a considerable role. Occasional poster campaigns, demonstrations, and evidence of private conversation shows that pervasive factionalism has allowed elements of freedom and consen-

255

sus into the system; recurrent repression, including imprisonment, equally shows the government's determination to keep dissent from becoming a threat to the system or its current leaders. Rights to travel and emigration are limited, as are religious freedoms. Rights to marry and have children are perhaps more closely controlled than in any other country in the world. Economic pressures have forced some, not wholly successful, rationalization of economic policy, including renunciation of guaranteed employment for youth. Introduction of private sector incentives has increased economic freedom, especially for small entrepreneurs and farmers. Small local strikes and slowdowns have been reported concerning wage increases and worker demands for greater control over choice of employment. Inequality derives from differences in political position and location rather than direct income.

Comparatively: China (Mainland) is as free as Algeria, freer than Mongolia, less free than China (Taiwan).

C H I N A (Taiwan)

Economy: capitalist-statist
Polity: centralized dominant party
Population: 19,600,000

Political Rights: 5
Civil Liberties: 5
Status: partly free

A quasi-ethnic state with a majority nonterritorial subnationality

Political Rights. Taiwan has been ruled by a single party organized according to a communist model (although anticommunist ideologically), and under strong military influence. Parliament includes some representatives from Taiwan, but most parliamentarians are still persons elected in 1947 as representatives of districts in China where elections could not be held subsequently because of communist control. Opposition legislators have been few and isolated. However, a new opposition party organized in late 1986 may herald a significant shift in the system. The campaigns of non-government candidates have been highly limited, particularly because the media are overwhelmingly pro-government. The indirect presidential election is pro forma. Some local and regional positions are elective, including those in the provincial assembly that are held by Taiwanese. Subnationalities: The people are eighty-six percent native Taiwanese (speaking two Chinese dialects); opposition movements in favor of transferring control from the mainland immigrants to the Taiwanese are repressed. The vice-president is Taiwanese. Small indigenous ethnic groups are discriminated against.

Civil Liberties. The media include government or party organs, but are mostly in private hands. Newspapers and magazines are subject to censorship or suspension, and most practice strict self-censorship. The dissenting journals of independent editors and publishers were unable to publish in most of 1986. In late 1986 the government spoke of ending the martial law that has been used to deny constitutional rights since 1947. Government thought-police and their agents also operate overseas. Television is one-sided. Rights to assembly are limited, but are sporadically granted. There are several hundred political prisoners, including prominent leaders of the moderate opposition. Union activity is restricted; strikes are forbidden. Private rights to property, education, and religion are generally respected; there is no recognized right to travel overseas, and travel to mainland China is criminal.

Comparatively: China (Taiwan) is as free as Hungary, freer than Burma, less free than South Korea.

C O L O M B I A

Economy: capitalist
Polity: centralized multiparty
Population: 29,400,000

Political Rights: 2
Civil Liberties: 3
Status: free

A relatively homogeneous population with scattered minorities

Political Rights. Colombia is a constitutional democracy. The president is directly elected, as are both houses of the legislature. Power alternates between the two major parties. Both have well-defined factions. The largest guerrilla group now participates in electoral politics. The provinces are directly administered by the national government. The military and police are not firmly under government control.

257

Civil Liberties. The press is private, with most papers under party control, and quite free. Radio includes both government and private stations; television is a government monopoly. All media have been limited in their freedom to report subversive activity. Personal rights are generally respected; courts are relatively strong and independent. Riots and guerrilla activity have led to periodic states of siege in which these rights are limited, and violence is endemic. Assemblies are often banned for fear of riots. In these conditions the security forces have infringed personal rights violently, especially those of leftist unions, peasants, and Amerindians in rural areas. Many persons are rounded up in antiguerrilla or antiterrorist campaigns, and may be tortured or killed. However, opponents are not given prison sentences simply for the nonviolent expression of political opinion, and the government and courts have attempted to control abuses. Human rights organizations are active. The government encourages private enterprise where possible; union activity and strikes for economic goals are legal.

Comparatively: Colombia is as free as India, freer than Guyana, less free than Venezuela.

C O M O R O S

Economy: noninclusive capitalist
Polity: centralized one-party
Population: 500,000

Political Rights: 6
Civil Liberties: 6
Status: not free

A relatively homogeneous population

Political Rights. The present Comoran leader returned to power with the aid of mercenaries in 1978, and they continue to protect him. His later election was an uncontested 99% event. The position of Prime Minister was subsequently abolished and autocratic rule enhanced. Coups have been attempted. Assembly elections have allowed choice within the one-party framework, and the Assembly has little power. Independents contest some elections. Elections may be manipulated. Each island has an appointed governor and council. (The island of Mayotte is formally a part of the Comoros, but it has chosen to be a French dependency.)

Civil Liberties. Radio is government owned and controlled. There is no independent press, but some outside publications and occasional underground dissident writings are available. People are detained for reasons of conscience, and there are many political prisoners. Pressure is reported against the opposition, but private criticism is allowed. There is a new emphasis on Islamic customs. The largely plantation economy has led to severe landlessness and concentrated wealth; emigration to the mainland for employment is very common. The concentration of wealth in a few hands closely connected to the government reduces choice.

Comparatively: Comoros is as free as Tanzania, freer than Mozambique, less free than Zambia.

C O N G O

Economy: noninclusive mixed socialist

Polity: socialist one-party (military dominated)

Population: 1,900,000

Political Rights: 7

Civil Liberties: 6

Status: not free

A formally transethnic heterogeneous state

Political Rights. Congo is an increasingly arbitrary military dictatorship with a very small ruling party based primarily in one section of the country. One-party elections allow no opposition, but criticism is aired in parliament.

Civil Liberties. The press and all publications are heavily censored. Radio is government owned. Criticism may lead to imprisonment, yet there is some private discussion and limited dissent. Executions and imprisonment of political opponents have occurred, but conditions have improved. The only union is state sponsored; strikes are illegal. Religious groups are limited but generally free. There is little judicial protection; passports are difficult to obtain. At the local and small entrepreneur level private property is generally respected; most large-scale commerce and industry are either nationalized or controlled by expatriates. Literacy is high for the region.

Comparatively: Congo is as free as Syria, freer than Iraq, less free than Kenya.

C O S T A   R I C A

Economy: capitalist
Polity: centralized multiparty
Population: 2,600,000

Political Rights: 1
Civil Liberties: 1
Status: free

A relatively homogeneous population

Political Rights. A parliamentary democracy, Costa Rica has a directly elected president and several important parties. No parties are prohibited, and intraparty democracy is highly developed. Much of the society and economy is administered by a large and diffuse network of autonomous public institutions. This structure is supplemented by an independent tribunal for overseeing elections. Elections are fair; rule alternates between parties. Lacking a regular army, politics are not under military influence. Provinces are under the direction of the central government.

Civil Liberties. The media are notably free, private, and varied; they serve a society ninety percent literate. A surprisingly onerous licensing requirement for journalists is an isolated stain on the country's otherwise exemplary freedom. The courts are fair, and private rights, such as those to movement, occupation, education, religion, and union organization, are respected.

Comparatively: Costa Rica is as free as Ireland, freer than Colombia.

C U B A

Economy: socialist
Polity: communist one-party
Population: 10,200,000

Political Rights: 6
Civil Liberties: 6
Status: not free

A complex but relatively homogeneous population

Political Rights. Cuba is a one-party communist state on the Soviet model. Real power lies, however, more in the person of Fidel Castro and in the Russian leaders upon whom he depends than is the case in other noncontiguous states adopting this model. Popular election at the municipal level is closely supervised. Provincial and national assemblies are elected by municipalities but can be recalled by popular vote. The whole system is largely a show: political opponents are excluded from nomination by law, many others are simply disqualified by Party fiat; no debate is allowed on major issues; once elected the assemblies do not oppose Party decisions.

Civil Liberties. All media are state controlled and express only what the government wishes. Although the population is literate, publications, foreign or domestic, are in very short supply. Cuba may have the longest serving prisoners of conscience in the world. Torture has been reported in the past; hundreds who have refused to recant their opposition to the system continue to be held in difficult conditions, and new arrests are frequent. There are hundreds of thousands of others who are formally discriminated against as opponents of the system. There is freedom to criticize policy administration through the press and the institutions of "popular democracy," but writing or speaking against the system, even in private is severely repressed. There are reports of psychiatric institutions also being used for incarceration. Independent human rights organizations are not allowed to function. Freedom to choose work, education, or residence is greatly restricted; new laws force people to work harder. It is generally illegal to leave Cuba, but some have been forced to leave.

Comparatively: Cuba is as free as Gabon, freer than Czechoslovakia, less free than Guyana.

C Y P R U S (G)

Economy: capitalist
Polity: multiparty
Population: 500,000

Political Rights: 1
Civil Liberties: 2
Status: free

An ethnic state

Political Rights. The "Greek" portion of Cyprus is a fully functioning parliamentary democracy on the Westminster model. Elections have been fair and highly competitive. However, the community continues to be under considerable political influence from mainland Greece. The atmosphere of confrontation with the Turkish side of the island may restrict freedoms, especially for the small number of remaining citizens of Turkish background.

Civil Liberties. The newspapers are free and varied in both sectors, but generally support their respective governments. Radio and television are under the control of governmental or semigovernmental bodies. The usual rights of free peoples are respected, including occupation, labor organization, and religion. Because of communal strife and invasion, property has often been taken from members of one group by force (or abandoned from fear of force) and given to the other. Under these conditions rights to choose one's sector of residence or to travel between sectors have been greatly restricted.

Comparatively: Cyprus (G) is as free as France, freer than Greece, less free than Denmark.

C Y P R U S (T)

Economy: capitalist
Polity: multiparty
Population: 150,000

Political Rights: 2
Civil Liberties: 3
Status: free

An ethnic state

Political Rights. "Turkish" Cyprus was created after Turkish troops intervened to prevent a feared Greek takeover. A large section of the island, including much territory formerly in Greek hands, is protected by Turkish military power from the larger Greek portion of the island, as well as the much larger Greek population. In spite of this limitation, parliamentary forms are functioning in the Turkish sector: 1985 witnessed three elections that fully confirmed the popularity of the present government. However, the continuing confrontation restricts choice for some, particularly the few remaining Greek Cypriots in the Turkish sector.

Civil Liberties. Publications are free and varied. Radio and television are under governmental or semigovernmental control. The usual rights of free peoples are respected, including occupation, labor, organization, and religion. However, travel between the sectors and the removal of property is restricted. Many people formerly resident in the Turkish part of the island have lost their property.

Comparatively: Cyprus (T) is as free as India, freer than Turkey, less free than Greece.

C Z E C H O S L O V A K I A

Economy: socialist
Polity: communist one-party
Population: 15,500,000

Political Rights: 7
Civil Liberties: 6
Status: not free

A binational state

Political Rights. Czechoslovakia is a Soviet style, one-party communist state, reinforced by the presence of Soviet troops. Elections are noncompetitive and there is essentially no legislative debate. Polls suggest passive opposition of the great majority of the people to the governing system. Subnationalities: The division of the state into separate Czech and Slovak socialist republics has only slight meaning since the Czechoslovak Communist Party continues to rule the country (under the guidance of the Soviet Communist Party). Although less numerous and poorer than the Czech people, the Slovaks are granted at least their rightful share of power within this framework.

Civil Liberties. Media are government or Party owned and rigidly censored. There is a general willingness to express dissent in private, and there are many serious, if small, underground publications. Freedoms of assembly, organization, and association are denied. Heavy pressures are placed on religious activities, especially through holding ministerial incomes at a very low level and curtailing religious education. There are a number of prisoners of conscience; exclusion of individuals from their chosen occupations and short detentions are more common sanctions. The beating of political suspects is common, and psychiatric detention is employed. Successful defense in political cases is possible, but lawyers may be arrested for overzealous defense. Human rights groups are persecuted. Travel to the West and emigration are restricted. Independent trade unions and strikes are forbidden. Rights to choice of occupation and to private property are restricted.

Comparatively: Czechoslovakia is as free as East Germany, freer than Bulgaria, less free than Poland.

D E N M A R K

Economy: mixed capitalist
Polity: centralized multiparty
Population: 5,100,000

Political Rights: 1
Civil Liberties: 1
Status: free

A relatively homogeneous population

Political Rights. Denmark is a constitutional monarchy with a unicameral parliament. Elections are fair. Since a wide variety of parties achieve success, resulting governments are based on coalitions. Referendums may be used to decide major issues. Districts have governors appointed from the center and elected councils; local administration is under community control.

Civil Liberties. The press is free (and more conservative politically than the electorate). Radio and television are government owned but relatively free. Labor unions are powerful both socially and politically. All other rights are guaranteed. The very high tax level constitutes more than usual constraint on private property in a capitalist state, but has provided a fairly equitable distribution of social benefits. Religion is free but state supported.

Comparatively: Denmark is as free as Norway, freer than Finland.

D J I B O U T I

Economy: noninclusive capitalist
Polity: nationalist one-party
Population: 300,000

Political Rights: 6
Civil Liberties: 6
Status: not free

A binational state with subordination

Political Rights. Djibouti is formally a parliamentary democracy under French protection. Only one party is allowed, and in recent elections there has been little if any choice. The party is tightly controlled by a small elite. Although all ethnic groups are carefully included in the single-party lists, one group is clearly dominant. A large French garrison continues to play a role.

Civil Liberties. The media are government owned and controlled and there is no right of assembly. There have recently been prisoners of conscience and torture. Unions are under a degree of government control, but there is a right to strike. An extremely poor country, its market economy is still dominated by French interests.

Comparatively: Djibouti is as free as Tanzania, freer than Somalia, less free than North Yemen.

D O M I N I C A

Economy: capitalist
Polity: centralized multiparty
Population: 100,000

Political Rights: 2
Civil Liberties: 2
Status: free

A relatively homogeneous population with a minority enclave

Political Rights. Dominica is a parliamentary democracy with competing political parties. An opposition party came to power in highly competitive 1980 elections. There have been several violent attempts to overthrow the government, and the military has subsequently been disbanded. The dissolution of the army has been accepted by the voters. There are local assemblies, but it is alleged that the rights of the native Caribs may not be fully respected.

265

Civil Liberties. The press is private; radio is both private and public. The press is generally free and critical, and the radio presents alternative views. Rights of assembly and organization are guaranteed. There is rule of law and no prisoners of conscience. States of emergency have recurrently limited rights to a small extent. Personal rights to travel, residence, and property are secured, as are the union rights of workers.

Comparatively: Dominica is as free as Nauru, freer than Guyana, less free than Barbados.

DOMINICAN REPUBLIC

Economy: capitalist
Polity: centralized multiparty
Population: 6,400,000

Political Rights: 1
Civil Liberties: 3
Status: free

A complex but relatively homogeneous population

Political Rights. The Dominican Republic is a presidential democracy on the American model. Elections are free and competitive. Military influence is greatly reduced. Provinces are under national control, municipalities under local.

Civil Liberties. The media are generally privately owned, free, and diverse, but government advertising may be denied unfavored papers, and stations may be closed for defamation. Communist materials are restricted. Broadcasting is highly varied, but subject to government review. Public expression is generally free; the spokesmen of a wide range of parties quite openly express their opinions. There are no prisoners of conscience; the security services seem to have been responsible for disappearances and many arbitrary arrests in recent years. The courts appear relatively independent, and human rights groups are active. Labor unions operate under constraints and strikes have been repressed. Travel overseas is sometimes restricted. State-owned lands are slowly being redistributed.

Comparatively: Dominican Republic is as free as Uruguay, freer than Colombia, less free than Barbados.

E C U A D O R

Economy: noninclusive capitalist
Polity: centralized multiparty
Population: 9,600,000

Political Rights: 2
Civil Liberties: 3
Status: free

An ethnic state with a potential subnationality

Political Rights. Ecuador is governed by an elected president and congress. 1984 witnessed a change of government by electoral process, an event rare in the country's history. There have been minor restrictions on party activity and nominations. Provinces and municipalities are directly administered, but local and provincial councils are elected. The struggle of an aggressive president with a hostile congress and rebellious military officers produced continuing instability in 1986. The government has openly ignored decisions of both congress and courts. Subnationalities: Forty percent of the population is Indian, most of whom speak Quechua. This population at present does not form a conscious subnationality in a distinct homeland.

Civil Liberties. Newspapers are under private or party control and quite outspoken. Radio and television are mostly under private control. However, programs have been cancelled, reporters fired, or advertising cancelled for falling out of government favor. There are no long-term prisoners of conscience, but persons are detained for criticizing government officials. Human rights organizations are active. The court system is not strongly independent, and imprisonment for belief may occur. Land reform has been hampered by resistance from landed elites. Although there are state firms, particularly in major industries, Ecuador is essentially a capitalist and traditional state.

Comparatively: Ecuador is as free as India, freer than Panama, less free than Venezuela.

E G Y P T

Economy: mixed socialist
Polity: dominant-party
    (military dominated)
Population: 50,500,000

Political Rights: 5
Civil Liberties: 4

Status: partly free

A relatively homogeneous population with a communal religious minority

Political Rights. Egypt is a controlled democracy. Within limits political parties may organize: communist and religious extremist parties are forbidden. The ruling party won about seventy-five percent of the vote in 1984 parliamentary elections, but opposition parties achieved increased representation. Participation rates were very low; electoral laws favored the government. Because of election regulations, the opposition boycotted 1986 elections to the upper house. The military is largely autonomous and self-sufficient. Neither house of parliament plays a powerful role. Subnationalities: Several million Coptic Christians live a distinct communal life.

Civil Liberties. The Egyptian press is mostly government owned, but presents critical discussions in many areas; weekly party papers are relatively free and increasingly influential. Radio and television are under governmental control. A fairly broad range of literary publications has recently developed. There is limited freedom of assembly. Severe riot laws and a variety of laws restricting dissent have led to large-scale imprisonment or banning from political or other organizational activity. Many prisoners of conscience have been held in the last few years, but very seldom for long periods. Women's rights have improved. In both agriculture and industry considerable diversity and choice exists within a mixed socialist framework. Unions have developed some independence from the government, but there is no right to strike. The predominance of state corporations contributes to the acquiescence of unions in official policy. Travel and other private rights are generally free. More substantial democratic development is retarded by corruption, poverty, population growth, and Islamic fundamentalism.

Comparatively: Egypt is as free as Morocco, freer than Algeria, less free than Brazil.

E L   S A L V A D O R

Economy: capitalist

Polity: centralized multiparty (military influenced)

Population: 5,100,000

Political Rights: 3

Civil Liberties: 4

Status: partly free

A relatively homogeneous population

Political Rights. El Salvador is ruled by an elected president and parliament. The 1984 election was fair, but the armed opposition did not participate. In the countryside a bloody struggle between government and guerrilla forces continues. On the government side, armed killers have prevented the establishment of normal political or civil relationships. Recent elections have legitimized the power of the civil, elected government and confirmed the political weakness of the guerrillas. But the army continues to operate outside government control, even in the area of rural development.

Civil Liberties. Newspapers and radio are largely in private hands. Under strong pressure from all sides, the media have been self-censored, but are showing more independence. Legal and illegal opposition papers and broadcasts appear, but no major critical voice has developed comparable to the La Prensas of Nicaragua (in 1985) and Panama. The rule of law is weak, assassination common, but improvement has occurred. Conscription by both sides has been a major rights problem. Atrocities are committed by both sides in the conflict, probably frequently without the authorization of leaders. On the government side, no military officer has yet been successfully tried for a human rights offense. Human rights organizations are active. The Catholic Church remains a force. The university has reopened, but faculty and students continue to live under threat. Union activities are common, and strikes, legal and illegal, have become a major means of political expression for groups on the left. Although still a heavily agricultural country, rural people are to a large extent involved in the wage and market economy. Banking and foreign trade of export crops have been nationalized; land reform has had limited but significant success.

Comparatively: El Salvador is as free as Nepal, freer than Nicaragua, less free than Dominican Republic.

E Q U A T O R I A L   G U I N E A

Economy: noninclusive   Political Rights: 7
        capitalist-statist
Polity: military nonparty   Civil Liberties: 7
Population: 400,000   Status: not free

An ethnic state with a territorial minority

Political Rights. Equatorial Guinea is a military dictatorship. The coup that replaced the former dictator was popular, but the population as a whole played and plays little part. The partially elected assembly seems irrelevant. A several-hundred-man Moroccan bodyguard protects the incumbent at Spanish expense.

Civil Liberties. The media are very limited, government owned, and do not report opposition viewpoints. The rule of law is tenuous; there are political prisoners, but perhaps none of conscience. Police brutality is common, and execution casual. Compulsory recruitment for plantation and other work occurs. Opposition parties are not tolerated, and there are no unions. Religious freedom was reestablished in 1979, and private property is recognized. Plantation and subsistence farming is still recovering from near destruction under the previous government.

Comparatively: Equatorial Guinea is as free as Zaire, less free than Tanzania.

E T H I O P I A

Economy: noninclusive socialist
Polity: communist one-party
    (military dominated)
Population: 43,900,000 (?)

Political Rights: 7
Civil Liberties: 7

Status: not free

An ethnic state with major territorial subnationalities

Political Rights. Ethiopia is ruled by a military committee that has successively slaughtered the leaders of the ancien regime and many of its own leaders. A spectrum of mass organizations has been established on the model of a one-party socialist state. Establishing locally elected village councils has been the primary effort to mobilize the people. In late 1984 a national communist (workers) party was established. **Subnationalities:** The heartland of Ethiopia is occupied by the traditionally dominant Amhara and acculturated subgroups of the diffuse Galla people. In the late nineteenth century Ethiopian rulers united what had been warring fragments of a former empire in this heartland, and proceeded to incorporate some entirely new areas. At that time the Somali of the south came under Ethiopian rule; Eritrea was incorporated as the result of a UN decision in 1952. Today Ethiopia is crosscut by linguistic and religious conflicts: most important is separatism due to historic allegiances to ancient provinces (especially Tigre), to different experiences (Eritrea), and to the population of a foreign nation (Somalia).

Civil Liberties. The media are controlled, serving the mobilization needs of the government. Individual rights are unprotected under conditions of despotism and anarchy. Political imprisonment, forced confession, execution, disappearance, and torture are common. There are no rights to assembly. Many thousands have been killed aside from tnose that died in civil war. Education is totally controlled. What freedom there was under the Ethiopian monarchy has been largely lost. Initially, land reform benefited many, but the subsequent villagization policy seriously disrupted agriculture. Choice of residence and workplace is often made by the government; there have been reports of forced transport to state farms, and of tne forced movement of ethnic groups. Religious groups have been persecuted, and religious freedom is limited.

271

Peasant and worker organizations are closely controlled. Travel outside the country is strictly controlled; hostages or guarantors are often required before exit. The words and actions of the regime indicate little respect for private rights in property. The economy is under increasing government control through nationalizations, state-sponsored peasant cooperatives, and the regulation of business licenses. Starvation has been a recurrent theme, with government ineffectiveness playing a part both before and after the accession of the present regime. Starvation is also used as a tool in the struggle against dissident peoples.

Comparatively: Ethiopia is as free as Cambodia, less free than Sudan.

E U R O P E A N   C O M M U N I T Y

Economy: capitalist-statist
Polity: decentralized multiparty
Population: 322,300,000

Political Rights: 2
Civil Liberties: 1
Status: free

An ethnically heterogeneous community of independent states

Political Rights. The Community has evolved a variety of institutions since World War II for the managing of economic and political affairs. As in most international organizations, major decision making is made through an international bureaucracy or commission representing the member countries, and through the periodic meeting of representatives of their respective governments—the Council of Ministers and European Council. However, the Community has also developed a directly elected parliament that is growing in influence, and a Community Court of Justice. Increasingly, tne law made by these institutions is coming to be considered superior to the national law of member countries. In addition, other institutions in Western Europe reinforce the operation of a system of free institutions within the Community itself.

Civil Liberties. The availability of information to the publics of the Community is characteristic of the free nature of these societies. In addition, the Council of Europe's court of human rights has striven to raise the level of respect for civil liberties.

Comparatively: The European Community is as free as France, less free than Denmark, freer than Turkey.

F I J I

Economy: noninclusive capitalist
Polity: centralized multiparty
Population: 700,000

Political Rights: 2
Civil Liberties: 2
Status: free

A binational state

Political Rights. Fiji has a complex political structure designed to protect the interests of both the original Fijians and the Fiji Indians, who now form a slight majority. The Lower House is directly elected on the basis of both communal and national rolls. The Upper House is indirectly elected by a variety of electors (including the council of chiefs, the prime minister, and the opposition leader). Local government is organized both by the central government and by a Fijian administration headed by the council of chiefs.

Civil Liberties. The press is free and private (but government positions must sometimes be published). The growth of Fiji as a center for South pacific regional publications has strengthened its print media. Government radio is under a separate and independent commission. Libel laws can restrict the media's political discussion. Freedom to assemble is not impeded. The full protection of the rule of law is supplemented by an ombudsman to investigate complaints against the government. Some rights to property may have been sacrificed to guarantee special rights of inalienability of land granted the Fijians. Strong unions have full rights. Religion, travel, and other personal rights are secured. The nation may be about evenly divided between a subsistence economy, based on agriculture and fishing, and a modern market economy.

Comparatively: Fiji is as free as Papua New Guinea, freer than Tonga, less free than New Zealand.

FINLAND

Economy: mixed capitalist
Polity: centralized multiparty
Population: 4,900,000

Political Rights: 2
Civil Liberties: 2
Status: free

An ethnic state with a small territorial subnationality

Political Rights. Finland has a parliamentary system with a strong, directly elected president. Since there are many relatively strong parties, government is almost always by coalition. Elections have resulted in shifts in coalition membership. By treaty foreign policy cannot be anti-Soviet, but the 1982 presidential election indicated a weakening of a more general Soviet veto on the political process. The provinces have centrally appointed governors. Subnationalities: The rural Swedish minority (seven percent) has its own political party and strong cultural ties to Sweden. The Swedish-speaking Aland Islands have local autonomy and other special rights.

Civil Liberties. The press is private, diverse, and uncensored. Government-press relations can be so hostile as to restrict communications. Most of the radio service is government controlled, but there is an important commercial television station. The government network has been manipulated at times. Discussion in the media is controlled by a political consensus that criticism of the Soviet Union should be circumspect. There is a complete rule of law; private rights are secured, as is freedom of religion, business, and labor.

Comparatively: Finland is as free as Mauritius, freer than Malta, less free than Sweden.

FRANCE

Economy: capitalist-statist
Polity: centralized multiparty
Population: 55,400,000

Political Rights: 1
Civil Liberties: 2
Status: free

An ethnic state with major territorial subnationalities

Political Rights.   France is a parliamentary democracy with many features of the American system, such as a strong presidency and a check and balance of several centers of power. Either the Senate or the more powerful Assembly can check the power of government.   If the president's party does not control parliament, experience in 1986 suggested that the prime minister can exercise powers comparable to those of the president. The constitutional council oversees elections and passes on the constitutionality of assembly or executive actions on the model of the United States Supreme Court.   Regional and local power has recently been greatly increased: communes, departments, and regions now have elected governments. Subnationalities: Territorial subnationalities continue to have limited rights as ethnic units, but the ethnic and self-determination rights of such groups as the Bretons, Corsicans, and Basques are increasingly observed.

Civil Liberties.   The French press is generally free.   There is government involvement in financing and registration of journalists; press laws restrict freedom more than in other Western states. Criticism of the president and top officials may be muted by government threats and court actions. The news agency is private. Radio is now free and plural; the government television monopoly has generally been pro-administration, but new systems are being added.   In spite of recent changes there is still an authoritarian attitude in government-citizen relations, publications may be banned at the behest of foreign governments, and arrest without explanation still occurs, particularly of members of subnationalities. Police brutality is commonly alleged.   Information and organization about conscientious objection is restricted.   France is, of course, under the rule of law, and rights to occupation, residence, religion, and property are secured.   A new Secretary of State for Human Rights, concerned primarily with internal issues, should improve governmental performance.   Both through extensive social programs and the creation of state enterprises France is quite far from a pure capitalist form.

Comparatively: France is as free as West Germany, freer than India, less free than the United Kingdom.

GABON

Economy: noninclusive capitalist
Polity: nationalist one-party
Population: 1,000,000

Political Rights: 6
Civil Liberties: 6
Status: not free

A transethnic heterogeneous state

Political Rights. Gabon is a moderate dictatorship operating in the guise of a one-party state, with controlled elections characteristic of this form. Candidates must be party approved but there may be limited competition. The system remains dependent on the French. Major cities have elected local governments but little independence; provinces are administered from the center.

Civil Liberties. All media are government owned and controlled; few legitimate opposition voices are raised; journalists may be arrested for expression. Some critical items appear in local or available foreign media. There are prisoners of conscience and mistreatment. There is no right of political assembly; only one labor union is sanctioned. Membership in the governing party is compulsory. The authoritarian government generally does not care to interfere in private lives, and respects religious freedom, private property, and the right to travel. The government is taking a more active role in the economy and is gradually replacing foreign managers with Gabonese.

Comparatively: Gabon is as free as Libya, freer than Angola, less free than Sudan.

GAMBIA

Economy: noninclusive capitalist
Polity: dominant party
Population: 800,000

Political Rights: 3
Civil Liberties: 4
Status: partly free

A transethnic heterogeneous state

Political Rights. This is a parliamentary democracy in which the same party and leader have been in power since independence in 1965; elections are won with substantial margins. In a recent election the opposition candidate campaigned from prison. There is local, mostly traditional autonomy, but not regional self-rule. The state is now in confederation with Senegal, and the system is protected by Senegalese troops.

Civil Liberties. The private and public newspapers and radio stations are generally free, but are subject to self-censorship. Arrests for antigovernment pamphlets occur. Although opposition leaders have been jailed following a major insurrection, the independent judiciary maintains the rule of law. The state of emergency was again extended in 1984; a threatening law against treason was passed in 1986. Labor unions operate within limits. The agricultural economy remains traditionally organized and is largely dependent on peanuts, the export of which is a state monopoly. Internal travel is limited by document checkpoints.

Comparatively: Gambia is as free as Nepal, freer than Sierra Leone, less free than Botswana.

G E R M A N Y, E A S T

Economy: socialist
Polity: communist one-party
Population: 16,700,000

Political Rights: 7
Civil Liberties: 6
Status: not free

A relatively homogeneous population

Political Rights. East Germany is in practice a one-party communist dictatorship. No electoral competition is allowed that involves policy questions; all citizens are compelled to vote; the government-selected list of candidates may offer limited choice. In addition, the presence of Soviet troops and direction from the Communist Party of the Soviet Union significantly reduces the sovereignty (or group freedom) of the East Germans.

Civil Liberties. Media are government-owned means of indoctrination. Dissidents are repressed by imprisonment and exclusion; the publication or importation of materials with opposing views is forbidden. One may be arrested for private criticism of the system, but complaints about policy implementation occur in all the media; a few favored dissidents have managed to exist and publish outside the country. Among the thousands of prisoners of conscience, the most common offenses are trying to leave the country illegally (or in some cases even seeking permission to leave), or propaganda against the state. Prisoners of conscience may be severely beaten or otherwise harmed. Political reeducation may be a condition of release. The average person is not allowed freedom of occupation or residence. Once defined as an enemy of the state, a person may be barred from his occupation and his children denied higher education. Particularly revealing has been the use of the "buying out scheme" by which West Germany has been able intermittently to obtain the release of prisoners in the East through cash payments and delivering goods such as bananas and coffee. There is considerable religious freedom, with the Catholic and Protestant hierarchies possessing some independence, as does the peace movement at times. Freedom exists within the family, although there is no right to privacy or the inviolability of the home, mail, or telephone. Agriculture is highly collectivized; virtually all industry is state controlled. Membership in unions, production cooperatives, and other associations is compulsory.

Comparatively: East Germany is as free as Saudi Arabia, freer than Bulgaria, less free than Poland.

G E R M A N Y ,   W E S T

Economy: capitalist
Polity: decentralized multiparty
Population: 60,700,000

Political Rights: 1
Civil Liberties: 2
Status: free

A relatively homogeneous population

Political Rights. West Germany is a parliamentary democracy with an indirectly elected and largely ceremonial president. Both major parties have ruled since the war. The weak Senate is elected by the assemblies of the constituent states and loyally defends states' rights. Successive national governments have been based on changing party balances in the powerful lower house. The recent success of the "Greens" at all levels suggests the openness of the system to change. The states have their own elected assemblies; they control education, internal security, and culture.

Civil Liberties. The papers are independent and free, with little governmental interference. Radio and television are organized in public corporations under the usually neutral direction of the state governments. Generally the rule of law has been carefully observed, and the full spectrum of private freedoms is available. Terrorist activities have led to tighter security regulations, invasions of privacy, and less acceptance of nonconformity. Arrests have been made for handling or producing inflammatory literature, for neo-Nazi propaganda, or for calling in question the courts or electoral system. Government participation in the economy is largely regulatory; in addition, complex social programs and mandated worker participation in management have limited certain private freedoms while possibly expanding others.

Comparatively: West Germany is as free as France, freer than Finland, less free than the United States of America.

G H A N A

Economy: mixed socialist
Polity: military nonparty
Population: 13,600,000

Political Rights: 7
Civil Liberties: 6
Status: not free

A transethnic heterogeneous state with subnationalities

Political Rights. A small military faction rules with the support of radical organizations. On the local level traditional sources of power are minimal. Local councils are elected, but are closely supervised where possible. Widespread violence suggests anarchy in many areas. Subnationalities: The country is composed of a variety of peoples, with those in the South most self-conscious. The latter are the descendants of a number of traditional kingdoms, of which the Ashanti are the most important. A north-south, Muslim-Christian opposition exists but is weakly developed, because of the numerical and economic weakness and incomplete hold of Islam in the north. In the south and center of the country a sense of Akan identity is developing among the Ashanti, Fanti, and others; since they include forty-five percent of the people, this amounts to strengthening the ethnic core of the nation. The one million Ewe in the southeast (a people divided between Ghana and Togo) play a major role in the new revolutionary government.

Civil Liberties. Radio and television and most of the press are government owned. All are under close government scrutiny. However, a degree of independence is suggested by the periodic suspension and banning of semi-independent publications. Private opinion is restrained. There have been hundreds of political arrests and political trials; many professionals have been murdered, apparently for "revolutionary" reasons. Soldiers are reported out of control. Papers and universities have been closed. Peoples' courts have been used to counter the previous judicial system. There has been a great deal of government control in some areas of the economy--especially in cocoa production, on which the economy depends, and in modern capital-intensive industry. The assets of many businesses have been frozen. Some groups, including the strong women's marketing associations, have resisted government attempts to impose price ceilings on all goods. Labor unions are controlled. Like Senegal, Ghana has a relatively highly developed industry and its agriculture is dependent on world markets. There is religious freedom; travel is controlled.

Comparatively: Ghana is as free as Niger, freer than Romania, less free than Ivory Coast.

G R E E C E

Economy: capitalist-statist
Polity: centralized multiparty
Population: 10,000,000

Political Rights: 2
Civil Liberties: 2
Status: free

A relatively homogeneous state

Political Rights. Greece is a parliamentary democracy with an indirectly elected president. The development and extension of free institutions has proceeded rapidly, and recent elections have been competitive and open to the full spectrum of parties. However, governmental actions in elections and parliament have led to serious accusations of misuse of authority. Provincial administration is centrally controlled; there is local self-government.

Civil Liberties. Newspapers are private and the judiciary is independent. Broadcast media are government owned and controlled; TV favors the government viewpoint. Government interference in journalism, broadcasting, and universities has recently been reported. There are no known prisoners of conscience. Because of the recent revolutionary situation all views are not freely expressed (a situation similar to that in post-fascist Portugal). One can be imprisoned for insulting the authorities or religion. The courts are not entirely independent. Pressures have been reported against the Turkish population in Western Thrace, in regard to education, property, and free movement. Union activity is under government influence, particularly in the dominant public sector. Private rights are respected.

Comparatively: Greece is as free as Finland, freer than Malta, less free than France.

G R E N A D A

Economy: capitalist-statist
Polity: centralized multiparty
Population: 118,000

Political Rights: 2
Civil Liberties: 2
Status: free

A relatively homogeneous population

Political Rights. Parliamentary rule has been effectively reestablished. The 1984 elections were free and fair, and included all major political forces. The legislature governs. There is no local government.

Civil Liberties. The newspapers are independent, varied, and free. Radio is government controlled—the government has been accused of restricting the development of private radio. There are no prisoners of conscience. Trade unions are strong and independent. The economy is largely private.

Comparatively: Grenada is as free as Colombia, freer than Panama, less free than Barbados.

G U A T E M A L A

Economy: noninclusive capitalist
Polity: centralized multiparty
    (military influenced)
Population: 8,600,000

Political Rights: 3
Civil Liberties: 3

Status: partly free

An ethnic state with a major potential territorial subnationality

Political Rights. Guatemala is in transition from military to civilian rule. Credible elections in November and December 1985 reestablished formal civilian rule. The executive and congress have moved slowly but steadily to reestablish civilian civilian institutions. However, military and other security forces maintain extra-constitutional power at all levels. The provinces are centrally administered; local government under elected officials is important is some areas. Subnationalities: Various groups of Mayan and other Indians make up half the population; they do not yet have a subnationalist sense of unity, but are involved both forcibly and voluntarily in guerrilla and antiguerrilla activity.

Civil Liberties. The press and a large portion of radio and television are privately controlled. Until recently self-censorship has been common because of the threat of torture and murder by political opponents. Expression is now relatively free, although many killings continue to occur. The struggle against rural guerrillas has led to frequent attacks on recalcitrant peasants or Indians by security forces. Tens of thousands have been killed in the last few years, primarily by the security forces. Thousands have sought refuge internally and in border areas. The judiciary is under both leftist and governmental pressure in political or subversive cases and has been relatively ineffective in these areas. Recent improvements in security have increased rights in many areas. Rights of assembly and demonstration are vigorously expressed. Political parties are active, and unions are reestablishing their strength.

Comparatively: Guatemala is as free as the Philippines, freer than Mexico, less free than Ecuador.

G U I N E A

Economy: noninclusive
      mixed socialist
Polity: military nonparty
Population: 6,200,000

Political Rights: 7

Civil Liberties: 5

Status: not free

A formally transethnic heterogeneous state

Political Rights. Guinea is under military rule. Local elective councils have been established.

Civil Liberties. The press has limited freedom. Unions are under government direction. Many political detainees have been tortured; some apparently executed. Unions appear to have achieved some independence. Industry is heavily nationalized.

Comparatively: Guinea is as free as Nigeria, freer than Ghana, less free than Senegal.

G U I N E A - B I S S A U

Economy: noninclusive socialist
Polity: socialist one-party
      (military dominated)
Population: 900,000

Political Rights: 6
Civil Liberties: 7

Status: not free

A transethnic heterogeneous state

Political Rights. Guinea-Bissau is administered by one party; other parties are illegal. Regional council elections lay the basis for indirect election of the assembly; party guidance is emphasized at all levels. Public pressure has caused the replacement of some local officials. Increasingly violent struggle among top leaders has resulted in many deaths.

Civil Liberties. The media are government controlled; criticism of the system is forbidden. Human rights is not protected by an adequate rule of law; many have been executed without adequate trial or died in detention. Union activity is government directed. Land ownership is public or communal. The small industrial sector remains mixed, but the continuing economic crisis has virtually halted all private sector activity. An additional block to further decollectivization is the Soviet and Cuban presence. Religion is relatively free, as are travel and other aspects of private life.

Comparatively: Guinea-Bissau is as free as Mozambique, freer than Somalia, less free than Libya.

G U Y A N A

Economy: mixed socialist
Polity: centralized multiparty
Population: 800,000

Political Rights: 5
Civil Liberties: 5
Status: partly free

An ethnically complex state

Political Rights. Guyana is a parliamentary democracy with a strong executive and an increasingly dominant ruling party. In recent elections the government has been responsibly charged with irregularities that resulted in its victory. In the last election (December 1985), the opposition was often excluded from the polling stations both to vote and observe the process. Opposition parties are denied equal access to the media, and their supporters are discriminated against in employment. Administration is generally centralized but some local officials are elected.

Civil Liberties. Radio is government owned. Several opposition newspapers have been nationalized; the opposition press has been nearly forced out of existence. However, a variety of foreign news media are still available. There is a right of assembly, but harassment occurs. Opposition parties remain well organized. There is an operating human rights organization. All private schools have been nationalized, and the government has interfered with university appointments. It is possible to win against the government in court; there are no prisoners of conscience, though torture of convicts may be practiced. Art and music are under considerable government control. The independence of unions has been greatly abridged. The private sector is stagnating under official intimidation and extensive state control of productive property, although a black market thrives. The opposition is terrorized by armed gangs and the police; the general public suffers under arbitrary and severe controls. Political patronage is extensive and some social benefits are allocated on a preferential basis. Internal exile has been used against political opponents.

Comparatively: Guyana is as free as North Yemen, freer than Nicaragua, less free than Guatemala.

H A I T I

Economy: noninclusive capitalist
Polity: interim nonparty
    (military dominated)
Population: 5,900,000

Political Rights: 5
Civil Liberties: 4

Status: partly free

A relatively homogeneous population

Political Rights. In 1986 Haiti came under the loose control of an initially popular military caretaker government. It has moved slowly and not very effectively toward establishing a legitimate democratic system. A constituent assembly election in late 1986 failed due to boycotts and inattention.

Civil Liberties. The media are private and public, highly varied and largely free. The prisons have been emptied. The main human rights problems in 1986 were those of anarchy—many have been killed or persecuted by the public without trial. Union activity remains restricted. Corruption and extreme poverty has seriously infringed rights to political equality.

Comparatively: Haiti is as free as Egypt, freer than Nicaragua, less free than Jamaica.

H O N D U R A S

Economy: noninclusive capitalist
Polity: centralized multiparty
Population: 4,600,000

Political Rights: 2
Civil Liberties: 3
Status: free

A relatively homogeneous population

Political Rights. The government is a parliamentary democracy with an elected president. The relationships between the president, congress, the supreme court, and the military are still in question. Military leaders have retained influence, but civilian government has been able to assert its dominance. Provincial government is centrally administered; local government is elected.

Civil Liberties. The media are largely private and free of prior censorship. Licensing requirements for journalists can limit freedom. Human rights organizations are active. Militant peasant organizations are quite active, and the struggle of peasants for land often leads to violence. The spreading of guerrilla war from neighboring countries has led to represssions of refugees and others. Most private rights are respected—in so far as government power reaches. Private killings, especially of leftists and with the involvement of security forces, have often been reported. Labor unions have suffered oppression, but are relatively strong, especially in plantation areas. There is freedom of religion and movement.

Comparatively: Honduras is as free as Colombia, freer than Panama, less free than Venezuela.

H U N G A R Y

Economy: socialist
Polity: communist one-party
Population: 10,600,000

Political Rights: 5
Civil Liberties: 5
Status: partly free

A relatively homogeneous population

Political Rights. Hungary is ruled as a one-party communist dictatorship. Although there is an elective national assembly as well as local assemblies, all candidates must be approved by the party, and the decisions of the politburo are decisive. Within this framework recent elections have allowed choice among candidates. Independents have been elected and in many cases run-offs have been required. Parliament has come to take a more meaningful part in the political process. The group rights of the Hungarian people are diminished by the government's official acceptance of the right of the Soviet government to intervene in the domestic affairs of Hungary by force. A council to represent the special interests of the large gypsy community has been established.

Civil Liberties. Media are under government or party control. Basic criticism of top leaders, communism, human rights performance, or the Soviet presence is inadmissable, but some criticism is allowed; this is expressed through papers, plays, books, the importation of foreign publications, or listening to foreign broadcasts. Radio and television give relatively balanced presentations, even of news. Informally organized dissident groups are allowed to exist. Individuals are regularly detained for reasons of conscience, though usually for short periods. Control over religious affairs is more relaxed than in most communist states. Although private rights are not guaranteed, in practice there is considerable private property, and permission to travel into and out of the country is easier to obtain than in most of Eastern Europe. The border with Austria is essentially open. Unions are party directed and have no right to strike; however, workers have gained some control over enterprise management and operations.

Comparatively: Hungary is as free as Bhutan, freer than Czechoslovakia, less free than Egypt.

I C E L A N D

Economy: capitalist
Polity: centralized multiparty
Population: 230,000

Political Rights: 1
Civil Liberties: 1
Status: free

A relatively homogeneous population

Political Rights. Iceland is governed by a parliamentary democracy. Recent years have seen important shifts in voter sentiment, resulting successively in right- and left-wing coalitions. Although a small country, Iceland pursues an independent foreign policy. Provinces are ruled by central government appointees.

Civil Liberties. The press is private or party and free of censorship. Radio and television are state owned but supervised by a state board representing major parties and interests. There are no political prisoners and the judiciary is independent. Private rights are respected; few are poor or illiterate.

Comparatively: Iceland is as free as Norway, freer than Portugal.

I N D I A

Economy: noninclusive   Political Rights: 2
          capitalist-statist
Polity: decentralized multiparty   Civil Liberties: 3
Population: 785,000,000   Status: free

A multinational and complex state

Political Rights. India is a parliamentary democracy in which the opposition has an opportunity to rule. The strong powers retained by the component states have been compromised in recent years by the central government's frequent imposition of direct rule. However, control of the states by regional political parties has increased. Use of criminal elements in politics in some local areas is a threat to fair participation. A 1985 law to prohibit change of party affiliation after election should strengthen voter rights.

Subnationalities. India contains a diverse collection of mostly territorially distinct peoples united by historical experience and the predominance of Hinduism. India's dominant peoples are those of the north central area that speak as a first language either the official language, Hindi (Hindustani), or a very closely related dialect of Sanskrit origin. The other major subnational peoples of India may be divided into several groups: (1) peoples with separate states that are linguistically and historically only marginally distinct from the dominant Hindi speakers (for example, the Marathi, Gujerati, or Oriya); (2) peoples with separate states that are of Sanskrit background linguistically, but have a relatively strong sense of separate identity (for example, Bengalis or Kashmiris); (3) peoples with separate states that are linguistically and to some extent racially quite distinct (for example, Telegu or Malayalam); and (4) peoples that were not originally granted states of their own, and often still do not have them. These peoples, such as the Santali, Bhuti-Lepcha, or Mizo, may be survivors of India's pre-Aryan peoples. The Indian federal system accords a fair amount of democratic rights to its peoples. Several peoples from groups (2), (3), and (4) have shown through legal (especially votes) and illegal means a strong desire by a significant part of the population for independence or greater autonomy (notably

Kashmiris, Nagas, and Gurkhas). In 1986, after a long struggle, the Mizos were granted a greater degree of self-determination. Sikh extremists continue to impede the successful reestablishment of elected state government in the Punjab. The Northeast is inflamed by hatred of encroaching Bengalis from both Indian Bengal and Bangladesh. This accounting leaves out many nonterritorial religious and caste minorities, although here again the system has granted relatively broad rights to such groups for reasonable self-determination.

Civil Liberties. The Indian press is diversified, independent, but often not strongly critical or investigative. Radio and television are government controlled in this largely illiterate country, and they serve government interests. There is freedom of organization and assembly, but there have been illegal arrests, questionable killings, and reports of torture by the police, which have often been out of control. Journalism can be dangerous. There is a remarkable extent of private political organization at many social levels and for a variety of causes. The judiciary is generally responsive, fair, and independent. The frequent approach to anarchy in Indian society offers many examples of both freedom and repression. There are few if any prisoners of conscience, but hundreds are imprisoned for real or "proposed" political violence; demonstrations often lead to fatalities and massive detentions. Due to the decentralized political structure, operation of the security laws varies from region to region. Kashmir has especially repressive security policies in relation to the press and political detention; Sikkim is treated as an Indian colony; the same might be said for some other border areas. Assam and the Punjab are necessarily under stricter supervision. Indians enjoy freedom to travel, to worship as they please, and to organize for mutual benefit, especially in unions and cooperatives. Lack of education, extreme poverty, and surviving traditional controls reduce the meaning of such liberties for large numbers.

Comparatively: India is as free as Colombia, freer than Malaysia, less free than Japan.

I N D O N E S I A

Economy: noninclusive
      capitalist-statist
Polity: centralized dominant-
      party (military dominated)
Population: 168,400,000

Political Rights: 5

Civil Liberties: 6

Status: partly free

A transethnic complex state with active and potential subnationalities

Political Rights. Indonesia is a controlled parliamentary democracy under miltary direction. Recent parliamentary elections allowed some competition but severely restricted opposition campaigning and organization. The number and character of opposition parties are carefully controlled, parties must refrain from criticizing one another, candidates of both government and opposition require government approval, and the opposition is not allowed to organize in rural areas. All parties must accept the broad outline of state policy and the state ideology. All civil servants are expected to vote for the government. In any event parliament does not have a great deal of power. Regional and local government is under central control, although there is limited autonomy in a few areas. Local and regional assemblies are elected. Military officers are included in most legislatures and play a major part in the economy as managers of both public and army corporations.

Subnationalities. Indonesia includes a variety of ethnic groups and is divided by crosscutting island identities. Although the island of Java is numerically dominant, the national language is not Javanese, and most groups or islands do not appear to have strong subnational identifications. There is discrimination against Chinese culture. Both civilian and military elites generally attempt to maintain religious, ethnic, and regional balance, but government-sponsored settlement of Javanese on outer islands results in the destruction of minority cultures and the denial of self-determination. Groups demanding independence exist in Sulawesi, the Moluccas, Timor, West Irian, and northern Sumatra. Today the most active movements are in West Irian and Timor—among peoples with little in common with Indonesians.

Civil Liberties. Most newspapers are private. All are subject to fairly close government supervision; there is heavy self-censorship and censorship. Criticism of the system is muted by periodic suppressions. Radio and television are government controlled, whether or not private. Freedom of assembly is restricted, but citizens are not compelled to attend meetings. All organizations must now conform to the official ideology. There are prisoners of conscience. Thousands of released prisoners remain in second-class status, especially in regard to residence and employment. In this area the army rather than the civilian judiciary is dominant. The army has been responsible for many thousands of unnecessary deaths in its suppression of revolt in, or conquest of, East Timor. Recently there have been many murders of nonpolitical criminals, apparently at the hands of "hit squads" allied to the security services. Union activity is closely regulated, but labor organization is widespread and strikes occur. Many people are not allowed to travel outside the country for political reasons. Movement, especially to the cities, is restricted; other private rights are generally respected. The Indonesian bureaucracy has an unenviable reputation for arbitrariness and corruption—practices that reduce the effective expression of human rights. The judiciary is not independent. There are many active human rights organizations. Much of industry and commercial agriculture is government owned; sharecropping and tenant farming are relatively common, particularly on Java.

Comparatively: Indonesia is as free as South Africa, freer than Burma, less free than Singapore.

I R A N

Economy: noninclusive
        capitalist-statist
Polity: quasi-dominant party
Population: 48,000,000

Political Rights: 5

Civil Liberties: 6

Status: partly free

An ethnic state with major territorial subnationalities

Political Rights. Iran has competitive elections, but the direction of the nonelective, theocratic leadership narrowly defines who may compete in the elections. Those who oppose the overall system on fundamentals are silenced or eliminated. Political parties are poorly defined. **Subnationalities:** Among the most important non-Persian peoples are the Kurds, the Azerbaijani Turks, the Baluch, and a variety of other (primarily Turkish) tribes. Many of these have striven for independence in the recent past when the opportunity arose. The Kurds are in active revolt.

Civil Liberties. Newspapers are semi-private or factional, and all are closely controlled. The other media are largely government-owned propaganda organs. The right of assembly is denied to those who do not approve of the new system. There are many prisoners of conscience, and executions for political offenses, often nonviolent, have been frequent. Unions have been suppressed. Vigilante groups compete with the official security system; many private rights have become highly insecure, as the goal of the Islamic system is control over most aspects of life. This is especially so for the Bahais and other religious minorities. Legal emigration is quite difficult. Education is subject to religious restrictions; the freedom and equality of women is radically curtailed. However, privacy has recently been reemphasized and there appears to be a good deal of freedom in the home. Diversity and choice still characterize economic activity.

Comparatively: Iran is as free as Yugoslavia, freer than Iraq, less free than Egypt.

I R A Q

Economy: noninclusive socialist
Polity: socialist one-party
Population: 16,000,000

Political Rights: 7
Civil Liberties: 7
Status: not free

An ethnic state with a major territorial subnationality

Political Rights. Iraq is a one-party state under dictatorial leadership. Elections allow some choice of individuals, but all candidates are carefully selected, and no policy choices are involved in the process. Resulting parliaments have little if any power. Provinces are governed from the center. **Subnationalities:** Many Kurds remain in open war with the regime, in spite of institutions ostensibly developed for them.

292

Civil Rights. Newspapers are public or party and are closely controlled by the government; foreign and domestic books and movies are censored. Radio and television are government monopolies. The strident media are emphasized as governmental means for active indoctrination. Political imprisonment, brutality, and torture are common, and execution frequent. Poisoning on release from prison is reported. The families of suspects are often imprisoned. Rights are largely de facto or those deriving from traditional religious law. Religious freedom or freedom to organize for any purpose is very limited. Education is intended to serve the party's purposes. Iraq has a dual economy with a large traditional sector. The government has taken over much of the modern petroleum-based economy; land reform is, however, now expanding private choice.

Comparatively: Iraq is as free as Bulgaria, less free than Lebanon.

IRELAND

Economy: capitalist
Polity: centralized multiparty
Population: 3,600,000

Political Rights: 1
Civil Liberties: 1
Status: free

A relatively homogeneous population

Political Rights. Ireland is a parliamentary democracy that successively shifts national power among parties. The bicameral legislature has an appointive upper house with powers only of delay. Local government is not powerful, but is elective rather than appointive. Referendums are also used for national decisions.

Civil Liberties. The press is free and private, and radio and television are under an autonomous corporation. Strong censorship has always been exercised over both publishers and the press, but since this is for social rather than political content, it lies within that sphere of control permitted a majority in a free democracy. The rule of law is firmly established and private rights are guaranteed.

Comparatively: Ireland is as free as Canada, freer than France.

ISRAEL

Economy: mixed capitalist
Polity: centralized multiparty
Population: 4,200,000

Political Rights: 2
Civil Liberties: 2
Status: free

An ethnic state with microterritorial subnationalities

Political Rights. Israel is governed under a parliamentary system. Recent elections have resulted in increasingly uneasy or unstable coalitions. Provinces are ruled from the center, although important local offices in the cities are elective. Subnationalities: National elections do not involve the Arabs in the occupied territories, but Arabs in Israel proper participate in Israeli elections as a minority grouping. Arabs both in Israel and the occupied territories must live in their homeland under the cultural and political domination of twentieth century immigrants.

Civil Liberties. Newspapers are private or party, and free of censorship except for restrictions relating to the always precarious national security. Radio and television are governmentally owned. In general the rule of law is observed, although Arabs in Israel are not accorded the full rights of citizens, and the orthodox Jewish faith holds a special position in the country's religious, customary, and legal life. Detentions, house arrest, and brutality have been reported against Arabs opposing Israel's Palestine policy. Because of the war, the socialist-cooperative ideology of its founders, and dependence on outside support, the role of private enterprise in the economy has been less than in most of Euro-America. Arabs are, in effect, not allowed to buy land from Jews, while Arab land has been expropriated for Jewish settlement. Unions are economically and politically powerful and control over twenty-five percent of industry. The Survey's rating of Israel is based on its judgment of the situation in Israel proper and not that in the occupied territories.

Comparatively: Israel is as free as Uruguay, freer than India, less free than France.

I T A L Y

Economy: capitalist-statist
Polity: centralized multiparty
Population: 57,200,000

Political Rights: 1
Civil Liberties: 1
Status: free

A relatively homogeneous population with small territorial subnationalities

Political Rights. Italy is a bicameral parliamentary democracy. Elections are free. Since the 1940s governments have been dominated by the Christian Democrats, with coalitions shifting between dependence on minor parties of the left or right. Recently premiers have often been from these smaller parties. At the same time, the major parties have improved their internal democracy and legitimacy. The fascist party is banned. Referendums are used to supplement parliamentary rule. Opposition parties gain local political power. Regional institutions are developing, and the judiciary's moves against mob influence at this level improves the legitimacy of the system.

Civil Liberties. Italian newspapers are free and cover a broad spectrum. Radio and television are both public and private and provide unusually diverse programming. Laws against defamation of the government and foreign and ecclesiastical officials exert a slight limiting effect on the media. Freedom of speech is inhibited in some areas and for many individuals by the violence of extremist groups or criminal organizations. Since the bureaucracy does not respond promptly to citizen desires, it represents, as in many countries, an additional impediment to full expression of the rule of law. The judiciary has recently shown strong independence and determination. Detention may last for years without trial. Unions are strong and independent. Catholicism is no longer a state religion but remains a favored religion. Major industries are managed by the government, and the government has undertaken extensive reallocations of land.

Comparatively: Italy is as free as the United Kingdom, freer than Greece.

I V O R Y   C O A S T

Economy: noninclusive capitalist
Polity: nationalist one-party
Population: 10,500,000

Political Rights: 6
Civil Liberties: 5
Status: partly free

A transethnic heterogeneous state

Political Rights. Ivory Coast is ruled by a one-party, capitalist dictatorship in which a variety of political elements have been integrated. Assembly elections have recently allowed choice of individuals, including nonparty, but not policies. Provinces are ruled directly from the center. Contested municipal elections occur.

Civil Liberties. Although the legal press is party or government controlled, it presents a limited spectrum of opinion. Foreign publications are widely available. While opposition is discouraged, there is no ideological conformity. Radio and television are government controlled. Short-term imprisonment and conscription are used to control opposition. Travel and religion are generally free. Rights to strike or organize unions are quite limited. All wage earners must contribute to the ruling party. Economically the country depends on small, private or traditional farms; in the modern sector private enterprise is encouraged.

Comparatively: Ivory Coast is as free as Transkei, freer than Guinea, less free than Senegal.

J A M A I C A

Economy: capitalist-statist
Polity: centralized multiparty
Population: 2,300,000

Political Rights: 2
Civil Liberties: 3
Status: free

A relatively homogeneous population

Political Rights. Jamaica is a parliamentary democracy in which power changes from one party to another. However, political life is violent; election campaigns have been accompanied by hundreds of deaths. The general neutrality of the civil service, police, and army preserves the system. Responses by both parties to the anomalous one-party parliament has been excellent (more open debate in parliament and a mock opposition parliament taking its arguments to the people). Public opinion polls are becoming an increasingly important part of the political process. Regional or local administrations have little independent power, but local elections have taken an increasing national significance.

Civil Liberties. The press is largely private; the broadcasting media largely public. The only major daily supports the party that currently forms the government. Critical media are widely available to the public. Freedom of assembly and organization are generally respected. The judiciary and much of the bureaucracy retain independence, although the police and legal system have been accused of countenancing brutality and severe punishments. The number of criminals shot by the police is remarkably high. Some foreign companies have been nationalized, but the economy remains largely in private hands. Labor is both politically and economically powerful.

Comparatively: Jamaica is as free as Colombia, freer than Panama, less free than Dominica.

J A P A N

Economy: capitalist
Polity: centralized multiparty
Population: 121,000,000

Political Rights: 1
Civil Liberties: 1
Status: free

A relatively homogeneous population

Political Rights. Japan is a bicameral, constitutional monarchy with a relatively weak upper house. The conservative-to-centrist Liberal Democratic Party has ruled since the mid-1950s, either alone or in coalition with independents. Concentrated business interests have played a strong role in maintaining Liberal Party hegemony through the use of their money, influence, and prestige. In addition, weighting of representation in favor of rural areas tends to maintain the Liberal Party position. Opposition parties are fragmented. They have local control in some areas, but the power of local and regional assemblies and officials is limited.

Democracy within the Liberal Party is increasing. The Supreme Court has the power of judicial review, but its voice is not yet powerful.

Civil Liberties. News media are generally private and free, although many radio and television stations are served by a public broadcasting corporation. Television is excellent and quite free. Courts of law are not as important in Japanese society as in Europe and America. Although the courts and police appear to be relatively fair, nearly all of those arrested confess and are convicted. Travel and change of residence are unrestricted. By tradition public expression and action are more restricted than in most modern democracies. Japanese style collectivism leads to strong social pressures, especially psychological pressures, in many spheres (unions, corporations, or religious-political groups, such as Soka Gakkai). Most unions are company unions. Human rights organizations are very active. Discrimination against Koreans and other minority groups remains a problem.

Comparatively: Japan is as free as Australia, freer than France.

J O R D A N

Economy: capitalist	Political Rights: 5
Polity: limited monarchy	Civil Liberties: 5
Population: 3,700,000	Status: partly free

A relatively homogeneous population

Political Rights. Although formally a constitutional monarchy, Jordan has had few elections and a very weak parliament. Provinces are ruled from the center; elected local governments have limited autonomy. The king and his ministers are regularly petitioned by citizens.

Civil Liberties. Papers are mostly private, but self-censored and occasionally suspended. Television and radio are government controlled. Free private conversation and mild public criticism are allowed. Under a continuing state of martial law normal legal guarantees for political suspects are suspended, and organized opposition is not permitted. There are prisoners of conscience and instances of torture. Labor has a limited right to organize and strike. Private rights such as those of property, travel, or religion appear to be respected. The government has partial control over many large corporations.

Comparatively: Jordan is as free as Guyana, freer than South Yemen, less free than Egypt.

K E N Y A

Economy: noninclusive capitalist
Polity: nationalist one-party
Population: 21,200,000

Political Rights: 6
Civil Liberties: 5
Status: partly free

A transethnic heterogeneous state with active and potential subnationalities

Political Rights. Kenya is a one-party nationalist state. Only members of the party can run for office, and political opponents are excluded or expelled. All civil servants have been ordered to join the party, which includes a large part of the population. Election results can express popular dissatisfaction, but candidates avoid discussion of basic policy or the president. Selection of top party and national leaders is by consensus or acclamation; there is some democracy within the party. The administration is centralized, but elements of tribal and communal government continue at the periphery. Subnationalities: Comprising twenty percent of the population, the Kikuyu are the largest tribal group. In a very heterogeneous society, the Luo are the second most important subnationality.

Civil Liberties. The press is private, but essentially no criticism of major policies is allowed. Radio and television are under government control. Rights of assembly, organization, and demonstration are severely limited, particularly for students and faculty. The courts have considerable independence. Prisoners of conscience, detained intermittently, include university lecturers and writers. Defending them in court is itself dangerous. Unions are active but strikes are de facto illegal. Private rights are generally respected. Land is gradually coming under private rather than tribal control.

Comparatively: Kenya is as free as Ivory Coast, freer than Tanzania, less free than Gambia.

K I R I B A T I

Economy: noninclusive
          capitalist-statist
Polity: decentralized nonparty
Population: 58,000

Political Rights: 1

Civil Liberties: 2
Status: free

A relatively homogeneous population with a territorial subnationality

Political Rights. Kiribati has a functioning parliamentary system. Although there are no formal parties, both the legislature and president are elected in a fully competitive system. Local government is significant.

Civil Liberties. The press is private; radio government owned. Public expression appears to be free and the rule of law guaranteed. The modern economy is dominated by investments from the now virtually depleted government-run phosphate industry. A free union operates, and most agriculture is small, private subsistence; land cannot be alienated to non-natives.

Comparatively: Kiribati is as free as France, freer than Western Samoa, less free than Australia.

K O R E A, N O R T H

Economy: socialist
Polity: quasi-communist one-party
Population: 20,500,000

Political Rights: 7
Civil Liberties: 7
Status: not free

A relatively homogeneous state

Political Rights. North Korea is a hard-line communist dictatorship in which the organs and assemblies of government are only a facade for party or individual rule. The communism and Marxism-Leninism on which the governing system is based seems to have been replaced by the ruler's personal ideology. National elections allow no choice. The politburo is under one-man rule; the dictator's son is the dictator's officially anointed successor. Military officers are very strong in top positions.

Civil Liberties. The media are all government controlled, with glorification of the leader a major responsibility. External publications are rigidly excluded, and those who listen to foreign broadcasts severely punished. No individual thoughts are advanced publicly or privately. Individual rights are minimal. Everyone is given a security rating that determines future success. Opponents are even kidnapped overseas. Rights to travel internally and externally are perhaps the most restricted in the world: tourism is unknown--even to communist countries. Social classes are politically defined in a rigidly controlled society; and differences between the standard of living of the elite and the general public are extreme. Thousands are long-term prisoners of conscience; torture is reportedly common. There are also reeducation centers and internal exile. There is no private business or agriculture.

Comparatively: North Korea is as free as Albania, less free than South Korea.

K O R E A, S O U T H

Economy: capitalist
Polity: centralized multiparty
Population: 43,300,000

Political Rights: 4
Civil Liberties: 5
Status: partly free

A relatively homogeneous state

Political Rights. South Korea is under a military regime with the support of a partly free legislature. Recent elections of both president and assembly have given the opposition a restricted right to compete. The opposition now controls a substantial bloc of legislators, but the legislature is relatively weak, and legislators have been arrested for their public statements. The method of allocating seats greatly favors the government party. Public campaigns can significantly affect government. Local government is not independent.

Civil Liberties. Although most newspapers are private, as well as many radio stations and one television station, they have been reorganized by government fiat. Independent broadcasting has almost ceased to exist. Freedom to express differing opinion has been repeatedly restricted only to reemerge, and the mobilization of public opinion by the opposition directly affects government policy. Because of government pressures, including detentions and beatings, self-censorship is the rule, and such censorship affects all media. Special laws against criticizing the constitution, the government, or its policies results in many prisoners of conscience; torture is used. The courts have not been able to effectively protect the rights of political suspects or prisoners. Many political opponents have been denied travel permits, but freedom of internal and external travel is otherwise unabridged. There is religious freedom (but not freedom of religious groups to criticize the government). Human rights organizations are active, but have been under heavy pressure. Outside this arena, private rights have been generally respected. Rapid capitalistic economic growth has been combined with a relatively egalitarian income distribution. Government controls most heavy industry; other sectors are private. Union activity remains severely curtailed under the 1980 labor law.

Comparatively: South Korea is as free as Pakistan, freer than China (Mainland), less free than Thailand.

K U W A I T

Economy: mixed capitalist-statist
Polity: traditional nonparty
Population: 1,800,000

Political Rights: 6
Civil Liberties: 5
Status: partly free

The citizenry is relatively homogeneous

Political Rights. Kuwait's limited parliament was again dissolved in 1986 when its criticisms of the government became too threatening to the ruling family. Citizens have access to the monarch. More than half the population are immigrants: their political, economic, and social rights are inferior to those of natives; they very seldom achieve citizenship for themselves or their children.

Civil Liberties. Although the private press presents diverse opinions and ideological viewpoints, papers are subject to suspension for "spreading dissension," or for criticism of the monarch, Islam, or friendly foreign states. Radio and television are government controlled. Imported media are censored. Freedom of assembly is curtailed. Public critics may be detained, expelled, or have their passports confiscated. Formal political parties are not allowed. Private discussion is open, and few, if any, political prisoners are held. Private freedoms are respected, and independent unions operate. There is a wide variety of enabling government activity in fields such as education, housing, and medicine that is not based on reducing choice through taxation.

Comparatively: Kuwait is as free as Nicaragua, freer than Cuba, less free than Egypt.

L A O S

Economy: noninclusive socialist
Polity: communist one-party
Population: 3,600,000

Political Rights: 7
Civil Liberties: 7
Status: not free

An ethnic state with active or potential subnationalities

Political Rights. Laos has established a traditional communist party dictatorship in which the party is superior to the external government at all levels. The government is subservient to the desires of the Vietnamese communist party, upon which the present leaders must depend. Vietnam continues to maintain five divisions in the country; it is strongly represented in nearly every government ministry. Resistance continues in rural areas, where many groups have been violently suppressed. Subnationalities: Pressure on the Hmong people has caused the majority of them to flee the country.

Civil Liberties. The media are all government controlled. There are prisoners of conscience; thousands have spent as long as a decade in reeducation camps. Few private rights are accepted, but there is relaxed opposition to traditional ways, particularly Buddhism. Collectivization has been halted since 1979 because of peasant resistance; most farms continue to be small and individually owned. The limited industry is nationalized. Travel within and exit from the country are highly restricted.

Comparatively: Laos is as free as Mongolia, less free than China (Mainland).

L E B A N O N

Economy: capitalist
Polity: decentralized multiparty
Population: 2,700,000

Political Rights: 5
Civil Liberties: 4
Status: partly free

A complex, multinational, microterritorial state

Political Rights. In theory Lebanon is a parliamentary democracy with a strong but indirectly elected president. In spite of the calamities of the last decade, the constitutional system still functions to varying degrees in some parts of the country. The parliament is elected, although the last general election was in 1972. Palestinians, local militias, Syrian and Israeli forces have all but erased national sovereignty in much of the country. Subnationalities: Leading administrative and parliamentary officials are allocated among the several religious or communal groups by complicated formulas. These groups have for years existed semi-autonomously within the state, although their territories are often intermixed.

Civil Liberties. Renowned for its independence, the press still offers a highly diverse selection to an attentive audience. Most censorship is now self-imposed, reflecting the views of locally dominant military forces. Radio is government and party; television is part government and now officially uncensored. Widespread killing in recent years has inhibited the nationwide expression of most freedoms and tightened communal controls on individuals. In many areas the courts cannot function effectively, but within its power the government secures most private rights. Few if any prisoners of conscience are detained by the government. Unions are government-supervised and subsidized and generally avoid political activity. There is little government intervention in the predominantly service-oriented economy. There is an active human rights organization.

Comparatively: Lebanon is as free as Morocco, freer than Syria, less free than Cyprus (T).

L E S O T H O

Economy: noninclusive capitalist
Polity: nonparty traditional
(military dominated)
Population: 1,600,000

Political Rights: 5
Civil Liberties: 5

Status: partly free

A relatively homogeneous population

Political Rights. After an early 1986 coup, Lesotho has been temporarily ruled by the military leader and the king. There is some local government, and the chiefs retain limited power at this level. Although there are frequent expressions of national independence, the country remains under considerable South African economic and political pressure. Lesotho is populated almost exclusively by Basotho people, and the land has never been alienated. A large percentage of the male citizenry works in South Africa.

Civil Liberties. The media are government and church; criticism is muted. Political activity or assembly is repressed, but not eliminated; some members of the previous government have been detained. The judiciary preserves considerable independence vis-a-vis the government: one can win against the government in political cases. Limited union activity is permitted; some strikes have occurred. Most private rights are respected, but political opponents may be denied foreign travel.

Comparatively: Lesotho is as free as North Yemen, freer than South Africa, less free than Botswana.

305

L I B E R I A

Economy: noninclusive capitalist
Polity: dominant party
   (military dominated)
Population: 2,200,000

Political Rights: 5
Civil Liberties: 5

Status: partly free

A transethnic heterogeneous state

Political Rights. Liberia's election of president and assembly in 1985 was marred by the exclusion of important candidates and parties from the process. Credible accusation of falsification led to an attempted coup in the aftermath and the subsequent detention of opposition leaders. There is some traditional local government.

Civil Liberties. The press is private, exercises self-censorship, but represents a variety of positions. Papers may be suspended or closed. Radio and television are largely government controlled. Lack of legal protection continues to characterize the country; anarchical conditions are common. Executions, coups, and accusations of coups are frequent. Disappearances and torture are reported. Prisoners of conscience are detained. Travel and other private rights are generally respected. Only blacks can become citizens. Religion is free. Union organization is partly free; illegal strikes have occurred, often without government interference. Most industry is government or foreign owned.

Comparatively: Liberia is as free as Sierra Leone, freer than Togo, less free than Senegal.

L I B Y A

Economy: mixed socialist
Polity: socialist quasi one-party
   (military dominated)
Population: 3,900,000

Political Rights: 6
Civil Liberties: 6

Status: not free

A relatively homogeneous state

Political Rights. Libya is a military dictatorship effectively under the control of one person. Although officially there is no party, the effort to mobilize and organize the entire population for state purposes follows the socialist one-party model. The place of a legislature is taken by the direct democracy of large congresses. Elections held at local levels reflect local interests and are relatively fair; some have been nullified by the central government on the basis that they too closely reflected "outworn" tribal loyalties. Whatever the form, no opposition is allowed on the larger questions of society. Institutional self-management has been widely introduced in the schools, hospitals, and factories. Sometimes the system works well enough to provide a meaningful degree of decentralized self-determination.

Civil Liberties. The media are government-controlled means for active indoctrination. Political discussion at local and private levels may be relatively open. There are many political prisoners; the use of military and people's courts for political cases suggests little respect for the rule of law, yet acquittals in political cases occur. All lawyers must work for the state. Torture and mistreatment are frequent; executions for crimes of conscience occur—even in foreign countries through assassination. Although ideologically socialist some of the press remains in private hands. Oil and oil-related industries are the major areas of government enterprise. Socialization tends to be announced at the top and imposed rather anarchically and sporadically at the bottom. Most private associations and trade organizations are being integrated into or replaced by state organizations. Employment is increasingly dependent on political loyalty. Respect for Islam provides some check on arbitrary government.

Comparatively: Libya is as free as Algeria, freer than Afghanistan, less free than Tunisia.

L U X E M B O U R G

Economy: capitalist
Polity: centralized multiparty
Population: 365,000

Political Rights: 1
Civil Liberties: 1
Status: free

A relatively homogeneous state

Political Rights. Luxembourg is a constitutional monarchy on the Belgian model, in which the monarchy is somewhat more powerful than in the United Kingdom or Scandinavia. The legislature is bicameral with the appointive upper house having only a delaying function. Recent votes have resulted in important shifts in the nature of the dominant coalition.

Civil Liberties. The media are private and free. The rule of law is thoroughly accepted in both public and private realms. Rights of assembly, organization, travel, property, and religion are protected.

Comparatively. Luxembourg is as free as Iceland, freer than France.

MADAGASCAR

Economy: noninclusive mixed socialist	Political Rights: 5
Polity: dominant party (military dominated)	Civil Liberties: 5
Population: 10,300,000	Status: partly free

A transethnic heterogeneous state

Political Rights. Madagascar is essentially a military dictatorship with a very weak legislature. Legislative elections have been restricted to candidates selected by the former political parties on the left grouped in a "national front"; resulting parliaments appear to play a very small part in government. The presidential election in late 1982 allowed vigorous opposition. Although the opposition candidate was later arrested, he subsequently won a seat in the 1983 parliamentary elections. Emphasis has been put on developing the autonomy of local Malagasy governmental institutions. The restriction of local elections to approved "front" candidates belies this emphasis, but contests are genuine. Although tribal rivalries are very important, all groups speak the same language.

Civil Liberties. There is a private press, but papers are carefully censored and may be suspended. Broadcasting is government controlled. Movie theaters have been nationalized. There is no right of assembly; still, election processes allow periods of intense criticism, and vocal, organized opposition persists. There are few long-term prisoners of conscience; short-term political detentions are common, often combined with ill-treatment. The rule of law is weak, but political prisoners may be acquitted. Labor unions are not strong and most are party-affiliated. Religion is free, and most private rights are respected. Public security is very weak. Overseas travel is restricted. While still encouraging private investment, most businesses and large farms are nationalized. Corruption is widespread.

Comparatively: Madagascar is as free as Liberia, freer than Mozambique, less free than Morocco.

M A L A W I

Economy: noninclusive capitalist
Polity: nationalist one-party
Population: 7,300,000

Political Rights: 6
Civil Liberties: 7
Status: not free

A transethnic heterogeneous state

Political Rights. Malawi is a one-man dictatorship with party and parliamentary forms. Elections allow some choice among individuals. Administration is centralized, but there are both traditional and modern local governments.

Civil Liberties. The private and religious press is under strict government control, as is the government-owned radio service. Even private criticism of the administration remains dangerous. Foreign publications are carefully screened. The country has been notable for the persecution of political opponents, including execution and torture. There are prisoners of conscience, and even slight criticism can lead to severe penalties. Asians suffer discrimination. Corruption and economic inequality are characteristic. The comparatively limited interests of the government offer considerable scope for individual rights. There is some protection by law in the modernized sector. Small-scale subsistence farming is dominant, with much of the labor force employed in southern Africa.

Comparatively: Malawi is as free as South Yemen, freer than Somalia, less free than Zambia.

M A L A Y S I A

Economy: capitalist
Polity: decentralized
　　　dominant-party
Population: 15,800,000

Political Rights: 3
Civil Liberties: 5

Status: partly free

An ethnic state with major nonterritorial subnationalities

Political Rights. Malaysia is a parliamentary democracy with a weak, indirectly elected and appointed senate and a powerful lower house. The relatively powerless head of state is a monarch; the position rotates among the traditional monarchs of the constituent states. A multinational front has dominated electoral and parliamentary politics. By such devices as imprisonment or the banning of demonstrations, the opposition is not given an equal opportunity to compete in elections. However, the ruling front incorporates a variety of parties and interests. For example, in 1985-86 a regional opposition party won its state elections. It was eventually allowed both to rule in the state and to displace the former ruling party in the front. The states of Malaysia have their own rulers, parliaments, and institutions, but it is doubtful if any state has the power to leave the federation. Elected local governments have limited power. Subnationalities: Political, economic, linguistic, and educational policies have favored the Malays (forty-four percent) over the Chinese (thirty-six percent), Indians (ten percent), and others. Malays dominate the army. Traditionally the Chinese had been the wealthier and better-educated people. Although there are Chinese in the ruling front, they are not allowed to question the policy of communal preference. Increasingly, Chinese voters are voting for the opposition.

Civil Liberties. The press is private and highly varied. However, nothing that might affect communal relations negatively can be printed, and editors are constrained to follow government advice on many issues by the need to renew their publishing licenses annually. "Undesirable" publications, defined in the broadest terms, may not be printed or distributed. Foreign journalists are closely controlled. Radio is mostly government owned, television entirely so: both present primarily the government's viewpoint. Academics are restrained from discussing sensitive issues. There have been reports of an atmosphere of fear in both academic and opposition political circles, as well as widespread discrimination against non-Malays. An attempt to establish a private university for Chinese-language students was blocked. About three hundred political suspects are detained, generally on suspicion of communist activity. Some are clearly prisoners of conscience; several have held responsible political positions. Confessions are often forcibly extracted. Nevertheless, significant criticism appears in the media and in parliament. The government regularly interferes with Muslim religious expression, restricting both those too modernist and too fundamentalist. Christians cannot proselytize. Chinese must convert to Islam before marrying a Muslim. Unions are permitted to strike and have successfully opposed restrictive legislation. Although the government has begun to assume control of strategic sectors of the economy, economic activity is generally free, except for government favoritism to the Malays.

Comparatively: Malaysia is as free as Mexico, freer than Indonesia, less free than India.

M A L D I V E S

Economy: noninclusive capitalist
Polity: traditional nonparty
Population: 200,000

Political Rights: 5
Civil Liberties: 6
Status: partly free

A relatively homogeneous population

Political Rights. The Maldives have a parliamentary government in which a president (elected by parliament and confirmed by the people) is predominant. The elected parliament has gained some freedom of discussion. Regional leaders are presidentially appointed, but there are elected councils. Both economic and political power are concentrated in the hands of a very small, wealthy elite. Islam places a check on absolutism.

Civil Liberties. Newspapers are private, but writers are subject to prosecution for expressing even modest criticism. The radio station is owned by the government. Foreign publications are received; political discussion is limited. Several persons have been arrested for their political associations since a coup attempt. The legal system is based on traditional Islamic law. There is no freedom of religion. No unions have been formed. Most of the people rely on a subsistence economy; the small elite has developed commercial fishing and tourism.

Comparatively: Maldives is as free as Brunei, freer than Seychelles, less free than Mauritius.

M A L I

Economy: noninclusive mixed socialist

Polity: nationalist one-party (military dominated)

Population: 7,900,000

Political Rights: 7

Civil Liberties: 6

Status: not free

A transethnic heterogeneous state

Political Rights. Mali is a military dictatorship with a recently constructed political party to lend support. The regime appears to function without broad popular consensus. Assembly and presidential elections allow no choice, though there is some at the local level. Military officers have a direct role in the assembly. Subnationalities: Although the government is ostensibly transethnic, repression of northern peoples has been reported.

Civil Liberties. The media are nearly all government owned and closely controlled. Antigovernment demonstrations are forbidden. Private conversation is relatively free, and foreign publications enter freely. There are prisoners of conscience, and reeducation centers are brutal. Student protests are controlled by conscription and detention. Religion is free; unions are controlled; travelers must submit to frequent police checks. There have been reports of slavery and forced labor. Private economic rights in the modern sector are minimal, but collectivization has recently been deemphasized for subsistence agriculturists—the majority of the people. Corruption, particularly in state enterprises, is widespread and costly.

Comparatively: Mali is as free as Ghana, freer than Somalia, less free than Liberia.

M A L T A

Economy: mixed capitalist-statist
Polity: centralized multiparty
Population: 400,000

Political Rights: 2
Civil Liberties: 4
Status: partly free

A relatively homogeneous population

Political Rights. Malta is a parliamentary democracy in which the governing party has become increasingly antidemocratic. The most recent election resulted in a government victory in spite of an opposition majority in the popular vote. There is little local government.

Civil Liberties: The press is free, but foreign and domestic journalists are under government pressure. Radio and television are government controlled and biased. The government has tried to prevent the opposition use of Italian stations and to forbid criticism of the system to foreigners. The rule of law is shaky: judges who cross the government are removed or demoted; and court orders are repeatedly ignored; violent attacks on the courts have been praised by government leaders. The government foments gang violence against its opponents, but there may be violence on both sides. The government has concentrated a great deal of the economy in its hands in a manner that reduces freedom by reducing pluralism. The governing party and major union have been amalgamated; one union confederation remains independent but subdued.

Comparatively: Malta is as free as Vanuatu, freer than Turkey, less free than Cyprus(G).

MAURITANIA

Economy: noninclusive
    capitalist-statist

Political Rights: 7

Polity: military nonparty

Civil Liberties: 6

Population: 1,900,000

Status: not free

An ethnic state with a major territorial subnationality

Political Rights. Mauritania has been ruled by a succession of military leaders without formal popular or traditional legitimation. Contested local elections in December 1986 may constitute a new opening. Subnationalities: There is a subnational movement, in the non-Arab, southern part of the country.

Civil Liberties. The media are government owned and censored, but foreign publications and broadcasts are freely available. There are few if any long-term prisoners of conscience. Arrests are common, particularly for voicing opposition to Arabicization. Conversation is free; no ideology is imposed, but no opposition organizations or assemblies are allowed. Travel may be restricted for political reasons. Internal exile has been imposed on some former officials. Union activity is government controlled. There is religious freedom within the limits of an Islamic country. The government controls much of industry and mining, as well as wholesale trade, but there have been recent moves to reduce government involvement. The large rural sector remains under tribal or family control. Only in 1980 was there a move to abolish slavery.

Comparatively: Mauritania is as free as Mali, freer than Ethiopia, less free than Algeria.

MAURITIUS

Economy: capitalist

Political Rights: 2

Polity: centralized multiparty

Civil Liberties: 2

Population: 1,000,000

Status: free

An ethnically complex state

Political Rights. Mauritius is a parliamentary democracy. Recent elections have shifted control from one party to another. However, the weakness of parties and political allegiances inhibits the development of stable and thoroughly legitimate government. A variety of different racial and religious communities are active in politics. There are guarantees in the electoral system to make sure no major group is unrepresented in parliament. Elected local governing bodies are important.

Civil Liberties. The press is private or party, pluralistic and uncensored. Nevertheless, there has been a struggle between journalists and the government over the imposition of restrictions, and rights of reply on television. Broadcasting is government owned; opposition views are aired. Opposition parties campaign freely and most rights are guaranteed under a rule of law. The security services have been accused of violating the privacy of dissenters. The labor union movement is quite strong, as are a variety of communal organizations. Strikes are common, but restrictive laws make most strikes both illegal and costly to the participants. There is religious and economic freedom; social services are financed through relatively high taxes.

Comparatively: Mauritius is as free as Papua New Guinea, freer than India, less free than France.

M E X I C O

Economy: capitalist-statist
Polity: decentralized
      dominant-party
Population: 81,700,000

Political Rights: 4
Civil Liberties: 4

Status: partly free

An ethnic state with potential subnationalities

Political Rights. Mexico is ruled by a governmental system formally modeled on that of the United States; in practice the president is much stronger and the legislative and judicial branches much weaker. The states have independent governors and legislatures, as do local municipalities. The ruling party has had a near monopoly of power on all levels since the 1920s. Political competition has been largely confined to factional struggles within the ruling party. Party conventions are controlled from the top down. Progress in opening the system to other parties has been reflected in recent elections, but 1985 elections were marred by irregularities. Plausible accusations include adding fictitious names, stuffing the ballot boxes, excluding opposition observers, and fraudulent counting. Government pressure on the bureaucracy and media for support is overwhelming. The clergy are not allowed to participate in the political process. Subnationalities: There is a large Mayan area in Yucatan that has formerly been restive; there are also other smaller Indian areas.

Civil Liberties. The media are mostly private, but operate under a variety of direct and indirect government controls (including subsidies and take-overs). Free of overt censorship, papers are subject to government "guidance." Literature and the arts are free. The judicial system is not strong. However, decisions can go against the government; it is possible to win a judicial decision that a law is unconstitutional in a particular application. Religion is free. Widespread bribery and lack of control over the behavior of security forces greatly limits freedom, especially in rural areas. Disappearances occur, detention is prolonged, torture and brutality have been common. Private economic rights are respected; government ownership predominates in major industries, graft is legendary. Access to land continues to be a problem despite reform efforts. Nearly all labor unions are associated with the ruling party. Their purpose is as much to control workers for the system as to represent them. There is a right to strike. Some union and student activity has been repressed. Critical human rights organizations exist.

Comparatively: Mexico is as free as Malaysia, freer than Nicaragua, less free than Colombia.

M O N G O L I A

Economy: socialist
Polity: communist one-party
Population: 1,900,000

Political Rights: 7
Civil Liberties: 7
Status: not free

A relatively homogeneous population

Political Rights. A one-party communist dictatorship, Mongolia has recently experienced a change of leader through a mysterious politburo shift of power. Power is organized at all levels through the party apparatus. Those who oppose the government cannot run for office. Parliamentary elections offer no choice and result in 99.9% victories. Mongolia has a subordinate relationship to the Soviet Union; 25,000 Soviet troops are maintained in the country. It must use the USSR as an outlet for nearly all of its trade, and its finances are under close Soviet supervision.

Civil Liberties. All media are government controlled. Religion is restricted; Lamaism is nearly wiped out. Freedom of travel, residence, and other civil liberties are denied. As in many communist countries, all typewriting and duplicating machines must be registered annually. Employment is assigned; workers committees are extensions of the party.

Comparatively. Mongolia is as free as Bulgaria, less free than China (Mainland).

M O R O C C O

Economy: noninclusive
    capitalist-statist
Polity: centralized multiparty
Population: 23,700,000

Political Rights: 4

Civil Liberties: 5

Status: partly free

An ethnic state with active and potential subnationalities

Political Rights. Morocco is a constitutional monarchy in which the king has retained major executive powers. Parliament is active and competitive, but not powerful. Referendums have been used to support the king's policies. Recent elections at both local and national levels have been well contested. Many parties participated; the moderate center was the chief victor. The autonomy of local and regional elected governments is limited.

Subnationalities. Although people in the newly acquired land of the Western Sahara participate in the electoral process, it has an important resistance movement—mostly in exile. In the rest of the country the large Berber minority is a subnationality whose self-expression is restricted.

317

Civil Liberties. Newspapers are private or party, and quite diverse. Recently there has been no formal censorship, but government guidance is common, and backed up with the confiscation of particular issues and the closing of publications. Monarchical power must not be criticized. Broadcasting stations are under government control, although they have recently been opened to the parties for campaign statements. In the past the use of torture has been quite common and may continue; the rule of law has also been weakened by the frequent use of prolonged detention without trial. There are many political prisoners; some are prisoners of conscience. Private organizational activity is vigorous and includes student, party, business, farmer, and human rights groups. There are strong independent labor unions in all sectors; religious and other private rights are respected. State intervention in the economy is increasing, particularly in agriculture and foreign trade.

Comparatively: Morocco is as free as South Korea, freer than Algeria, less free than Spain.

MOZAMBIQUE

Economy: noninclusive socialist
Polity: socialist one-party
Population: 14,000,000 (?)

Political Rights: 6
Civil Liberties: 7
Status: not free

A transethnic heterogeneous state

Political Rights. Mozambique is a one-party communist dictatorship in which all power resides in the "vanguard party." All candidates are selected by the party at all levels, but there is some popular control of selection at local levels. Discussion in party congresses and other meetings can be quite critical. Regional administration is controlled from the center. Southerners and non-Africans dominate the government. Much of the country is under guerrilla control.

Civil Liberties. All media are rigidly controlled. Rights of assembly and foreign travel do not exist. There are no private lawyers. Secret police are powerful; thousands are in reeducation camps, and executions occur. Police brutality is common. Unions are prohibited. Pressure has been put on several religious groups, especially the Catholic clergy and Jehovah's Witnesses, although there has been some recent relaxation. Villagers are being forced into communes, leading to revolts in some areas. However, the socialization of private entrepreneurs has been partially reversed. The emigration of citizens is restricted, although seasonal movement of workers across borders is unrecorded.

Comparatively: Mozambique is as free as Malawi, freer than Somalia, less free than Tanzania.

N A U R U

Economy: mixed capitalist-statist
Polity: traditional nonparty
Population: 9,000

Political Rights: 2
Civil Liberties: 2
Status: free

An ethnically complex state

Political Rights. Nauru is a parliamentary democracy in which governments change by elective and parliamentary means. All MP's are elected as independents, although there are informal alignments. The cabinet currently represents a coalition of factions. The country is under Australian influence.

Civil Liberties. The media are free of censorship but little developed. The island's major industry is controlled by the government under a complex system of royalties and profit-sharing. No taxes are levied; phosphate revenues finance a wide range of social services. The major cooperative and union are independent.

Comparatively: Nauru is as free as Fiji, freer than Tonga, less free than New Zealand.

N E P A L

Economy: noninclusive capitalist
Polity: traditional nonparty
Population: 17,400,000

Political Rights: 3
Civil Liberties: 4
Status: partly free

An ethnic state with active and potential subnationalities

Political Rights. Nepal is a constitutional monarchy in which the king is dominant. A relatively free referendum held in 1980 rejected a move toward party government, but the new constitution opened the system to direct elections for most members of parliament. In practice, neither king nor government determines who is elected, but the king appoints many MPs. Although parliament acts independently, and is able to change governments, as in Morocco, the king has almost unlimited power to make final decisions.

Subnationalities. There are a variety of different peoples, with only fifty percent of the people speaking Nepali as their first language. Hinduism is a unifying force for the majority. Historically powerful Hindu castes continue to dominate.

Civil Liberties. Principal newspapers are public and print only what the government wishes; private journals carry criticism of the government but not the king. Some offending publications have been suspended in the recent past. Radio is government owned. Private contacts are relatively open. Political detention is common, sometimes probably for little more than expression of opinion. Parties are banned as the result of the referendum, but human rights organizations function. Union organization is under government control. The judiciary is not independent. Religious proselytizing and conversion is prohibited, and the emigration of those with valuable skills or education is restricted. The population is nearly all engaged in traditional occupations; sharecropping and tenant farming is common. Illiteracy levels are very high.

Comparatively: Nepal is as free as Turkey, freer than Bhutan, less free than Mauritius.

N E T H E R L A N D S

Economy: mixed capitalist
Polity: centralized multiparty
Population: 14,500,000

Political Rights: 1
Civil Liberties: 1
Status: free

A relatively homogeneous population

Political Rights. Netherlands is a constitutional monarchy in which nearly all the power is vested in a directly elected legislature. The results of elections have periodically transferred power to coalitions of the left and right. There is some diffusion of political power below this level, but not a great deal. The monarch retains more power than in the United Kingdom through the activity of appointing governments in frequently stalemated situations, and through the advisory Council of State.

Civil Liberties. The press is free and private. Radio and television are provided by private associations under state ownership. Commercial services have been introduced. A wide range of views is broadcast. The courts are independent, and the full spectrum of private rights guaranteed. Non-European immigrants are not well accepted by the society. The burden of exceptionally heavy taxes limits some economic choice, but benefits offer the opportunity to choose not to work.

Comparatively: The Netherlands is as free as Belgium, freer than Portugal.

N E W   Z E A L A N D

Economy: capitalist
Polity: centralized multiparty
Population: 3,300,000

Political Rights: 1
Civil Liberties: 1
Status: free

A relatively homogeneous state with a native subnationality

Political Liberties. New Zealand is a parliamentary democracy in which power alternates between the two major parties. There is elected local government, but it is not independently powerful. Subnationalities: About ten percent of the population are Maori, the original inhabitants. Their rights are now a growing concern.

Civil Liberties. The press is private and free. Television and most radio stations are government owned, but without reducing their independence significantly. The rule of law and private rights are thoroughly respected. Since taxes (a direct restriction on choice) are not exceptionally high, and industry is not government owned, we label New Zealand capitalist. Others, emphasizing the government's highly developed social programs and penchant for controlling prices, wages, and credit, might place New Zealand further toward the socialist end of the economic spectrum.

Comparatively: New Zealand is as free as the United States, freer than France.

N I C A R A G U A

Economy: noninclusive mixed socialist

Polity: dominant-party

Population: 3,300,000

Political Rights: 5

Civil Liberties: 6

Status: partly free

A relatively homogeneous population

Political Rights. Government is in the hands of the Sandinista political-military movement. Major opposition parties chose not to participate in the November 1984 elections, because of Sandinista controls on the media and harassment of the opposition campaigns. Detailed Sandinista controls over livelihood makes a free vote impossible. Still, there is a small, legal, elected opposition in the legislature. The legislature has little significance in the political system; in the Marxist-Leninist style, the government is controlled by the Party rather than the legislature. Subnationalities: Several thousand Miskito Indians have been forcibly settled and resettled with many killed in the process.

Civil Liberties. Newspapers and radio stations are under direct or indirect government control; private television is not allowed. Essentially all opposition publications have been forbidden. Government gangs regularly break up opposition rallies. Political activity by parties outside the Sandinista movement is restricted. There are thousands of political prisoners: most are former national guardsmen; many detainees, including labor leaders, are clearly prisoners of conscience. Neighborhood watch committees have been established. Killing and intimidation occur, especially in rural areas. Thousand of disappearances have been reported. The independence of the judiciary is not well developed, although the government does not always win in court. A parallel judiciary has constricted the rule of law. Foreign travel is restricted for some political opponents. Internal travel is restricted in much of the country. Nongovernment labor unions are not allowed to function. A private human rights organization is active, but its publications have been censored and then suspended. The Catholic Church retains its critical independence, as do many individuals and small groups. Some enterprises and farms have been nationalized; much of the economy remains formally private, though supplies must generally be bought from, and products sold to, the government.

Comparatively: Nicaragua is as free as Tunisia, freer than Cuba, less free than El Salvador.

N I G E R

Economy: noninclusive capitalist
Polity: military nonparty
Population: 6,700,000

Political Rights: 7
Civil Liberties: 6
Status: not free

A transethnic heterogeneous state

Political Rights. Niger is a military dictatorship with no elected assembly or legal parties. A civilian "development assembly" has recently been appointed. All districts are administered from the center.

Civil Liberties. Niger's very limited media are government owned and operated, and are used to mobilize the population. Dissent is seldom tolerated, although ideological conformity is not demanded, and foreign publications are available. There is little overt censorship, but also no barrier to censorship. A military court has taken the place of a suspended Supreme Court; a few political prisoners are held under severe conditions. Unions and religious organizations are relatively independent but nonpolitical. Foreign travel is relatively open; outside of politics the government does not regulate individual behavior. The economy is largely subsistence farming based on communal tenure; direct taxes on the poor have been abolished; agriculture has been honestly supported.

Comparatively: Niger is as free as Mali, freer than North Korea, less free than Liberia.

N I G E R I A

Economy: noninclusive
          capitalist-statist

Polity: military nonparty

Population: 100,000,000

Political Rights: 7

Civil Liberties: 5

Status: not free

A multinational state

Political Rights. After successive coups, Nigeria is under the direct rule of the military. The full spectrum of political positions has been replaced by the military command. Subnationalities: Nigeria is made up of a number of powerful subnational groupings. The numerical dominance of Muslims, and agitation for an Islamic state, makes full majoritarian democracy unattractive to many non-Muslims. Speaking mainly Hausa, the people of the north are Muslim. The highly urbanized southwest is dominated by the Yoruba; and the east by the Ibo. Within each of these areas and along their borders there are other peoples, some of which are conscious of their identity and number more than one million persons. Strong loyalties to traditional political units—lineages or kingdoms—throughout the country further complicate the regional picture.

Civil Liberties. The status of civil liberties remains in flux. Television and radio are now wholly federal or state owned, as are all but two of the major papers, in part as the result of a Nigerianization program. Still, the media have limited editorial independence, and, between clampdowns, express diverse and critical opinions.   Political organization, assembly, and publication are largely eliminated.   The universities, secondary schools, and trade unions are under close government control or reorganization in the last few years. The national student association has been banned. The courts have demonstrated their independence on occasion. Police are often brutal, and military riot control has led to many deaths. Tnere is freedom of religion and travel, but rights of married women are quite restricted. The country is in the process of moving from a subsistence to industrial economy—largely on the basis of government-controlled oil and oil-related industry. Government intervention elsewhere in agriculture (cooperatives and plantations) and industry has been considerable. Since private business and industry are also encouraged, this is still far from a program of massive redistribution. General corruption in political and economic life has frequently diminished the rule of law. Freedom is respected in most other areas of life.

Comparatively: Nigeria is as free as Tanzania, freer than Benin, less free than Senegal.

NORWAY

Economy: mixed capitalist
Polity: centralized multiparty
Population: 4,200,000

Political Rights: 1
Civil Liberties: 1
Status: free

A relatively homogeneous population with a small Lapp minority

Political Rights. Norway is a centralized, constitutional monarchy. Labor remains the strongest party, but other parties have formed several governments since the mid-1960s. There is relatively little separation of powers. Regional governments have appointed governors, and cities and towns their own elected officials.

Civil Liberties. Newspapers are privately or party owned; radio and television are state monopolies, but are not used for propaganda. This is a pluralistic state with independent power in the churches and labor unions. Relatively strong family structures have also been preserved. Norway is capitalistic, yet the government's control over the new oil resource and general reliance on centralized economic plans reduce the freedom of economic activity. Wages are equalized to an unusual degree; private hospitals are all but forbidden.

Comparatively: Norway is as free as the United Kingdom, freer than West Germany.

OMAN

Economy: noninclusive
          capitalist-statist
Polity: centralized nonparty
Population: 1,300,000

Political Rights: 6

Civil Liberties: 6
Status: not free

An ethnic state with a territorial subnationality

Political Rights. Oman is an absolute monarchy with no political parties or elected assemblies. There is an appointed consultative assembly. Regional rule is by centrally appointed governors, but the remaining tribal structure at the local and regional level gives a measure of local autonomy. British influence remains strong. Subnationalities: The people of Dhofar constitute a small regional subnationality.

Civil Liberties. Broadcasting is government owned; the daily papers are government owned, weeklies are subsidized. There is little or no criticism. Foreign publications are censored regularly. Although the preservation of traditional institutions provides a check on arbitrary action, the right to a fair trial is not guaranteed in political cases. Freedom of assembly is curtailed, and there are no independent unions. With all this, there are few if any prisoners of conscience. Travel is not restricted; private property is respected. Proselytizing for non-Muslim faiths is illegal. The population is largely involved in subsistence agriculture.

Comparatively: Oman is as free as Algeria, freer than Saudi Arabia, less free than the United Arab Emirates.

P A K I S T A N

Economy: noninclusive capitalist-statist	Political Rights: 4
Polity: quasi-multiparty (military dominated)	Civil Liberties: 5
Population: 101,900,000	Status: partly free

A multinational state

Political Rights. Pakistan is under mixed military and civilian rule. A December 1984 referendum on the President's rule and Islam was a farce—it was almost impossible to vote against it. However, in 1985 nonparty assembly elections created a parliament that has increasingly shown its independence. Although the established political parties did not compete, many of their individual members did. Campaigning for a boycott was illegal. Local elections of limited significance have been held. Military officers have positions throughout the bureaucracy and private industry.

Subnationalities. Millions of Pathans, Baluch, and Sindis have a long record of struggle for greater regional autonomy or independence. Provincial organization has sporadically offered a measure of self-determination, but at least the Baluch and Sindis continue to feel oppressed.

Civil Liberties. Newspapers are censored; the frequent detention of journalists and closing of papers lead to self-censorship. Radio and television are government controlled; movies are closely controlled for political content. For ordinary crimes punishments are often severe; torture is alleged, and executions have been common. Thousands of members of the opposition have been imprisoned or flogged in the violent political climate. Although political party activity is again legal, major parties have refused to accept the conditions for their registration. Rights of assembly are limited, as well as travel for political persons. Courts preserve some independence. Union activity is restricted but strikes and demonstrations occur; student unions are banned. Emphasis on Islamic conservatism curtails private rights, especially freedom of religion and women's rights: religious minorities suffer discrimination. Prayer wardens attempt to ensure general observance of five prayers a day. Teaching must conform to Islam. Private property is respected; some basic industries have been nationalized. Over half the rural population consists of sharecroppers and tenant farmers.

Comparatively: Pakistan is as free as Bangladesh, freer than Iran, less free than India.

P A N A M A

Economy: capitalist-statist
Polity: centralized multiparty
      (military dominated)
Population: 2,200,000

Political Rights: 6
Civil Liberties: 3

Status: partly free

A relatively homogeneous population with small subnationalities

Political Rights. Panama is formally organized as a democracy on the American model. The 1984 election that was to return power to a civilian government was influenced by the military. In 1985 the military forced the resignation of the president they had chosen, replacing him with the relatively unknown vice-president. The provinces are administered by presidential appointees, with elected councils; there is considerable local power in Indian areas.

Civil Liberties. There are oppposition papers, and critical opposition positions are reported in the news media. Through regulation, sanctions, threats, and special arrangements, the government ensures a preponderance of pro-government reporting in all media. Political parties maintain their opposition role, and rights to organization and assembly are generally respected. The judiciary is not independent; the rule of law is weak in both political and nonpolitical areas. There are few if any prisoners of conscience, but individuals dangerous to the military's interests may be eliminated. Labor unions are under some restrictions. There is freedom of religion, although foreign priests are not allowed. In general, travel is free and private property respected. Major firms are state owned; land reform has been largely ineffective in reducing inequities in land ownership.

Comparatively: Panama is as free as Singapore, freer than Nicaragua, less free than Colombia.

P A P U A   N E W   G U I N E A

Economy: noninclusive capitalist
Polity: decentralized multiparty
Population: 3,400,000

Political Rights: 2
Civil Liberties: 2
Status: free

A transethnic heterogeneous state with many subnationalities

Political Rights. Papua New Guinea is an independent parliamentary democracy, although it remains partially dependent on Australia economically, technically, and militarily. Elections are fair and seats are divided among a number of major and minor parties. Since party allegiances are still fluid, there is considerable party-switching after elections. Parties are weakened by the overwhelming desire of politicians for government positions and their perquisites. Because of its dispersed and tribal nature, local government is in some ways quite decentralized. Elected provincial governments with extensive powers have been established, but only a few have firm public support. **Subnationalities:** The nation is being created from an amalgam of small tribal peoples with similar racial and cultural backgrounds. Development of provincial governments has quieted secessionist sentiments in Bougainville, Papua, and elsewhere.

Civil Liberties. The press is free, but not highly developed. Radio is government controlled but presents critical views; Australian stations are also received. There are no political prisoners. Rights to travel, organize, demonstrate, and practice religion are secure. The legal system adapted from Australia is operational, but a large proportion of the population lives in a preindustrial world with traditional controls, including violence, that limit freedom of speech, travel, occupation, and other private rights. In the cities wide disparities in income and violent crime are major social issues; in the country, continued tribal warfare. Land ownership is widely distributed.

Comparatively: Papua New Guinea is as free as St. Vincent, freer than Vanuatu, less free than Australia.

PARAGUAY

Economy: noninclusive
    capitalist-statist

Polity: centralized dominant-
    party (military dominated)

Population: 4,100,000

Political Rights: 5

Civil Liberties: 6

Status: partly free

A relatively homogeneous state with small Indian groups

Political Rights. Paraguay has been ruled as a modified dictatorship since 1954. In addition to an elected president, there is a parliament that includes members of opposition parties. Presidential election results determine parliamentary representation. Elections are regularly held, but they have limited meaning: the ruling party receives about ninety percent of the vote, a result guaranteed by direct and indirect pressures on the media, massive government pressure on voters, especially in the countryside, interference with opposition party organization, and perhaps electoral fraud. The most important regional and local officials are appointed by the president. **Subnationalities:** The population represents a mixture of Indian (Guarani) and Spanish peoples; ninety percent continue to speak Guarani as well as Spanish—a bilingualism the government has promoted. Several small tribes of primitive forest people are under heavy pressure from both the government and the public.

Civil Liberties. The government closely controls both press and broadcasting; nongovernmental stations and papers have very limited editorial independence. Dissenting opinion is expressed, especially by the church hierarchy. Opposition political organization continues, as do human rights organizations, but there is open discrimination in favor of members of the ruling party in education, government, business, and other areas. A limited right of assembly and demonstration is exercised. Imprisonment, torture, and execution of political opponents, particularly peasants, have been and, to a limited extent, still are an important part of a sociopolitical situation that includes general corruption and anarchy. Political opponents or dissident writers may also be refused passports or exiled. There are now few if any long-term prisoners of conscience, but the rule of law is very weak. Most unions are dominated by the ruling party, but some demonstrate independence. Beyond the subsistence sector, private economic rights are restricted by government intervention, control, and favoritism. A large proportion of peasants work their own land, partly as a result of government land reform.

Comparatively: Paraguay is as free as Nicaragua, freer than Cuba, less free than Guatemala.

P E R U

Economy: noninclusive capitalist-statist	Political Rights: 2
Polity: centralized multiparty	Civil Liberties: 3
Population: 20,200,000	Status: free

An ethnic state with a major potential territorial subnationality

Political Rights. Peru is ruled by an elected multiparty parliamentary system. Won by the opposition, 1985 elections have led to strong assertion of civilian control over security forces. Provincial administration is not independent, but local elections are significant. Subnationalities: Several million people speak Quechua in the highlands, and it is now an official language. There are other important Indian groups.

Civil Liberties. The media are largely private. Censorship has been abolished. Essentially all positions are freely expressed, but there is still the shadow of the military and the recent past. There is little if any imprisonment for conscience, but many are killed or imprisoned in the course of antiguerrilla and antiterrorist campaigns; torture occurs. However, thousands of members of the security forces have been censored or arrested for excesses, and even generals have been held responsible. Periodic states of emergency reduce freedoms, especially in certain areas. Travel is not restrained, and rights to religion and occupation are generally respected. Labor is independent and politically active; strikes are common. The public sector remains dominant, but private property has regained governmental acceptance.

Comparatively: Peru is as free as Ecuador, freer than Mexico, less free than Venezuela.

PHILIPPINES

Economy: noninclusive
    capitalist-statist
Polity: dominant party
Population: 58,100,000

Political Rights: 4

Civil Liberties: 2

Status: partly free

A transethnic heterogeneous state with active and potential subnationalities

Political Rights. The early February presidential election in 1986 led to a disputed result. With American backing, the popular candidate of the middle classes was able to enforce her claim to victory. Although she may have actually "won" the election fairly, no effort was made to have a recount establish this as a fact—nor was a new election held. Instead, a new government was installed on the basis of a decreed interim constitution. Local and provincial officials were then replaced throughout the country without electoral or other legitimization. Subnationalities: The Philippines includes a variety of different peoples of which the Tagalog speaking are the most important (although a minority). A portion of the Muslim (Moro) subnationality is in active revolt along the front of Christian-Muslim opposition. There are several major potential subnationalities that may request autonomy in the future on the basis of both territorial and linguistic identity.

Civil Liberties. Newspapers and broadcasting are largely private, free, and pluralistic. Diverse foreign publications are available. Radio is free and varied, but television seems to continue under more government influence. Demonstrations by groups from the far right to the far left have been massive. Unions are again developing independence, and strikes occur. Military actions against insurgents have led to many unnecessary arrests, killings, and destruction. Disappearances occur, as do private, progovernment killings. The Catholic Church maintains its independence. The private economy is marginally capitalist, but rapid growth in government intervention, favoritism, and direct ownership of industries by government and government favorites brings the economy closer to capitalist-statist.

Comparatively: The Philippines is as free as Malta, freer than Singapore, less free than Peru.

P O L A N D

Economy: mixed socialist
Polity: communist one-party
    (military dominated)
Population: 37,500,000

Political Rights: 6
Civil Liberties: 5

Status: partly free

A relatively homogeneous population

Political Rights. Poland is a one-party communist and military dictatorship. Assembly elections in 1985 allowed some competition. All candidates must support the system. More generally, in recent years a few nonparty persons have gained election to the assembly, and some sessions have evidenced more than pro forma debate.

There are elected councils at provincial levels. Although party
and military hierarchies operating from the top down are the loci
of power, the Catholic Church, academics, peasants, and workers
must be considered by any government. The Soviet Union's claim
to a right of interference and continual pressure diminishes
Poland's independence.

Civil Liberties. The Polish newspapers are both private and
government; broadcasting is government owned. Censorship is pervasive, but legal media are opening their discussion to a wider
range of opinions. Underground publication on a massive scale
exists in a variety of fields. Private expression is relatively free.
There are no formal rights of assembly or organization, nor concept
of an independent judiciary. The church remains a major
independent voice, as do the leaders of the formally disallowed
Solidarity. Detention, beating, and harassment are common means
of restricting opposition. Illegal attempts to leave Poland have
frequently led to arrest, but opponents have been forced into exile.
For most people passports are now relatively easy to obtain. Most
agriculture and considerable commerce remain in private hands;
industry is fully nationalized.

Comparatively: Poland is as free as South Africa, freer than
Czechoslovakia, less free than Mexico.

P O R T U G A L

Economy: mixed capitalist
Polity: centralized multiparty
Population: 10,100,000

Political Rights: 1
Civil Liberties: 2
Status: free

A relatively homogeneous population

Political Rights. Portugal is a parliamentary democracy with a
more powerful president than is common in Europe. There is vigorous party competition over most of the spectrum (except the far
right), and fair elections. The overwhelming majority of voters are
centrist. Elections are competitive and power is shared by several
groups. Provincial government is centrally directed.

Civil Liberties. In spite of government or party ownership of
most major papers, journalism is now quite free. Radio and tele-

vision are government owned, except for one Catholic station. They are both relatively free editorially. The government has restored the rule of law. There are few if any prisoners of conscience, yet one can be imprisoned for insult to the military or government. Long periods of detention without trial occur in isolated instances. Imprisonment for "fascist" organization or discussion was promulgated in 1978. The Catholic Church, unions, peasant organizations, and military services remain alternative institutions of power. Although there is a large nationalized sector, capitalism is the accepted form for much of the economy.

Comparatively: Portugal is as free as France, freer than Jamaica, less free than United Kingdom.

Q A T A R

Economy: mixed capitalist-statist
Polity: traditional nonparty
Population: 300,000

Political Rights: 5
Civil Liberties: 5
Status: partly free

A relatively homogeneous citizenry

Political Rights. Qatar is a traditional monarchy. The majority of the residents are recently arrived foreigners; of the native population perhaps one-fourth are members of the ruling family. Open receptions are regularly held for the public to present grievances. Consensus plays an important role in the system.

Civil Liberties. The media are public or subsidized private, and loyalist. Discussion is fairly open; foreign publications are controlled. Political parties are forbidden. This is a traditional state still responsive to Islamic and tribal laws that moderate the absolutism of government. The family government controls the nation's wealth through control over oil, but there are also independently powerful merchant and religious classes. There are no income taxes, and many public services are free. There are no organized unions or strikes. The rights of women and religious minorities are quite limited: only native Muslim males have the full rights of citizens.

Comparatively: Qatar is as free as the United Arab Emirates, freer than Saudi Arabia, less free than Lebanon.

R O M A N I A

Economy: socialist
Polity: communist one-party
Population: 22,800,000

Political Rights: 7
Civil Liberties: 7
Status: not free

An ethnic state with territorial subnationalities

Political Rights. Romania is a traditional communist state. Assemblies at national and regional levels are subservient to the party hierarchy. Although the party is not large, all decisions are made by a small elite and especially the dictator. Elections involve only candidates or issues chosen by the party or dictator; for some assembly positions the party may propose several candidates. Soviet influence is relatively slight. **Subnationalities:** The Magyar and German minorities are territorially based. If offered self-determination, one Magyar area would surely opt for rejoining neighboring Hungary; many of the Germans evidently wish to migrate to Germany, and many have. In Romania the cultural rights of both groups are narrowly limited.

Civil Liberties. The media include only government or party organs; self-censorship committees replace centralized censorship. Private discussion is guarded; police are omnipresent. Dissenters are frequently imprisoned. Forced confessions, false charges, and psychiatric incarceration are characteristic. Treatment may be brutal; physical threats are common. Many arrests have been made for attempting to leave the country or importing foreign literature (especially Bibles and publications in minority languages). Contacts with foreigners must be reported if not given prior approval. Religious and other personal freedoms, such as the right not to have children, are quite restricted. Outside travel and emigration are not considered rights; potential emigrants may suffer economic discrimination, but many have been allowed to leave the country. Private museums have been closed. Independent labor and management rights are essentially nonexistent. Attempts to form a trade union in 1979 were crushed, as was a major coal strike in 1981. Pressure on workers and consumers to provide a greater surplus is heavy. Central planning is pervasive throughout the highly nationalized economy.

335

Comparatively: Romania is as free as the USSR, less free than Hungary.

R W A N D A

Economy: noninclusive mixed   Political Rights: 6
       socialist
Polity: nationalist one-party   Civil Liberties: 6
      (military dominated)
Population: 6,500,000   Status: not free

An ethnic state with a minor nonterritorial subnationality

Political Rights. Rwanda is a military dictatorship with an auxiliary party organization. Elections are not free and candidates are pre-selected, but voters have some choice. Districts are administered by the central government. Everyone must belong to the party, but party elections and deliberations have some competitive and critical aspects. There are elected local councils and officials. Subnationalities: The former ruling people, the Tutsi, have been persecuted and heavily discriminated against, but the situation has improved.

Civil Liberties. The weak media are governmental or religious; Only the mildest criticism is voiced; there is no right of assembly. Political prisoners are held. The courts have some independence. Hundreds of followers of religious sects were sentenced in 1986 for crimes such as failing to salute or to pay mandatory party contributions. Travel is restricted both within the country and across its borders. Labor unions are very weak. There are no great extremes of wealth. The government is socialist in intent, but missionary cooperatives dominate trade, and private business is active in the small nonsubsistence sector. Traditional ways of life rather than government orders regulate the lives of most.

Comparatively: Rwanda is as free as Tanzania, freer than Burundi, less free than Zambia.

ST. KITTS — NEVIS
(ST. CHRISTOPHER AND NEVIS)

Economy: capitalist
Polity: decentralized multiparty
Population: 42,000

Political Rights: 1
Civil Liberties: 1
Status: free

A relatively homogeneous state

Political Rights. St. Kitts-Nevis has a fully functioning parliamentary system in which the smaller Nevis has a relatively large share of power, internal self-government, and an open option to secede. Both unicameral parliaments include several appointed senators.

Civil Liberties. The media are free; there is a constitutional rule of law.

Comparatively: St. Kitts-Nevis is as free as Costa Rica, freer than Jamaica.

ST. LUCIA

Economy: capitalist
Polity: centralized multiparty
Population: 115,000

Political Rights: 1
Civil Liberties: 2
Status: free

A relatively homogeneous state

Political Rights. This is a functioning parliamentary democracy in which power alternates between parties, most recently in 1982. There are elected local governments.

Civil Liberties. The papers are largely private or party controlled, and uncensored. Radio is government and private; television private. Organization and assembly are free, but harassment and violence accompany their expression. There are strong business, labor, and religious organizations. Massive strikes played a role in forcing the resignation of the prime minister in early 1982. Personal rights generally are secured, although travel to Libya has been limited for potential dissidents.

Country Summaries

Comparatively: St. Lucia is as free as Venezuela, freer than Jamaica, less free than the United States.

ST. VINCENT AND THE GRENADINES

Economy: capitalist
Polity: centralized multiparty
Population: 123,000

Political Rights: 2
Civil Liberties: 2
Status: free

A relatively homogeneous state

Political Rights. St. Vincent is an operating multiparty state. In a 1984 election the ruling party was defeated.

Civil Liberties. Weekly papers present a variety of uncensored opinion, although there may be some government favoritism. Radio is government owned and has been accused of bias. Foreign media are readily available. There is a full right to assembly and organization; effective opposition to government policies is easily organized and often successful. There is a rule of law, but accusations of police brutality. Much of economic activity is based on agriculture.

Comparatively: St. Vincent is as free as Finland, freer than Colombia, less free than Barbados.

SAO TOME AND PRINCIPE

Economy: socialist
Polity: socialist one-party
Population: 85,000

Political Rights: 7
Civil Liberties: 7
Status: not free

A relatively homogeneous population

Political Rights. Sao Tome and Principe are governed under strongman leadership by the revolutionary party that led the country to independence. There is an indirectly elected assembly. Popular dissatisfaction and factional struggles occasionally appear, but no public opposition is allowed. Local elections allow greater freedom. Angolan and other foreign troops have been used to maintain the regime.

338

Civil Liberties. The media are government owned and controlled; opposition voices are not heard; there is no effective right of political assembly. Labor unions are not independent. The rule of law does not extend to political questions; persons are detained for expression of wrong opinions; many opponents are in exile. There is little evidence of brutality or torture. Union activity is minimal and controlled. The largely plantation agriculture has been socialized, as has most of the economy. Illiteracy is particularly high.

Comparatively: Sao Tome and Principe appear to be as free as Angola, less free than Comoros.

SAUDI ARABIA

Economy: capitalist-statist
Polity: traditional nonparty
Population: 10,000,000

Political Rights: 6
Civil Liberties: 7
Status: not free

A relatively homogeneous population

Political Rights. Saudi Arabia is a traditional family monarchy ruling without representative assemblies. Political parties are prohibited. The right of petition is guaranteed, and religious leaders provide a check on arbitrary government. Regional government is by appointive officers; there are some local elective assemblies.

Civil Liberties. The press is both private and governmental; strict self-censorship is expected. Radio and television are mostly government owned, although ARAMCO also has stations. Private conversation is relatively free; there is no right of political assembly or political organization. Islamic law limits arbitrary government, but the rule of law is not fully institutionalized. There are political prisoners, and torture is reported; there may be prisoners of conscience. Citizens have no freedom of religion—all must be Muslims, and must observe Muslim rites. Strikes and unions are forbidden. Private rights in areas such as occupation or residence are generally respected, but marriage to a non-Muslim or non-Saudi is closely controlled. Women may not marry non-Muslims, and suffer other special disabilities, particularly in the right to travel. The economy is overwhelmingly dominated by petroleum or petroleum-related industry that is directly or indirectly under government control. The commercial and agricultural sectors are private, but connection to the royal family may be critical for success. Extreme economic inequality is maintained by the political system.

Comparatively: Saudi Arabia is as free as Mauritania, freer than Ethiopia, less free than Bahrain.

S E N E G A L

Economy: mixed capitalist	Political Rights: 3
Polity: centralized	Civil Liberties: 4
dominant-party	
Population: 6,900,000	Status: partly free

A transethnic heterogeneous state

Political Rights. Although elections are fairly open and parties represent a variety of positions, one party continues to dominate elections, and not without help from the government. Opposition parties are not allowed to form coalitions, and election regulations do not provide for adequate supervision. Contested elections occur on the local level. Subnationalities: Ethnically eighty percent are Muslims; the Wolof people represent thirty-six percent of the population, including most of the elite, the urban population, and the more prosperous farmers. However, regional loyalties, both within and outside of this linguistic grouping, seem to be at least as important as communal groupings in defining potential subnationalities. Rapid assimilation of rural migrants in the cities to Wolof culture has reduced the tendency toward ethnic cleavage, but a separatist movement in the far south has shown increasing activity.

Civil Liberties. The press is predominantly public; the independence of private publications is somewhat constrained, although opposition papers and journals appear. Radio and television are under an autonomous government body, but not fully impartial. Rights of assembly and demonstration are often denied. There are at least separatist prisoners of conscience. Unions have gained increasing independence. Religion, travel, occupation, and other private rights are respected. The government sometimes loses in the courts. Although much of the land remains tribally owned, government-organized cooperatives, a strong internal private market, and dependence on external markets have transformed the preindustrial society. Many inefficient and corrupt state and quasi-public enterprises are now being dismantled.

Comparatively: Senegal is as free as Gambia, freer than Ivory Coast, less free than Botswana.

SEYCHELLES

Economy: mixed capitalist
Polity: socialist one-party
Population: 65,000

Political Rights: 6
Civil Liberties: 6
Status: not free

A relatively homogeneous population

Political Rights. Seychelles is a one-party state allowing little political competition for parliament and none for president. The former ruling party is said to have "simply disappeared." Tanzanian military support has largely been replaced by North Korean. There is no local government.

Civil Liberties. Aside from an occasional, mildly critical Catholic publication, there is no independent opinion press; radio is government owned. No opposition in publication or even conversation is legal. Individuals have little judicial protection. There is no right of political assembly, and the security services have broad powers of arrest. Opposition party activities are banned; people have frequently been arrested on political charges. Critics are often urged to leave, exiled, or refused permission to leave. Labor and government are interconnected. Private rights, including private property, are generally respected. Religious institutions maintain some independence. Quasi-government enterprises are being established; state monopolies control the marketing of all export crops. Government services in this largely impoverished country are extensive.

Comparatively: Seychelles is as free as Tanzania, freer than Somalia, less free than Maldives.

SIERRA LEONE

Economy: noninclusive capitalist
Polity: socialist one-party
Population: 3,700,000

Political Rights: 5
Civil Liberties: 5
Status: partly free

A formally transethnic heterogeneous state

Political Rights. Sierra Leone's one-party system has coopted many members of the previous opposition. The 1985 presidential election allowed no choices; participation was suspiciously high. The 1986 parliamentary election allowed choice, but many candidates were arbitrarily excluded. Military influence in government is critical. There are some elected and traditional local governments.

Civil Liberties. The press is private and governmental. Radio is government controlled. There is occasional independence in the press, but it is under heavy pressure; still there is considerable freedom of private speech. The courts do not appear to be very powerful or independent. Special emergency powers have sporadically given the government untrammeled powers of detention, censorship, restriction of assembly, and search. There may now be no prisoners of conscience. Identity cards have recently been required of all citizens. Labor unions are relatively independent, and travel is freely permitted. The largely subsistence economy has an essentially capitalist modern sector. Corruption is pervasive and costly.

Comparatively: Sierra Leone is as free as Zimbabwe, freer than Gabon, less free than Senegal.

SINGAPORE

Economy: mixed capitalist
Polity: centralized dominant-party
Population: 2,600,000

Political Rights: 4
Civil Liberties: 5
Status: partly free

An ethnically complex state

Political Rights.   Singapore is a parliamentary democracy in which the ruling party traditionally wins all legislative seats. Economic and other pressures against all opposition groups (exerted in part through control of the media) make elections very unfair.   Opposition leaders have been sentenced and bankrupted for such crimes as defaming the prime minister during the campaign. The opposition still obtains thirty percent of the vote.   In December 1984 the opposition won two seats and greatly improved its vote.   Alarmed, the government continued to bring actions against one MP until he was jailed and expelled from parliament. There is no local government.

Civil Liberties.   The press is nominally free, but owners of shares with policy-making power must be officially approved—in some cases the government owns the shares.   By closing papers and imprisoning editors and reporters, the press is kept under close control.   Government argues that the press has a duty to support government positions.   Letters to the editors do express opposition opinion.   Broadcasting is largely a government monopoly and completely controlled.   The prime minister has publicly pressed the law society to expel members of which he disapproves.   University faculties are under pressure to conform.   Rights of assembly are restricted.   Most opposition is treated as a communist threat and, therefore, treasonable.   Prisoners of conscience are held; in internal security cases the protection of the law is weak—prosecution's main task appears to be obtaining forced confessions of communist activity.   Torture is alleged.   Trade union freedom is inhibited by the close association of government and union.   Private rights of religion, occupation, or property are generally observed, although a large and increasing percentage of manufacturing and service companies are government owned.   Natalist policy favors better educated.   Many youths have reportedly been forcibly drafted into construction brigades.

Comparatively: Singapore is as free as Uganda, freer than Indonesia, less free than Malaysia.

S O L O M O N   I S L A N D S

Economy: noninclusive capitalist
Polity: decentralized multiparty
Population: 300,000

Political Rights: 2
Civil Liberties: 2
Status: free

A relatively homogeneous state with subnational strains

Political Rights. The Solomon Islands are a parliamentary democracy under the British monarch. Elections are intensely contested; party discipline is weak. There is some decentralization of power at the local level; further decentralization to the provincial level is planned.

Civil Liberties. Radio is government controlled; the limited press is both private and governmental. There is no censorshp. Although some pressures against journalists have been reported, discussion in both media is varied and critical. The rule of law is maintained in the British manner alongside traditional ideas of justice. Published incitement to inter-island conflict has led to banishment for several persons. Union activity is free, and strikes occur. The government is involved in major businesses. Most land is held communally but farmed individually.

Comparatively: The Solomon Islands are as free as Fiji, freer than Vanuatu, less free than New Zealand.

S O M A L I A

Economy: noninclusive mixed
    socialist
Polity: socialist one-party
    (military dominated)
Population: 7,800,000

Political Rights: 7
Civil Liberties: 7
Status: not free

A relatively homogeneous state

Political Rights. The Somali Republic is under one-man military rule combining glorification of the ruler with one-party socialist legitimization. Elections in 1984 with ninety-nine percent approval allowed no choice. Ethnically the state is homogeneous,

although until the military coup in 1969 tne six main clan groupings and their subdivisions were the major means of organizing
loyalty and power. While politics is still understood in lineage
terms, in its centralizing drive the government has tried to elimi-
nate both tribal and religious power. Opposition guerrilla activity
is frequently reported.

Civil Liberties. The media are under strict government control, private conversation is controlled, and those who do not
follow the government are considered to be against it. There are
many political prisoners, including prisoners of conscience. There
have been jailings for strikes and executions for reasons of
conscience. Travel is restricted. Some state farms and industries
have been established beyond the dominant subsistence economy.
A large black market circumvents official distribution channels;
corruption is widespread in government and business.

Comparatively: Somalia is as free as Ethiopia, less free than
Kenya.

S O U T H   A F R I C A

Economy: capitalist-statist
Polity: centralized multiparty
Population: 26,000,000

Political Rights: 5
Civil Liberties: 6
Status: partly free

An ethnic state with major territorial and nonterritorial subnationalities

Political Rights. South Africa is a parliamentary democracy in
whicn the black majority is excluded from participation in the
national political process because of race. Recent constitutional
changes add over ten percent more to the politically accepted
population; the great majority black population remains excluded.
For the nonblack population elections appear fair and open. There
is a limited scope for blacks to influence affairs within their own
communities. Subnationalities: Most of the black majority is
ascribed to a variety of "homelands" that they may or may not live
in, although thousands have been forced to move to these limited
areas. Several of these have become independent states in the
eyes of South Africa, but they have not received such recognition

345

elsewhere. (Except for Transkei, we see these as dependent territories; because of their close integration into South Africa politically and economically we treat these states as part of South Africa for most purposes. The dependent governments of these states are generally unpopular and tyrannical, although this is less so in Bophuthatswana. Geographically and historically Transkei does have a reasonable claim to statehood, in spite of the reasons that may have brought it into being. It is in many ways comparable to Lesotho, Swaziland, or, further afield, states such as Bhutan or Mongolia.) In the several homelands that have not yet separated from the country officially, black leaders have some power and support from their people. Most black political parties are banned, but operating political parties among Indians and people of mixed blood represent the interests of their peoples. Regionally, government within the white community includes both central government officials and elected councils.

Civil Liberties. The white South African press is private and quite outspoken, although often censored or restricted. Unlike other repressive societies, restrictions apply more to reportage and access than to opinion. The nonwhite press is closely restricted, but nevertheless shows critical independence on occasion. Broadcasting is under government control. The courts are independent on many issues, including apartheid, but have not effectively controlled the security forces. There are political prisoners and torture—especially for black activists, who live in an atmosphere of terror. Nevertheless, black organizations regularly denounce the government's racial and economic policies, hold conferences, and issue statements. Academic groups publish highly critical well-publicized studies of the system. Private rights are generally respected for whites. Blacks have rights to labor organization, although political activity is restricted. Legal separation of the races remains, but has been relaxed in a number of ways. Rights to choice of residence and occupation have improved for nonwhites, but hundreds of thousands have been forcibly moved, and such expulsions continue. Human rights organizations are active in both white and black communities. Church organizations have become centers of opposition to apartheid. Escalating violence and counterviolence, and the emergency powers that accompany the violence, obscure these gains.

Comparatively: South Africa is as free as Yugoslavia, freer than Tanzania, less free than Morocco.

S P A I N

Economy: capitalist
Polity: centralized multiparty
Population: 38,800,000

Political Rights: 1
Civil Liberties: 2
Status: free

An ethnic state with major territorial subnationalities

Political Rights. Spain is a constitutional monarchy with a fully functioning democratic system. In the last few years it has managed to largely overcome or pacify military, far right, and Basque dissidence. Elected regional and local governments are of increasing importance. Referendums are also used for major issues. Subnationalities: The Basque and Catalan territorial subnationalities have had their rights greatly expanded in recent years.

Civil Liberties. The press is private and is now largely free. The television network and some radio stations are government owned. National television is controlled by an all-party committee, but there are autonomous regional channels. There are few prisoners of conscience; imprisonment still threatens those who insult the security services, the courts, the state, or the flag. Short detention periods are often used with little legal redress. Police brutality and torture still occur, and the government has been slow to punish the civil guardsmen often responsible. Criticism of the government and of suspected human rights violators are quite freely expressed both publicly and privately. Private freedoms are respected. Continued terrorism and reactions to terrorism affect some areas. Union organization is free and independent.

Comparatively: Spain is as free as France, freer than Brazil, less free than Norway.

SRI LANKA

Economy: mixed capitalist-statist
Polity: centralized multiparty
Population: 16,600,000

Political Rights: 3
Civil Liberties: 4
Status: partly free

An ethnic state with a major subnationality

Political Rights. Sri Lanka is a parliamentary democracy in which opposition groups have been partially excluded. In late 1982 tne government used its then current popularity to guarantee by referendum a six-year extension of its rule. The referendum was held under a state of emergency restricting opposition campaigning. Regional government is centrally controlled; local government is by elected councils. **Subnationalities:** Receiving a large vote in the most recent election, the Tamil minority constitutes a serious secessionist tendency. Tamil guerrillas control parts of the country. Tne government has been unable to protect Tamils against the army, guerrillas, and private mobs.

Civil Liberties. The well-developed governmental press is under strong pressure to follow the governmental line. Broadcasting is government controlled and presents a narrow range of views. Censorship is used particularly in regard to the guerrilla war. The rule of law has been threatened by this communal violence, as well as by the use and misuse of state-of-emergency powers to detain political opponents. Courts remain independent of the government; an important human rights movement supports their independence. However, their decisions can be overruled by parliament. A few prisoners of conscience have been arrested, at least for advocating Tamil independence; torture and brutality is alleged. There is freedom of assembly but not demonstration. Private rights to movement, residence, religion, and occupation are respected in theory, but gangs and the army have been guilty of widespread looting, destruction, and killing in Tamil areas. Strikes in public services are restricted, but unions are well developed and politically influential. There has been extensive land reform; the state has nationalized a number of enterprises in this largely plantation economy. The system has done an excellent job in providing for basic nutrition, health, and educational needs within a democratic framework.

Comparatively: Sri Lanka is as free as El Salvador, freer than Indonesia, less free than India.

S U D A N

Economy: noninclusive mixed
      capitalist

Polity: multiparty

Population: 22,900,000

Political Rights: 4

Civil Liberties: 5

Status: partly free

An ethnic state with major but highly diverse subnationalities

Political Rights. 1986 saw the return of parliamentary government to the northern two-thirds of the country. Much of the south is effectively under rebel or military control. Subnationalities: The peoples of the south are ethnically and religiously distinct. The national government remains overwhelmingly northern. A war for southern independence is again underway. Other major ethnic groups are also interested in regional autonomy.

Civil Liberties. The press is being privatized. Radio and television are government controlled. There is considerable independence of expression, at least in the capital city. Arrests for expression still occur, however, and violence or its threat limits expression elsewhere. Worker and professional organizations are politically effective.

Comparatively: Sudan is as free as Egypt, freer than Ethiopia, less free than Turkey.

S U R I N A M E

Economy: noninclusive mixed
      socialist

Polity: military nonparty

Population: 375,000

Political Rights: 6

Civil Liberties: 6

Status: not free

An ethnically complex state

Political Rights. Suriname is ruled by a military leader and council without legitimization by elections. An appointed assembly and alliances with some business and labor groups have broadened the base of power marginally. The government faces a rebel force along its frontier.

Civil Liberties. Although press and radio are largely private and varied, they are under strong government pressure to conform. Political organization or assembly is forbidden. The leaders of all major opposition groups (of former political parties, unions, journalists, and academia) were executed without trial in late 1982. Prisoners of conscience have been detained and treated brutally. Courts and unions retain some independence. Houses are searched at will.

Comparatively: Suriname is as free as Tanzania, freer than Albania, less free than Guyana.

S W A Z I L A N D

Economy: noninclusive capitalist
Polity: traditional nonparty
Population: 700,000

Political Rights: 5
Civil Liberties: 6
Status: partly free

A relatively homogeneous population

Political Rights. Swaziland is ruled by a king. Indirect elections for part of an advisory legislature are held, but only one party is allowed. Local councils invite popular participation. South African political and economic influence is pervasive.

Civil Liberties. Private media exist alongside the dominant government media; little criticism is allowed; South African and other foreign media provide an alternative. Opposition leaders have been repeatedly detained, and partisan activity is forbidden. Criticism is common in parliament and other councils, but public assemblies are restricted, unions limited, emigration difficult. The rule of law is very insecure. Religious, economic, and other private rights are maintained. The traditional way of life is continued, especially on the local level. Several thousand whites in the country and in neighboring Transvaal own the most productive land and business.

Comparatively: Swaziland is as free as South Africa, freer than Mozambique, less free than Botswana.

S W E D E N

Economy: mixed capitalist
Polity: centralized multiparty
Population: 8,400,000

Political Rights: 1
Civil Liberties: 1
Status: free

A relatively homogeneous population

Political Rights. Sweden is a parliamentary democracy in which no party monopolizes power, and the king's power has been all but extinguished. Referendums are held. Although there are some representative institutions at regional and local levels, the system is relatively centralized. Resident aliens have a right to vote in local elections. The tendency of modern bureaucracies to regard issues as technical rather than political has progressed further in Sweden than elsewhere.

Civil Liberties. The press is private or party; broadcasting is by state-licensed monopolies. Although free of censorship; the media are accused of presenting a narrow range of views, but this may be changing as politics become polarized. There is the rule of law. The defense of those accused by the government may not be as spirited as elsewhere, but, on the other hand, the ombudsman office gives special means of redress against administrative arbitrariness. Most private rights are respected. State interference in family life is unusually strong, with many children unjustly taken from their parents. The national church has a special position. In many areas, such as housing, individual choice is restricted more than in other capitalist states—as it is of course by the very high tax load. Unions are a powerful part of the system. The state intervenes in the economy mainly through extensive business regulation rather than direct ownership.

Comparatively: Sweden is as free as Denmark, freer than West Germany.

S W I T Z E R L A N D

Economy: capitalist
Polity: decentralized multiparty
Population: 6,500,000

Political Rights: 1
Civil Liberties: 1
Status: free

A trinational state

Political Rights. Switzerland is a parliamentary democracy in which all major parties are given cabinet positions on the basis of the size of the vote for each party. The president and vice-president are elected on a rotating basis from this cabinet. Parties that increase their vote above a certain level are invited to join the government, although such changes in party strength rarely occur. The lack of a decisive shift in power from one party to another in tne last fifty years is a major limitation on the democratic effectiveness of the Swiss system. However, its dependence on the grand coalition style of government is a partial substitute, and the Swiss grant political rights in other ways that compensate for the lack of a transfer of power. Many issues are decided by the citizenry through national referendums or popular initiatives. After referendums, in keeping with the Swiss attitude, even the losing side is given part of what it wants if its vote is sufficiently large. **Subnationalities:** The three major linguistic groups have separate areas under their partial control. Their regional and local elected governments have autonomous rights and determine directly much of the country's business. National governments try to balance the representatives of the primary religious and linguistic groups; this is accomplished in another way by the upper house that directly represents the cantons (regions) on an equal basis.

Civil Liberties. The high-quality press is private and independent. Broadcasting is government operated, although with the considerable independence of comparable West European systems. Unions are free. Strikes are few because of a 1937 labor peace agreement requiring arbitration. The rule of law is strongly upheld; as in Germany it is against the law to question the intentions of judges. 1985 saw a major extension of women's rights. Private rights are thoroughly respected.

Comparatively: Switzerland is as free as the United States, freer than West Germany.

S Y R I A

Economy: mixed socialist
Polity: centralized dominant-party
    (military dominated)
Population: 10,500,000

Political Rights: 6
Civil Liberties: 7

Status: not free

A relatively homogeneous population

Political Rights. Syria is a military dictatorship assisted by an elected parliament. The election of the military president is largely pro forma; in assembly elections a variety of parties and independents compete within and without the National Front, organized under the leadership of the governing party. Many "independents" serve in the cabinet, but their independence is minimal. Because of its control of the army, the Alawite minority (ten percent) has a very unequal share of national power. Provinces have little separate power, but local elections are contested.

Civil Liberties. The media are in the hands of government or party. Broadcasting services are government owned. The media are used as governmental means for active indoctrination. Medical, bar, and engineering associations have been dissolved. Thousands have been arrested and many executed. Other thousands have been killed in punitive expeditions. The courts are neither strongly independent nor effective in political cases where long-term detention without trial occurs. Political prisoners are often arrested following violence, but there are also prisoners of conscience. Political opponents may even be killed overseas. Torture has frequently been employed in interrogation. Religious freedom is restricted. Rights to choice of occupation or residence are generally respected; foreign travel and emigration are closely controlled for certain groups. Much of industry has been nationalized; the commercial sector remains private. Land reform has successfully expanded private ownership. There is no independent labor movement.

Comparatively: Syria is as free as South Yemen, freer than Somalia, less free than Kuwait.

T A N Z A N I A

Economy: noninclusive socialist
Polity: socialist one-party
Population: 22,400,000

Political Rights: 6
Civil Liberties: 6
Status: not free

A transethnic heterogeneous nation in union with Zanzibar

Political Rights. Tanzania is an unequal union of two states. The single parties of each state have joined to form one all-Tanzanian party. Elections offer choice between individuals, but no issues are to be discussed in campaigns; all decisions come down from above, including the choice of candidates. Over half of the MP's are appointed. The resulting parliament is not, however, simply a rubber stamp. Local government is an extension of party government. Subnationalities: Ethnically, the country is divided into a large number of peoples (none larger than thirteen percent); most are not yet at the subnational level. The use of English and Swahili as national languages enhances national unity. Recent resistance by some Zanzibar leaders to continued association with the mainland has been defused by the appointment of a Zanzibari as president.

Civil Liberties. Civil liberties are subordinated to the goals of the socialist leadership. No contradiction of official policy is allowed to appear in the media, nearly all of which is government owned, or in educational institutions; private and limited criticism of implementation appears. The people learn only of those events the government wishes them to know. There is no right of assembly or organization. Millions of people have been forced into communal villages; people from the cities have been abruptly transported to the countryside; forced labor on the farms is still a problem. Thousands have been detained for political crimes. There are prisoners of conscience. Lack of respect for the independence of the judiciary and individual rights is especially apparent in Zanzibar. Union activity is government controlled. Neither labor nor capital have legally recognized rights—strikes are illegal. Most business and trade and much of agriculture are nationalized. Religion is free, at least on the mainland; overseas travel is restricted.

Comparatively: Tanzania is as free as Algeria, freer than Malawi, less free than Zambia.

THAILAND

Economy: noninclusive capitalist
Polity: centralized multiparty
(military dominated)
Population: 52,800,000

Political Rights: 3
Civil Liberties: 3

Status: partly free

An ethnic state with a major territorial subnationality

Political Rights. Thailand is a constitutional monarchy with continuing military influence. Both parties and parliament are, however, significant. The politics are those of consensus. Provincial government is under national control; there are elected and traditional institutions at the local level. **Subnationalities:** There is a Muslim Malay community in the far south, and other small ethnic enclaves in the north.

Civil Liberties. The press is private, but periodic suppressions and warnings lead to limited self-censorship. Casting doubt on the monarchy is illegal. Most broadcasting is government or military controlled. Some books are banned as subversive. There are few long-term prisoners of conscience, but many are periodically detained for communist activity. Human rights and other public interest organizations are active. Labor activity is relatively free. Private rights to property, choice of religion, or residence are secure; foreign travel or emigration is not restricted. However, corruption limits the expression of all rights. Government enterprise is quite important in the basically capitalist modern economy.

Comparatively: Thailand is as free as Philippines, freer than Malaysia, less free than India.

T O G O

Economy: noninclusive mixed
Polity: nationalist one-party
  (military dominated)
Population: 3,000,000

Political Rights: 6
Civil Liberties: 6

Status: not free

A transethnic heterogeneous state

Political Rights. Togo is a military dictatorship ruled in the name of a one-party state. In this spirit there is a deliberate denial of the rights of separate branches of government, including a separate judiciary, or even of private groups. National elections allow choice among party-approved candidates. Campaigns allow no policy discussion. But essentially everyone can join the party and there is some discussion in parliament and party organs. Below the national level only the cities have a semblance of self-government. The government depends on French troops to protect it against internal enemies. **Subnationalities:** The southern Ewe are culturally dominant and the largest group (twenty percent), but militant northerners now rule.

Civil Liberties. No criticism of the government is allowed in the government or church media, and foreign publications may be confiscated. There are prisoners of conscience, and torture occurs. Jehovah's Witnesses are banned. There is occasional restriction of foreign travel. Union organization is closely regulated. In this largely subsistence economy the government is heavily involved in trade, production, and the provision of services. All wage earners must contribute to the ruling party.

Comparatively: Togo is as free as Gabon, freer than Ethiopia, less free than Zambia.

T O N G A

Economy: noninclusive capitalist
Polity: traditional nonparty
Population: 100,000

Political Rights: 5
Civil Liberties: 3
Status: partly free

A relatively homogeneous population

Political Rights. Tonga is a constitutional monarchy in which the king and nobles retain power. Only a minority of the members of the legislative assembly are elected directly by the people; but the veto power of the assembly can be effectively expressed. Regional administration is centralized; there are some elected local officials.

Civil Liberties. The main paper is a government weekly; radio is under government control. Other foreign and local media are available. There is a rule of law, but the king's decision is still a very important part of the system. Private rights within the traditional Tonga context seem guaranteed.

Comparatively: Tonga is as free as Mexico, freer than Seychelles, less free than Western Samoa.

T R A N S K E I

Economy: noninclusive capitalist

Polity: centralized
         dominant-party

Population: 2,500,000

Political Rights: 5

Civil Liberties: 6

Status: partly free

A relatively homogeneous population

Political Rights. In form Transkei is a multiparty parliamentary democracy; in fact it is under the strongman rule of a paramount chief supported by his party's majority. The meaning of recent elections has been partly nullified by governmental interference, including the jailing of some opposition leaders. Chiefs form half of the assembly by appointment. The balancing of tribal interests remains very important in the system, but beyond that there is little decentralization of power. South Africa has a great deal of de facto power over the state, particularly because of the large number of nationals that work in South Africa. However, Transkei is at least as independent as several Soviet satellites; it has had continuing public disputes with South Africa.

Civil Liberties. The press is private, but under strong government pressure. Broadcasting is government controlled. Many members of the opposition have been imprisoned; new retroactive laws render it illegal to criticize Transkei or its rulers. Freedom

of organization is very limited, although an opposition party still
exists. Private rights are respected within the limits of South
African and Transkei custom. Capitalist and traditional economic
rights are diminished by the necessity of a large portion of the
labor force to work in South Africa.

Comparatively: Transkei is as free as Swaziland, freer than
Mozambique, less free than Zimbabwe.

T R I N I D A D   A N D   T O B A G O

Economy: capitalist-statist
Polity: decentralized multiparty
Population: 1,200,000

Political Rights: 1
Civil Liberties: 2
Status: free

An ethnically complex state

Political Rights. Trinidad and Tobago is a parliamentary democracy in which one party has managed to retain power since 1956
(in part because of the division of the electorate among ethnic
groups). However, there has been a decentralization of power, and
elections have been vigorously contested by a variety of parties.
Local government is elected. Tobago's elected regional government is controlled by an opposition party.

Civil Liberties. The private or party press is generally free of
restriction; broadcasting is under both government and private
control. Opposition is regularly voiced, although the government-
owned television is said to favor the government. There is a full
spectrum of private rights. Violence and communal feeling reduce
the effectiveness of such rights for many, as does police violence.
Many sectors of the economy are government owned. Human rights
organizations are active. Labor is powerful and strikes frequent.

Comparatively: Trinidad and Tobago is as free as Venezuela,
freer than Guyana, less free than Belgium.

T U N I S I A

Economy: mixed capitalist
Polity: dominant party
Population: 7,200,000

Political Rights: 6
Civil Liberties: 5
Status: partly free

A relatively homogeneous population

Political Rights. Tunisia has a dominant party system, but is essentially under one-man rule. Elections to the assembly are contested primarily within the one-party framework; opposition parties and opposition factions in the ruling party have recently been forced outside the process by increasingly authoritarian rule. Regional government is centrally directed; there is elected local government.

Civil Liberties. The private, party, and government press is under government pressure. Frequently banned or fined, opposition papers have almost ceased to exist after government suspensions. Broadcasting is government controlled. Distribution of cassettes and video tapes give a modest dimension of freedom. Private conversation is relatively free, but there is no right of assembly. Organizational activity is generally free, including that of the Tunisian Human Rights League. The courts demonstrate only a limited independence, but it is possible to win against the government. Unions have been relatively independent despite periods of repression. There are few if any long-term prisoners of conscience, but arrests for unauthorized political activity or expression occur. The unemployed young are drafted for government work. Overseas travel is occasionally blocked. Most private rights seem to be respected, including economic freedoms since doctrinaire socialism was abandoned and much of agriculture returned to private hands.

Comparatively: Tunisia is as free as Kuwait, freer than Algeria, less free than Egypt.

T U R K E Y

Economy: capitalist-statist
Polity: multiparty
      (military dominated)
Population: 52,300,000

Political Rights: 3
Civil Liberties: 4

Status: partly free

An ethnic state with a major territorial subnationality

Political Rights. Power is divided between a military president and a civilian prime minister. The current president was confirmed in power on a questionable adjunct to a constitutional referendum in late 1982. Opposition campaigning was restricted and the vote not entirely secret. Although controls on party formation and candidature greatly reduced the significance of the legislative election in November 1983, subsequent events have, in effect, restored the old parties and shown the ruling party to represent an authentic democratic force. Power is centralized, but local and provincial elections are significant. Subnationalities: Several million Kurds are denied self-determination; it is illegal to teach or publish in Kurdish.

Civil Liberties. The press is private; the government controls the broadcasting system directly or indirectly. Suspensions and arrests by the government have produced self-censorship, but the press has become increasingly outspoken. Kurds and Armenians are prohibited topics, even in books. There remain many prisoners of conscience under martial law, and petitioners to expand rights have been detained. Religious expression is free only if religion is not related to law and way of life. Torture has been common, but the government has made arrests of some accused torturers. The courts exhibit some independence in political decisions. Independent union activity has been curtailed; but strikes are now permitted. Nearly fifty percent of the people are subsistence agriculturists. State enterprises make up more than half of Turkey's industry.

Comparatively: Turkey is as free as Sri Lanka, freer than Yugoslavia, less free than Spain.

T U V A L U

Economy: noninclusive capitalist
Polity: traditional nonparty
Population: 8,000

Political Rights: 1
Civil Liberties: 1
Status: free

A relatively homogeneous state

Political Rights. Tuvalu is a parliamentary democracy under the British monarch. Each island is represented; seats are contested individually. Opposition blocs have been formed in the assembly and have been able to achieve power. There are local councils for each island. Continued dependence on the United Kingdom is self-chosen and economically unavoidable.

Civil Liberties. Media are government owned but little developed. The rule of law is maintained in the British manner, alongside traditional ideals of justice. The economy is largely subsistence farming; much of the labor force is employed overseas.

Comparatively: Tuvalu is as free as New Zealand, freer than Mauritius.

U G A N D A

Economy: noninclusive
         capitalist-statist
Polity: transitional military
Population: 15,200,000

Political Rights: 5

Civil Liberties: 4
Status: partly free

A transethnic heterogeneous state with major subnationalities

Political Rights. A rebel movement representing ethnically the majority of the population attained power by military victory in 1986. The announced goal is to build a democratic society; the inclusion of a variety of former political leaders in government reenforces this presumption. **Subnationalities:** The population is divided among a wide variety of peoples, some of which are subnationalities based on kingdoms that preceded the present state. The most important of these was Buganda.

361

Civil Liberties. Newspapers are private, party, or government; radio and television are government owned. In 1986 the new regime banned an obstreperous newspaper. Free discussion has again emerged. Assembly and travel are restricted within the country. Unions are weak and government influenced. The murder of opposition politicians has declined, and over 1,000 political prisoners have been released. The courts have some independence. Religious freedom has been partially reestablished, and the churches play a balancing role to a limited extent. The economy has suffered severe dislocation: property is not secure, the black market flourishes.

Comparatively: Uganda is as free as Lebanon, freer than Tanzania, less free than Brazil.

UNION OF
SOVIET SOCIALIST REPUBLICS

Economy: socialist
Polity: communist one-party
Population: 280,000,000

Political Rights: 7
Civil Liberties: 7
Status: not free

A complex ethnic state with major territorial subnationalities

Political Rights. The Soviet Union is ruled by parallel party and governmental systems: the party system is dominant. Elections are held for both systems, but in neither is it possible for the rank and file to determine policy. Candidacy and voting are closely controlled, and the resulting assemblies do not seriously question the policies developed by party leaders (varying by time or issue from one individual to twenty-five). The Soviet Union is in theory elaborately divided into subnational units, but in fact the all-embracing party structure renders local power minimal.

Subnationalities. Russians account for half the Soviet population. The rest belong to a variety of subnational groupings ranging down in size from the forty million Ukrainians. Most groups are territorial, with a developed sense of subnational identity. The political rights of all of these to self-determination, either within the USSR or through secession, is effectively denied. In many cases Russians or other non-native peoples have been settled in subnational territories in such numbers as to make the native people a minority in their own land (for example, Kazakhstan). Expression of opinion in favor of increased self-determination is repressed at least as much as anticommunist opinion. Most of these peoples have had independence movements or movements for enhanced self-determination since the founding of the USSR. Several movements have been quite strong since World War II (for example, in the Ukraine or Lithuania); the blockage of communication by the Soviet government makes it very difficult to estimate either the overt or latent support such movements might have. In 1978 popular movements in Georgia and Armenia led to the retention of the official status of local languages in the Republics of the Caucasus; freedoms, such as that to move in and out of the country, are notable in Armenia.

Civil Liberties. The media are totally owned by the government or party and are, in addition, regularly censored. Major deviations from the party line are found only in rare and very small underground publications. Arrest and exile have silenced nearly all dissident criticism. However, official discussion of policy issues has become more diversified among writers, economists, and others. Crimes against the state, including insanity (demonstrated by perverse willingness to oppose the state), are broadly defined; as a result, political prisoners are present in large numbers both in jails and insane asylums. Nearly all imprisonment and mistreatment of prisoners in the Soviet Union are carried out in accordance with Soviet security laws—even though these laws conflict with other Soviet laws written to accord with international standards. Since the Bolshevik Revolution there has never been an acquittal in a major political trial. Insofar as private rights, such as those to religion, education, or choice of occupation, exist, they are de facto rights that may be denied at any time. Travel within and outside of the USSR is highly controlled; many areas of the country are still off-limits to foreigners—especially those used as areal prisons for dissidents. Some private entrepreneurial activity has now been legalized; there are rights to nonproductive personal property. Other rights, such as those to organize independent labor unions, are strictly denied. Literacy is high, few starve, and private oppression is no more.

Comparatively: The USSR is as free as Romania, less free than Hungary.

U N I T E D   A R A B   E M I R A T E S

Economy: capitalist-statist
Polity: decentralized nonparty
Population: 1,400,000

Political Rights: 5
Civil Liberties: 5
Status: partly free

A relatively homogeneous citizenry

Political Rights. The UAE is a confederation of seven shaikh-doms in which the larger are given the greater power both in the appointed assembly and the administrative hierarchy. There is a great deal of consultation in the traditional pattern. Below the confederation level there are no electoral procedures or parties. Each shaikhdom is relatively autonomous in its internal affairs. The majority of the people are recent immigrants and noncitizens. The army, enlisted men and officers, are generally foreign.

Civil Liberties. The press is private or governmental. There is self-censorship, but some criticism is expressed. Broadcasting is under federal or shaikhdom control. There are no political assemblies, but there are also few, if any, prisoners of conscience. The courts dispense a combination of British, tribal, and Islamic law. Labor unions are prohibited, but illegal strikes have occurred. Private rights are generally respected; there is freedom of travel. As in most Muslim countries there is freedom of worship for established religions, but only the favored Muslims may prose-lytize. Many persons may still accept the feudal privileges and restraints of their tribal position. The rights of the alien majority are less secure: "troublemakers" are deported. Private economic activity exists alongside the dominance of government petroleum and petroleum-related activities.

Comparatively: United Arab Emirates are as free as Bahrain, freer than Saudi Arabia, less free than Sudan.

UNITED KINGDOM

Economy: mixed capitalist
Polity: centralized multiparty
Population: 56,600,000

Political Rights: 1
Civil Liberties: 1
Status: free

An ethnic state with major subnationalities

Political Rights. The United Kingdom is a parliamentary democracy with a symbolic monarch. Plurality elections from single-member districts on the basis of party affiliation rather than personal record lead to strong parties and political stability. Fair elections are open to all parties, including those advocating secession. Unchecked by a written constitution or judicial review, parliament is restrained only by tradition. Between elections this means potentially great powers for the prime minister. There are elected local and regional governments, and their limited powers are gradually being increased. **Subnationalities:** Scots, Welsh, Ulster Scots, and Ulster Irish are significant and highly self-conscious territorial minorities. In 1978 parliament approved home rule for Scotland and Wales, but the Welsh and (more ambiguously) the Scots voters rejected this opportunity in 1979. Northern Ireland's home rule has been in abeyance because of an ethnic impasse, but is being reestablished. Ulster Scot and Irish live in intermixed territories in Northern Ireland. Both want more self-determination—the majority Ulster Scots as an autonomous part of the United Kingdom, the minority Ulster Irish as an area within Ireland.

Civil Liberties. The press is private and powerful; broadcasting has statutory independence although it is indirectly under government control. British media are comparatively restrained because of strict libel and national security laws, and a tradition of accepting government suggestions for the handling of sensitive news. In Northern Ireland a severe security situation has led to the curtailment of private rights, to imprisonment, and on occasion to torture and brutality. However, these conditions have been relatively limited, thoroughly investigated by the government, and improved as a result. Elsewhere the rule of law is entrenched, and private rights generally respected. Unions are independent and powerful. In certain areas, such as medicine, housing, inheritance, and general disposability of income, socialist government policies have limited choice for some while improving opportunities for others.

Comparatively: The United Kingdom is as free as the United States, freer than West Germany.

U N I T E D   S T A T E S   O F   A M E R I C A

Economy: capitalist
Polity: decentralized multiparty
Population: 241,000,000

Political Rights: 1
Civil Liberties: 1
Status: free

An ethnically complex state with minor territorial subnationalities

Political Rights. The United States is a constitutional democracy with three strong but separate centers of power: president, congress, and judiciary. Elections are fair and competitive, but voter participation is frequently less than fifty percent. Parties are remarkably weak: in some areas they are little more than temporary means of organizing primary elections. States, and to a less extent cities, have powers in their own rights; they often successfully oppose the desires of national administrations. Each state has equal representation in the upper house, which in the USA is the more powerful half of parliament.

Subnationalities. There are many significant ethnic groups, but the only clearly territorial subnationalities are the native peoples. The largest Indian tribes, the Navaho and Sioux, number 100,000 or more each. About 150,000 Hawaiians still reside on their native islands, intermingled with a much larger white and oriental population. Spanish-speaking Americans number in the millions; except for a few thousand residing in an area of northern New Mexico, they are mostly twentieth-century immigrants living among English-speaking Americans, particularly in the large cities. Black Americans make up over one-tenth of the U.S. population; residing primarily in large cities, they have no major territorial base. Black and Spanish-speaking Americans are of special concern because of their relative poverty; their ethnic status is comparable to that of many other groups in America, including Chinese, Japanese, Filipinos, Italians, or Jews.

Civil Liberties. The press is private and free; both private and public radio and television are government regulated. There are virtually no government controls on the content of the printed media (except in nonpolitical areas such as pornography) and few on broadcasting. There are no prisoners of conscience or sanctioned uses of torture; some regional miscarriages of justice and police brutality have political and social overtones. Widespread use of surveillance techniques and clandestine interference with radical groups or groups thought to be radical have occurred sporadically; as a reduction of liberties the threat has remained largely potential. A new threat is control over the expression of former government employees. Wherever and whenever publicity penetrates, the rule of law is generally secure, even against the most powerful. The government often loses in the courts. Private rights in most spheres are respected, but rights to travel to particular places, such as Cuba, are circumscribed. Unions are independent and politically influential. Although a relatively capitalistic country, the combination of tax loads and the decisive government role in agriculture, energy, defense, and other industries restricts individual choice as it increases majority power.

Comparatively: The United States is as free as Australia, freer than West Germany.

U R U G U A Y

Economy: mixed capitalist
Polity: centralized multiparty
Population: 3,000,000

Political Rights: 2
Civil Liberties: 2
Status: free

A relatively homogeneous population

Political Rights. Uruguay has a democratically elected president and parliament. All parties have been legalized; the former guerrilla movement has joined the political process. Since the military is not completely under civilian control, trials of military officers implicated in human rights offenses have been delayed.

Civil Liberties. The press is private, and broadcasting private and public. Both are free, as are books and journals. Foreign media are widely available. Rights of assembly and organization as well as the independence of the judiciary and the civil service have been reestablished. All prisoners of conscience have been released. Private rights are generally respected. The tax load of an overbuilt bureaucracy and emphasis on private and government monopolies in major sectors still restrict choice in this now impoverished welfare state.

Comparatively: Uruguay is as free as Mauritius, freer than Paraguay, less free than Venezuela.

V A N U A T U

Economy: noninclusive capitalist-statist	Political Rights: 2
Polity: decentralized mutiparty	Civil Liberties: 4
Population: 120,000	Status: partly free

A relatively homogeneous society with geographical subnationalities

Political Rights. Vanuatu has a parliamentary system with an indirectly elected president. Elections have been freely contested by multiple parties. Opposition exists between islands and between the French- and English-educated. Local government is elected; a decentralized federal system of regional government is being developed.

Civil Liberties. Government controls both print and broadcast media; the only critical paper was closed by government order in 1983. The full spectrum of civil freedoms is observed, but in the aftermath of the suppression of a secessionist (largely French supported) movement at independence, many political arrests and trials occurred; mistreatment was reported. The judiciary is independent. Rights to political, economic, and union organization are observed, but unions have been under pressure. There is a general right to travel.

Comparatively: Vanuatu is as free as Malta, freer than Maldives, less free than Belize.

VENEZUELA

Economy: capitalist-statist
Polity: centralized multiparty
Population: 17,800,000

Political Rights: 1
Civil Liberties: 2
Status: free

A relatively homogeneous population

Political Rights. Venezuela is a constitutional democracy in which power has alternated between major parties in recent years. Campaigns and voting are fair and open. Regional and local assemblies are relatively powerful, but governors are centrally appointed. Each state has equal representation in the upper house.

Civil Liberties. The press is private and generally free; most broadcasting is also in private hands. Censorship occurs only in emergencies, but television scripts on certain subjects must be approved in advance; journalists have been warned or arrested, and programs suspended, for normal reportage. The rule of law is generally secure, except apparently in areas of guerrilla actions where disappearances occur. However, there are no prisoners of conscience, and the government has taken steps to prevent torture. The court can rule against the government, and charges are brought against the security forces. Most private rights are respected; government involvement in the petroleum industry has given it a predominant economic role. Human rights organizations are very active. Unions are well organized and powerful.

Comparatively: Venezuela is as free as France, freer than Ecuador, less free than Costa Rica.

VIETNAM

Economy: socialist
Polity: communist one-party
Population: 62,000,000

Political Rights: 7
Civil Liberties: 7
Status: not free

An ethnic state with subnationalities

Political Rights. Vietnam is a traditional communist dictatorship with the forms of parliamentary democracy. Actual power is in the hands of the communist party; this is, in turn, dominated by a small group at the top. Officially there is a ruling national front, as in several other communist states, but the noncommunist parties are facades. Administration is highly centralized, with provincial boundaries arbitrarily determined by the central government. The flow of refugees and other evidence suggest that the present regime is very unpopular, especially in the South which is treated as an occupied country. **Subnationalities:** Continued fighting has been reported in the Montagnard areas in the South. Combined with new resettlement schemes, non-Vietnamese peoples are under pressure in both North and South Vietnam. Many Chinese have been driven out of the country.

Civil Liberties. The media are under direct government, party, or army control; only the approved line is presented. While the people have essentially no rights against the state, there is occasional public criticism and passive resistance, especially in the South. Arbitrary arrest is frequent. Repression of religious groups has eased, at least in the South. Perhaps one-half million persons have been put through reeducation camps, hundreds of thousands have been forced to move into new areas, or to change occupations; thousands are prisoners of conscience or in internal exile. Former anticommunist and other groups are regularly discriminated against in employment, health care, and travel. There are no independent labor union rights, rights to travel, or choice of education; many have been forced into collectives.

Comparatively: Vietnam is as free as USSR, less free than China (Mainland).

W E S T E R N   S A M O A

Economy: noninclusive capitalist
Polity: centralized multiparty
Population: 160,000

Political Rights: 4
Civil Liberties: 3
Status: partly free

A relatively homogeneous population

Political Rights. Western Samoa is a constitutional monarchy in which the assembly is elected by 16,000 "family heads." There have been important shifts of power among parties in the assembly as the result of elections, or the shift of allegiance of factions without elections. A recent election was voided in the courts on a corruption issue. Campaigning by lavish distribution of gifts is common. Village government has preserved traditional forms and considerable autonomy; it is also based on rule by "family heads."

Civil Liberties. The press is private and government; radio is government owned; television is received only from outside. Government media have limited independence. There is general freedom of expression, organization, and assembly. The judiciary is independent and the rule of law and private rights are respected within the limits set by the traditional system. Most arable land is held in customary tenure. Health and literacy standards are very high for a poor country.

Comparatively: Western Samoa is as free as Senegal, freer than Indonesia, less free than Nauru.

Y E M E N,   N O R T H

Economy: noninclusive capitalist
Polity: military nonparty
Population: 6,300,000

Political Rights: 5
Civil Liberties: 5
Status: partly free

A complex but relatively homogeneous population

Political Rights. North Yemen is a military dictatorship supplemented by an appointive and elected advisory assembly. Leaders are frequently assassinated. The tribal and religious structures still retain considerable authority, and the government must rely on a wide variety of different groups in an essentially nonideological consensual regime. Local elections allow meaningful competition. Political parties are forbidden. The country is divided between city and country, a variety of tribes, and two major religious groupings, and faces a major revolutionary challenge.

Civil Liberties. The weak media are largely government owned; the papers have occasional criticisms—the broadcast media have none. Foreign publications are routinely censored. Yet proponents of both royalist and far left persuasions are openly accepted in a society with few known prisoners of conscience.

There is no right of assembly. Politically active opponents may be encouraged to go into exile. The traditional Islamic courts give some protection; many private rights are respected. There is no right to strike or to engage in religious proselytizing. Unions and professional associations are government sponsored. Economically the government has concentrated on improving the infrastructure of Yemen's still overwhelmingly traditional economy. Most farmers are tenants; half the labor force is employed abroad.

Comparatively: North Yemen is as free as Bhutan, freer than South Yemen, less free than Egypt.

Y E M E N,   S O U T H

Economy: noninclusive socialist
Polity: socialist one-party
      (military influenced)
Population: 2,300,000

Political Rights: 6
Civil Liberties: 7

Status: not free

A relatively homogeneous population

Political Rights. South Yemen is formally organized according to the Marxist-Leninist one-party model. In practice, it is government by coup and violence. Elections follow the one-party model; there is some choice among individuals, particularly on the local level. Soviet influence in internal and external affairs is powerful.

Civil Liberties. The media are government owned or controlled, and employed actively as means of indoctrination. Even conversation with foreigners is highly restricted. In the political and security areas the rule of law hardly applies. Political imprisonments, torture, and "disappearances" have instilled a pervasive fear in those who would speak up. Death sentences against protesting farmers have been handed down by people's courts. Independent private rights are few, although some traditional law and institutions remain. Unions are under government control. Industry and commerce have been nationalized, some of the land collectivized.

Comparatively: South Yemen is as free as Malawi, freer than Somalia, less free than Oman.

Y U G O S L A V I A

Economy: mixed socialist
Polity: communist one-party
Population: 23,200,000

Political Rights: 6
Civil Liberties: 5
Status: partly free

A multinational state

Political Rights. Yugoslavia is governed on the model of the USSR, but with the addition of unique elements. These include: the greater role given the governments of the constituent republics; and the greater power given the managers and workers of the self-managed communities and industrial enterprises. The Federal Assembly is elected indirectly by those successful in lower level elections. The country has been directed by a small elite of the communist party, but measures to increase in-party democracy seem genuine. No opposition member is elected to state or national position, nor is there public opposition in the assemblies to government policy on the national level.

Subnationalities. The several peoples of Yugoslavia live largely in their historical homelands. The population consists of forty percent Serbs, twenty-two percent Croats, eight percent Slovenes, eight percent Bosnian Muslims, six percent Macedonians, six percent Albanians, two percent Montenegrins, and many others. The Croats have an especially active independence movement; Albanians have agitated for more self-determination. Yet there is a degree of authentic defense of cultural differences. For example, both politically and economically Slovenia is developing western rather than eastern-bloc traditions—while remaining within the official limits of the system.

Civil Liberties. The media in Yugoslavia are controlled directly or indirectly by the government, although there is ostensible worker control. The range of ideas and criticism of government policy in domestic and available foreign publications is greater than in most communist states: there is no prepublication censorship. There is no right of assembly, but some assemblies are allowed outside of government direction. Hundreds have been imprisoned for ideas expressed verbally or in print that deviated from the official line (primarily through subnationalist enthusiasm, anticommunism, or communist deviationism). Dissidents are even pursued overseas. Torture and brutality occur; psychiatric hospitals are also used to confine prisoners of conscience. As long as the issue is not political, however, the courts have some independence; there is a realm of de facto individual freedom that includes the right to seek employment outside the country. Travel outside Yugoslavia is often denied to dissidents; religious proselytizing is forbidden, but sanctioned religious activity is increasing. Labor is not independent, but has rights through the working of the "self-management" system; local strikes are common, but illegal. Although the economy is socialist or communalist in most respects, agriculture in this most agricultural of European countries remains overwhelmingly private.

Comparatively: Yugoslavia is as free as Poland, freer than Romania, less free than Morocco.

Z A I R E

Economy: noninclusive
       capitalist-statist

Political Rights: 7

Polity: nationalist one-party
      (military dominated)

Civil Liberties: 7

Population: 33,300,000

Status: not free

A transethnic heterogeneous state with subnationalities

Political Rights. Zaire is under one-man military rule, with the ruling party essentially an extension of the ruler's personality. Presidential elections are farces. Elections at both local and parliamentary levels are restricted to one party, but allow for extensive choice among individuals. Parliament has little if any power. Regions are deliberately organized to avoid ethnic identity: regional officers all are appointed from the center, generally from outside the area, as are officers of the ruling party. The president's personal exploitation of the system delegitimizes it.

Subnationalities. There are such a variety of tribes or linguistic groups in Zaire that no one group has as much as twenty percent of the population. The fact that French remains the dominant language reflects the degree of this dispersion. Until recently most Zaire citizens have seen themselves only in local terms without broader ethnic identification. The revolts and wars of the early 1960s saw continually shifting patterns of affiliation, with the European provincial, but not ethnic, realities of Katanga and South Kasai being most important. The most self-conscious ethnic groups are the Kongo people living in the west (and Congo and Angola) and the Luba in the center of the country. In both cases ethnicity goes back to important ancient kingdoms. There is continuing disaffection among the Lunda and other ethnic groups.

Civil Liberties. Private newspaper ownership remains only in name. Broadcasting is government owned and directed. Censorship and self-censorship are pervasive. There is no right of assembly, and union organization is controlled. Government has been arbitrary and capricious. The judiciary is not independent; prisoners of conscience are numerous, and execution and torture common. Ethnic organizations are closely restricted. Arrested conspirators have been forbidden their own lawyers. There is relative religious freedom; the Catholic church retains some power. Through the misuse of government power, the extravagance and business dealings of those in high places reduces economic freedom. Nationalization of land has often been a prelude to private development by powerful bureaucrats. Pervasive corruption and anarchy reduce human rights. There is also considerable government enterprise.

Comparatively: Zaire is as free as Vietnam, less free than Zambia.

Z A M B I A

Economy: noninclusive mixed socialist	Political Rights: 5
Polity: socialist one-party	Civil Liberties: 5
Population: 7,100,000	Status: partly free

A transethnic heterogeneous state

Political Rights. Zambia is ruled as a one-party dictatorship, although there have been elements of freedom within that party. Party organs are constitutionally more important than governmental ministries. Although elections have some meaning within this framework, the government has suppressed opposition movements within the party. Perhaps uniquely, parliament managed to block a government bill in 1985. Expression of dissent is possible through abstention or negative votes. There are some town councils with elected members.

Civil Liberties. All media are government controlled. A considerable variety of opinion is expressed, but it is a crime to criticize the president, the parliament, or the ideology. Foreign publications are censored. There is a rule of law and the courts have some independence; political cases are won against the government. Political opponents are often detained, and occasionally tortured, yet most people talk without fear. Traditional life continues. The government does not fully accept private or traditional rights in property or religion; important parts of the economy, especially copper mining, have been nationalized. Union, business, and professional organizations are under government pressure but retain significant independence.

Comparatively: Zambia is as free as Guyana, freer than Angola, less free than Morocco.

Z I M B A B W E

Economy: noninclusive capitalist-statist	Political Rights: 4
Polity: centralized dominant party	Civil Liberties: 6
Population: 9,000,000	Status: partly free

An ethnically complex state with a territorial subnationality

Political Rights. Zimbabwe is a parliamentary democracy. The ruling party has achieved power through elections marked by coercion of the electorate both before and after the actual process. The whites retain special minority political rights in a transitional phase. All military forces are still not controlled. Pressure to form a one-party state is growing with the increasing repression of the main opposition party. Subnationalities: The formerly dominant white, Indian, and colored populations (five percent altogether) are largely urban. The emerging dominant people are the majority Shona-speaking groups (seventy-four percent). The Ndebele (eighteen percent) are territorially distinct and politically self-conscious. Their allegiance to a minority party is being violently reduced.

Civil Liberties. The major papers are indirectly government owned and follow the government line, except occasionally in the letters columns. The government-owned broadcast media are active organs of government propaganda. The rule of law is increasingly threatened; opposition politicians have been forced into exile or imprisoned. Acquittals in political cases are often followed by rearrests. Racial discrimination is officially outlawed, especially in residence, occupation, and conscription. Many citizens live in fear of the nationalist parties and their former guerrilla forces. Many have been killed or beaten in an attempt to force change of party allegiance. Unions and private associations retain some independence, but are increasingly being unified under government direction. The economy has capitalist, socialist, and statist aspects. The white population still wields disproportionate economic power.

Comparatively: Zimbabwe is as free as Sierre Leone, freer than South Africa, less free than Senegal.

PART V

Related Territory Summaries

Related Territory Summaries

Using the same format as the Country Summaries, the dependent territories of each superordinate country are discussed below as a group. Exceptions to the general pattern are pointed out. It is often unclear whether a political unit should be regarded as a territory or an integral unit of its ruling state. For example, only the history of the Survey explains why the "independent" homelands of South Africa are considered dependent territories while the Republics of the USSR are not. Depending on the historical background, geographical separation—as by water and distance—often leads to the political unit being defined as a related territory. Many additional separated islands, such as those of India or Indonesia, could well be defined as dependent territories rather than as an integral part of the state. In general, if a unit is considered a full equal of the units of the superordinate state, it is not a territory.

A U S T R A L I A

CHRISTMAS ISLAND

Economy: capitalist-statist
Polity: agent
Population: 3,300

Political Rights: 4
Civil Liberties: 2
Status: partly free

An ethnically complex territory

COCOS ISLANDS

Economy: capitalist-statist
Polity: agent and council
Population: 600

Political Rights: 4
Civil Liberties: 2
Status: partly free

A relatively homogeneous population (nonwhite)

NORFOLK ISLAND

Economy: capitalist
Polity: council & administrator
Population: 2,200

Political Rights: 4
Civil Liberties: 2
Status: partly free

A relatively homogeneous population

Australia apparently follows democratic practices in so far as possible. Christmas Island is economically based on a state-run phosphate mine, which is soon to be depleted. The population is Chinese and Malay. Formerly a personal fiefdom, Cocos Islands has been placed under Australian administration, with the assistance of a local council. In 1984 the people voted in a UN supervised referendum to be integrated with Australia. Yet distance, the Malay population, and the plantation economy may make this difficult in more than theory. There appears to be free expression and a rule of law, but in neither are communications media developed.

Norfolk Island has a freely elected legislative assembly. It is in large measure self-governing; the wish of some residents for more independence is currently under consideration. An Australian "administrator" remains appointed. At least one lively free newspaper is published—in spite of threats and arson against the editor. Other rights of organization and law appear to be guaranteed.

C H I L E

EASTER ISLAND

Economy: capitalist-statist
Polity: governor
Population: 2,000

Political Rights: 5
Civil Liberties: 5
Status: partly free

A relatively homogeneous population (nonwhite)

The Island is granted limited autonomy within the generally repressive Chilean context. In 1984 the appointed governor was for the first time a native of the island. Discussion of local problems is quite open, and local elective institutions function.

D E N M A R K

FAROE ISLANDS

Economy: mixed capitalist
Polity: multiparty
Population: 44,000

Political Rights: 1
Civil Liberties: 1
Status: free

A relatively homogeneous population

GREENLAND

Economy: mixed capitalist
Polity: multiparty
Population: 51,000

Political Rights: 1
Civil Liberties: 1
Status: free

An ethnically complex population (nonwhite majority)

Both territories have elected parliamentary governments responsible for internal administration, and free to discuss their relationship to Denmark. In addition they elect representatives to the Danish parliament. They also have considerable freedom in international affairs—such as Greenland's ability to opt out of the European Economic Community in 1985. On major issues referendums are also held. Full freedoms of expression and organization are recognized. The local languages are dominant in both territories. The majority Inuit population is now politically in charge of Greenland.

F R A N C E

FRENCH GUIANA

Economy: noninclusive capitalist-statist
Polity: dependent multiparty (limited)
Population: 73,000

Political Rights: 3
Civil Liberties: 2
Status: partly free

An ethnically complex state (nonwhite majority)

FRENCH POLYNESIA

Economy: capitalist-statist
Polity: dependent multiparty
Population: 170,000

Political Rights: 3
Civil Liberties: 2
Status: partly free

A relatively homogeneous population (few French)

GUADELOUPE

Economy: capitalist-statist
Polity: dependent multiparty (limited)
Population: 324,000

Political Rights: 3
Civil Liberties: 2
Status: partly free

Relatively homogeneous with a small, dominant French minority

MARTINIQUE

Economy: capitalist-statist
Polity: dependent multiparty
    (limited)
Population: 342,000

Political Rights: 3
Civil Liberties: 2

Status: partly free

Relatively homogeneous with a small, dominant French minority

MAHORE (formerly MAYOTTE)

Economy: noninclusive capitalist
Polity: dependent multiparty
    (limited)
Population: 47,000

Political Rights: 2
Civil Liberties: 2

Status: free

A relatively homogeneous population (non-French)

MONACO

Economy: capitalist-statist
Polity: dependent constitutional
    monarchy (limited)
Population: 26,000

Political Rights: 4
Civil Liberties: 2

Status: partly free

An ethnically heterogeneous population

NEW CALEDONIA

Economy: capitalist-statist
Polity: dependent multiparty
Population: 150,000

Political Rights: 3
Civil Liberties: 2
Status: free

An ethnically complex territory (large French component)

Territory Summaries

REUNION

Economy: capitalist-statist
Polity: dependent multiparty
(limited)
Population: 495,000

Political Rights: 3
Civil Liberties: 2

Status: partly free

An ethnically complex territory (few French)

ST. PIERRE AND MIQUELON

Economy: capitalist
Polity: dependent multiparty
(limited)
Population: 6,260

Political Rights: 2
Civil Liberties: 2

Status: free

A relatively homogeneous territory (French)

WALLIS AND FUTUNA

Economy: capitalist-statist
Polity: dependent assembly
Population: 12,300

Political Rights: 4
Civil Liberties: 3

Status: partly free

A relatively homogeneous population (non-French)

The territories of French Guiana, Guadeloupe, Martinique, and Reunion are considered overseas departments of France. They have elected representatives in the French parliament (who need not be from the territory) and local councils. However, French law applies; a French administrator is the chief executive; both French subsidies and numbers of French bureaucrats, and sometimes troops or police are substantial. Open advocacy of independence in such integral parts of France is often repressed. Nevertheless, small independence movements exist in at least Guadeloupe and Martinique. Local elected governments have little power. The governance of the "collectivities" of Mahore (Mayotte) and St. Pierre and Miquelon is similar. Two recent referendums in Mahore have confirmed the desire of the people for their island to remain a part of France (because the Christian population would otherwise be ruled by the Muslim Comoros). Women are especially active in the anti-Comoros movement. Beyond the special colonial position, French law and its civil guarantees are maintained in the group.

The overseas territories of French Polynesia, New Caledonia, and Wallis and Futuna in the South Pacific are more traditional colonies in theory. In practice, the adminstrative structure is similar to that of the overseas departments. Assemblies have limited powers, although in the large territories perhaps as great as those in the overseas departments since, there is not the automatic application of French law. Independence appears here to be a lively and accepted issue, especially in New Caledonia. France seems willing to go toward independence even though a 1985 election shows the majority to be against independence. The native people, the Kanaks (about forty percent), are highly organized and pro-independence—if the post-independence system guaranteed their control. French reluctance to grant full freedom led to New Caledonia threatening an election boycott and an alternative government in 1984. Wallis and Futuna chose territorial status by referendum in 1959.

Monaco is not normally considered a dependent territory. However, by treaty with France, Monacan policy must conform to French security, political, and economic interests; the head minister must be chosen from a list submitted by the French government, and France controls foreign relations. The hereditary ruler appoints the government, but shares legislative power with an elected council. There is also elected local government. Foreign publications are freely available. Civil freedoms approximate those in France. The government owns the casino and major hotels.

Of the traditional colonial powers only France retains a grip on its colonies that seems to be resented by important segments of their populations. For example, independence movements in Guadeloupe and New Caledonia have not had the opportunity for fair electoral tests of their desires that those in American and British colonies have had. France does not allow such electoral tests of independence sentiment in its overseas departments, and seldom elsewhere.

I S R A E L

OCCUPIED AREAS

Economy: capitalist
Polity: external administration;
      local government
Population: 1,150,000

Political Rights: 5
Civil Liberties: 5

Status: partly free

A complex population with a dominant minority

The Gaza Strip and the West Bank have had some elected local government; the decisive power is in the hands of the occupying force. Opposition to the occupation is expressed in local elections and the media, but heavy pressure against any organized opposition is applied in an atmosphere of violence on both sides. There is censorship as well as other controls on the media and on movement. Settlement by the occupying people has steadily infringed upon the rights of the Arab majority.

I T A L Y

SAN MARINO

Economy: capitalist
Polity: dependent multiparty
Population: 19,380

Political Rights: 1
Civil Liberties: 1
Status: free

A relatively homogeneous state

VATICAN

Economy: statist
Polity: elected monarchy
Population: 860

Political Rights: 6
Civil Liberties: 4
Status: partly free

A relatively homogeneous population

San Marino is ruled by a multiparty parliamentary government with active elected local governments. The media are independent; in addition, Italian media are available. Although often considered independent, the influence of Italy is overwhelming. Defense and many foreign-relations areas are handled by the Italian government; major court cases are tried in Italian courts; the political parties are essentially branches of the respective Italian parties. Citizenship was recently extended to long-term residents for the first time.

The political situation of the Vatican is anomalous. On the one hand, the Vatican is ostensibly an independent state under absolutist rule, with the ruler chosen for life by a small international elite, which also has advisory functions. On the other hand, the international relations of the state are actually based on its ruler's status as head of a church rather than as head of a state. The people of the Vatican live more as Italian citizens than as citizens of the Vatican, regardless of their formal status. Vatican media represent the views of the church, yet Italian media and avenues of expression are fully available, and the dissatisfied can leave the context of the Vatican with minimal effort.

N E T H E R L A N D S

ARUBA

Economy: mixed capitalist
Polity: multiparty internal
Population: 65,000

Political Rughts: 1
Civil Liberties: 1
Status: free

An ethnically complex territory (few Dutch)

NETHERLANDS ANTILLES

Economy: mixed capitalist
Polity: multiparty internal
Population: 190,000

Political Rights: 1
Civil Liberties: 1
Status: free

An ethnically complex territory (few Dutch)

The **Netherlands Antilles** consist of two groups of islands in the Caribbean. Although the governor is appointed, the islands are largely self-governing at both the territory and island levels. The parliament is freely elected. The Netherlands has been urging the islands to accept independence, but the smaller islands have resisted independence in federation with the dominant island, Curacao. Full freedom of party organization, expression, and abstention are fully recognized. The press, radio, and television are private, free, and highly varied.

Aruba achieved autonomy in 1986 and is expected to attain full independence in 1996. The pattern of government is similar to that of the Netherlands Antilles.

N E W   Z E A L A N D

COOK ISLANDS

Economy: capitalist-statist
Polity: multiparty internal
Population: 18,000

Political Rights: 2
Civil Liberties: 2
Status: free

A relatively homogeneous population (nonwhite)

NIUE

Economy: capitalist-statist
Polity: internal parliamentary
Population: 3,000

Political Rights: 2
Civil Liberties: 2
Status: free

A relatively homogeneous population (nonwhite)

TOKELAU ISLANDS

Economy: capitalist-statist   **Political Rights:** 4
Polity: limited assembly   **Civil Liberties:** 2
Population: 1,600   **Status:** partly free

A relatively homogeneous population (nonwhite)

The **Cook Islands** and **Niue** are largely self-governing territories with elected parliaments. There is continuing oversight by New Zealand, particularly in defense, foreign affairs, and justice. Niue has been unable to arrest a steady decline in population. Tokelau is administered by appointed officials with the help of an elected assembly. Political life, particularly in the Cook Islands, has been vigorous and free.

P O R T U G A L

AZORES

Economy: capitalist-statist   **Political Rights:** 2
Polity: internal multiparty   **Civil Liberties:** 2
Population: 292,000   **Status:** free

A relatively homogeneous population

MACAO

Economy: capitalist-statist   **Political Rights:** 3
Polity: limited internal assembly **Civil Liberties:** 4
Population: 400,000   **Status:** partly free

An ethnically complex population (majority Chinese)

MADEIRA

Economy: capitalist-statist
Polity: internal multiparty
Population: 266,000

Political Rights: 2
Civil Liberties: 2
Status: free

An ethnically complex but relatively homogeneous population

The Azores and Madeira are considered "autonomous regions," whose multiparty governments have a large degree of internal self-rule, including the right to issue their own stamps. The islands also have elected representatives in the Portuguese parliament. They have the same civil freedoms as on the mainland. Both regions have independence movements. Land holding has traditionally been very concentrated on Madeira. With populations made up largely of Portuguese settlers of past centuries, neither island group has been seen as a colony. Macao is administered by a Lisbon-appointed governor with the help of an elected local assembly. Peking and its supporters affect all levels of government and constrain the news media, as well as rights of assembly and organization. However, democratic institutions are more developed here than in Hong Kong.

SOUTH AFRICA

BOPHUTHATSWANA

Economy: capitalist-statist
Polity: dependent dominant party
Population: 1,400,000

Political Rights: 6
Civil Liberties: 5
Status: partly free

An ethnically complex population

CISKEI

Economy: capitalist-statist
Polity: dependent dominant party
Population: 740,000

Political Rights: 6
Civil Liberties: 6
Status: not free

An ethnically homogeneous territory

SOUTH WEST AFRICA (NAMIBIA)

Economy: capitalist-traditional
Polity: appointed multiparty-
    traditional
Population: 1,100,000

Political Rights: 6
Civil Liberties: 5

Status: partly free

An ethnically heterogeneous territory

VENDA

Economy: capitalist-statist
Polity: dependent multiparty
Population: 550,000

Political Rights: 6
Civil Liberties: 6
Status: not free

A relatively homogeneous territory

South West Africa, or Namibia, is ruled as a colony of South Africa, with the help of a multiparty government appointed in 1985. Tnere is considerable freedom of the press, of discussion, and organization—although with occasional interventions. The judiciary is relatively free. Native chiefs and councils play political and judicial roles in their home areas. The northern or Ovambo half of the country is under police rule in a guerrilla war setting.

The other territories are homelands that have accepted formal independence—except for Transkei, which the Survey accepts as independent. Characteristically, most wage earners ascribed to these states work in South Africa proper; the states receive extensive South African aid, and they are not viable units geographically. South Africa exerts considerable control over their foreign

393

affairs and security, although there are often disputes. Formally governed by parliamentary systems, the control of political organization and expression, the large number of appointed parliamentarians, and the violent atmosphere makes them more dictatorial than democratic. Expression of opinion in regard to the existence of the state is especially perilous. There are arrests for reasons of conscience and reports of torture. Nevertheless, these territories protect their peoples from many of the worst insults of apartheid, and, in Bophuthatswana, a much closer approximation to justice exists for blacks than in South Africa itself.

S P A I N

CANARY ISLANDS

Economy: capitalist
Polity: centralized multiparty
Population: 1,500,000

Political Rights: 1
Civil Liberties: 2
Status: free

A complex but relatively homogeneous population

C E U T A

Economy: capitalist-statist
Polity: dependent, unrecognized
Population: 78,000 (including
             12,000 soldiers)
An ethnically homogeneous population

Political Rights: 2
Civil Liberties: 3
Status: free

M E L I L L A

Economy: capitalist-statist
Polity: dependent, unrecognized
Population: 63,000

Political Rights: 2
Civil Liberties: 3
Status: free

An ethnically complex population

Spain has no official colonies. Its outposts in North Africa, Ceuta and Melilla, ruled as parts of the Spanish provinces across from them, remain anomalies. Both have been Spanish for centuries. Only after demonstrations in Melilla in 1986 did the government move to give most Muslims citizenship—but the process will evidently be very slow.

The **Canary Islands** are governed as two provinces. Although the people are of diverse origins and preserve many pre-Spanish customs, the culture today is largely Hispanic. There is an independence movement, but the development of internal self-determination on a regional basis may help to reduce the desire for separation. Spanish law guarantees rights as in Spain itself.

S W I T Z E R L A N D

LIECHTENSTEIN

Economy: capitalist-statist
Polity: constitutional monarchy
Population: 124,000

Political Rights: 3
Civil Liberties: 1
Status: free

A relatively homogeneous population

Foreign affairs, defense, and some economic regulations are controlled by Switzerland. Swiss money is used, as is the Swiss postal service. The government is responsible both to the hereditary monarch and an elected parliament. Referendums supplement parliamentary rule. There is local government. Women have recently attained the right to vote and have entered parliament. The media are mostly Swiss, although there are local papers.

U N I T E D   K I N G D O M

ANGUILLA

Economy: mixed capitalist
Polity: dependent limited
    assembly
Population: 6,500

Political Rights: 2
Civil Liberties: 2

Status: free

A relatively homogeneous population (nonwhite)

BERMUDA

Economy: mixed capitalist
Polity: multiparty
Population: 55,000

Political Rights: 2
Civil Liberties: 1
Status: free

An ethnically complex state (largely nonwhite)

BRITISH VIRGIN ISLANDS

Economy: mixed socialist
Polity: limited internal
    assembly
Population: 11,000

Political Rights: 2
Civil Liberties: 1

Status: free

A relatively homogeneous population (nonwhite)

CAYMAN ISLANDS

Economy: capitalist
Polity: limited internal
    assembly
Population: 17,000

Political Rights: 2
Civil Liberties: 2

Status: free

An ethnically mixed population (largely white)

CHANNEL ISLANDS

Economy: capitalist
Polity: traditional
    parliamentary
Population: 132,000

Political Rights: 2
Civil Liberties: 1

Status: free

An ethnically mixed population (white)

FALKLAND ISLANDS

Economy: capitalist-statist
Polity: limited representative
Population: 1,800

Political Rights: 2
Civil Liberties: 2
Status: free

A relatively homogeneous population (white)

GIBRALTAR

Economy: capitalist-statist
Polity: internal parliamentary
Population: 30,000

Political Rights: 1
Civil Liberties: 2
Status: free

An ethnically complex population

HONG KONG

Economy: capitalist
Polity: colonial
Population: 5,700,000

Political Rights: 4
Civil Liberties: 2
Status: partly free

A relatively homogeneous population (Chinese)

Territory Summaries

ISLE OF MAN

Economy: capitalist
Polity: parliamentary
Population: 65,000

Political Rights: 1
Civil Liberties: 1
Status: free

A relatively homogeneous population (white)

MONTSERRAT

Economy: capitalist
Polity: colonial legislative
Population: 12,000

Political Rights: 2
Civil Liberties: 2
Status: free

A relatively homogeneous population (nonwhite)

ST. HELENA

Economy: capitalist-statist
Polity: colonial legislative
Population: 5,200

Political Rights: 2
Civil Liberties: 2
Status: free

A relatively homogeneous population (white)

TURKS AND CAICOS

Economy: capitalist
Polity: colonial legislative
Population: 7,400

Political Rights: 2
Civil Liberties: 2
Status: free

A relatively homogeneous population (nonwhite)

The dependencies of the United Kingdom all have the civil rights common to the homeland. Nearly all have expressed, through elections, elected representatives, or simply lack of controversy in a free atmosphere, a desire to stay a dependency of the United Kingdom under present arrangements. For example, the

398

party winning decisively in 1984 in Turks and Caicos ran on an anti-independence stand. The people of Gibraltar have often affirmed their desire to remain a colony. For the other colonies, there is little evidence of a significant denial of political or civil liberties.

Constitutionally, the dependencies may be divided into three groups. The first consists of those units with essentially full internal autonomy, expressed through freely elected parliaments. The second group is administered by a strong appointed governor and a largely elected assembly or council. The third group consists of colonies with little if any power in elected assemblies or officials. The first group includes the Channel Islands, the Isle of Man, and possibly Bermuda. Midway between the first and second groups are the British Virgin Islands, Cayman Islands, Gibraltar, and possibly Montserrat. In the second group are Anguilla, Falkland Islands, St. Helena, and Turks and Caicos. The last group consists only of Hong Kong, whose political development, and to some extent even civil liberties have been arrested by the presence of communist China. In preparation for the turning back of sovereignty to China in 1997 legislative institutions are being developed, and political consciousness is growing. To date the suffrage is very limited. At the same time the self-censorship of the press is increasing.

UNITED STATES OF AMERICA

AMERICAN SAMOA

Economy: capitalist-communal
Polity: parliamentary self-
      governing
Population: 32,000

Political Rights: 2
Civil Liberties: 2

Status: free

A relatively homogeneous population (nonwhite)

Territory Summaries

BELAU

Economy: capitalist-communal	Political Rights: 2
Polity: parliamentary self-governing	Civil Liberties: 2
Population: 12,000	Status: free

A relatively homogeneous population (nonwhite)

FEDERATED STATES OF MICRONESIA

Economy: capitalist-communal	Political Rights: 2
Polity: parlimentary self-governing	Civil Liberties: 2
Population: 74,000	Status: free

A relatively homogeneous population (nonwhite)

GUAM

Economy: capitalist-statist	Political Rights: 3
Polity: parliamentary self-governing	Civil Liberties: 2
Population: 106,000	Status: partly free

An ethnically complex population (mostly nonwhite)

MARSHALL ISLANDS

Economy: capitalist-statist	Political Rights: 2
Polity: parliamentary self-governing	Civil Liberties: 2
Population: 31,000	Status: free

A relatively homogeneous population (nonwhite)

NORTHERN MARIANAS

Economy: capitalist
Polity: parliamentary self-
      governing
Population: 17,000

Political Rights: 1
Civil Liberties: 2

Status: free

A relatively homogeneous population (nonwhite)

PUERTO RICO

Economy: capitalist
Polity: self governing quasi-state
Population: 3,300,000

Political Rights: 2
Civil Liberties: 1
Status: free

A relatively homogeneous population (Spanish speaking)

VIRGIN ISLANDS

Economy: capitalist
Polity: appointed governorship
Population: 97,000

Political Rights: 2
Civil Liberties: 3
Status: free

A complex population (mostly nonwhite)

Puerto Rico is an internally self-governing commonwealth with a political system modeled on that of the states of the United States. Control alternates between the major regional parties. Both directly and indirectly the Puerto Ricans have voted to remain related to the United States. (Independence parties have never received more than a small fraction of the vote.) There is full freedom of discussion and organization. The press and broadcast media are highly varied and critical. There are political prisoners, and instances of brutality and unnecessary killings, but no good evidence of imprisonment or killing simply for expression of opinion.

The rest of America's dependent territories are now either internally self-governing or have accepted in free referenda their present status. The territories have elective institutions including in most cases an elected governor or chief adminstrator. There have been a number of recent referendums approving free association with the United States in the Micronesian territories. However, except for the commonwealth of Northern Marianas, the agreements are not yet fully approved by the American Congress. Full independence was not discussed extensively by either the United States or the islanders. Belaus's majority has approved the compact, but not the three-fourths that its constitution requires. The heavy American military presence in Guam may reduce its independence. Guamanians also may soon wish to achieve commonwealth status similar to that of the Northern Marianas. Traditional chiefs have special powers in most other Pacific territories. The island groupings, such as the Marshalls or the Federated States have strong local governments on the separate islands, and are really loose federations. Overdependence on American largesse is arguably the greatest hindrance to complete freedom in the Pacific territories. Freedom of expression, assembly, and organization are recognized in all territories.

FRANCE-SPAIN CONDOMINIUM

ANDORRA

Economy: capitalist
Polity: limited multiparty
Population: 31,000

Political Rights: 3
Civil Liberties: 3
Status: partly free

A relatively homogeneous population (Catalan)

Andorra has a parliamentary government overseen by the representatives of the French President and the Bishop of Urgel. Formal parties are not permitted, but "groupings" contest the elections in their stead. There has been agitation for more self-determination. External relations are handled primarily by France, a responsibility France has insisted on in recent discussions with the EEC. An independent weekly is supplemented by French and Spanish publications. Only recently has the Andorra Council been able to regulate its own radio stations.

Index

See also Country and Related Territory Summaries, as well as page vii.

Index

Communications
  international, 99
Communications media
  freedom of, 17
Comparative Survey, 29
  and human rights, 84
  and positive indicators, 88
  categories of, **7**
  changes in, 66
  comparisons with, 81, **87**
  criteria of, 82
  criticisms of, 79
  history of, **48**
  inadequate data for, 85
  inclusion in, 39
  influence of Board on, 80
  methodology of, 81, 85, **89**
  methods of, 25
  period covered by, 39
  purposes of, 5
  rating system for, 8
  scales for, 8
Congress party, 13, 196
Consensus
  in political systems, 158
Conservatism, 172
Contributions
  campaign, 12
Corruption, 24
Covenant on Political and Civil
    Rights, 87
credibility
  loss of, 100
Criticisms of Survey
  ideological, 79
  methodological, 81
Cuba, 82
Czechoslovakia, 38, 82

D
Dahl, Robert, 6, 85, 160, 174
Daniloff, Nicholas, 100, 103
Decentralization, 16
Democracy
  and Africa, 209
  and economic equality, 5
  and elites, 160
  and Japan, 175
  and Marxism, 158, 160
  and people's democracy, 5
  and primaries, 181

and repression, 161
and ruling elites, 180
as liberal democracy, 4
bourgeois, 158
in Mauritius, **209**
in the United Kingdom, 180
in the United States, 179
in third world, **193**
participatory, 170
pluralism, 158
problems of, **157**
role of the press in, 185
role of the upper house, 185
struggle for, 78
unitary processes in, 175
Democracy, consensual, 175
Democracy, U. S.
  compared to other democracies,
    179
Democracy, liberal
  and American experience, 159
  and elections, **162**
  definition of, **157**
  enemies of, 160
  Hayek's criticism of, 173
  Marxist critique of, 169
  possible modifications of, 173
  radical criticism of, 161
  Rousseauian critics, 167
  traditionalist critique, 171
Democracy, problem of popular
    rule, 160
Democracy, strong, 174
Democracy, thin, 174
Demonstration
  right of, 201
Demonstration, right of, 20
Diego Garcia, 214
Dominant-party systems, 14, **77**
Disappearances, 21
Dissent, in USSR, 102
Donahue, Phil, 107

E
East Asia
  forms of government in, 158
Easter Island, **46**
Economic Daily, 119
Economic Information, 119
Economic systems
  types of, 72

Index